Henry Kiddle

Brown's Grammar Improved

Henry Kiddle

Brown's Grammar Improved

ISBN/EAN: 9783741123313

Manufactured in Europe, USA, Canada, Australia, Japa

Cover: Foto ©Suzi / pixelio.de

Manufactured and distributed by brebook publishing software
(www.brebook.com)

Henry Kiddle

Brown's Grammar Improved

OF

NGLISH GRAMMAR,

METHODICALLY ARRANGED;

WITH

FORMS OF PARSING AND CORRECTING, EXAMPLES FOR PARSING,
QUESTIONS FOR EXAMINATION, FALSE SYNTAX FOR COR-
RECTION, EXERCISES FOR WRITING, OBSERVATIONS
FOR THE ADVANCED STUDENT, FIVE
METHODS OF ANALYSIS,

AND

A KEY TO THE ORAL EXERCISES:

TO WHICH ARE ADDED FOUR APPENDIXES.

SIGNED FOR THE USE OF SCHOOLS, ACADEMIES, AND PRIVATE LEARNERS.

BY GOOLD BROWN,

PRINCIPAL OF AN ENGLISH AND ⬛⬛⬛ ACADEMY, NEW YORK.

"Ne quis igitur tanquam parva fastidiat ⬛⬛⬛ elementa."—QUINTILIAN.

A NEW ⬛⬛

WITH EXERCISES IN A⬛⬛ PARSING,

BY HENRY K⬛

ASSISTANT SUPERINTENDENT OF CO⬛

NEW Y⬛

WILLIAM WOOD, 61 ⬛

vent an other less objectionable. Such attempts have generally met the reception they deserved. Their history will give no encouragement to future innovators.

7. While some have thus wasted their energies in eccentric flights, vainly supposing that the learning of ages would give place to their whimsical theories; others, with more success, not better deserved, have multiplied grammars almost innumerably, by abridging or modifying the books they had used in childhood. So that they who are at all acquainted with the origin and character of the various compends thus introduced into our schools, cannot but desire a work which shall deserve a more extensive and more permanent patronage, based upon better claims. For, as Lord Bacon observes, the number of ill-written books is not to be diminished by ceasing to write, but by writing others which, like Aaron's serpent, shall swallow up the spurious.

8. The nature of the subject almost entirely precludes invention. The author has, however, aimed at that kind and degree of originality, which are to be commended in works of this sort; and has borrowed no more from others than did the most learned and popular of his predecessors. And, though he has taken the liberty to think and write for himself, he trusts it will be evident that few have excelled him in diligence of research, or have followed more implicitly the dictates of that authority which gives law to language.

9. All science is laid in the nature of things; and he only who seeks it there, can rightly guide others in the paths of knowledge. He alone can know whether his predecessors went right or wrong, who is capable of a judgement independent of theirs. But with what shameful servility have many false or faulty definitions and rules been copied and copied from one grammar to another, as if authority had canonized their errors, or none had eyes to see them! Whatsoever is dignified and fair, is also modest and reasonable; but modesty does not consist in having no opinion of one's own, nor reason in following with blind partiality the footsteps of others. Grammar unsupported by authority, is indeed mere fiction. But what apology is this, for that authorship which has produced so many grammars without originality? Shall he who cannot write for himself, improve upon him who can? It is not deference to merit, but impudent pretence, practising on the credulity of ignorance! Commonness alone exempts it from scrutiny, and the success it has, is but the wages of its own worthlessness! To read and be informed, is to make a proper use of books for the advancement of learning; but to assume to be an author by editing mere commonplaces and stolen criticisms, is equally beneath the ambition of a scholar and the honesty of a man.

10. Grammar being a practical art, with the principles of which every intelligent person is more or less acquainted, it might be expected that a book written professedly on the subject, should exhibit some evidence of its author's skill. But it would seem that a multitude of bad or indifferent writers have judged themselves qualified to teach the art of speaking and writing well; so that correctness of language and neatness of style are as rarely to be found in grammars as in other books. There have been, however, several excellent scholars, who have thought it an object not unworthy of their talents, to prescribe and elucidate the principles of English Grammar. But these, for an obvious reason, have executed their designs with various degrees of success; and even the most meritorious have left ample room for improvement, though some have evinced an ability which does honour to themselves, while it gives cause to regret their lack of an inducement to further labour. The mere grammarian can neither aspire to praise, nor stipulate for a reward; and to those who were best qualified to write, the subject could offer no adequate motive for diligence.

11. Having devoted many years to studies of this nature, and being conversant with most of the grammatical treatises already published, the author conceived that the objects above enumerated, might, perhaps, be better effected than they had been in any work within his knowledge. And he persuades himself that the improvements here offered, are neither few nor inconsiderable. He does not mean, however, to depreciate the labours, or to detract from the merits of those who have gone before him and taught with acknowledged skill. He has studiously endeavoured to avail himself of all the light they have thrown upon the subject. For his own information, he has carefully perused more than two hundred English grammars, and has glanced over many others that were not worth reading. With this publication in view, he has al o resorted to the original sources of grammatical knowledge, and has not only critically considered what he has seen and heard of our vernacular tongue, but has sought with some diligence the analogies of speech in the structure of several other languages.

12. His progress in compiling this work has been slow, and not unattended with labour and difficulty. Amidst the contrarieties of opinion, that appear in the various treatises already before the public, and the perplexities inseparable from so complicated a subject, he has, after deliberate consideration, adopted those views and explanations which appeared to him the least liable to objection, and the most compatible with his ultimate object—the production of a practical school grammar.

13. Ambitious of making not a large but an acceptable book, he has compressed into this volume the most essential parts of a mass of materials from which he could as easily have formed a folio. Whether the toil be compensated or not, is a matter of little consequence; he has neither written for bread, nor built castles in the air. He is too well versed in the history of his theme, too well aware of the precarious fortune

of authors, to indulge any confident anticipations of success; yet he will not deny that his hopes are large, being conscious of having cherished them with a liberality of feeling which cannot fear disappointment. In this temper he would invite the reader to a thorough perusal of the following pages. A grammar should speak for itself. In a work of this nature, every word or tittle which does not recommend the performance to the understanding and taste of the skillful, is, so far as it goes, a certificate against it. Yet, if some small errors have escaped detection, let it be recollected that it is almost impossible to print with perfect accuracy a work of this size, in which so many little things should be observed, remembered, and made exactly to correspond. There is no human vigilance which multiplicity may not sometimes baffle, and minuteness sometimes elude. To most persons grammar seems a dry and difficult subject; but there is a disposition of mind, to which what is arduous, is for that very reason alluring. The difficulties encountered in boyhood from the use of a miserable epitome, and the deep impression of a few mortifying blunders made in public, first gave the author a fondness for grammar; circumstances having since favoured this turn of his genius, he has voluntarily pursued the study, with an assiduity which no man will ever imitate for the sake of pecuniary recompense.

14. This work contains a full series of exercises adapted to its several parts, with notices of the manner in which they are to be used, according to the place assigned them. The examples of false syntax placed under the rules, are to be corrected *orally;* the four chapters of exercises adapted to the four parts of the subject, are to be *written* out by the learner. In selecting examples for these exercises, the author has been studious to economize the learner's and the teacher's time, by admitting those only which were very short. He has, in general, reduced each example to a single line. And, in this manner, he has been able to present, in this small volume, a series of exercises, more various than are given in any other grammar, and nearly equal in number to all that are contained in Murray's two octavoes. It is believed that a grammatical treatise at once so comprehensive and concise, has not before been offered to the public.

15. The only successful method of teaching grammar, is, to cause the principal definitions and rules to be committed thoroughly to memory, that they may ever afterwards be readily applied. Oral instruction may smooth the way, and facilitate the labour of the learner; but the notion of communicating a competent knowledge of grammar without imposing this task, is disproved by universal experience. Nor will it avail any thing for the student to rehearse definitions and rules of which he makes no practical application. In etymology and syntax, he should be alternately exercised in learning small portions of his book, and then applying them in *parsing*, till the whole is rendered familiar. To a good reader, the achievement will be neither great nor difficult; and the exercise is well calculated to improve the memory, and strengthen all the faculties of the mind.

16. The mode of instruction here recommended is the result of long and successful experience. There is nothing in it, which any person of common abilities will find it difficult to understand or adopt. It is the plain didactic method of definition and example, rule and praxis; which no man who means to teach grammar well, will ever desert, with the hope of finding an other more rational or more easy. The book itself will make any one a grammarian, who will take the trouble to observe and practise what it teaches; and even if some instructors should not adopt the readiest and most efficient method of making their pupils familiar with its contents, they will not fail to instruct by it as effectually as they can by any other. Whoever is acquainted with the grammar of our language, so as to have some tolerable skill in teaching it, will here find almost every thing that is true in his own instructions, clearly embraced under its proper head, so as to be easy of reference. And perhaps there are few, however learned, who, on a perusal of the volume, would not be furnished with some important rules and facts which had not before occurred to their own observation.

17. The greatest peculiarity of the method is, that it requires the pupil to speak or write a great deal, and the teacher very little. But both should constantly remember that grammar is the art of speaking and writing well; an art which can no more be acquired without practice than that of dancing or swimming. And each should be careful to perform his part handsomely—without drawling, omitting, stopping, hesitating, faltering, miscalling, reiterating, stuttering, hurrying, slurring, mouthing, misquoting, mispronouncing, or any of the thousand faults which render utterance disagreeable and inelegant. It is the learner's diction that is to be improved; and the system will be found well calculated to effect that object; because it demands of him, not only to answer questions on grammar, but also to make a prompt and practical application of what he has just learned. If the class be tolerable readers, it will not be necessary for the teacher to say much; and, in general, he ought not to take up the time by so doing. He should, however, carefully superintend their rehearsals; give the word to the next, when any one errs; and order the exercise in such a manner that either his own voice, or the example of his best scholars, may gradually correct the ill habits of the awkward, till all learn to recite with clearness, understanding well what they say, and making it intelligible to others.

18. The exercise of parsing commences immediately after the first lesson of etymology, and is carried on progressively till it embraces all the doctrines that are applica-

ble to it. If it be performed according to the order prescribed, it will soon make the student perfectly familiar with all the primary definitions and rules of grammar. It requires just enough of thought to keep the mind attentive to what the lips are utter- ing; while it advances by such easy gradations and constant repetitions as leave the pupil utterly without excuse, if he does not know what to say. Being neither wholly extemporaneous nor wholly rehearsed by rote, it has more dignity than a school-boy's conversation, and more ease than a formal recitation, or declamation ; and is therefore an exercise well calculated to induce a habit of uniting correctness with fluency in or- dinary speech—a species of elocution as valuable as any other.

19. The best instruction is that which ultimately gives the greatest facility and skill in practice; and grammar is best taught by that process which brings its doctrines most directly home to the habits as well as to the thoughts of the pupil—which the most effectually conquers inattention, and leaves the deepest impress of shame upon blundering ignorance. In the whole range of school exercises, there is none of greater importance than that of parsing; and yet perhaps there is none which is, in general, more defectively conducted. Scarcely less useful, as a means of instruction, is the practice of correcting false syntax orally, by regular and logical forms of argument; nor does this appear to have been more ably directed towards the purposes of disci- pline. There is so much to be done, in order to effect what is desirable in the man- agement of these things; and so little prospect that education will ever be generally raised to a just appreciation of that study which, more than all others, forms the mind to habits of correct thinking; that, in reflecting upon the state of the science at the present time, and upon the means of its improvement, the author cannot but sympa- thize, in some degree, with the sadness of the learned Sanctius; who tells us, that he had "always lamented, and often with tears, that while other branches of learning were excellently taught, grammar, which is the foundation of all others, lay so much neglected, and that for this neglect there seemed to be no adequate remedy."—*Pref. to Minerva.* The grammatical use of language is in sweet alliance with the moral; and a similar regret seems to have prompted the following exclamation of the Christian poet:

> "Sacred Interpreter of human thought,
> How few respect or use thee as they ought!"—*Cowper.*

20. No directions, either oral or written, can ever enable the heedless and the un- thinking to speak or write well. That must indeed be an admirable book, which can attract levity to sober reflection, teach thoughtlessness the true meaning of words, raise vulgarity from its fondness for low examples, awaken the spirit which attains to excellency of speech, and cause grammatical exercises to be skillfully managed, where teachers themselves are so often lamentably deficient in them. Yet something may be effected by means of a better book, if a better can be introduced. And what with- stands?—Whatever there is of ignorance or error in relation to the premises. And is it arrogant to say there is much? Alas! in regard to this, as well as to many a weightier matter, one may too truly affirm, *Mulla non sunt sicut multis videntur—* Many things are not as they seem to many. Common errors are apt to conceal them- selves from the common mind; and the appeal to reason and just authority is often frustrated, because a wrong head defies both. But, apart from this, there are difficul- ties: multiplicity perplexes choice; inconvenience attends change; improvement re- quires effort; conflicting theories demand examination; the principles of the science are unprofitably disputed; the end is often divorced from the means; and much that belies the title, has been published under the name.

21. It is certain, that the printed formularies most commonly furnished for the im- portant exercises of parsing and correcting, are either so awkwardly written, or so negligently followed, as to make grammar, in the mouths of our juvenile orators, little else than a crude and faltering jargon. Murray evidently intended that his book of exercises should be constantly used with his grammar; but he made the examples in the former so dull and prolix, that few learners, if any, have ever gone through the series agreeably to his direction. The publishing of them in a separate volume, has probably given rise to the absurd practice of endeavouring to teach his grammar with- out them. The forms of parsing and correcting which this author furnishes, are also misplaced; and when found by the learner, are of little use. They are so verbose, awkward, irregular, and deficient, that the pupil must be a dull boy, or utterly igno- rant of grammar, if he cannot express the facts extemporaneously in better English. When we consider how exceedingly important it is, that the business of a school should proceed without loss of time, and that, in the oral exercises here spoken of, each pupil should go through his part promptly, clearly, correctly, and fully, we can- not think it a light objection that these forms, so often to be repeated, are badly writ- ten. Nor does the objection lie against this writer only: *Ab uno disce omnes.* But the reader may demand some illustrations.

22. First—from his etymological parsing: "O Virtue! how amiable thou art!" Here his form for the word *Virtue* is—" *Virtue* is a *common substantive of* the *neuter* gender, *of the third* person, *in the* singular number, *and the* nominative case." It should have been—" *Virtue* is a common *noun*, personified *proper*, of the *second per- son*, singular number, *feminine* gender, and nominative case." And, then the defini- tions of all these things should have followed in regular numerical order. He gives

the class of this noun wrong, for virtue addressed becomes an individual; he gives the gender wrong, and in direct contradiction of what he says of the word, in his section on gender; he gives the person wrong; as may be seen by the pronoun *thou;* he repeats the definite article three times unnecessarily, and inserts two needless prepositions, making them different where the relation is precisely the same: and all this, in a sentence of two lines, to tell the properties of the noun *Virtue!*—But, in etymological parsing, the definitions explaining the properties of the parts of speech, ought to be regularly and rapidly rehearsed by the pupil, till all of them are perfectly familiar, and till he can discern, with the quickness of thought, what is true or false in the description of any word in any intelligible sentence. All these the author omits; and, on account of this omission, his whole method of etymological parsing is miserably deficient.

23. Secondly—from his syntactical parsing: "*Vice* degrades us." Here his form for the word *Vice* is—"*Vice* is a common substantive of the third person, *in the* singular number, *and the* nominative case." Now, when the learner is told that this is the syntactical parsing of a noun, and the other the etymological, he will of course conclude, that to advance from the etymology to the syntax of this part of speech, is merely *to omit the gender*—this being the only difference between the two forms. But even this difference had no other origin than the compiler's carelessness in preparing his octavo book of exercises—the gender being inserted in the duodecimo. And what then? Is the syntactical parsing of a noun to be precisely the same as the etymological? Never. But Murray, and all who admire and follow his work, are content to parse many words by halves—making a distinction, and yet often omitting, in both parts of the exercise, every thing which constitutes the difference. He should here have said—"*Vice* is a common noun of the third person, singular number, neuter gender, and nominative case: and is the subject of *degrades;* according to the rule which says, 'A noun or a pronoun which is the subject of a verb, must be in the nominative case.' Because the meaning is—*vice degrades.*" This is the whole description of the word, with its construction; and to say less, is to leave the matter unfinished.

24. Thirdly—from his "mode of verbally correcting erroneous sentences: 'The man is prudent which speaks little.' This sentence," says Murray, "is incorrect; because *which* is a pronoun *of the neuter gender, and does not agree in gender* with its antecedent *man,* which is masculine. But a pronoun should agree with its antecedent in gender, &c., according to the fifth rule of syntax. *Which* should *therefore* be *who,* a relative pronoun, agreeing with its antecedent *man;* and the sentence should stand thus: 'The man is prudent *who* speaks little.'" Again: "'After I visited Europe, I returned to America.' *This sentence,*" says he, "*is not correct;* because the verb *visited* is in the imperfect tense, and yet used here to express an action, not only past, but prior to the time referred to by the verb *returned,* to which it relates. By the thirteenth rule of syntax, when verbs are used that, in point of time, relate to each other, the order of time should be observed. The imperfect tense *visited,* should therefore have been *had visited,* in the pluperfect tense, representing the action of *visiting,* not only as past, but also as prior to the time of *returning. The sentence corrected would stand thus:* 'After I *had visited* Europe, I returned to America.'" These are the first two examples of Murray's verbal corrections, and the only ones retained by Alger, in his *improved, recopy-righted edition* of Murray's Exercises. Yet, in each of them, is the argumentation palpably false! In the former, truly, *which* should be *who;* but not because *which* is of the *neuter gender;* but because the application of that relative to *persons,* is now nearly obsolete. Can any grammarian forget that, in speaking of brute animals, male or female, we commonly use *which,* and never *who?* But if *which* must needs be *neuter,* the world is wrong in this.—As for the latter example, it is right as it stands: and the correction is, in some sort, tautological. The conjunctive adverb *after* makes one of the actions subsequent to the other, and gives to the *visiting* all the priority that is signified by the pluperfect tense. "*After* I *visited* Europe," is equivalent to "*When* I *had visited* Europe." The whole argument is therefore void.

25. These few brief illustrations, out of thousands that might be adduced in proof of the faultiness of the common manuals, the author has reluctantly introduced, to show that, even in the most popular books, the grammar of our language has not been treated with that care and ability which its importance demands. It is hardly to be supposed that men unused to a teacher's duties, can be qualified to compose such books as will most facilitate his labours. Practice is a better pilot than theory. And while, in respect to grammar, the evidences of failure are constantly inducing changes from one system to another, and almost daily giving birth to new expedients as constantly to end in the same disappointment; perhaps the practical instructions of an experienced teacher, long and assiduously devoted to the study, may approve themselves to many, as seasonably supplying the aid and guidance which they require.

26. From the doctrines of grammar, novelty is rigidly excluded. They consist of details to which taste can lend no charm, and genius no embellishment. A writer may express them with neatness and perspicuity—their importance alone can commend them to notice. Yet, in drawing his illustrations from the stores of literature, the grammarian may select some gems of thought, which will fasten on the memory a

worthy sentiment, or relieve the dullness of minute instruction.   Such examples have
been taken from various authors, and interspersed through the following pages.

27.   The moral effect of early lessons being a point of the utmost importance, it is especially incumbent on all those who are endeavouring to confer the benefits of intel-
lectual culture, to guard against the admission or the inculcation of any principle which
may have an improper tendency, and be ultimately prejudicial to those whom they instruct.   In preparing this treatise for publication, the author has been solicitous to
avoid every thing that could be offensive to the most delicate and scrupulous reader ;
and, of the several thousands of quotations given, he trusts that the greater part will
be considered valuable on account of the sentiments they contain.

28.   He has not thought it needful, in a work of this kind, to encumber his pages
with a useless parade of names and references, or to distinguish very minutely what is
copied and what is original.   All strict definitions of the same thing are necessarily
similar.   The doctrines of the work are, for the most part, expressed in his own language, and illustrated by that of others.   Where authority was requisite, names have
been inserted ; and in general also where there was room.   In the doctrinal parts of
the volume, not only quotations from others, but most examples made for the occasion,
are marked with guillemets, to distinguish them from the main text; while, to almost every thing which is really taken from any other known writer, a name or reference is added.   In the exercises for correction, few references have been given; because it is no credit to any author, to have written bad English.   But the intelligent
reader will recognize as quotations a large portion of the examples, and know from
what works they are taken.   To the school-boy this knowledge is neither important
nor interesting

29.   Many of the definitions and rules of grammar have so long been public property,
and have been printed under so many names, that it is difficult, if not impossible, to
know to whom they originally belonged.   Of these the author has freely availed himself, though seldom without some amendment; while he has carefully abstained from
every thing on which he supposed there could now be any individual claim.   He has
therefore fewer personal obligations to acknowledge, than most of those who are reputed to have written with sufficient originality on the subject.

30.   In truth, not a line has here been copied with any view to save the labour of composition; for, not to compile an English grammar from others already extant, but to
compose one directly from the sources of the art, was the task which the writer
proposed to himself.   And though the theme is not one upon which a man may hope
to write well with little reflection, it is true, that the parts of this treatise which have
cost him the most labour, are those which "consist chiefly of materials selected from
the writings of others."   These, however, are not the didactical portions of the book,
but the proofs and examples ; which, according to the custom of the ancient grammarians, ought to be taken from other authors.   But so much have the makers of our
modern grammars been allowed to presume upon the respect and acquiescence of their
readers, that the ancient exactness on this point would often appear pedantic.   Many
phrases and sentences either original or anonymous will therefore be found among the
illustrations of the following work ; for it was not supposed that any reader would demand for every thing of this kind the authority of a great name.   Anonymous examples are sufficient to elucidate principles, if not to establish them; and elucidation is
often the sole purpose for which an example is needed.

31.   The author is well aware that no writer on grammar has any right to propose
himself as authority for what he teaches ; for every language, being the common property of all who use it, ought to be carefully guarded against any caprice of individuals,
and especially against that which might attempt to impose erroneous or arbitrary definitions and rules.   "Since the matter of which we are treating," says the philologist
of Salamanca, "is to be verified, first by reason, and then by testimony and usage,
none ought to wonder if we sometimes deviate from the track of great men ; for, with
whatever authority any grammarian may weigh with me, unless he shall have confirmed his assertions by reason and also by examples, he shall win no confidence in
respect to grammar.   For, as Seneca says, Epistle 95, ' Grammarians are the *guard-
ians*, not the *authors*, of language.' "—*Minerva*, Lib. i, Cap. ii.   Yet, as what is in-
tuitively seen to be true or false, is already sufficiently proved or detected, many
points in grammar need nothing more than to be clearly stated and illustrated ; nay, it
would seem an injurious reflection on the understanding of the reader, to accumulate
proofs of what cannot but be evident to all who speak the language.

32.   Among men of the same profession, there is an unavoidable rivalry, so far as
they become competitors for the same prize ; but in competition there is nothing dishonourable, while excellence alone obtains distinction, and no advantage is sought by
unfair means.   It is evident that we ought to account him the best grammarian, who
has the most completely executed the worthiest design.   But no worthy design can
need a false apology ; and it is worse than idle to prevaricate.   That is but a spurious
modesty, which prompts a man to disclaim in one way what he assumes in an other
—or to underrate the duties of his office, that he may boast of having "done all that
could reasonably be expected."   Whoever professes to have improved the science of
English grammar, must claim to know more of the matter than the generality of English grammarians ; and he who begins with saying that "little can be expected" from

the office he assumes, must be wrongfully contradicted when he is held to have done much. Neither the ordinary power of speech, nor even the ability to write respectably on common topics, makes a man a critic among critics, or enables him to judge of literary merit. And if, by virtue of these qualifications alone, a man will become a grammarian or a connoisseur, he can hold the rank only by courtesy—a courtesy which is content to degrade the character, that his inferior pretensions may be accepted and honoured under the name.

33. By the force of a late popular example, still too widely influential, grammatical authorship has been reduced in the view of many, to little or nothing more than a mere serving-up of materials anonymously borrowed; and, what is most remarkable, even for an indifferent performance of this low office, not only unnamed reviewers, but several writers of note, have not scrupled to bestow the highest praise of grammatical excellence! And thus the palm of superior skill in grammar, has been borne away by a *professed compiler;* who had so mean an opinion of what his theme required, as to deny it even the common courtesies of compilation. What marvel is it, that, under the wing of such authority, many writers have since sprung up, to improve upon this most happy design : while all who were competent to the task, have been discouraged from attempting any thing like a complete grammar of our language? What motive shall excite a man to long-continued diligence, where such notions prevail as give mastership no hope of preference, and where the praise of his ingenuity and the reward of his labour must needs be inconsiderable, till some honoured compiler usurp them both, and bring his "most useful matter" before the world under better auspices? If the love of learning supply such a motive, who that has generously yielded to the impulse, will not now, like Johnson, feel himself reduced to an "humble drudge"—or, like Perizonius, apologize for the apparent folly of devoting his time to such a subject as grammar?

34. Since the first edition of this work, more than two hundred new compends, many of them professing to be abstracts of *Murray* with improvements, have been added to our list of English grammars. The author has examined about one hundred and fifty, and seen advertisements or notices of nearly half as many more. Being various in character, they will of course be variously estimated; but, so far as he can judge, they are, without exception, works of little or no real merit, and not likely to be much patronized or long preserved from oblivion. For which reason, he would have been inclined entirely to disregard the petty depredations which the writers of several of them have committed upon the following digest, were it not possible that by such a frittering-away of his work he himself might one day seem to some to have copied that from others which was first taken from him. Trusting to make it manifest to men of learning, that in the production of these Institutes far more has been done for the grammar of our language, than any single hand had before achieved within the limits of a school-book, and that with perfect fairness towards other writers; he cannot but feel a wish that the integrity of his text should be preserved, whatever else may befall; and that the multitude of scribblers who judge it so needful to remodel Murray's defective compilation, would forbear to publish under his name or their own what they find only in the following pages.

35. The mere rivalry of their authorship is no subject of concern; but it is enough for any ingenuous man to have toiled for years in solitude to complete a work of public utility, without entering a warfare for life to defend and preserve it. Accidental coincidences in books are unfrequent, and not often such as to excite the suspicion of the most sensitive. But, though the criteria of plagiarism are neither obscure nor disputable, it is not easy, in this beaten track of literature, for persons of little reading to know what is, or is not, original. Dates must be accurately observed. Many things must be minutely compared. And who will undertake such a task, but he that is personally interested? Of the thousands who are forced into the paths of learning, few ever care to know, by what pioneer, or with what labour, their way was cast up for them. And even of those who are honestly engaged in teaching, not many are adequate judges of the comparative merits of the great number of books on this subject. The common notions of mankind conform more easily to fashion than to truth: and, even of some things within their reach, the majority seem content to take their opinions upon trust. Hence, it is vain to expect that that which is intrinsically best, will be everywhere preferred , or that which is meritoriously elaborate, adequately appreciated. But common sense might dictate that learning is not encouraged or respected by those who, for the making of books, prefer a pair of scissors to the pen.

36. The real history of grammar is little known ; and many erroneous impressions are entertained concerning it: because the story of the systems most generally received, has never been fully told ; and that of a multitude now gone to oblivion, was never worth telling. In the distribution of grammatical fame, which has chiefly been made by the hand of interest, we have had a strange illustration of the saying : " Unto every one that hath shall be given, and he shall have abundance: but from him that hath not, shall be taken away even that which he hath." Some whom fortune has made popular, have been greatly overrated, if learning and talents are to be taken into the account ; since it is manifest, that with no extraordinary claims to either, they have taken the very foremost rank among grammarians, and thrown the learning and talents of others into the shade, or made them tributary to their own success and popularity.

1*

37. Few writers on grammar have been more noted than Lily and Murray. A law was made in England by Henry the Eighth, commanding Lily's grammar " only everywhere to be taught, for the use of learners and for the hurt in changing of schoolmaisters."—*Pref. to Lily*, p. xiv. Being long kept in force by means of a special inquiry directed to be made by the bishops at their stated visitations, this law, for three hundred years, imposed the book on all the established schools of the realm. Yet it is certain, that about one half of what has thus gone under the name of Lily, (" because," says one of the patentees, " he had *so considerable a hand* in the composition,") was written by Dr. Colet, by Erasmus, or by others who improved the work after Lily's death. (See Ward's Preface to the book, 1793.) And of the other half, history incidentally tells, that neither the scheme nor the text was original. The Printer's Grammar, London, 1787, speaking of the art of type-foundery, says : " The Italians in a short time brought it to that perfection, that in the beginning of the year 1474, they cast a letter not much inferior to the best types of the present age; as may be seen in a Latin Grammar written by Omnibonus Leonicenus, and printed at Padua on the 14th of January, 1474 ; *from whom our grammarian, Lily, has taken the entire scheme of his grammar, and transcribed the greatest part thereof, without paying any regard to the memory of this author.*" The historian then proceeds to speak about types. See also the History of Printing, 8vo, London, 1770. This is the grammar which bears upon its titlépage: " *Quam solam Regia Majestas in omnibus scholis docendam præcipit.*"

38. Murray was an intelligent and very worthy man, to whose various labours in the compilation of books our schools are under many obligations. But in original thought and critical skill he fell far below most of " the authors to whom," he confesses, " the grammatical part of his compilation is *principally indebted for its materials;* namely, Harris, Johnson, Lowth, Priestley, Beattie, Sheridan, Walker, Coote, Blair, and Campbell."—*Introd. to Gram.*, p. 7. It is certain and evident that he entered upon his task with a very insufficient preparation. His biography informs us, that, " Grammar did not particularly engage his attention, until a short time before the publication of his first work on that subject ;" that, " His grammar, as it appeared in the first edition, was completed in rather less than a year—though he had an intervening illness, which for several weeks stopped the progress of the work ;" and that, " the Exercises and Key were also composed in about a year."—*Life of L. Murray*, p. 183. From the very first sentence of his book, it appears that he entertained but a low and most erroneous idea of the duties of that sort of character in which he was about to come before the public. He improperly imagined, as many others have done, that " little can be expected" from a modern grammarian, or (as he chose to express it) " from a *new compilation*, besides a careful selection of the most useful matter, and some degree of improvement in the mode of adapting it to the understanding, and the gradual progress of learners."—*Introd. to Gram.*, 8vo, p. 5 ; 12mo, p. 3. As if, to be master of his own art—to think and write well himself, were no part of a grammarian's business! And again, as if the jewels of scholarship, thus carefully selected, could need a burnish or a foil from other hands than those which fashioned them!

39. Murray's general idea of the doctrines of grammar was judicious. He attempted no broad innovation on what had been previously taught ; for he had neither the vanity to suppose he could give currency to novelties, nor the folly to waste his time in labours utterly nugatory. By turning his own abilities to their best account, he seems to have done much to promote and facilitate the study of our language. But his notion of grammatical authorship, cuts off from it all pretence to literary merit, for the sake of doing good ; and, taken in any other sense than as a forced apology for his own assumptions, his language on this point is highly injurious towards the very authors whom he copied. To justify himself, he ungenerously places them, in common with others, under a degrading necessity which no able grammarian ever felt, and which every man of genius or learning must repudiate. If none of our older grammars disprove his assertion, it is time to have a new one that will; for, to expect the perfection of grammar from him who cannot treat the subject in a style at once original and pure, is absurd. He says, " The greater part of an English grammar *must necessarily be a compilation;*" and adds, with reference to his own, " originality belongs to but a small portion of it. This I have acknowledged ; and I trust *this acknowledgement* will protect me from all attacks, grounded on any supposed unjust and irregular assumptions."—*Letter*, 1811. The acknowledgement on which he thus relies does not appear to have been made, till his grammar had gone through several editions. It was then inserted as follows: " In a work which professes to be a compilation, and which, *from the nature and design of it*, must consist chiefly of materials selected from the writings of others, *it is scarcely necessary to apologize* for the use which the compiler has made of his predecessors' labours, or for *omitting to insert* their names."—*Introd. to Gram.*, 8vo, p. 7 ; 12mo, p. 4.

40. For the nature and design *of a book*, whatever they may be, the author alone is answerable ; but the nature and design *of grammar*, are no less repugnant to the strain of this apology, than to the vast number of errors and defects which were overlooked by Murray in his work of compilation. There is no part of the volume more accurate, than that which he literally copied from Lowth. To the Short Introduction alone he was indebted for more than a hundred and twenty paragraphs ; and even in these

there are many things obviously erroneous. Many of the best practical notes were taken from Priestley; yet it was he, at whose doctrines were pointed most of those "positions and discussions," which alone the author claims as original. To some, however, his own alterations may have given rise; for, where he "persuades himself he is not destitute of originality," he is often arguing against the text of his own earlier editions. Webster's well-known complaints of Murray's unfairness, had a far better cause than requital; for there was no generosity in ascribing them to peevishness, though the passages in question were not worth copying. On perspicuity and accuracy, about sixty pages were extracted from Blair, and it requires no great critical acumen to discover, that they are miserably deficient in both. On the law of language, there are fifteen pages from Campbell; which, with a few exceptions, are well written. The rules for spelling are the same as Walker's: the third one, however, is a gross blunder; and the fourth, a needless repetition. Were this a place for minute criticism, blemishes almost innumerable might be pointed out. It might easily be shown that almost every rule laid down in the book for the observance of the learner, was repeatedly violated by the hand of the master. Nor is there among all those who have since abridged or modified the work, an abler grammarian than he who compiled it. Who will pretend that Flint, Alden, Comly, Jaudon, Russell, Bacon, Lyon, Miller, Alger, Maltby, Ingersoll, Fisk, Greenleaf, Merchant, Kirkham, Cooper, R. G. Greene, Woodworth, Smith, or Frost, has exhibited greater skill? It is curious to observe, how frequently a grammatical blunder committed by Murray, or some one of his predecessors, has escaped the notice of all these, as well as of many others who have found it easier to copy him than to write for themselves.

41. But Murray's grammatical works, being at once extolled in the reviews, and made common stock in trade,—being published, both in England and in America, by booksellers of the most extensive correspondence, and highly commended even by those who were most interested in the sale of them,—have been eminently successful with the public; and, in the opinion of the world, success is the strongest proof of merit. Nor has the force of this argument been overlooked by those who have written in aid of his popularity. It is the strong point in most of the commendations which have been bestowed upon Murray as a grammarian. A recent eulogist computes, that, "at least five millions of copies of his various school-books have been printed;" particularly commends him for his "candour and liberality towards rival authors;" avers that, "he went on, examining and correcting his grammar, through all its forty editions, till he brought it to a degree of perfection which will render it as permanent as the English language itself;" censures (and not without reason) the "presumption" of those "superficial critics" who have attempted to amend the work, and usurp his honours; and, regarding the compiler's confession of his indebtedness to others, but as a mark of "his exemplary diffidence of his own merits," adds, (in very bad English,) "Perhaps there never was an author whose success and fame were *more unexpected by himself, than Lindley Murray.*"—*The Friend*, Vol. iii, p. 33.

42. In a New-York edition of Murray's Grammar, printed in 1812, there was inserted a "Caution to the Public," by Collins & Co., his American correspondents and publishers, in which are set forth the unparalleled success and merit of the work, "as it came *in purity* from the pen of the author;" with an earnest remonstrance against the several *revised editions* which had appeared at Boston, Philadelphia, and other places, and against the unwarrantable liberties taken by American teachers, in altering the work, under pretence of improving it. In this article it is stated, "that *the whole* of these mutilated editions *have been seen* and examined by Lindley Murray himself, and that they have met with his *decided disapprobation*. Every rational mind," continue these gentlemen, "will agree with him, that, 'the *rights of living authors,* and the *interests of science and literature,* demand the abolition of this *ungenerous practice.*'" Here, then, we have the opinion and feeling of Murray himself upon this tender point of right. Here we see the tables turned, and other men judging it "scarcely necessary to apologize for the use which *they have made* of their predecessors' labours."

43. It is not intended by the introduction of these notices, to impute to Murray any thing more or less than what his own words plainly imply; except those inaccuracies and deficiencies which still disgrace his work as a literary performance, and which of course he did not discover. He himself knew that he had not brought the book to such perfection as has been ascribed to it; for, by way of apology for his frequent alterations, he says, "Works of this nature admit of repeated improvements; and are, perhaps, never complete." But it is due to truth to correct erroneous impressions; and, in order to obtain from some an impartial examination of the following pages, it seems necessary first to convince them that it is *possible,* to compose a better grammar than Murray's, without being particularly indebted to him. If this treatise is not such, a great deal of time has been thrown away upon a useless project; and if it is, the achievement is no fit subject for either pride or envy. It differs from his, and from every grammar based upon his, as a new map, drawn from actual and minute surveys, differs from an old one, compiled chiefly from others still older and confessedly still more imperfect. The region and the scope are essentially the same; the tracing and the colouring are more original; and (if the reader can pardon the suggestion) perhaps more accurate and vivid.

44. He who makes a new grammar, does nothing for the advancement of learning, unless his performance excel all earlier ones designed for the same purpose; and nothing for his own honour, unless such excellence result from the exercise of his own ingenuity and taste. A good style naturally commends itself to every reader—even to him who cannot tell why it is worthy of preference. Hence there is reason to believe, that the true principles of practical grammar, deduced from custom and sanctioned by time, will never be generally superseded by any thing which individual caprice may substitute. In the republic of letters, there will always be one who can distinguish merit; and it is impossible that these should ever be converted to any whimsical theory of language, which goes to make void the learning of past ages. There will always be some who can discern the difference between originality of style, and innovation in doctrine—between a due regard to the opinions of others, and an actual usurpation of their text; and it is incredible that these should ever be satisfied with any mere compilation of grammar, or with any such authorship as either confesses or betrays the writer's own incompetence. For it is not true, that "an English grammar must necessarily be," in any considerable degree, if at all, "a compilation;" nay, on such a theme, and in "the grammatical part" of the work, all compilation, beyond a fair use of authorities regularly quoted, or of materials either voluntarily furnished or free to all, most unavoidably implies—not conscious "ability," generously doing honour to rival merit—nor "exemplary diffidence," modestly veiling its own—but inadequate skill and inferior talents, bribing the public by the spoils of genius, and seeking precedence by such means as not even the purest desire of doing good can justify.

45. All praise of excellence must needs be comparative, because the thing itself is so. To excel in grammar, is but to know better than others wherein grammatical excellence consists. Hence there is no fixed point of perfection beyond which such learning may not be carried. The limit to improvement is not so much in the nature of the subject, as in the powers of the mind, and in the inducements to exert them upon a theme so humble and so uninviting. Dr. Johnson suggests in his masterly preface, "that a whole life cannot be spent upon syntax and etymology, and that even a whole life would not be sufficient." Who then will suppose, in the face of such facts and confessions as have been exhibited, that either in the faulty publications of Murray, or among the various modifications of them by other hands, we have any such work as deserves to be made a permanent standard of instruction in English grammar?— The author of this treatise will not pretend that it is perfect; though he has bestowed upon it no inconsiderable pains, that the narrow limits to which it must needs be confined, might be filled up to the utmost advantage of the learner, as well as to the best direction and greatest relief of the teacher.

46. A KEY *to the Oral Exercises in False Syntax*, is inserted in the Grammar, that the pupil may be enabled fully to prepare himself for that kind of class recitations. Being acquainted with the rule, and having seen the correction, he may be expected to state the error and the reason for the change, without embarrassment or delay. It is the opinion of some teachers, that no Key in aid of the student should be given. Accordingly many grammars, not destitute of exercises in false syntax, are published without either formules of correction, or a Key to show the right reading. But English grammar, in any extensive exhibition of it, is a study dry and difficult enough for the young, when we have used our best endeavours to free it from all obscurities and doubts. The author thinks he has learned from experience, that, with explicit help of this sort, most pupils will not only gain more knowledge of the art in a given time, but in the end find their acquisitions more satisfactory and more permanent.

47. A separate KEY *to the Exercises for Writing*, is published for the convenience of teachers and private learners. For an obvious reason this Key should not be put into the hands of the school-boy. Being a distinct volume, it may be had, bound by itself or with the Grammar. Those teachers who desire to exercise their pupils orally in correcting false grammar without a Key, can at any time make use of this series of examples for such purpose.

48. From the first edition of the following treatise, there was made by the author, for the use of young learners, a brief abstract, entitled, *"The First Lines of English Grammar;"* in which are embraced all the leading doctrines of the original work, with a new series of examples for their application in parsing. Much that is important in the grammar of the language, was necessarily excluded from this epitome; nor was it designed for those who can learn a larger book without wearing it out. But economy, as well as convenience, demands small and cheap treatises for children; and those teachers who approve of this system of grammatical instruction, will find many reasons for preferring the First Lines to any other compend, as an introduction to the study of these Institutes.

49. Having undertaken and prosecuted this work, with the hope of facilitating the study of the English Language, and thus promoting the improvement of the young, the author now presents his finished labours to the candour and discernment of those to whom is committed the important business of instruction. How far he has succeeded in the execution of his design, is willingly left to the just decision of those who are qualified to judge. GOOLD BROWN.

Revised, Lynn, Mass., 1854.

POSTSCRIPT TO THE PREFACE.

THE school-book now pretty well-known as "Brown's Institutes of English Grammar," was my first attempt at authorship in the character of a grammarian; and, satisfactory as it has been to the many thousands who have used it, it has nevertheless, like all other not incorrigible attempts in this line, been found susceptible of sundry important emendations. So that I must believe with Murray, that, "Works of this nature admit of *repeated improvements;* and are, perhaps, never complete." It cannot, however, be said in my favour, as it has been in commendation of this author, that, "He went on examining and correcting his grammar *through all its forty editions,* till he brought it to the utmost degree of perfection;" but something has been done in this way, three or four of the early editions of the Institutes having been severally retouched and improved by the author's hand; and now, an undiminished demand for the work having continued to spread its reputation, I have at length the satisfaction to have endeavoured yet once again to render it still more worthy of the public favour.

The time which has elapsed since the author first published this work, has been mainly spent in labours and studies tending very directly to enlarge and mature his knowledge of English Grammar; and, especially, to better his acquaintance with the great variety of books and essays which have been written upon it. The principal result of these labours and studies has been given to the world in his large work entitled "The Grammar of English Grammars." To conform the future editions of these Institutes more nearly to the text of this large Grammar, to supply some deficiences which have been thought to lessen the comparative value of the former work, to divide the book more systematically into chapters and subdivisions, and to correct a few typographical errors which had crept in, were the objects contemplated in the revision which has now been effected.

In making these improvements, I have not forgotten that alterations in a popular class-book are, on some accounts, exceedingly undesirable. The writer who ventures at all upon them, is ever liable to subject his patrons and best friends to more or less inconvenience; and for this he should be very sure of having presented, in every instance, an ample compensation. It is believed that the changes which the present revision exhibits, though they are neither few nor unimportant, need not prevent, in schools, a concurrent use of old editions with the new, till the former may be sufficiently worn out. What has been added or changed, will therefore lack no justification; and the author will rest, with sufficient assurance, in the hope that the intelligent patronage which has hitherto been giving more and more publicity to his earliest teachings, will find, decidedly, and without mistake, in this improved form of the work, the best common school Grammar now extant.

GOOLD BROWN.

Lynn, Mass., 1855.

TABLE OF CONTENTS.

PART III.—SYNTAX.

PART IV.—PROSODY.

THE

INSTITUTES

OF

ENGLISH GRAMMAR.

ENGLISH GRAMMAR is the art of speaking, reading, and writing the English language correctly.

It is divided into four parts; namely, Orthography, Etymology, Syntax, and Prosody.

Orthography treats of letters, syllables, separate words, and spelling.

Etymology treats of the different parts of speech, with their classes and modifications.

Syntax treats of the relation, agreement, government, and arrangement, of words in sentences.

Prosody treats of punctuation, utterance, figures, and versification.

PART I.

ORTHOGRAPHY.

Orthography treats of letters, syllables, separate words, and spelling.

CHAPTER I.—OF LETTERS.

A *Letter* is an alphabetic mark, or character, commonly representing some elementary sound of a word.

An elementary sound of a word, is a simple or primary sound of the human voice, used in speaking.

The sound of a letter is commonly called its *power :* when any letter of a word is not sounded, it is said to be *silent* or *mute.*

2*

The letters in the English alphabet, are twenty-six; the simple or primary sounds in the language, are about thirty-six or thirty-seven.

A knowledge of the letters consists in an acquaintance with these *four sorts of things;* their *names*, their *classes*, their *powers*, and their *forms*.

The letters are written, or printed, or painted, or engraved, or embossed, in an infinite variety of shapes and sizes; and yet are always *the same*, because their essential properties do not change, and their names, classes, and powers, are mostly permanent.

The following are some of the different sorts of types, or *styles* of letters, with which every reader should be early acquainted:—

1. The Roman: A a, B b, C c, D d, E e, F f, G g, H h, I i, J j, K k, L l, M m, N n, O o, P p, Q q, R r, S s, T t, U u, V v, W w, X x, Y y, Z z.

2. The Italic: *A a, B b, C c, D d, E e, F f, G g, H h, I i, J j, K k, L l, M m, N n, O o, P p, Q q, R r, S s, T t, U u, V v, W w, X x, Y y, Z z.*

3. The Script: *A a, B b, C c, D d, E e, F f, G g, H h, I i, J j, K k, L l, M m, N n, O o, P p, Q q, R r, S s, T t, U u, V v, W w, X x, Y y, Z z.*

4. The Old English: A a, B b, C c, D d, E e, F f, G g, H h, I i, J j, K k, L l, M m, N n, O o, P p, Q q, R r, S s, T t, U u, V v, W w, X x, Y y, Z z.

OBSERVATIONS.

Obs. 1.—Language, in the primitive sense of the term, embraced only vocal expression, or human speech uttered by the mouth; but, after letters were invented to represent articulate sounds, language became twofold, *spoken* and *written;* so that the term *language*, now signifies, *any series of sounds or letters formed into words and employed for the expression of thought.*

Obs. 2.—Letters claim to be a part of language, not merely because they represent articulate sounds, or spoken words, but because they form words of themselves, and have the power to become intelligible signs of thought, even independently of sound. Literature being the counterpart of speech, and more plenteous in words, the person who cannot read and write, is about as deficient in language, as the well instructed deaf mute: perhaps more so; for *copiousness*, even of speech, results from letters.

Obs. 3.—For the formation of words, letters have some important advantages over articulate or syllabic sounds, though the latter communicate thought more expeditiously. The written symbols subdivide even the least parts of spoken language, which are syllables, reducing them to a few combinable elements; and are themselves thereby reduced to a manageable number,—even to fewer than the elements which they represent. But the great advantage of recorded language is its *permanence*, with its unlimited power of *circulation* and *transmission.*

Obs. 4.—As a letter taken singly is commonly the sign of some elementary sound, and of nothing more, so the primary combinations of letters are often exhibited as mere notations of syllabic sounds, and not as having the signification of *words.* Silent letters occur only in the particular positions which custom or etymology has given them in certain *words;* and, though mute, they are still named and classed according to the powers usually pertaining to the same characters.

Obs. 5.—It is suggested above, that a knowledge of the letters implies an acquaintance with their *names,* their *classes,* their *powers,* and their *forms.* Under these four heads, therefore, I shall briefly present the facts which seem to be most worthy of the learner's attention at first, and shall reserve for the appendix a more particular account of these important elements.

I. NAMES OF THE LETTERS.

The *names* of the letters, as now commonly spoken and written in English, are *A, Bee, Cee, Dee, E, Eff, Gee, Aitch, I, Jay, Kay, Ell, Em, En, O, Pee, Kue, Ar, Ess, Tee, U, Vee, Double-u, Ex, Wy, Zee.*

OBSERVATIONS.

Obs. 1.—The names of the letters, as expressed in the modern languages, are mostly framed *with reference* to their powers, or sounds. Yet is there in English no letter of which the name is always identical with its power; for *A, E, I, O,* and *U,* are the only letters which can name themselves, and all these have other sounds than those which their names express. The consonants are so manifestly insufficient to form any name of themselves alone, and so palpable is the difference between the nature and the name of each, that, did we not know how education has been trifled with, it would be hard to believe the assertion of Murray, that, "They are frequently confounded by writers on grammar!"

Obs. 2.—Those letters which name themselves, take for their names those sounds which they usually represent at the end of an accented syllable; thus the names, *A, E, I, O, U,* are uttered with the sounds given to the same letters in the first syllables of the other names, *Abel, Enoch, Isaac, Obed, Urim;* or in the first syllables of the common words, *paper, penal, pilot, potent, pupil.* The other letters, most of which can never be perfectly sounded alone, have names in which their powers are combined with other sounds more vocal; as, *Bee, Cee, Dee,—Ell, Em, En,—Jay, Kay, Kue.* But, in this respect, the terms *Aitch* and *Double-u* are irregular; because they have no obvious reference to the powers of the letters thus named.

Obs. 3.—The names of the letters, like those of the days of the week, are words of a very peculiar kind; being nouns that are at once *both proper and common.* For, in respect to rank, character, and design, each letter is a thing strictly individual and identical—that is, it is ever one and the same; yet, in an other respect, it is a comprehensive sort, embracing individuals both various and numberless. The name of a letter, therefore, should always be written with a capital, as a proper noun, at least in the singular number; and should form the plural regularly, as an ordinary appellative. Thus: (if we adopt, as we ought, the names now most generally used in English schools:) *A, Aes; Bee, Bees; Cee, Cees; Dee, Dees; E, Ees; Eff, Effs; Gee, Gees; Aitch, Aitches; I, Ies; Jay, Jays; Kay, Kays; Ell, Ells; Em, Ems; En, Ens; O, Oes; Pee, Pees; Kue, Kues; Ar, Ars; Ess, Esses; Tee, Tees; U, Ues; Vee, Vees; Double-u, Double-ues; Ex, Exes; Wy, Wies; Zee, Zees.*

Obs. 4.—Letters, like all other things, must be learned and spoken of *by their names;* nor can they be spoken of otherwise; yet, as the simple characters are better known and more easily exhibited than their written names, the former are often substituted for the latter, and are read as the words for which they are assumed. Hence the orthography of these words has hitherto been left too much to mere fancy or caprice; no certain method of writing them has been generally inculcated; so that many who think themselves well educated, would be puzzled to name on paper these simple elements of all learning.

OBS. 5.—In many, if not in all languages, the five vowels, A, E, I, O, U, name themselves; but they name themselves differently to the ear, according to the different ways of uttering them in different languages. And as the name of a consonant necessarily requires one or more vowels, that also may be affected in the same manner. But, in every language, there should be a known way both of writing and of speaking every name in the series; and that, if there is nothing to hinder, should be made conformable to *the genius of the language.* For the names of the letters, in any language, are, in reality, *words of that language,* and not likely to be very suitable for the same purpose in any other.

OBS. 6.—The letters, once learned, may be used *unnamed;* and so are they used, always, except in oral spelling, or when some of their own number are to be particularized. The chief use of the *written* names is, to preserve and teach those which are *spoken;*—to record current practice, in the hope of thereby preventing or lessening diversity: for, as Walker observes, "*The names of the letters ought to have no diversity.*"—*Principles,* No. 483.

OBS. 7.—The occasions, however, for naming the letters are so frequent, and lists of their names are given in so many books, that one cannot but marvel at the absence of these words from the columns of our dictionaries, and at the errors found elsewhere concerning them. So discrepant and erroneous are the modes of writing them adopted by authors of spelling-books, and even by our best authorities—Walker, Webster, Murray, Churchill, W. Allen, and others—that any common school-boy would *guess* their forms quite as well. Even John Walker, in his "Principles of English Pronunciation," spells five or six of them wrong; commences all of them with small type, as reckoning them common nouns only; fixes a gratuitous and silly "*diversity*" in five of them with his own hand; and contradicts himself by preferring *zed* to *izzard* at first, and *izzard* to *zed* at last!

OBS. 8.—In every nation that is not totally illiterate, custom must have established for the letters a certain set of names, which are *the only true ones,* and which are of course to be preferred to such as are local, or obsolete, or unauthorized. Sundry examples of these objectionable sorts of names may indeed be cited from our school literature; for, in the lapse of ages, usage has changed in a few instances, and, in their rash ignorance, some authors of A-Bee-Cee books have taught, in lieu of the right names, both archaisms and innovations at the same time; while many others, thinking the naming of letters a matter not worth their attention, have omitted it altogether. I have recorded above the *true* English names of all the letters, as they are now used, and as they have been most fitly, and perhaps most generally, used thus far in the nineteenth century; and, if there could be in human works any thing unchangeable, I should wish, (with due deference to all schemers and fault-finders,) that these names might remain the same and in good use forever.

II. CLASSES OF THE LETTERS.

The letters are divided into two general classes, *vowels* and *consonants.*

A *vowel* is a letter which forms a perfect sound when uttered alone; as, *a, e, o.*

A *consonant* is a letter which cannot be perfectly uttered till joined to a vowel; as, *b, c, d.*

The vowels are *a, e, i, o, u,* and sometimes *w* and *y.* All the other letters are consonants.

W or *y* is called a consonant when it precedes a vowel heard in the same syllable; as in *wine, twine, whine; ye, yet, youth:* in all other cases, these letters are vowels; as in *newly, dewy, eye-brow; Yssel, Ystadt, yttria.*

<h3 style="text-align:center">CLASSES OF CONSONANTS.</h3>

The consonants are divided into *semivowels* and *mutes.*

A *semivowel* is a consonant which can be imperfectly sounded without a vowel, so that at the end of a syllable its sound may be protracted; as, *l, n, z,* in *al, an, az.*

A *mute* is a consonant which cannot be sounded at all without a vowel, and which at the end of a syllable suddenly stops the breath; as, *k, p, t,* in *ak, ap, at.*

The semivowels are *f, h, j, l, m, n, r, s, v, w, x, y, z,* and *c* and *g* soft: but *w* or *y* at the end of a syllable, is a vowel; and the sound of *c, f, g, h, j, s,* or *x,* can be protracted only as an *aspirate,* or strong breath.

Four of the semivowels,—*l, m, n,* and *r,*—are termed *liquids,* on account of the fluency of their sounds; and four others,—*v, w, y,* and *z,*—are likewise more vocal than the aspirates.

The mutes are eight; *b, d, k, p, q, t,* and *c* and *g* hard: three of these,—*k, q,* and *c* hard,—sound exactly alike: *b, d,* and *g* hard, stop the voice less suddenly than the rest.

<h3 style="text-align:center">OBSERVATIONS.</h3>

Obs. 1.—The foregoing division of the letters is of very great antiquity, and, in respect to its principal features, sanctioned by almost universal authority. Aristotle, three hundred and thirty years before Christ, divided the Greek letters into *vowels, semivowels,* and *mutes,* and declared that no syllable could be formed without a vowel. Some modern writers, however, not well satisfied with this ancient distribution of the elements of learning, have contradicted the Stagirite, and divided both sounds and letters into new classes, with various new names. But, so far as I can see, they have thereby effected no important improvement; and, since mere innovation is not in itself desirable in such cases, the old scheme is here still preferred.

Obs. 2.—Dr. Rush, author of "the Philosophy of the Human Voice," resolves the letters into "*tonics, subtonics,* and *atonics;*" and avers that "consonants alone may form syllables." S. Kirkham too, though his *Grammar* teaches the old doctrine as given by Murray, prefers in his *Elocution* the instructions of Rush; disparages "the *hoary* division of the letters of our alphabet into *vowels* and *consonants;*" affirms that, "A consonant is not only capable of being perfectly sounded without the help of a vowel, but, moreover, of forming, like a vowel, a *separate syllable;*" (p. 32;) commends Rush's new "division and classification of the elementary *characters* of our language, in accordance with their use in *intonation;*" puts an obsolete *k* into each of the Doctor's new names, giving to novelties the garb of antiques; tells of "the *Tonicks,* the *Subtonicks,* and the *Atonicks;*" and, under these three heads, exhibits his thirty-five "elements" of the English tongue, by means of Italics and the splitting of syllables, thus:—

1. "The *Tonicks*, twelve: *A*-te, *a*-rk, *a*-ll, *a*-t, *ee*-l, *e*-rr, *e*-nd, *i*-de, *i*-t, *o*-ld, *oo*-ze, *ou*-t.

2. "The *Subtonicks*, fourteen: *B*-oat, *d*-are, *g*-ilt, *v*-ice, *z*-one, *y*-e, *w*-o, *th*-at, a-*z*-ure, so-*ng*, *l*-ate, *m*-ate, *n*-ot, *r*-oe.

3. "The *Atonicks*, nine: U-*p*, a-*t*, lur-*k*, i-*f*, thi-*s*, *h*-e, *wh*-at, *th*-in, blu-*sh*."
—*Kirkham's Elocution*, pp. 32 and 33.

Obs. 3.—As a mode of classing the *letters* of the alphabet, (which character is claimed for it,) this arrangement has no fitness whatever. As a classification of the *sounds* of the language, it is less objectionable, but still very faulty. Its vowel powers are too few, and yet the list contains two which are questionable: for *ou* in *out* is a proper diphthong; and, according to Walker, *e* in *err* and *e* in *end* are sounded alike. The term "*i*-de," which is given for a "word," is not properly such; and the term "*g*-ilt" is an ill example of the hard *g*, because *g* before *i* is usually soft, like *j*. How the power of *wh* differs from the sounds of *h* and *w* united, I see not, though sundry modern authors affirm that it is simple and elementary. The assertion, that "consonants alone may form syllables," is a flat absurdity; it implies that consonants are not consonants, but vowels!

Obs. 4.—In Comstock's Elocution, we have the following statement: "The elements, as well as the letters by which they are represented, are usually divided into two classes, *Vowels* and *Consonants*. A more philosophical division, however, is into three classes, *Vowels*, *Subvowels*, and *Aspirates*. The *vowels* are pure vocal sounds; their number is fifteen: they are heard in *ale*, *arm*, *all*, *an*, *eve*, *end*, *ile*, *in*, *old*, *lose*, *on*, *tube*, *up*, *full*, *our*. The *subvocals* have a vocality, but inferior to that of the vowels; their number is fourteen: they are heard in *bow*, *day*, *gay*, *light*, *mind*, *no*, *song*, *roll*, *then*, *vile*, *wo*, *yoke*, *zone*, *azure*. The *aspirates* are made with the whispering breath, and, consequently, have no vocality; they are nine in number; and are heard in *fame*, *hut*, *kite*, *pit*, *sin*, *shade*, *tin*, *thin*, *what*."—Pp. 19 and 20.

Obs. 5.—This again is a classification of *sounds*, and not of the *letters*. To call it "a more philosophical division" of the letters, is a ridiculous absurdity. For, of the twenty-six letters, it throws out four,—*c*, *j*, *q*, and *x*,—because their sounds may be otherwise expressed; while ten repetitions of the same letter with a different sound, and six combinations of different letters, making sixteen unalphabetical items, are allowed to swell the number of "elements" to thirty-eight; *ou* and *wh* being improperly reckoned among them. The definitions, too, are each of them inconsistent with the fact that all these elements may be either *whispered* or *spoken aloud*, at pleasure.

Obs. 6.—The elementary sounds of the language being more numerous than the letters of the alphabet, and not very philosophically distributed among them, no accurate classification of either species can be exactly adapted to the other; and to divide the powers of the letters into one set of classes, and then divide the letters themselves, with reference to their powers, into an other set, as a few late writers have done, seems to be neither free from objection, nor very necessary to the purposes of instruction. Such is the scheme in Covell's "Digest," and also in Greene's "Elements of English Grammar;" where the sounds used in English, being reckoned forty by the latter author, and forty-one by the former, are divided into "*Vocals*, *Subvocals*, and *Aspirates*," with an additional class of "*Cognates*," or "*Correlatives*;" and then the letters are classed as "*vowels* and *consonants*;" with the suggestion that consonants are either "subvocals" or "aspirates."

Obs. 7.—By way of definition, Covell says, "*Vocals* consist of *pure voice* only. *Subvocals* consist of *voice and breath* united. *Aspirates* consist of *pure breath* only. A *vowel* is a letter used to represent a *vocal*. A *consonant* is a letter used to represent a *subvocal* or *aspirate*."—Pp. 11 and 16. Greene says, "The *vocals* consist of *pure tone only*. The *subvocals* consist of *tone* united with *breath*. The *aspirates* consist of *pure breath only*. Those letters which represent *vocals* are called *vowels*. Those letters which represent *subvocals and aspirates* are called *consonants*."—Pp. 2 and 5. Now, since all the elements of words, except silent letters, may be *whispered*, and whispering consists in the articulation "*of pure breath only*," may not a little whispering show the unfitness of all these definitions?

OBS. 8.—Greene says, "By what rule such sounds as *f, s,* or *c* soft, which have no vocality whatever, can be called *semivowels,* it *is impossible* to see."—*Elements of E. Gram.,* p. 3. This remark must have originated in some wrong notion of what vocality is. Again, it is forgotten that not "sounds," but *letters,* are by the definition made semivowels. If there is any error in regarding a hiss as half a voice, or in calling "*f, s,* or *c* soft" a semivowel, Aristotle himself is answerable for it, as may be seen in the twentieth chapter of his Poetics. But S. S. Greene contradicts the old philosopher not only by denying all vocality to some of his semivowels, but also by finding the nature of "*subvocals*" in both of his examples of a *mute;* namely in *g* hard and *d,* or the corresponding Greek letters. See "Table of Elementary Sounds," in Greene's Elements, edition of 1853; wherein our sibilant *s* is blunderingly stereotyped as being an element of two or three different sorts, and as having *v* for its "*correlative.*"

OBS. 9.—By an improper recognition of sounds for letters, and of combinations for simples, some authors absurdly reckon the consonants alone to be more numerous than are all the alphabetic characters together. Thus the Rev. Dr. Mandeville: "A consonant is a letter which, as the name implies, cannot be sounded without the aid of a vowel. The consonants are *b, c, d, f, g, h, i, j, k, l, m, n, p, q, r, s, t, v, w, x, y, z;* to which must be added *th, ch, sh, zh, wh, ng:* being plainly elementary sounds, and as such *belonging to the alphabet,* though not formally included in it."—*Course of Reading,* p. 13.

OBS. 10.—The distinction between vowels and consonants is generally obvious and easy enough; and yet, in reference to certain sounds or letters, when not pure, but combined, it is often very difficult and arbitrary. Some few of our grammarians have long taught that *w* and *y,* as well as *a, e, i, o, u,* are always vowels. The most common doctrine is, that *w* and *y* are sometimes vowels and sometimes consonants, and that *a, e, i, o,* and *u,* are always vowels. But, the sound of initial *w* being thought to be sometimes heard in *u,* likewise in *o,* and the sound of initial *y* sometimes in *e,* or *i,* or *u,* some writers have recognized one; some, two; some, three; and a few, all four, of these letters, as well as *w* and *y,* as being sometimes consonants; thus making a vast diversity of teaching concerning the classification of the six—a diversity which also extends itself equally into each of the new schemes of elements remarked upon above.

OBS. 11.—Dr. Lowth, and his improver, Churchill, also Sheridan, and his copier, Jones, represent *a, e, i, o, u, w,* and *y* as being invariably vowels, and as having no sounds peculiar to consonants. This opinion makes easy and simple the division of the letters, but it greatly swells the number of diphthongs, shows not why the initial *w* or *y* follows a vowel without hiatus, and accounts not for the use of *a,* in preference to *an,* before nouns beginning with *w* or *y:* as, *a wall, a yard;* not *an wall, an yard.*

OBS. 12.—Dr. Webster, in his great American Dictionary, says, "*Y* is sometimes used as a consonant."—*Introd.,* p. lxxviii. Concerning *a, e, i, o, u,* and *w,* he appears to agree with Lowth, and the others above named. Fisher, a London grammarian of the last century, treated *w* as being always a *consonant,* and *y* as being sometimes such. Brightland, Johnson, Murray, Walker, Ward Wells, Worcester, and others,—a majority of those who treat of the letters,—maintain the division which I have adopted above.

OBS. 13.—Dr. Mandeville says, "*I, y,* and *w,* are sometimes consonants."—*Course of Reading,* p. 9. Dr. Pinneo, uttering a strange solecism, and ambiguity of construction, says, "All the letters of the alphabet, except the vowels, and sometimes *i, u, w,* and *y,* are consonants."—*Analytical Gram., Stereotype Edition of* 1853, p. 7. L. T. Covell says, "All, except *a,* may be consonants."—*Digest of E. Gram.,* p. 16.

OBS. 14.—Sheridan and Jones divide the consonants into mutes and semivowels, then subdivide the mutes into "*pure* and *impure,*" and the semivowels into "*vocal* and *aspirated.*" In lieu of this, some, among whom are Herries and Bicknell, divide the consonants into *three* sorts, "*half vowels, aspirates,* and *mutes.*" Many divide them into *labials, dentals, linguals, palatals,* and *nasals;* classes which refer to the lips, teeth, tongue, palate, and nose, as the effective organs of their utterance.

Obs. 15.—Certain consonants or consonantal sounds are often distinguished in pairs, by way of contrast with each other, the one being called *flat* and the other *sharp:* as, *b* and *p; d* and *t; g* hard and *k; j* and *ch; v* and *f; th* flat and *th* sharp; *z* and sharp *s; zh* and *sh.* These, with reference to each other, are sometimes termed *correlatives* or *cognates.*

III. POWERS OF THE LETTERS.

The *powers* of the letters are properly those element-ary sounds which their figures are used to represent; but letters formed into words, are capable of communi-cating thought independently of sound.

The *vowel* sounds which form the basis of the English language, and which ought therefore to be perfectly familiar to every one who speaks it, are those which are heard at the beginning of the words, *ate, at, ah, all, eel, ell, isle, ill, old, on, ooze, use, us,* and that of *u* in *bull.*

In the formation of words or syllables, some of these fourteen primary sounds may be joined together, as in *ay, oil, out, owl;* and all of them may be preceded or followed by certain motions and positions of the lips and tongue, which will severally convert them into other terms in speech. Thus the same essential sounds may be changed into a new series of words by an *f;* as, *fate, fat, far, fall, feel, fell, file, fill, fold, fond, fool, fuse, fuss, full.* Again, into as many more with a *p ;* as, *pate, pat, par, pall, peel, pell, pile, pill, pole, pond, pool, pule, purl, pull.*

The simple *consonant* sounds in English are twenty-two : they are marked by *b, d, f, g* hard, *h, k, l, m, n, ng, p, r, s, sh, t, th* sharp, *th* flat, *v, w, y, z,* and *zh.* But *zh* is written only to show the sound of other letters; as of *s* in *pleasure,* or *z* in *azure.*

All these sounds are heard distinctly in the following words: *buy, die, fie, guy, high, kie, lie, my, nigh, eying, pie, rye, sigh, shy, tie, thigh, thy, vie, we, ye, zebra, seizure.* Again : most of them may be repeated in the same word, if not in the same syllable; as in *bibber, diddle, fifty, giggle, high-hung, cackle, lily, mimic, ninny, singing, pippin, mirror, hissest, flesh-brush, tittle, thinketh, thither, vivid, witwal, union, dizzies, vision.*

The possible combinations and mutations of the twenty-six letters of our alphabet, are many millions of millions. But those clusters which are unpronounceable, are useless. Of such as may be easily uttered, there are more than enough for all the purposes of useful writing, or the recording of speech.

Thus it is, that from principles so few and simple as about six or seven and thirty plain elementary sounds, represented by characters still fewer, we derive such a variety of oral and written signs, as may suffice to explain or record all the sentiments and transactions of all men in all ages.

OBSERVATIONS.

Obs. 1.—Different vowel sounds are produced by opening the mouth differently, and placing the tongue in a peculiar manner for each; but the voice may vary in loudness, pitch, or time, and still utter the same vowel power.

Obs. 2.—Each of the vowel sounds may be variously expressed by letters. About half of them are sometimes words: the rest are seldom, if ever, used alone even to form syllables. But the reader may easily learn to utter them all, separately, according to the foregoing series. Let us note them as plainly as possible: eigh, ä, ah, awe, ēh, ĕ, eye, ĭ, oh, ŏ, yew, ŭ, û. Thus the eight long sounds, *eigh, ah, awe, eh, eye, oh, ooh, yew,* are, or may be words; but the six less vocal, called the short vowel sounds, as in *at, et, it, ot, ut, put,* are commonly heard only in connexion with consonants; except the first, which is perhaps the most frequent sound of the vowel *A* or *a*—a sound sometimes given to the *word* a, perhaps most generally; as in the phrase, "twice ă day."

Obs. 3.—With us, the consonants J and X represent, not simple, but complex sounds: hence they are never doubled. J is equivalent to *dzh;* and X, either to *ks* or to *gz.* The former ends no English word, and the latter begins none. To the initial X of foreign words, we always give the simple sound of Z; as in *Xerxes, xebec.*

Obs. 4.—The consonants C and Q have no sounds peculiar to themselves. Q has always the power of *k,* and is constantly followed by *u* and some vowel or two more in the same syllable; as in *quake, quest, quit, quoit.* C is hard, like *k,* before *a, o,* and *u;* and soft, like *s,* before *e, i,* and *y:* thus the syllables *ca, ce, ci, co, cu, cy,* are pronounced *ka, se, si, ko, ku, sy. S* before *c* preserves the former sound, but coalesces with the latter; hence the syllables, *sca, sce, sci, sco, scu, scy,* are sounded *ska, se, si, sko, sku, sy. Ce* and *ci* have sometimes the sound of *sh;* as in *ocean, social. Ch* commonly represents the sound of *tsh;* as in *church.*

Obs. 5.—G, as well as C, has different sounds before different vowels. G is always hard, or guttural, before *a, o,* and *u;* and generally soft, like *j,* before *e, i,* or *y:* thus the syllables, *ga, ge, gi, go, gu, gy,* are pronounced *ga, je, ji, go, gu, jy.*

Obs. 6.—The imperfections of the English alphabet have been the subject of much comment, and sundry schemes for its reformation have successively appeared and disappeared without effecting the purpose of any one of their authors. It has been thought that there ought to be one character, and only one, for each simple sound in the language; but, in attempting to count the several elementary sounds which we use, our orthoepists have arrived at a remarkable diversity of conclusions. Bicknell, copying Martin's Physico-Grammatical Essay, says, "The simple sounds," originally necessary to speech, "were in no wise to be reckoned of any certain number: by the first men they were determined to no more than *ten,* as some suppose; as others, *fifteen* or twenty; it is however certain that mankind in general *never exceed twenty* simple sounds; and of these only *five* are reckoned strictly such."—*Bicknell's Gram.,* Part ii, p. 4.

Obs. 7.—The number of oral elements is differently reckoned by our

2

critics, because they do not agree among themselves concerning the identity or the simpleness, the sameness or the singleness, of some of the sounds in question ; and also because it is the practice of all, or nearly all, to admit as elementary some sounds which differ from each other only in length or shortness, and some which are not conceived to be entirely simple in themselves. The circumstances of the case seem to make it impossible to find out *for a certainty* what would be a perfect alphabet for our tongue.

Obs. 8.—Sheridan, taking *i* and *u* for diphthongs, *h* for "no letter," and the power of *h* for no sound, made the elements of his oratory twenty-eight. Jones followed him implicitly, saying, "The number of simple sounds in our tongue is *twenty-eight*, 9 Vowels, and 19 Consonants. H is no letter, but merely a mark of aspiration."—*Prosodial Gram.*, p. xiv. Bolles says, "The number of simple vowel and consonant sounds in our tongue is twenty-eight, and one pure aspiration *h*, making in all twenty-nine."—*Octavo Dict.*, *Introd.*, p. 9. Walker recognized several more ; but I know not whether he has anywhere told us *how many there are.*

Obs. 9.—Lindley Murray enumerates at first *thirty-six* well known sounds, and the same thirty-six that are given in the main text above; but he afterwards, contradicting certain teachings of his Spelling-Book, acknowledges *one more*, making *thirty-seven*—the third sound of *e*—"An obscure and scarcely perceptible sound : as in *open, lucre, participle.*"—*Gram.*, p. 11. Comstock, who does not admit the obscure *e*, says, "There are *thirty-eight elements* in the English alphabet, and * * * a deficiency of *twelve letters.*" —*Elocution*, p. 19. Wells, deducting C, Q, and X, says, "The remaining twenty-three letters are employed to represent *about forty* elementary sounds." *School Gram.*, 113th Th., p. 42. His first edition stated the number of sounds to be "*forty-one.*"—P. 36.

Obs. 10.—For the sake of the general principle, which we always regard in writing, a principle of universal grammar, as old at least as the writings of Aristotle, that *there can be no syllable without a vowel, or without some vowel power*, I am inclined to teach, with Brightland, Dr. Johnson, L. Murray, and others, that, in English, as in French, there is given to the vowel *e*, in some unaccented syllables a certain very obscure sound, which approaches, but amounts not to an absolute suppression, though it is commonly so regarded by the writers of our dictionaries. See Murray's examples above. If the *e* in "*open*" or *able* be supposed to have some faint sound, the oral elements of our language may be reckoned *thirty-seven*.

Obs. 11.—It is also a general principle, necessarily following from this, that, where the vowel of a syllable is suppressed or left entirely mute, any part which remains, of such syllable, falls to another vowel, and becomes part of another syllable : thus Cowper, in the phrase "'*Tis desp'rate*," reduces five syllables to three. But Wells, in arguing against the common definition of a consonant, says, "We have many syllables in which the vowel, though written, is *not heard at all* in pronunciation, as in the words *taken, burdened*, which are pronounced *tak-n, burd-nd.*" And he adds, "There are instances, also, in which *a consonant is sounded as a distinct syllable*, without the use even of a written vowel, as in the words *chas-m, rhyth-m.*"—*School Gram.*, p. 31. Here a very excellent teacher evidently inculcates error; for *chasm, rhythm*, or even *chasmed*, is only a monosyllable, and to call a consonant a syllable, is a contradiction in terms.

IV. FORMS OF THE LETTERS.

In the English language, the Roman characters are generally employed; sometimes, the *Italic;* and occasionally, the 𝕺𝖑𝖉 𝕰𝖓𝖌𝖑𝖎𝖘𝖍. In *writing*, we use the *Script.*

The letters have severally *two forms*, by which they are distinguished as *capitals* and *small letters.*

Small letters constitute the body of every work; and capitals are used for the sake of eminence and distinction.

RULES FOR THE USE OF CAPITALS.

RULE I.—TITLES OF BOOKS.

The titles of books, and the heads of their principal divisions, should be printed in capitals. When books are merely mentioned, the chief words in their titles begin with capitals, and the other letters are small; as, " Pope's Essay on Man."

RULE II.—FIRST WORDS.

The first word of every distinct sentence, or of any clause separately numbered or paragraphed, should begin with a capital.

RULE III.—NAMES OF DEITY.

All names of the Deity should begin with capitals; as, *God, Jehovah, the Almighty, the Supreme Being.*

RULE IV.—PROPER NAMES.

Titles of office or honour, and proper names of every description, should begin with capitals; as, *Chief Justice Hale, William, London, the Park, the Albion, the Spectator, the Thames.*

RULE V.—OBJECTS PERSONIFIED.

The name of an object personified, when it conveys an idea strictly individual, should begin with a capital; as,
" Come, gentle *Spring,* ethereal mildness, come."

RULE VI.—WORDS DERIVED.

Words derived from proper names of persons or places, should begin with capitals; as, *Newtonian, Grecian, Roman.*

RULE VII.—I AND O.

The words *I* and *O* should always be capitals; as, " Out of the depths have *I* cried unto thee *O* Lord."—*Psalms,* cxxx, 1.

RULE VIII.—IN POETRY.

Every line in poetry, except what is regarded as making but one verse with the line preceding, should begin with a capital ; as,
" Our sons their fathers' failing language see,
And such as Chaucer is, shall Dryden be."—*Pope.*

RULE IX.—EXAMPLES, ETC.

A full example, a distinct speech, or a direct quotation, should begin with a capital; as, "Remember this maxim: 'Know thyself.'"—"Virgil says, 'Labour conquers all things.'"

RULE X.—CHIEF WORDS.

Other words of particular importance, and such as denote the principal subjects of discourse, may be distinguished by capitals. Proper names frequently have capitals throughout.

CHAPTER II.—OF SYLLABLES.

A *Syllable* is one or more letters pronounced in one sound, and is either a word or a part of a word; as, *a, an, ant.*

In every word there are as many syllables as there are distinct sounds; as, *gram-ma-ri-an.*

A word of one syllable is called a *monosyllable;* a word of two syllables, a *dissyllable;* a word of three syllables, a *trissyllable;* and a word of four or more syllables, a *polysyllable.*

DIPHTHONGS AND TRIPHTHONGS.

A *diphthong* is two vowels joined in one syllable; as, *ea* in *beat, ou* in *sound.*

A *proper diphthong,* is a diphthong in which both the vowels are sounded; as, *oi* in *voice.*

An *improper diphthong,* is a diphthong in which only one of the vowels is sounded; as, *oa* in *loaf.*

A *triphthong* is three vowels joined in one syllable; as, *eau* in *beau, iew* in *view.*

A *proper triphthong,* is a triphthong in which all the vowels are sounded; as, *uoy* in *buoy.*

An *improper triphthong,* is a triphthong in which only one or two of the vowels are sounded; as, *eau* in *beauty, iou* in *anxious.*

SYLLABICATION.

In dividing words into syllables, we are to be directed chiefly by the ear; it may however be proper to observe, as far as practicable, the following rules.

RULE I.—CONSONANTS.

Consonants should generally be joined to the vowels or diphthongs which they modify in utterance ; as, *ap-os-tol-i-cal.*

RULE II.—VOWELS.

Two vowels, coming together, if they make not a diphthong, must be parted in dividing the syllables ; as, *a-e-ri-al.*

RULE III.—TERMINATIONS.

Derivative and grammatical terminations should generally be separated from the radical words to which they have been added ; as, *harm-less, great-ly, con-nect-ed.*

RULE IV.—PREFIXES.

Prefixes in general form separate syllables ; as, *mis-place, out-ride, up-lift:* but if their own primitive meaning be disregarded, the case may be otherwise ; thus *re-create* and *rec-reate* are words of different import.

RULE V.—COMPOUNDS.

Compounds, when divided, should be divided into the simple words which compose them ; as, *no-where.*

RULE VI.—LINES FULL.

At the end of a line, a word may be divided, if necessary ; but a syllable must never be broken.

CHAPTER III.—OF WORDS.

A *Word* is one or more syllables spoken or written as the sign of some idea, or of some manner of thought.

SPECIES AND FIGURE OF WORDS.

Words are distinguished as *primitive* or *derivative,* and as *simple* or *compound.* The former division is called their *species ;* the latter, their *figure.*

A *primitive* word is one that is not formed from any simpler word in the language ; as, *harm, great, connect.*

A *derivative* word is one that is formed from some simpler word in the language ; as, *harmless, greatly, connected, disconnect, unconnected.*

3*

A *simple* word is one that is not compounded, not composed of other words; as, *watch, man, never, the, less.*

A *compound* word is one that is composed of two or more simple words; as, *watchman, nevertheless.*

Permanent compounds are consolidated; as, *book-seller, schoolmaster:* others, which may be called tempo-rary compounds, are formed by the hyphen; as, *glass-house, negro-merchant.*

RULES FOR THE FIGURE OF WORDS.

RULE I.——COMPOUNDS.

Words regularly or analogically united, and commonly known as forming a compound, should never be needlessly broken apart.

RULE II.——SIMPLES.

When the simple words would only form a regular phrase, of the same meaning, the compounding of any of them ought to be avoided.

RULE III.——THE SENSE.

Words otherwise liable to be misunderstood, must be joined together or written separately, as the sense and construction may happen to require.

RULE IV.——ELLIPSES.

When two or more compounds are connected in one sentence, none of them should be split to make an ellipsis of half a word.

RULE V.——THE HYPHEN.

When the parts of a compound do not fully coalesce, as *to-day, to-night, to-morrow;* or when each retains its original accent, so that the compound has more than one, or one that is movable, as *first-born, hanger-on, laughter-loving,* the hyphen should be inserted between them.

RULE VI.——NO HYPHEN.

When a compound has but one accented syllable in pro-nunciation, as *watchword, statesman, gentleman,* and the parts are such as admit of a complete coalescence, no hyphen should be inserted between them.

CHAPTER IV.—OF SPELLING.

Spelling is the art of expressing words by their proper letters.

Obs.—This important art is to be acquired rather by means of the spelling-book or dictionary, and by observation in reading, than by the study of written rules. The orthography of our language is attended with much uncertainty and perplexity: many words are variously spelled by the best scholars, and many others are not usually written according to the analogy of similar words. But to be ignorant of the orthography of such words as are uniformly spelled and frequently used, is justly considered disgraceful. The following rules may prevent some embarrassment, and thus be of service to those who wish to be accurate.

RULES FOR SPELLING.

RULE I.—FINAL F, L, OR S.

Monosyllables ending in *f, l,* or *s,* preceded by a single vowel, double the final consonant ; as, *staff, mill, pass :* except three in *f—clef, if, of ;* four in *l—bul, nul, sal, sol ;* and eleven in *s—as, gas, has, was, yes, is, his, this, us, thus, pus.*

RULE II.—OTHER FINALS.

Words ending in any other consonant than *f, l,* or *s,* do not double the final letter : except *abb, ebb, add, odd, egg, inn, err, burr, purr, yarr, butt, buzz, fuzz,* and some proper names.

RULE III.—DOUBLING.

Monosyllables, and words accented on the last syllable, when they end with a single consonant preceded by a single vowel, or by a vowel after *qu,* double their final consonant before an additional syllable that begins with a vowel : as, *rob, robber ; permit, permitting ; acquit, acquittal, acquitting.*

Exc.—X final, being equivalent to *ks,* is never doubled.

RULE IV.—NO DOUBLING.

A final consonant, when it is not preceded by a single vowel, or when the accent is not on the last syllable, should remain single before an additional syllable : as, *toil, toiling ; visit, visited ; general, generalize.*

Exc.—But *l* and *s* final are usually doubled, (though perhaps improperly,) when the last syllable is not accented : as, *travel, traveller ; bias, biassed.*

RULE V.—RETAINING.

Words ending with any double letter, preserve it double

before any additional termination, not beginning with the same letter ; as in the following derivatives : *seeing, blissful, oddly, hilly, stiffness, illness, smallness, carelessness, agreement, agreeable.*

Exc.—The irregular words, *fled, sold, told, dwelt, spelt, spilt, shalt, wilt, blest, past,* and the derivatives from the word *pontiff,* are exceptions to this rule.

RULE VI.—FINAL E.

The final *e mute* of a primitive word, is generally omitted before an additional termination beginning with a vowel : as, *rate, ratable ; force, forcible ; rave, raving ; eye, eying.*

Exc.—Words ending in *ce* or *ge,* retain the *e* before *able* or *ous,* to preserve the soft sounds of *c* and *g :* as, *peace, peaceable ; change, changeable ; outrage, outrageous.*

RULE VII.—FINAL E.

The final *e* of a primitive word, is generally retained before an additional termination beginning with a consonant : as, *pale, paleness ; lodge, lodgement.*

Exc.—When the *e* is preceded by a vowel, it is sometimes omitted ; as, *true, truly ; awe, awful:* and sometimes retained ; as, *rue, rueful ; shoe, shoeless.*

RULE VIII.—FINAL Y.

The final *y* of a primitive word, when preceded by a consonant, is changed into *i* before an additional termination : as, *merry, merrier, merriest, merrily, merriment ; pity, pitied, pities, pitiest, pitiless, pitiful, pitiable.*

·Exc.—Before *ing, y* is retained to prevent the doubling of *i ;* as, *pity, pitying.* Words ending in *ie,* dropping the *e* by Rule 6th, change *i* into *y,* for the same reason ; as, *die, dying.*

Obs.—When a vowel precedes, *y* should not be changed : as, *day, days ; valley, valleys ; money, moneys ; monkey, monkeys.*

RULE IX.—COMPOUNDS.

Compounds generally retain the orthography of the simple words which compose them ; as, *hereof, wherein, horseman, recall, uphill, shellfish.*

Exc.—In permanent compounds, the words *full* and *all* drop one *l ;* as, *handful, careful, always, withal :* in others, they retain both ; as, *full-eyed, all-wise, save-all.*

Obs.—Other words ending in *ll,* sometimes improperly drop one *l,* when taken into composition ; as, *miscal, downhil.* This excision is reprehensible, because it is contrary to general analogy, and because both letters are necessary to preserve the sound, and show the derivation of the compound.

Where is the consistency of writing, *recall, miscal,—inthrall, bethral,—wind-fall, downfal,—laystall, thumbstal,—waterfall, overfal,—molehill, dunghil,—windmill, twibil,—clodpoll, enrol?* [See Johnson's Dictionary, first American ed. 4to.]

CHAPTER V.—EXAMINATION.

LESSON I.—GENERAL DIVISION.

What is English Grammar?
How is it divided?
Of what does Orthography treat?
Of what does Etymology treat?
Of what does Syntax treat?
Of what does Prosody treat?

QUESTIONS ON ORTHOGRAPHY.

LESSON II.—LETTERS.

Of what does Orthography treat?
What is a *Letter?*
What is an elementary sound of a word?
What name is given to the sound of a letter? and what epithet, to a letter not sounded?
How many letters are there in English? and how many sounds do they represent?
In what does a knowledge of the letters consist?
What variety is noticed in letters that are always the same?
What different sorts of types, or letters, are used in English?
What are the names of the letters in English?
Which of the letters name themselves? and which do not?
What are the names of all in both numbers, singular and plural?

LESSON III.—CLASSES OF LETTERS.

Into what general classes are the letters divided?
What is a vowel?
What is a consonant?
What letters are vowels? and what, consonants?
When are *w* and *y* consonants? and when vowels?
How are the consonants divided?
What is a semivowel?
What is a mute?
What letters are semivowels? and which of these are aspirates?
What letters are called liquids, and why?
How many and which are the letters reckoned mutes?

LESSON IV.—POWERS, OR SOUNDS.

What is meant, when we speak of "the *powers* of the letters?"
In what series of short words are heard our chief vowel sounds?
How may these sounds be modified to form words or syllables?
Can you form a word from each by means of an *f?*
Will you form an other such series with a *p?*
How many and what are the consonant sounds in English?
In what series of words may all these sounds be heard?
In what series of words is each of them heard more than once?
Do our letters admit of combinations enough?
What do we derive from these elements of language?

3*

LESSON V.—FORMS OF THE LETTERS.

What is said of the employment of the several styles of letters in English ?
What distinction of form do we make in each of the letters ?
What is said of small letters ? and why are capitals used ?
How many rules for capitals are given? and what are their heads ?
What says Rule 1st of *titles of books ?*—Rule 2d of *first words ?*—Rule 3d of
   names of Deity ?—Rule 4th of *proper names ?*—Rule 5th of *objects personi-*
   fied ?—Rule 6th of *words derived ?*—Rule 7th of *I and O ?*—Rule 8th of
   poetry ?—Rule 9th of *examples,* &c. *?*—Rule 10th of *chief words ?*

LESSON VI.—SYLLABLES.

What is a syllable ?
Can the syllables of a word be perceived by the ear ?
What is a word of one syllable called?—a word of two ?—of three ?—of four
   or more ?
What is a diphthong ?
What is a proper diphthong ?—an improper diphthong ?
What is a triphthong ?
What is a proper triphthong ?—an improper triphthong ?
What chiefly directs us in dividing words into syllables ?
How many rules of syllabication are given ? and what are their heads ?
What says Rule 1st of *consonants ?*—Rule 2d of *vowels ?*—Rule 3d of *termina-*
   tions ?—Rule 4th of *prefixes?*—Rule 5th of *compounds?*—Rule 6th of *lines*
   full ?

LESSON VII.—WORDS.

What is a word ?
How are words distinguished in regard to species and figure ?
What is a primitive word?
What is a derivative word ?
What is a simple word?
What is a compound word?
How do permanent compounds differ from others ?
How many are the rules for the figure of words? and what, their heads ?
What says Rule 1st of *compounds?*—Rule 2d of *simples ?*—Rule 3d of *the
sense ?*—Rule 4th of *ellipses ?*—Rule 5th of *the hyphen ?*—Rule 6th of using
no hyphen ?

LESSON VIII.—SPELLING.

What is *spelling ?*
How is this art to be acquired ?
How many rules for spelling are there ? and what are their heads ?
What says Rule 1st of *final f, l, or s ?*—Rule 2d of *other finals ?*—Rule 3d of
   the *doubling* of consonants ?—Rule 4th *against the doubling* of consonants ?
   —Rule 5th of *retaining ?*—Rule 6th of *final e ?*—Rule 7th of *final e ?*—
   Rule 8th of *final y ?*—Rule 9th of *compounds ?*

CHAPTER VI.—FOR WRITING.

EXERCISES IN ORTHOGRAPHY.

☞ [Spelling is to be taught by example, rather than by rule. For *oral exercises*
in this branch of learning, a spelling-book or vocabulary should be employed. The
following examples of false orthography are inserted, that they may be corrected by
the pupil *in writing.* They are selected with direct reference to the rules; which
are at first indicated by figures. For it is evident, that exercises of this kind, without
express rules for their correction, would rather perplex than instruct the learner;
and that his ability to correct them without reference to the rules, must presuppose
such knowledge as would render them useless.

EXERCISE I.—CAPITALS.

1. The pedant quoted Johnson's dictionary of the english language, Gregory's dictionary of arts and sciences, Crabb's english synonymes, Walker's key to the pronunciation of proper names, Sheridan's rhetorical grammar, and the diversions of purley.

2. gratitude is a delightful emotion. the grateful heart at once performs its duty and endears itself to others.

3. What madness and folly, to deny the great first cause! Shall mortal man presume against his maker? shall he not fear the omnipotent? shall he not reverence the everlasting one?—'The fear of the lord is the beginning of wisdom.'

4. xerxes the great, emperor of persia, united the medes, persians, bactrians, lydians, assyrians, hyrcanians, and many other nations, in an expedition against greece.

5. I observed that, when the votaries of religion were led aside, she commonly recalled them by her emissary conscience, before habit had time to enchain them.

6. Hercules is said to have killed the nemean lion, the erymanthian boar, the lernean serpent, and the stymphalian birds. The christian religion has brought all mythologic stories and milesian fables into disrepute.

7. i live as i did, i think as i did, i love you as i did; but all these are to no purpose; the world will not live, think, or love as i do.—o wretched prince! o cruel reverse of fortune! o father Micipsa!

8. are these thy views? proceed, illustrious youth,
   and virtue guard thee to the throne of truth!

9. Those who pretend to love peace, should remember this maxim: "it is the second blow that makes the battle."

EXERCISE II.—CAPITALS.

'time and i will challenge any other two,' said philip.—'thus,' said diogenes, 'do i trample on the pride of plato.'—'true,' replied plato; 'but is it not with the greater pride of diogenes?'

the father in a transport of joy, burst into the following words: 'o excellent scipio! heaven has given thee more than human virtue! o glorious leader! o wondrous youth!'

epaminondas, the theban general, was remarkable for his love of truth. he never told a lie, even in jest.

and pharaoh said to joseph, "say to thy brethren, 'do this—lade your beasts, and go to the land of canaan.'"

who is she that, with graceful steps and a lively air, trips over yonder plain? her name is health: she is the daughter of exercise and temperance.

to the penitent sinner, a mediator and intercessor with the sovereign of the universe, appear comfortable names.

the murder of abel, the curse and rejection of cain, and the birth and adoption of seth, are almost the only events related of the immediate family of adam, after his fall.

on what foundation stands the warrior's pride,
how just his hopes, let swedish charles decide.

in every leaf that trembles to the breeze,
i hear the voice of god among the trees.

EXERCISE III.—SYLLABLES.

1. Correct Murray's division of the following words: "ci-vil, co-lour, co-py, da-mask, do-zen, e-ver, fea-ther, ga-ther, hea-ven, le-mon, mea-dow, ne-ver, o-range, pu-nish, ro-bin, sho-vel, ti-mid, whi-ther;—be-ne-fit, ca-nis-ter, ge-ne-rous, le-ve-ret, li-be-ral, se-ve-ral;—mi-se-ra-ble, to-le-ra-ble, e-pi-de-mic, pa-ra-ly-tic;—a-ca-de-mi-cal, cha-rac-te-ris-tic, ex-pe-ri-ment-al."—*Murray's Spelling-Book.*

2. Correct Webster's division of the following words: "oy-er, fol-io, gen-ial, gen-ius, jun-ior, sa-tiate, vi-tiate;—am-bro-sia, par-hel-ion, con-ven-ient, in-gen-ious, om-nis-cience, pe-cul-iar, so-cia-ble, par-tial-i-ty, pe-cun-ia-ry;—an-nun-ciate, e-nun-ciate, ap-pre-ciate, as-so-ciate, ex-pa-tiate, ne-go-tiate, sub-stan-tiate."—*Webster's Spelling-Books.*

3. Correct Cobb's division of the following words: "dres-ser, has-ty, pas-try, sei-zure, rol-ler, jes-ter, wea-ver, vam per, han-dy, dros-sy, glos-sy, mo-ver, mo-ving, oo-zy, ful-ler, trus-ty, weigh-ty, noi-sy, drow-sy, swar-thy."—*Cobb's Standard Spell-ing-Book.* And these: "eas-tern, full-y, pull-et, rill-et, scan-ty, nee-dy."—*Webster.* Also these: "woo-dy, stor-my, clou-dy, ex-al-ted, at-ten-dance."—*Murray.*

4. Divide the following words into their proper syllables: adit, ado, adorn, adown, adrift, anoint, athwart, awry, bespeak, bestow, between, bifold, encroach, incrust, foreknow, forestall, forswear, mishear, mistell, misyoke, outrap, overtire, preterit, retrace, unoiled, unrepaid, unresting, underbid, underanged, uphand, upholder, uprouse, withal.

5. Divide the following compounds into syllables: England, anthill, cowslip, farewell, foresail, foretop, hogshead, homeward, sandstone, forever, husbandman, painstaker.

EXERCISE IV.—FIGURE OF WORDS.

1. The shine of the plough share is the farmer's wealth.
The cross row has ever had some thing of a magic spell in it.
The old fashioned are apt to think the world grows worse.
The stealing of water melons may lead to house breaking.
A good clothes brush helps greatly to make a gentle man.
2. An ill-tongue is a fearful corrupter of good-manners.
Envy not the good-luck of prosperous transgressors.
St. Paul admonishes Timothy to refuse old-wives'-fables.
Lawmakers have often been partial to male-descendants.
New-year's-gifts brighten many a face on new-year's day.
3. They that live in glass-houses, should not throw stones.
A glass house is a house in which glass is manufactured.
A spirit stirring discourse is seldom a long winded one.
Knowledge and virtue are the stepping stones to honour.
The American whip poor Will is a night warbling bird.
4. Let school and meeting-houses be pleasantly located.
The teapot and kettle are now deemed indispensable.
Both the ten and the eight syllable verses are iambics.
Most, at six or seventeen years of age, are men and women.
A ketch is a vessel with two masts, a main and mizzen-mast.
5. The bloodyminded man seldom dwells long in safety.
A tiresmith puts on wheelbands redhot, then cools them.
Plato was so called because he was broadshouldered.
Timehonoured custom may be souldestroying folly.
Is evenhanded honesty expected in slavemerchants?
6. A good pay-master is always a man of some fore-thought.
The glory of the common-wealth is the states-man's boast.
Rain-bows are made of sun-shine dissolved in sky-water.

EXERCISE V.—SPELLING.

1. Few know the value of a friend, til they lose him.
Good men pas by offences, and take no revenge.
Hear patiently, iff thou wouldst speak wel.
2. The business of warr is devastation and destruction.
To er is human; to forgive, divine.
A bad speller should not pretend to scholarshipp.
3. It often requires deep diging, to obtain pure water.
Praise is most shuned by the praiseworthy.
He that hoists too much sail, runs a risk of overseting.
4. Quarrels are more easily begun than endded.
Contempt leaves a deepper scar than anger.
Of all tame animals the flatterrer is the most mischievous.

4

5. Smalness with talness makes the figure too slender.
Heedlesness is always in danger of embarrasment.
The recklesness of license is no attribute of fredom.
6. Good examples are very convinceing teachers.
Doubts should not excite contention, but inquirey.
Obligeing conduct procures deserved esteem.
7. Wise men measure time by their improvment of it.
Learn to estimate all things by their real usfulness.
Encouragment increases with success
8. Nothing essential to happyness is unattainable.
Vices, though near relations, are all at varyance.
Before thou denyest a favour, consider the request.
9. Good-wil is a more powerful motive than constraint.
A wel-spent day prepares us for sweet repose.
The path of fame is altogether an uphil road.

EXERCISE VI.—SPELLING.

1. He is tal enough who walks uprightly.
Repetition makes smal transgressions great.
Religion regulates the wil and affections.
2. To carry a ful cupp even, requires a steady hand.
Idleness is the nest in which mischief lays its egs.
The whole journey of life is besett with foes.
3. Peace of mind should be prefered to bodily safety.
A bad begining is unfavourable to success.
Very fruitful trees often need to be proped.
4. None ever gained esteem by tattling and gossipping.
Religion purifies, fortifies, and tranquillizes the mind.
They had all been closetted together a long time.
5. Blesed is he whose transgresion is forgiven.
Indolence and listlesness are foes to happiness.
Carelesness has occasioned many a wearisome step.
6. In all thy undertakeings, ponder the motive and the end.
We cannot wrong others without injureing ourselves.
A dureable good cannot spring from an external cause.
7. Duely appreciate and improve your privileges.
To borrow of future time, is thriftless managment.
He who is truely a freman is above mean compliances.
8. Pitiing friends cannot save us in a diing hour.
Wisdom rescues the decaies of age from aversion.
Vallies are generally more fertile than hills.
9. Cold numness had quite bereft her of sense.
A cascade, or waterfal, is a charming object in scenery.

Nettles grow in the vinyard of the slothfull.
Tuition is lost on idlers and numbsculs.

EXERCISE VII.—SPELLING.

1. He that scofs at the crooked, should beware of stooping.
Pictures that resemble flowers, smel only of paint.
Misdemeanours are the pioneers of gros vices.
2. To remitt a wrong, leaves the offender in debt.
Superlative commendation is near akinn to detraction.
Piety admitts not of excessive sorrow.
3. You are safe in forgeting benefits you have confered.
He has run well who has outstriped his own errors.
See that you have ballast proportionate to your riging.
4. The biasses of prejudice often preclude convincement.
Rather follow the wise than lead the foollish.
To reason with the angry, is like whisperring to the deaf.
A bigotted judge needs no time for deliberation.
The gods of this world have many worshippers.
5. Crosness has more subjects than admirers.
Fearlesness conquers where Blamelesness is armour-bearer.
6. Many things are chiefly valued for their rareity.
Vicious old age is hopeless and deploreable.
Irreconcileable animosity is always blameable.
7. Treachery lurks beneath a guilful tongue.
Disobedience and mischief deserve chastisment.
By self-examination, we discover the lodgments of sin.
The passions often mislead the judgment.
8. To be happy without holyness is impossible.
And, all within, were walks and allies wide.
Call imperfection what thou fancy'st such.
Without fire chimnies are useless.
9. The true philanthropist deserves a universal pasport.
Ridicule is generally but the froth of il-nature.
All mispent time will one day be regretted.

EXERCISE VIII.—SPELLING.

Fiction may soften, without improveing the heart.
Affectation is a sprout that should be niped in the bud.
A covettous person is always in want.
Fashion is compareable to an ignis-fatuus.
Fair appearances somtimes cover foul purposes.
Garnish not your commendations with flatterry.
Never utter a falshood even for truth's sake.

Medicines should be administerred with caution.
We have here no continueing city, no abideing rest.
Many a trapp is laid to ensnare the feet of youth.
We are caught as sillyly as the bird in the net.
By defering repentance, we accumulate sorrows.
To preach to the droneish, is to waste your words.
We are often benefitted by what we have dreaded.
We may be succesful, and yet disappointed.
In rebusses, pictures are used to represent words.
He is in great danger who parlies with conscience.
Your men of forhead are magnificent in promises.
A true friend is a most valueable acquisition.
It is not a bad memory that forgets injuryes.
Weigh your subject wel, before you speak positivly.
Difficulties are often increased by mismanagment.
Diseases are more easyly prevented than cured.
Contrivers of mischief often entrapp themselves.
Corrupt speech indicates a distemperred mind.
Asseveration does not allways remove doubt.
Hypocrites are like wolves in sheeps' clotheing.
Ostentatious liberallity is its own paymaster.

EXERCISE IX.—SPELLING.

A downhil road may be travelled with ease.
Distempered fancy can swel a molehil to a mountain.
Let your own unbiassed judgment determine.
A knave can often undersel his honest neighbours.
Xenophanes prefered reputation to wealth.
True politeness is the ofspring of benevolence.
Levellers are generally the dupes of designning men.
Rewards are for those who have fullfiled their duty.
Who trusts a hungry boy in a cubburd of dainties?
Misery acquaints a man with strange bedfellers.
The liberal man ties his purse with a beau-not.
Double-deelers are seldom long in favour.
The characters of the crosrow have wrought wonders.
The plagiary is a jacdaw decked with stolen plumes.
All virtues are in agrement; all vices, at varyance.
Personnal liberty is every man's natural birthrite.
There, wrapt in clouds, the blueish hills ascend.
The birds frame to thy song, their chearfull cherupping.
There figgs, skydyed, a purple hue disclose.
Lysander goes twice a day to the choccolat-house.
Years following years, steal sumthing every day.

The soul of the slothfull, does but drowse in his body.
What think you of a clergiman in a soldier's dres?
Justice is here holding the stilliards for a balance.
The huming-bird is somtimes no biger than a bumble-be.
The muskittoes will make you as spoted as a samon-trout.
Cruelty to animals is a malicious and lo-lived vice.
Absolute Necessity must sign their deth-warrant.
He who catches flies, emulates the nat-snaper.
The froggs had long lived unmolested in a horspond.
'These are villanous creatures,' says a blokheded boy.

     The robbin-read-breast til of late had rest;
     And children sacred held a martin's nest.

PART II.

ETYMOLOGY.

Etymology treats of the different parts of speech, with their classes and modifications.

CHAPTER I.—THE PARTS OF SPEECH.

The Parts of Speech, or sorts of words, in English, are ten; namely, the Article, the Noun, the Adjective, the Pronoun, the Verb, the Participle, the Adverb, the Conjunction, the Preposition, and the Interjection.

1. THE ARTICLE.

An Article is the word *the, an,* or *a,* which we put before nouns to limit their signification: as, *The* air, *the* stars; *an* island, *a* ship.

2. THE NOUN.

A Noun is the name of any person, place, or thing, that·can be known or mentioned: as, *George, York, man, apple, truth.*

3. THE ADJECTIVE.

An Adjective is a word added to a noun or pronoun, and generally expresses quality: as, A *wise* man; a *new* book.   You *two* are *diligent.*

4. THE PRONOUN.

A Pronoun is a word used in stead of a noun: as, The boy loves *his* book; *he* has long lessons, and *he* learns *them* well.

5. THE VERB.

A Verb is a word that signifies *to be, to act,* or *to be acted upon:* as, I *am,* I *rule,* I *am ruled;* I *love,* thou *lovest,* he *loves.*

6. THE PARTICIPLE.

A Participle is a word derived from a verb, participating the properties of a verb, and of an adjective or a noun; and is generally formed by adding *ing*, *d*, or *ed*, to the verb: thus, from the verb *rule*, are formed three participles, two simple and one compound; as, 1. *ruling*, 2. *ruled*, 3. *having ruled*.

7. THE ADVERB.

An Adverb is a word added to a verb, a participle, an adjective, or an other adverb; and generally expresses time, place, degree, or manner: as, They are now *here*, studying *very diligently*.

8. THE CONJUNCTION.

A Conjunction is a word used to connect words or sentences in construction, and to show the dependence of the terms so connected: as, "Thou *and* he are happy, *because* you are good."—*L. Murray.*

9. THE PREPOSITION.

A Preposition is a word used to express some relation of different things or thoughts to each other, and is generally placed before a noun or a pronoun: as, The paper lies *before* me *on* the desk.

10. THE INTERJECTION.

An Interjection is a word that is uttered merely to indicate some strong or sudden emotion of the mind: as, *Oh! alas! ah! poh! pshaw! avaunt!*

PARSING.

Parsing is the resolving or explaining of a sentence, or of some related word or words, according to the definitions and rules of grammar.

A *sentence* is an assemblage of words, making complete sense; as, "Reward sweetens labor.—"The fear of the Lord is the beginning of wisdom."

A *definition* of any thing or class of things is such a description of it, as distinguishes that entire thing or class from every thing else, by briefly telling *what it is.*

A *rule of grammar* is some law, more or less general, by which custom regulates· and prescribes the right use of language.

A *praxis* is a method of exercise, showing the learner how to proceed. (The word literally signifies action, doing, practice, or formal use.)

An *example* is a particular instance or model, serving to prove or illustrate some given proposition or truth.

An *exercise* is some technical performance required of the learner in order to test his knowledge or skill by use.

EXERCISES IN PARSING.

PRAXIS I.—ETYMOLOGICAL.

In the First Praxis, it is required of the pupil—to distinguish the different parts of speech, and to assign a reason for such distinction, by citing the proper definition, and adapting it to each particular case. Thus :—

XAMPLE PARSED.

" The patient ox submits to the yoke, and meekly performs the labor required of him."

1.*Submits is a verb, because it signifies action ;
  Performs is also a verb, for the same reason.
2. *Ox* is a noun, because it is the name of a thing ;
  Yoke and *labor* are nouns, for the same reason.
3. *The* is an article, because it limits the signification of *ox, yoke,* or *labor*—the noun before which it is placed.
4. *Patient* is an adjective, because it expresses the quality of *ox.*
5. *Him* is a pronoun, because it is used instead of the noun *ox.*
6. *Required* is a participle, because it expresses action like a verb, and qualifies the noun *labor* like an adjective.

---

* ☞ The numbers are here used to indicate the order in which the pupil should, at first, be required to distinguish the parts of speech in any sentence. The verb is made the first in this series, because it is the word to which all others have an immediate or remote relation, and because it is easily recognized, and, when discovered, leads the mind necessarily to a knowledge of the other parts of speech comprehended in the sentence, by showing the particular office of every word. This cannot be done, at this stage of the pupil's progress, with a proper degree of intelligence and precision, by mechanically examining each word in succession; for the reason that to do so requires him to compare the distinctive office of *each part of speech* with the word examined ; while in these preliminary exercises, he is only required to keep in mind the character of a *single* part of speech, and compare it with *each word* of the sentence in succession. Besides, an *eclectic* process like that indicated, is better calculated to keep the interest and attention of the pupil awake, the constant desire of *discovery* continually stimulating mental activity.

7. *Meekly* is an adverb, because it is added to the verb *performs*, and expresses manner.
8. *And* is a conjunction, because it connects *submits* and *performs*.
9. *To* is a preposition, because it expresses the relation of the verb *submits* to the noun *yoke*.

EXERCISE I.

Parse, in the following sentences, the verb, the noun, and the article, in the order, and according to the method, indicated in Praxis I.

The tree bears fruit.   Pizarro invaded Peru.   Avarice causes crime.   The miser loves gold.   The ox bears a yoke.   The river overflowed the banks.   John's brother has entered college. The carpenter is using a saw.   John Smith explored Virginia. Columbus was a Genoese.   Napoleon Bonaparte died an exile. Lend Charles a book.   The merchant has made a fortune. Did the candidate obtain the office?   The elephant is a quadruped.   Virgil praised the emperor Augustus.   The boys have told an untruth.   The scholar's diligence deserves a reward. Could the criminal have escaped punishment?   Queen Dido founded Carthage.   Scipio defeated Hannibal.

EXERCISE II.

Parse, in the following sentences, the verb, the noun, the article, the adjective, the pronoun, and the adverb, in the order, and according to the method, indicated in Praxis I.

The industrious boys have recited their lessons well.
The architect who planned that fine building, is named Brown.
Demosthenes was a very famous Grecian orator.
A child who disobeys his parents, is very ungrateful.
Human happiness is exceedingly transient.
The man who has not virtue, is not truly wise.
I saw the whole transaction; both parties disgraced themselves.   They had a fierce dispute.
Perseverance finally overcomes all obstacles.
I, who was present, know all the particulars.
A Being infinitely wise will not unnecessarily afflict his creatures.
Passionate men are very easily irritated.
Good books always deserve a careful perusal.
Evil communications corrupt good manners.

EXERCISE III.

Parse all the parts of speech to be found in the following sentences, according to Praxis I.

The rose, the lily, and the pink, are fragrant flowers.

A landscape presents a pleasing variety of objects.

The eagle has a strong and piercing eye.

The swallow builds her nest of mud, and lines it with soft feathers.

The setting sun gives a beautiful brilliancy to the western sky.

Virtuous youth gradually brings forward accomplished and flourishing manhood.

Sloth enfeebles equally the bodily and the mental powers. It saps the foundation of every virtue, and pours upon us a deluge of crimes and evils.

O Virtue! how miserable are they who forfeit thy rewards!

Alas! such miseries are too common among mankind!

Industry is needful in every condition of life; the price of all improvement is labor.

When spring returns, the trees resume their verdure, and the plants and flowers display their beauty.

CHAPTER II.—OF ARTICLES.

An Article is the word *the, an,* or *a,* which we put before nouns to limit their signification: as, *The* air, *the* stars; *an* island, *a* ship.

An and *a* are one and the same article. *An* is used whenever the following word begins with a *vowel sound;* as, *An* art, *an* end, *an* heir, *an* inch, *an* ounce, *an* hour, *an* urn.—*A* is used whenever the following word begins with a *consonant sound;* as, *A* man, *a* house, *a* wonder, *a* one, *a* yew, *a* use, *a* ewer. Thus the consonant sounds of *w* and *y*, even when expressed by other letters, require *a* and not *an* before them.

CLASSES.

The articles are distinguished as the *definite* and the *indefinite.*

I. The *definite article* is *the,* which denotes some particular thing or things; as, *The* boy, *the* oranges.

II. The *indefinite article* is *an* or *a,* which denotes one thing of a kind, but not any particular one; as, *A* boy, *an* orange.

Obs. 1.—The English articles have no grammatical modifications; they are not varied by numbers, genders, and cases, as are those of some other languages. In respect to class, each is *sui generis*.

Obs. 2.—A common noun without an article or other word to limit its signification, is generally taken in its widest sense; as, "A candid temper is proper for *man;* that is, *for all mankind.*"—*Murray.*

CHAPTER III.—OF NOUNS.

A Noun is the name of any person, place, or thing, that can be known or mentioned : as, *George, York, man, apple, truth.*

Obs. 1.—All words and signs taken *technically,* (that is, independently of their meaning, and merely as things spoken of,) are *nouns;* or, rather, are *things* read and construed *as nouns;* as, " *Us* is a personal pronoun."—*Murray.* " *Th* has two sounds."—*Id.* " *Control* is probably contracted from *counterroll.*"—*Crabb.* " Without one *if* or *but.*"—*Cowper.* " *A* is sometimes a noun; as, a great *A.*"—*Todd's Johnson.* " Formerly *sp* was cast in a piece, as *st's* are now."—*Hist. of Printing,* 1770.

Obs. 2.—In parsing, the learner must observe the *sense* and *use* of each word, and class it accordingly: many words commonly belonging to other parts of speech, are occasionally used as *nouns,* and must be parsed as such; as, 1. " The *Ancient* of days."—*Bible.* " Of the *ancients.*"—*Swift.* " For such *impertinents.*"—*Steele.* " He is an *ignorant* in it."—*Id.* " To the *nines.*"—*Burns.* 2. " Or any *he,* the proudest of thy sort."—*Shak.* " I am the happiest *she* in Kent."—*Steele.* "The *shes* of Italy."—*Shak.* " The *hes* in birds."—*Bacon.* 3. " Avaunt all attitude, and *stare,* and *start,* theatric !" —*Cowper.* " A *may-be* of mercy is insufficient."—*Bridge.* 4. " For the *producing* of real happiness."—*Crabb.* " *Reading, writing,* and *ciphering,* are indispensable to civilized man." 5. " An *hereafter.*"—*Addison.* " The dread of a *hereafter.*"—*Fuller.* "The deep *amen.*"—*Scott.* " The *while.*"—*Milton.* 6. " With *hark,* and *whoop,* and wild *halloo.*"—*Scott.* " Will cuts him short with a '*What then ?*'"—*Addison.*

CLASSES.

Nouns are divided into two general classes; *proper* and *common.*

I. A *proper noun* is the name of some particular individual, or people, or group; as, *Adam, Boston,* the *Hudson,* the *Romans,* the *Azores,* the *Alps.*

II. A *common noun* is the name of a sort, kind, or class, of beings or things; as, *Beast, bird, fish, insect,— creatures, persons, children.*

The particular classes, *collective, abstract,* and *verbal* or *participial,* are usually included among common nouns. The name of a thing *sui generis* is also called common.

1. A *collective noun,* or *noun of multitude,* is the name of many individuals together; as, *Council, meeting, committee, flock.*

2. An *abstract noun* is the name of some particular quality con idere l apart from its substance ; as, *Goodness, hardness, pride, frailty.*

3. A *verbal* or *participial noun* is the name of some action or state of being ; and is formed from a verb, like a participle, but employed as a noun : as, " The *triumphing* of the wicked is short."—*Job*, xx, 5.

4. A thing *sui generis*, (i. e., *of its own peculiar kind*,) is something which is distinguished, not as an individual of a species, but as a sort by itself, without plurality in either the noun or the sort of thing ; as, *Galvanism, music, geometry.*

Obs. 1.—The proper name of a person or place with an article prefixed, is generally used as a common noun ; as, " He is *the Cicero* of his age,"—that is, *the orator.* " Many a fiery *Alp*,"—that is, *mountain :* except when a common noun is understood ; as, *The* [river] *Hudson*,—*The* [ship] *Amity*,—*The treacherous* [man] *Judas.*

Obs. 2.—A common noun with the definite article prefixed to it, sometimes becomes proper ; as, *The Park*,—*The Strand.*

Obs. 3.—The common name of a thing or quality personified often becomes proper ; as, " ' My power,' said *Reason*, ' is to advise, not to compel.' "—*Johnson.*

MODIFICATIONS.

Nouns have modifications of four kinds ; namely, *Persons, Numbers, Genders*, and *Cases.*

PERSONS.

Persons, in grammar, are modifications that distin- guish the speaker, the hearer, and the person or thing merely spoken of.

Obs.—The distinction of persons is founded on the different relations which the objects mentioned may bear to the discourse itself. It belongs to nouns, pronouns, and finite verbs ; and to these it is always applied, either by peculiarity of form or construction, or by inference from the principles of concord. Pronouns are like their antecedents, and verbs are like their subjects, in person.

There are three persons ; the *first*, the *second*, and the *third.*

The *first person* is that which denotes the speaker or writer ; as " I *Paul* have written it."

The *second person* is that which denotes the hearer, or the person addressed ; as, " *Robert*, who did this ?"

The *third person* is that which denotes the person or thing merely spoken of; as, " *James* loves his *book*."

Obs. 1.—In *written* language, the *first person* denotes the writer or author ; and the *second*, the reader or person addressed : except when the writer describes not himself, but some one else, as uttering to another the words which he records.

Obs. 2.—The speaker seldom refers to himself *by name*, as the speaker; consequently, *nouns* are rarely used in the first person; and when they are, a pronoun is usually prefixed to them. Hence some grammarians deny the first person to *nouns* altogether; others ascribe it; and many are silent on the subject. Analogy clearly requires it; as may be seen by the following examples: "*Adsum* Troius Æneas."—*Virg.* "*Calliopius recensui.*"—*Ter. Com. apud finem.* "Paul, an apostle, &c., unto Timothy, *my* own son in the faith." —1 *Tim.*, i. 1.

Obs. 3.—When a speaker or writer does not choose to declare himself in the *first* person, or to address his hearer or reader in the *second*, he speaks of both or either in the *third*. Thus Moses relates what *Moses* did, and Cæsar records the achievements of *Cæsar.* So Judah humbly beseeches Joseph: "Let *thy servant* abide in stead of the lad a bondman to *my lord.*"—*Gen.*, xliv, 33. And Abraham reverently intercedes with God: "Oh! let not *the Lord* be angry, and I will speak."—*Gen.*, xviii, 30.

Obs. 4.—When inanimate things are spoken to, they are *personified;* and their names are put in the second person, because by the figure the objects are *supposed* to be capable of hearing.

NUMBERS.

Numbers, in grammar, are modifications that distinguish unity and plurality.

Obs.—The distinction of numbers serves merely to show whether we speak of one object, or of more. It belongs to nouns, pronouns, and finite verbs; and to these it is always applied, either by peculiarity of form, or by inference from the principles of concord. Pronouns are like their antecedents, and verbs are like their subjects, in number.

There are two numbers; the *singular* and the *plural.*

The *singular number* is that which denotes but one; as, The *boy* learns.

The *plural number* is that which denotes more than one; as, The *boys* learn.

The plural number of *nouns* is regularly formed by adding *s* or *es* to the singular : as, *book, books; box, boxes.*

RULE I.—When the singular ends in a sound which will unite with that of *s*, the plural is generally formed by adding *s* only, and the number of syllables is not increased : as, *pen, pens; grape, grapes.*

RULE II.—But when the sound of *s* cannot be united with that of the primitive word, the plural adds *s* to final *e*, and *es* to other terminations, and forms a separate syllable : as, *page, pages; fox, foxes.*

Obs. 1.—English nouns ending in *o* preceded by a consonant, add *es*, but do not increase their syllables: as, *wo, woes; hero, heroes; negro, negroes; potato, potatoes; muskitto, muskittoes; octavo, octavoes.* The exceptions to this rule appear to be in such nouns as are not properly and fully Anglicized; thus many write *cantos, juntos, solos,* &c. Other nouns in *o* add *s* only; as, *folio, folios; bamboo, bamboos.* The plural of *two* is commonly written *twos*, but some prefer *twoes.*

Obs. 2.—Common nouns ending in *y* preceded by a consonant, change *y* into *i*, and add *es*, without increase of syllables: as, *fly, flies; duty, duties.*

3

Other nouns in *y* add *s* only: as, *day, days ; valley, valleys.* So likewise proper names in *y* are sometimes varied ; as, *Henry,* the *Henrys.*

OBS. 3.—The following nouns in *f,* change *f* into *v,* and add *es,* for the plural; *sheaf, leaf, loaf, beef, thief, calf, half, elf, shelf, self, wolf, wharf :* as, *sheaves, leaves,* &c. *Life, lives ; knife, knives ; wife, wives ;* are similar. *Staff* makes *staves :* though the compounds of *staff* are regular ; as, *flagstaff, flagstaffs.* The greater number of nouns in *f* and *fe,* are regular ; as, *fifes, strifes, chiefs, griefs, gulfs,* &c.

OBS. 4.—The following are still more irregular : *man, men ; woman, women ; child, children ; brother, brethren* [or *brothers] ; foot, feet ; ox, oxen ; tooth, teeth ; goose, geese ; louse, lice ; mouse, mice ; die, dice ; penny, pence ; Dies,* stamps, and *pennies,* coins, are regular.

OBS. 5.—Many foreign nouns retain their original plural : as, *arcanum, arcana ; datum, data ; erratum, errata ; effluvium, effluvia ; medium, media* [or *mediums] ; minutia, minutiæ ; stratum, strata ; stamen, stamina ; genus, genera ; genius, genii* [*geniuses,* for men of wit]; *magus, magi ; radius, radii ; appendix, appendices* [or *appendixes] ; calx, calces ; index, indices* [or *indexes] ; vortex, vortices ; axis, axes ; basis, bases ; crisis, crises ; thesis, theses ; antithesis, antitheses ; diæresis, diæreses ; ellipsis, ellipses ; emphasis, emphases ; hypothesis, hypotheses ; metamorphosis, metamorphoses ; automaton, automata ; criterion, criteria* [or *criterions] ; phænomenon, phænomena ; cherub, cherubim ; seraph, seraphim ; beau, beaux* [or *beaus].*

OBS. 6.—Some nouns (from the nature of the things meant) have no plural ; as, *gold, pride, meekness.*

OBS. 7.—Proper names of *individuals,* strictly used as such, have no plural. But when several persons of the same name are spoken of, the noun becomes in some degree common, and admits the plural form and an article ; as, *The Stuarts,—The Cæsars :* so likewise when such nouns are used to denote character; as, " *The Aristotles,* the *Tullys,* and the *Livys."—Burgh.*

OBS. 8.—The proper names of *nations* and *societies* are generally plural ; and, except in a direct address, they are usually construed with the definite article : as, *The Greeks,—The Jesuits.*

OBS. 9.—When a title is prefixed to a proper name so as to form a sort of compound, the name, and not the title, is varied to form the plural ; as, *The Miss Howards,—The two Mr. Clarks.* But a title not regarded as a part of one compound name, must be made plural, if it refer to more than one ; as, *Messrs. Lambert and Son,—The Lords Calthorpe and Erskine,—The Lords Bishops of Durham and St. David's,—The Lords Commissioners of Justiciary.*

OBS. 10.—Some nouns have no singular ; as, *embers, ides, oats, scissors, tongs, vespers, literati.*

OBS. 11.—Some nouns are alike in both numbers; as, *sheep, deer, vermin, swine, hose, means, odds, news, species, series, apparatus.* The following are sometimes construed as singular, but more frequently, and more properly, as plural: *alms, amends, pains, riches ; ethics, mathematics, metaphysics, optics, politics, pneumatics,* and other similar names of sciences. *Bellows* and *gallows* are properly alike in both numbers ; (as, " Let a *gallows* be made."— *Esther,* v, 14. " The *bellows are* burned."—*Jer.,* vi., 29 ;) but they have a regular plural in vulgar use. *Bolus, fungus, isthmus, prospectus,* and *rebus,* admit the regular plural.

OBS. 12.—Compounds in which the principal word is put first, vary the principal word to form the plural, and the adjunct to form the possessive case : as, Sing. *father-in-law,* Plur. *fathers-in-law,* Poss. *father-in-law's ;*— Sing. *court-martial,* Plur. *courts-martial,* Poss. *court-martial's.* The Possessive plural of such nouns is never used.

OBS. 13.—Compounds ending in *ful,* and all those in which the principal word is put last, form the plural in the same manner as other nouns ; as, *handfuls, spoonfuls, mouthfuls, fellow-servants, man-servants, outpourings, ingatherings, downsittings.*

OBS. 14.—Nouns of multitude, when taken collectively, generally admit the plural form ; as, *meeting, meetings :* but when taken distributively, they have a plural signification, without the form ; as, " The *jury were* divided."

OBS. 15.—When other parts of speech become nouns, they either want the plural, or form it *regularly*, like common nouns of the same endings; as, "His affairs went on at *sixes* and *sevens*."—*Arbuthnot.* "Some mathematicians have proposed to compute by *twoes; others,* by *fours; others,* by *twelves.*" —*Churchill.* "Three *fourths,* nine *tenths.*"—*Id.* "Time's *takings* and *leavings.*"—*Barton.* "The *yeas* and *nays.*"—*Newspaper.* "The *ays* and *noes.*" —*Ibid.* "The *ins* and the *outs.*"—*Ibid.* "His *ands* and his *ors.*"—*Mott.* "One of the *buts.*"—*Fowle.* "In raising the mirth of *stupids.*"—*Steele.*

GENDERS.

Genders, in grammar, are modifications that distinguish objects in regard to sex.

OBS.—The different genders are founded on the natural distinction of sex in animals, and on the absence of sex in other things. In English, they belong only to nouns and pronouns; and to these they are usually applied agreeably to the order of nature. Pronouns are of the same gender as the nouns for which they stand.

There are three genders; the *masculine*, the *feminine*, and the *neuter*.

The *masculine gender* is that which denotes persons or animals of the male kind; as, *man, father, king.*

The *feminine gender* is that which denotes persons or animals of the female kind; as, *woman, mother, queen.*

The *neuter gender* is that which denotes things that are neither male nor female; as, *pen, ink, paper.*

OBS. 1.—Some nouns are equally applicable to both sexes; as, *cousin, friend, neighbour, parent, person, servant.* The gender of these is usually determined by the context. To such words, some grammarians have applied the unnecessary and improper term *common gender.* Murray justly observes, "There is no such gender belonging to the language. The business of parsing, can be effectually performed without having recourse to a *common gender.*" The term is more useful, and less liable to objection, as applied to the learned languages; but with us it is plainly a solecism.

OBS. 2.—Generic names, even when construed as masculine or feminine, often virtually include both sexes; as, "Hast thou given the *horse* strength? hast thou clothed *his* neck with thunder?"—"Doth the *hawk* fly by thy wisdom, and stretch *her* wings toward the south?"—*Job.* These have been called *epicene* nouns—that is, *supercommon;* but they are to be parsed each according to the gender of the pronoun which is put for it.

OBS. 3.—Those terms which are equally applicable to both sexes, (if they are not expressly applied to females,) and those plurals which are known to include both sexes, should be called masculine in parsing; for, in all languages, the masculine gender is considered the most worthy, and is generally employed when both sexes are included under one common term.

OBS. 4.—The sexes are distinguished in three ways:

I. By the use of different names: as, *bachelor, maid; boy, girl; brother, sister; buck, doe; bull, cow; cock, hen; drake, duck; earl, countess; father, mother; friar, nun; gander, goose; hart, roe; horse, mare; husband, wife; king, queen; lad, lass; lord, lady; man, woman; master, mistress; milter, spawner; nephew, niece; ram, ewe; sloven, slut; son, daughter; stag, hind; steer, heifer; uncle, aunt; wizard, witch.*

II. By the use of different terminations: as, *abbot, abbess; administrator, administratrix; adulterer, adulteress; bridegroom, bride; caterer, cateress; duke, duchess; emperor, emperess or empress; executor, executrix; governor, governess; hero, heroine; landgrave, landgravine; margrave, margravine;*

marquis, marchioness; sorcerer, sorceress; sultan, sultaness or *sultana; testator, testatrix; tutor, tutoress* or *tutress; widower, widow.*

The following nouns become feminine by merely adding *ess; baron, deacon, heir, host, jew, lion, mayor, patron, peer, poet, priest, prior, prophet, shepherd, viscount.*

The following nouns become feminine by rejecting the last vowel, and adding *ess; actor, ambassador, arbiter, benefactor, chanter, conductor, doctor, elector, enchanter, founder, hunter, idolator, inventor, prince, protector, songster, spectator, suitor, tiger, traitor, votary.*

III. By prefixing an attribute of distinction: as, *cock-sparrow, hen-sparrow; man-servant, maid-servant; he-goat, she-goat; male relations, female relations.*

Obs. 5.—The names of things without life, used literally, are always of the neuter gender. But inanimate objects are often represented figuratively, as having sex. Things remarkable for power, greatness, or sublimity, are spoken of as masculine; as, the *sun, time, death, sleep, fear, anger, winter, war.* Things beautiful, amiable, or prolific, are spoken of as feminine; as, the *moon, earth, nature, fortune, knowledge, hope, spring, peace.*

Obs. 6.—Nouns of multitude, when they convey the idea of unity, or take the plural form, are of the neuter gender; but when they convey the idea of plurality without the form, they follow the gender of the individuals that compose the assemblage.

Obs. 7.—Creatures whose sex is unknown, or unnecessary to be regarded, are generally spoken of as neuter; as, "He fired at the *deer,* and wounded *it.*"—"If a man shall steal an *ox* or a *sheep,* and kill *it* or sell *it ;*" &c.— *Exodus,* xxii, 1.

CASES.

Cases, in grammar, are modifications that distinguish the relations of nouns and pronouns to other words.

Obs.—The cases are founded on the different relations under which things are represented in discourse, and from which the words acquire correspondent relations, or become dependent one on an other, according to the sense. In English, these modifications, or relations, belong only to nouns and pronouns. Pronouns are not necessarily like their antecedents, in case.

There are three cases; the *nominative,* the *possessive,* and the *objective.*

The *nominative case* is that form or state of a noun or pronoun, which usually denotes the subject of a finite verb: as, The *boy* runs; *I* run.

Obs.—The *subject* of a finite verb is that which answers to *who* or *what* before it; as, "The boy runs"—*Who* runs? The *boy.* *Boy* is therefore here in the *nominative* case.

The *possessive case* is that form or state of a noun or pronoun, which usually denotes the relation of property: as, The *boy's* hat; *my* hat.

Obs. 1.—The possessive case of nouns is formed, in the singular number, by adding to the nominative *s preceded by an apostrophe ;* and, in the plural, when the nominative ends in *s,* by adding *an apostrophe only:* as, singular, *boy's ;* plural, *boys' ;*—sounded alike, but written differently.

Obs. 2.—Plural nouns that do not end in *s,* usually form the possessive case in the same manner as the singular; as, *man's, men's.*

Obs. 3.—When the singular and the plural are alike in the nominative, the apostrophe, which (as Dr. Johnson has shown) is merely a sign of the case, and not of elision, ought to follow the *s* in the plural, to distinguish it from the singular; as, *sheep's, sheeps'*.

Obs. 4.—The *apostrophic s* adds a syllable to the noun, when it will not unite with the sound in which the nominative ends; as, *torch's*, pronounced *torchiz*.

Obs. 5.—The apostrophe and *s* are sometimes added to mere characters, to denote *plurality*, and not the possessive case; as, Two *a*'s—three *b*'s—four 9's. In the following example, they are used to give the sound of a verbal termination to words that are not properly verbs: "When a man in a soliloquy reasons with himself, and *pro's* and *con's*, and weighs all his designs," &c.—*Congreve*.

The *objective case* is that form or state of a noun or pronoun, which usually denotes the object of a verb, participle, or preposition: as, I know the *boy*; he knows *me*.

Obs. 1.—The *object* of a verb, participle, or preposition, is that which answers to *whom* or *what* after it; as, "I know the boy."—I know *whom?* The boy. *Boy* is therefore here in the *objective* case.

Obs. 2.—The nominative and the objective of nouns, are always alike in form, being distinguishable from each other only by their place in a sentence, or their simple dependence according to the sense.

THE DECLENSION OF NOUNS.

The declension of a noun is a regular arrangement of its numbers and cases. Thus:—

EXAMPLE I.—FRIEND.

Sing.	Nom.	friend,	Plur.	Nom.	friends,
	Poss.	friend's,		Poss.	friends',
	Obj.	friend;		Obj.	friends.

EXAMPLE II.—MAN.

Sing.	Nom.	man,	Plur.	Nom.	men,
	Poss.	man's,		Poss.	men's,
	Obj.	man;		Obj.	men.

EXAMPLE III.—FOX.

Sing.	Nom.	fox,	Plur.	Nom.	foxes,
	Poss.	fox's,		Poss.	foxes',
	Obj.	fox;		Obj.	foxes.

EXAMPLE IV.—FLY.

Sing.	Nom.	fly,	Plur.	Nom.	flies,
	Poss.	fly's,		Poss.	flies',
	Obj.	fly;		Obj.	flies.

5*

ANALYSIS.

Analysis is the separation of a sentence into the parts which compose it.

Every sentence must contain, at least, two principal parts ; namely, the *subject* and the *predicate.*

The *subject* of a sentence is that of which it treats ; as, " The *sun* has set."—" Can *you* write ?"

The *predicate* is that which expresses the action, being, or passion, as belonging to the subject.   It is therefore always a verb.

Any combination of the subject and predicate is called a *proposition.*

A simple sentence is one that contains only one proposition ; as, " Fire burns."—" The truth will prevail."

Sentences are divided, with respect to the nature of the propositions which they contain, into four classes ; *declarative, interrogative, imperative,* and *exclamatory.*

A sentence is *declarative* when it expresses an affirmation or negation ; *interrogative,* when it expresses a question ; *imperative,* when it expresses a command ; and *exclamatory,* when it expresses an exclamation.

Obs. 1.—The predicate being always a verb, the subject of the sentence is the subject of the verb, as defined in *Obs. page* 52.   The *object of the verb,* when the latter is the predicate of a sentence, may be considered one of the principal parts of the sentence.   It properly, however, modifies the verb, and is not a *primary element* of the sentence.   In imperative sentences, the subject is the pronoun *thou* or *you* (understood).   For the definition of the *object* of a verb, see *Obs.* 1, *page* 53.

Obs. 2.—There are sometimes used in connection with a sentence, words that form no part of its structure.   Such words are said to be *independent.* A noun or a pronoun may be independent in various ways ; as,
1. The name of a person or thing addressed ; as, " *John,* when will you go ?"—" O *ye* of little faith !"
2. The name of a person or thing which is the subject of an exclamation ; as, " Alas, poor *Yorick ?*"
3. An expletive word used merely to make the subject or object emphatic ; as, " The *Spring*—she is a blessed thing !"—" *Gad,* a troop shall overcome him."

Such nouns and pronouns, although independent in *state,* require the *form* of the nominative case, and therefore, in parsing, should be said to be in that case.   Interjections are always independent.

EXERCISES IN ANALYSIS AND PARSING.

PRAXIS II.—ETYMOLOGICAL.

In the Second Praxis, it is required of the pupil—to state whether the sentence is declarative, interrogative, imperative, or exclamatory ; to analyze it by pointing out the subject, pred-icate, and object ; and to parse it by distinguishing the different parts of speech, and the classes and modifications of the nouns. Thus :—

" Columbus studied geography."

ANALYSIS.—This is a simple declarative sentence. The subject is *Columbus ;* the predicate, *studied ;* the object, *geography.*

PARSING.—*Columbus* is a proper noun, because it is the name of a particular individual ; it is of the third person, because it is the name of a person spoken of ; of the singular number, because it denotes but one ; of the masculine gender, because it is the name of a male ; and in the nominative case, because it is the subject of the verb *studied.*

Studied is a verb, because it signifies action.

Geography is a common noun, because it is the name of a thing *sui generis ;* (see page 48). It is of the third person, because it is spoken of ; of the singular number, because it denotes but one ; of the neuter gender, because it is neither male nor female ; and in the objective case, because it is the object of the verb *studied.*

Generosity makes friends. Can indolence bestow wealth ? Despise meanness. Can man avoid errors ? Does Eliza under-stand Italian ? Love truth. Perseverance overcomes obstacles. What did you say ? Diligence deserves praise. It should be rewarded. Could he have avoided disgrace ? Romulus founded Rome. Forgetfulness cures sorrow. Can liars respect them-selves ? Do they fear God ? Birds sing. Cowards fear death. Sinners feel remorse. Has John returned ? Time flies. Plants produce fruit. Observation increases knowledge. Mortal, prepare. Take warning, youth ! Liberty, it has fled ! Elec-tricity causes lightning. Avarice extinguishes generosity. In-tegrity inspires confidence. Who can trust liars ?

CHAPTER IV.—OF ADJECTIVES.

An Adjective is a word added to a noun or pronoun, and generally expresses quality : as, A *wise* man ; a *new* book. You *two* are *diligent.*

CLASSES.

Adjectives may be divided into six classes ; namely, *common, proper, numeral, pronominal, participial,* and *compound.*

I. A *common adjective* is any ordinary epithet, or adjective denoting quality or situation; as, *Good, bad, peaceful, warlike—eastern, western, outer, inner.*

II. A *proper adjective* is one that is formed from a proper name; as, *American, English, Platonic.*

III. A *numeral adjective* is one that expresses a definite number; as, *One, two, three, four, five, six, &c.*

IV. A *pronominal adjective* is a definitive word which may either accompany its noun, or represent it understood; as, "*All* join to guard what *each* desires to gain."—*Pope.* That is, *All men* join to guard what *each man* desires to gain.

V. A *participial adjective* is one that has the form of a participle, but differs from it by rejecting the idea of time; as, An *amusing* story.

VI. A *compound adjective,* is one that consists of two or more words joined together; as, *Nut-brown, laughter-loving, four-footed.*

Obs. 1.—Numeral adjectives are of three kinds: namely,
1. *Cardinal;* as, One, two, three, four, five, six, seven, eight, nine, ten, eleven, twelve, thirteen, fourteen, fifteen, &c.
2. *Ordinal;* as, First, second, third, fourth, fifth, sixth, seventh, eighth, ninth, tenth, eleventh, twelfth, thirteenth, &c.
3. *Multiplicative;* as, Single or alone, double or twofold, triple or threefold, quadruple or fourfold, quintuple or fivefold, sextuple or sixfold, septuple or sevenfold, octuple or eightfold, &c.
Obs. 2.—Compound adjectives, being formed at pleasure, are very numerous and various. Many of them embrace numerals, and run on in a series; as, *one-leaved, two-leaved, three-leaved, four-leaved,* &c.

MODIFICATIONS.

Adjectives have, commonly, no modifications but the forms of *comparison.*

Comparison is a variation of the adjective to express quality in different degrees; as, *hard, harder, hardest.*

There are three degrees of comparison; the *positive,* the *comparative,* and the *superlative.*

The *positive degree* is that which is expressed by the adjective in its simple form; as, *hard, soft, good.*

The *comparative degree* is that which exceeds the positive; as, *harder, softer, better.*

The *superlative degree* is that which is not exceeded; as, *hardest, softest, best.*

Those adjectives whose signification does not admit of

different degrees, cannot be compared; as, *two, second, all, total, immortal, infinite.*

Those adjectives which may be varied in sense, but not in form, are compared by means of adverbs; as, skillful, *more* skillful, *most* skillful—skillful, *less* skillful, *least* skillful.

REGULAR COMPARISON.

Adjectives are regularly compared, when the comparative degree is expressed by adding *er,* and the superlative, by adding *est* to them ; as,

Positive.	*Comparative.*	*Superlative.*
great,	greater,	greatest.
*wide,	wider,	widest.
hot,	hotter,	hottest.

The regular method of comparison is chiefly applicable to monosyllables, and to dissyllables ending in *y* or mute *e.*

COMPARISON BY ADVERBS.

The different degrees of a quality may also be expressed, with precisely the same import, by prefixing to the adjective the adverbs *more* and *most:* as, *wise, more wise, most wise ; famous, more famous, most famous ; amiable, more amiable, most amiable.*

The degrees of diminution are expressed, in like manner, by the adverbs *less* and *least:* as, *wise, less wise, least wise ; famous, less famous, least famous ; amiable, less amiable, least amiable.*

Obs. 1.—Adjectives of more than one syllable, except dissyllables ending in *y* or mute *e,* rarely admit a change of termination, but are rather compared by means of the adverbs : thus we say, *virtuous, more virtuous, most virtuous ;* but not *virtuous, virtuouser, virtuousest.*

Obs. 2.—The prefixing of an *adverb* can hardly be called a *variation* of the adjective ; the words may with more propriety be parsed separately, the *degree* being ascribed to the *adverb*—or, if you please, to *both* words ; for both are varied *in sense* by the inflection of the former.

Obs. 3.—The degrees in which qualities may exist in nature, are infinitely various ; but the only degrees with which the grammarian is concerned, are those which our *variation* of the adjective or adverb enables us to express. Whenever the *adjective itself* denotes these degrees, they properly belong to it ; as, *worthy, worthier, worthiest.* If an *adverb* is employed for this purpose, that also is compared, and the two degrees formed are properly its own ; as, worthy, *more* worthy, *most* worthy. But these same degrees may be *otherwise* expressed ; as, worthy, *in a higher degree* worthy, *in the highest degree* worthy. Here also the adjective *worthy* is virtually compared as before ; but only the adjective *high* is grammatically modified. Many grammarians have erroneously parsed the adverbs *more* and *most, less* and *least,* as parts of the adjective.

---

* See Rules for Spelling III. and VI.

3*

IRREGULAR COMPARISON.

The following adjectives are compared irregularly: *good, better, best; bad* or *ill, worse, worst; little, less, least; much, more, most; many, more, most.*

OBS. 1.—In *English,* and also in *Latin,* most adjectives that denote *place* or *situation,* not only form the superlative irregularly, but are also either redundant or defective in comparison. Thus:—

I. The following nine have more than one superlative: *far, farther, farthest, farmost* or *farthermost; near, nearer, nearest* or *next; fore, former, foremost* or *first; hind, hinder, hindmost* or *hindermost; in, inner, inmost* or *innermost; out, outer* or *utter, outmost* or *utmost, outermost* or *uttermost; up, upper, upmost* or *uppermost; low, lower, lowest* or *lowermost; late, later,* or *latter, latest* or *last.*

II. The following five want the positive: [*aft,* adv.,] *after, aftmost,* or *aftermost;* [*forth,* adv.,] *further, furthest* or *furthermost; hither, hithermost; nether, nethermost; under, undermost.*

III. The following want the comparative: *front, frontmost; rear, rearmost; head, headmost; end, endmost; top, topmost; bottom, bottommost; mid* or *middle, midst, midmost* or *middlemost; north, northmost; south, southmost; northern, northernmost; southern, southernmost; eastern, easternmost; western, westernmost.*

OBS. 2.—Many of these irregular adjectives are also in common use, as nouns, adverbs, or prepositions; the sense in which they are employed will show to what class they belong.

OBS. 3.—The words *fore* and *hind, front* and *rear, head* and *end, right* and *left, in* and *out, high* and *low, top* and *bottom, up* and *down, upper* and *under, mid* and *after,* are often joined in composition with other words; and some of them, when used as adjectives of place, are rarely separated from their nouns; as, *in*-land, *mid*-sea, *after*-ages, &c.

OBS. 4.—It may be remarked of the comparatives, *former* and *latter* or *hinder, upper* and *under* or *nether, inner* and *outer* or *utter, after* and *hither;* as well as of the Latin *superior* and *inferior, anterior* and *posterior, interior* and *exterior, prior* and *ulterior, senior* and *junior, major* and *minor;* that they cannot, like other comparatives, be construed with the conjunction *than,* introducing the latter term of comparison; for we never say, one thing is *former, superior,* &c., THAN an other.

OBS. 5.—*Common adjectives,* or epithets denoting quality, are more numerous than all the other classes put together. Many of these, and a few that are *pronominal,* may be varied by comparison; and some *participial* adjectives may be compared by means of the adverbs. But adjectives formed from *proper names,* all the *numerals,* and most of the *compounds,* are in no way susceptible of comparison.

OBS. 6.—Nouns are often used as adjectives; as, An *iron* bar—An *evening* school—A *mahogany* chair—A *South-Sea* dream. These also are incapable of comparison.

OBS. 7.—The numerals are often used as nouns; and, as such, are regularly declined; as, Such a *one*—*One's* own self—The little *ones*—By *tens*—For *twenty's* sake—By *fifties*—Two *millions.*

OBS. 8.—Comparatives, and the word *other,* are sometimes also employed as nouns, and have the regular declension; as, Our *superiors*—His *betters*—The *elder's* advice—An* *other's* wo—Let *others* do as they will. But, as adjectives, these words are invariable.

OBS. 9.—Pronominal adjectives, when their nouns are expressed, simply relate to them, and have no modifications: except *this* and *that,* which form

---

* There seems to be no good reason for joining *an* and *other.* *An* here excludes any other article; and analogy and consistency require that the words be separated. Their union has led sometimes to an improper repetition of the article; as, ' *Another* such a man,'—for, ' An other such man.'

the plural *these* and *those;* and *much, many,* and a few others, which are compared.

Obs. 10.—Pronominal adjectives, when their nouns are not expressed, may be parsed as representing them in *person, number, gender,* and *case:* but those who prefer it, may supply the ellipsis, and parse the adjective *simply as an adjective.*

Obs. 11.—The following are the principal pronominal adjectives : *All, any, both, certain, divers, each, either, else, enough, every, few, former, first, latter, last, little, less, least, much, many, more, most, neither, no* or *none,** *one, only, other, own, same, several, some, such, this, that, these, those, which, what.*

Obs. 12.— *Which* and *what,* when they are not prefixed to nouns, are, for the most part, relative or interrogative pronouns.

ANALYSIS.

Words, added to either of the principal parts of a sentence to modify or limit its meaning, are called *adjuncts.* Adjuncts are sometimes called *modifications.*

They are divided into two classes, *primary* and *secondary adjuncts.*

Primary adjuncts are those added directly to either of the principal parts; as, " *Good* books *always* deserve *a careful* perusal."

Secondary adjuncts are those added to other adjuncts; as, " *Suddenly* acquired wealth *very* rarely brings happiness."

Adjuncts are divided, with respect to their office, into three classes; namely, *adjective, adverbial,* and *explanatory.*

An adjective adjunct is one used to modify or limit a noun or a pronoun; as, " *Both those bad* boys deserve *severe* punishment."

An adverbial adjunct is one used like an adverb; as, " Remember *now* thy Creator *in the days of thy youth.*"

An explanatory adjunct is one used to explain a preceding noun or pronoun; as, " The emperor *Napoleon* was banished."—" We, *the people*, ordain this constitution."

The *subject* or the *object* in a sentence, may be modified by *adjective* or *explanatory adjuncts* of various forms; as,

---

* *No* and *none* seem to be only different forms of the same adjective; the former being used before a noun expressed, and the latter when the noun is understood, or not placed after the adjective; as, " For *none* of us liveth to himself, and *no* man dieth to himself."—*Romans,* xiv. 7.

1. By an *article* or an *adjective ;* as, "*The diligent* scholar improves."
2. By a *noun* or *pronoun* in the possessive case; as, "*William's* sister has lost *her* book."
3. By a *verb* used as an adjective; as, "The desire *to excel* is laudable."
4. By a *preposition and its object,* used together as an adjective; as, "A man *of integrity* obeys the dictates *of conscience.*"
5. By a *noun* or *pronoun* used as an explanatory adjunct; as, "His brother, *Charles,* is idle."

The predicate of a sentence may be modified by *adverbial adjuncts* of various forms; as,

1. By an *adverb ;* as, "The sun shines *brightly.*"
2. By a *preposition and its object,* used together as an adverb; as, "He came *from Boston.*"

EXERCISES IN ANALYSIS AND PARSING.

PRAXIS III.—ETYMOLOGICAL.

In the Third Praxis, it is required of the pupil—to classify and analyze the sentence as in the preceding praxis ; to point out, in addition, the adjuncts of each of the principal parts, and distinguish their classes ; and to parse the sentence by distinguishing the different parts of speech, and the classes and modifications of the nouns, and adjectives, distinguishing also the article as definite or indefinite.   Thus:—

EXAMPLE ANALYZED AND PARSED.

"The Athenians carefully observed Solon's wise laws."

ANALYSIS.—This is a simple declarative sentence.
The subject is *Athenians ;* the predicate, *observed ;* the object, *laws.*
The subject is limited by the adjective adjunct, *the ;* the predicate is modified by the adverbial adjunct, *carefully ;* and the object is modified by the adjective adjuncts, *Solon's* and *wise.*

PARSING.—*The* is the definite article, because it limits the noun *Athenians.*

Athenians is a proper noun, because it is the name of a particular people. (Modifications as in the preceding praxis.)
Carefully is an adverb, because it is added to the verb *observed,* and expresses manner.
Observed is a verb, because it expresses action.
Solon's is a proper noun, because it is the name of a particular individual; it is of the third person, singular number, masculine gender, and in the possessive case, because it indicates the possession of *laws.*
Wise is a common adjective, because it simply expresses the quality of laws.
Laws is a common noun, because it is the name of a class of things.

Pleasure's call always wins an eager attention.

Avarice rapidly extinguishes every generous emotion.

King Belshazzar made a great feast.

Every person highly praised William's noble conduct.

Where did your kind father buy that interesting book ?

The French ambassador immediately presented his credentials.

This benevolent young lady kindly teaches many poor children.

Riotous indulgence rapidly destroys the bodily vigor.

This enterprising merchant has just returned from Europe.

The study of astronomy greatly elevates the mind.

Indulgence in sloth can never lead to prosperity.

Charles's resignation filled all Europe with astonishment.

The beautiful prospects of nature always excite the warmest admiration of mankind.

The powerful eloquence of Demosthenes excited the fierce indignation of Athens against Philip of Macedon.

CHAPTER V.—OF PRONOUNS.

A Pronoun is a word used in stead of a noun : as, The boy loves *his* book; *he* has long lessons, and *he* learns *them* well.

Obs. 1.—The word for which a pronoun stands, is called its *antecedent*, because it usually precedes the pronoun. But some have limited the term *antecedent*, to the word represented by a relative.

Obs. 2.—The pronouns *I* and *thou* in their different modifications, stand immediately for persons that are, in general, sufficiently known without being named; (*I* meaning the *speaker*, and *thou* the *hearer*;) their antecedents are therefore generally *understood*.

Obs. 3.—The other personal pronouns are sometimes taken in a general or absolute sense, to denote persons or things not previously mentioned; as, "*He* that hath knowledge, spareth his words."

Obs. 4.—A pronoun with which a question is asked, stands for some person or thing unknown to the speaker; the noun, therefore, cannot occur before it, but may be used after it or instead of it.

Obs. 5.—The personal and the interrogative pronouns often stand in construction as the antecedents to other pronouns; as, *He that* arms his intent with virtue is invincible."—" *Who that* has any moral sense, dares tell lies ?"

CLASSES.

Pronouns are divided into three classes; *personal, relative,* and *interrogative.*

I. A *personal pronoun* is a pronoun that shows, by its form, of what person it is.

The *simple* personal pronouns are five : namely, *I,* of

the first person ; *thou*, of the second person ; *he, she,* and *it*, of the third person.

The *compound* personal pronouns are also five : namely, *myself*, of the first person ; *thyself*, of the second person ; *himself, herself,* and *itself*, of the third person.

II. A *relative pronoun* is a pronoun that represents an antecedent word or phrase, and connects different clauses of a sentence.

The relative pronouns are *who, which, what,* and *that ;* and the compounds *whoever* or *whosoever, whichever* or *whichsoever, whatever* or *whatsoever.*

What is a kind of double relative, equivalent to *that* or *those which;* and is to be parsed, first *as antecedent,* and then *as relative.*

III. An *interrogative pronoun* is a pronoun with which a question is asked.

The interrogative pronouns are *who, which,* and *wltat;* being the same in form as relatives.

Obs 1.—*Who* is usually applied to persons only; *which*, though formerly applied to persons, is now confined to animals and inanimate things . *what* (as a mere pronoun) is applied to things only: *that* is applied indifferently to persons, animals, or things.

Obs. 2.—The pronoun *what* has a twofold relation, and is often used (by ellipsis of the noun) both as antecedent and relative, being equivalent to *that which*, or *the thing which*. In this double relation, *what* represents two cases at the same time: as, " He is ashamed of *what* he has done ;" that is, of *that* [thing] *which* he has done. It is usually of the singular number, though sometimes plural; as, " I must turn to the faults, or *what appear* such to me."—*Byron.* "All distortions and mimicries, as such, are *what raise* aversion in stead of pleasure.—*Steele.*

Obs. 3.— *What* is sometimes used both as an *adjective* and a *relative* at the same time, and is placed before the noun which it represents : as, " *What* money we had was taken away ;" that is, *All the* money *that* we had, &c. ——" *What* man but enters, dies ;" that is, *Any* man *who*, &c. " *What* god but enters you forbidden field."—*Pope.* Indeed, it does not admit of being construed after a noun, as a simple relative. The compound *whatever* or *whatsoever* has the same peculiarities of construction; as, " We will certainly do *whatsoever thing* goeth forth out of our own mouth."—*Jer.,* xliv, 17.

Obs. 4.— *Who, which,* and *what,* when the affix *ever* or *soever* is added, have an unlimited signification ; and, as some general term, such as *any person*, or *any thing*, is usually employed as the antecedent, they are all commonly followed by two verbs : as, " *Whoever* attends, will improve ;" that is, *Any person who* attends, will improve. In parsing, supply the antecedent.

Obs. 5.— *Which* and *what* are often prefixed to nouns as definitive or interrogative adjectives ; and, as such, may be applied to persons as well as to things : as, " *What* man ?"—" *Which* boy ?"

Obs. 6.—The word *that* is a relative pronoun, when it is equivalent to *who, whom,* or *which ;* as, " The days *that* [which] are past, are gone forever." It is a definitive or pronominal adjective, when 'it relates to a noun expressed or understood after it; as, " *That* book is new." In other cases, it is a conjunction, as, " Live well, *that* you may die well."

Obs. 7.—The relative *that* has this peculiarity, that it cannot follow the word on which its case depends: thus, it is said, [*John,* xiii, 29,]   " Buy those things *that* we have need *of ;*" but we cannot say, "Buy those things *of that* we have need."

Obs. 8.—The word *as*, though usually a conjunction or an adverb, has sometimes the construction of a relative pronoun; as, "The Lord added to the church daily such [persons] *as* should be saved."—*Acts*, ii, 47.

Obs. 9.— *Whether* was formerly used as an interrogative pronoun, referring to one of two things ; as, " *Whether* is greater, the gold or the temple ?" —*Matt.*, xxiii, 17.

Obs. 10.—Interrogative pronouns differ from relatives chiefly in this ; that, as the subject referred to is unknown to the speaker, they do not relate to a *preceding* noun, but to something which is to be expressed in the answer to the question. Their *person, number,* and *gender,* therefore, are not regulated by an *antecedent* noun ; but by what the speaker supposes of a subject which may, or may not, agree with them in these respects : as, " *What* lies there ?" Ans. " Two *men* asleep."

MODIFICATIONS.

Pronouns have the same modifications as nouns; namely, *Persons, Numbers, Genders,* and *Cases.*

Obs. 1.—In the personal pronouns, most of these properties are distinguished by the words themselves ; in the relative and the interrogative pronouns, they are ascertained chiefly by the antecedent and the verb.

Obs. 2.—The personal pronouns of the first and second persons, are equally applicable to both sexes ; and should be considered masculine or feminine according to the known application of them. [See *Levizac's French Gram.*, p. 73.] The speaker and the hearer, being present to each other, of course know the sex to which they respectively belong ; and, whenever they appear in narrative, we are told who they are. In *Latin,* an adjective or a participle relating to these pronouns, is varied to *agree* with them in *number, gender,* and *case ;* as,

> *Miseræ* hoc tamen unum
> Exequere, Anna, *mihi : solam* nam perfidus ille
> *Te* colere, arcanos etiam tibi credere sensus ;
> *Sola* viri molles aditus et tempora nòras.—*Virgil.*

Obs. 3.—Many grammarians deny the first person of nouns, and the gender of pronouns of the first and second persons ; and at the same time teach, that, "Pronouns must always agree with their antecedents, and the nouns for which they stand. in *gender, number,* and *person.*"—*Murray's Gram.*, 2d *Ed.*, 1796. Now, no two words *can agree* in any property which belongs not to both !

THE DECLENSION OF PRONOUNS.

The declension of a pronoun is a regular arrangement of its numbers and cases.

SIMPLE PERSONALS.

The simple personal pronouns are thus declined :—

I, *of the* FIRST PERSON, *any* of the genders.*

Sing.			Plur.		
Nom.	I,		Nom.	we,	
Poss.	my, *or* mine,		Poss.	our, *or* ours,	
Obj.	me ;		Obj.	us.	

---

* That the pronouns of the first and second persons are sometimes masculine and sometimes feminine, is perfectly certain ; but whether they can or cannot be neuter, is a question difficult to be decided. To things inanimate they are only applied figur-

THOU, *of the* SECOND PERSON, *any of the genders.*

Sing.		Plur.	
Nom.	thou,	Nom.	ye,* *or* you,
Poss.	thy, *or* thine,	Poss.	your, *or* yours,
Obj.	thee;	Obj.	you.

HE, *of the* THIRD PERSON, *masculine gender.*

Sing.		Plur.	
Nom.	he,	Nom.	they,
Poss.	his,	Poss.	their, *or* theirs,
Obj.	him;	Obj.	them.

SHE, *of the* THIRD PERSON, *feminine gender.*

Sing.		Plur.	
Nom.	she,	Nom.	they,
Poss.	her, *or* hers,	Poss.	their, *or* theirs,
Obj.	her;	Obj.	them.

IT, *of the* THIRD PERSON, *neuter gender.*

Sing.		Plur.	
Nom.	it,	Nom.	they,
Poss.	its,†	Poss.	their, *or* theirs,
Obj.	it;	Obj.	them.

OBS. 1.—Most of the personal pronouns have two forms of the possessive case, in each number; as, *my* or *mine, our* or *ours; thy* or *thine, you* or *yours; her* or *hers, their* or *theirs.* The former is used before a noun expressed; the latter, when the governing noun is *understood,* or so placed as not immediately to follow the pronoun; as, "*My* powers are *thine.*"—*Montgomery.*

OBS. 2.—*Mine* and *thine* were formerly used before all words beginning with a vowel sound; *my* and *thy,* before others: as, "It was thou, a man, *mine* equal, *my* guide, and *mine* acquaintance."—*Psalm.* But this usage is now obsolete, or peculiar to the poets; as,

"Time writes no wrinkle on *thine* azure brow."—*Byron.*

COMPOUND PERSONALS.

The word *self*‡ added to the simple personal pronouns, forms the class of *compound personal pronouns;* which are used when an action reverts upon the agent, and also when

---

atively; and the question is, whether the figure always necessarily changes the gender of the antecedent noun. Pronouns are of the same gender as the nouns for which they stand; and if, in the following example, *gold* and *diamond* are neuter, so is the pronoun *me.* And, if not neuter, of what gender are they?

"Where thy true treasure? *Gold* says, 'Not in *me;*'
And, 'Not in *me,*' the *diamond.* Gold is poor."—*Young.*

* The use of the pronoun *ye* is mostly confined to the solemn style, and to the burlesque. In the latter, it is sometimes used for the objective case.

† In ancient times, *he, his,* and *him,* were applied to things neuter. In our translation of the Bible, the pronoun *it* is employed in the nominative and the objective, but *his* is retained in the possessive, neuter; as, "Look not thou upon the wine, when *it is* red, when *it* giveth *his* color in the cup, when *it* moveth *itself* aright."—*Prov.,* xxiii, 31. *Its* is not found in the Bible, except by misprint.

‡ The word *self* was originally an *adjective;* but when used alone, it is now generally a *noun.* This may have occasioned the diversity in the formation of the compound personal pronouns. Dr. Johnson calls *self* a *pronoun;* but he explains it as being both *adjective* and *substantive.*

some persons are to be distinguished from others : as, sing. *myself,* plur. *ourselves;* sing. *thyself,* plur. *yourselves;* sing. *himself,** plur. *themselves;* sing. *herself,* plur. *themselves;* sing. *itself,* plur. *themselves.* They all want the possessive case, and are alike in the nominative and objective.

RELATIVES AND INTERROGATIVES.

The relative and the interrogative pronouns are thus declined :—

WHO, *applied only to persons.*

Sing.	Nom.	who,	Plur.	Nom.	who,
	Poss.	whose,		Poss.	whose,
	Obj.	whom;		Obj.	whom,

WHICH, *applied to animals and things.*

Sing.	Nom.	which,	Plur.	Nom.	which,
	Poss.	†——		Poss.	——
	Obj.	which;		Obj.	which.

WHAT, *generally applied to things.*

Sing.	Nom.	what,	Plur.	Nom.	what, ·
	Poss.	——		Poss.	——
	Obj.	what;		Obj.	what.

THAT, *applied to persons, animals, and things.*

Sing.	Nom.	that,	Plur.	Nom.	that,
	Poss.	——		Poss.	——
	Obj.	that ;		Obj.	that.

COMPOUND RELATIVES.

The compound relative pronouns, *whoever* or *whosoever,* *whichever* or *whichsoever,* and *whatever* or *whatsoever,* are declined in the same manner as the simples, *who, which, what.*

ANALYSIS.

A *clause* is a sentence that forms a part of another sentence. Clauses are either *dependent* or *independent.*

A *dependent clause* is one used as an adjunct, or as

---

* *Hisself, itsself,* and *theirselves,* are more analogical than *himself, itsself,* *themselves;* but custom has rejected the former, and established the latter. When an adjective is prefixed to *self,* the pronouns are written separately in the possessive case ; as, *My* single self,—*My* own self,—*His* own self,—*Their* own selves.

† *Whose* is sometimes used as the possessive case of *which ;* as, "A religion *whose* origin is divine."—*Blair.*

one of the principal parts of a sentence.   The clause on
which it depends, is called the *principal clause.*

Clauses may be connected by conjunctions, relative
pronouns, or adverbs.

A *complex sentence* is one composed of a principal
clause, and one or more dependent clauses.

A *compound sentence* is one composed of two or more
independent clauses.

Compound or complex clauses are sometimes called
members.

Obs.—A clause introduced by a relative pronoun, is often called a *relative
clause;* it may be dependent or independent; thus the sentence, " This is
the man *who committed the deed,*" is complex; because the relative clause is
an adjunct of man, modifying it like an adjective; but " I gave the book to
John, *who has lost it,*" is a compound sentence, the relative clause not being
an adjunct, but expressing an *additional fact,* and equivalent to " *and he has
lost it.*"

EXERCISES IN ANALYSIS AND PARSING.

PRAXIS IV.—ETYMOLOGICAL.

*In the Fourth Praxis, it is required of the pupil—to clas-
sify the sentences ; to point out the component clauses ; to
analyze and parse each as in the preceding praxis ; and to
state the classes and modifications of the pronouns.   Thus :—*

EXAMPLE ANALYZED AND PARSED.

" Children who disobey their parents, deserve punishment."

ANALYSIS.—This is a complex declarative sentence; the principal clause is,
Children deserve punishment, and the dependent clause is, *Who disobey
their parents,* an adjective adjunct of *children;* the connective word
is *who.*

The subject of the principal clause is *children;* the predicate is *deserve;*
and the object is *punishment.*   The adjunct of the subject is the dependent clause ; the other parts have no adjuncts.   The subject of the
dependent clause is *who;* the predicate is *disobey;* the object is
parents.   The subject and the predicate have no adjuncts ; the adjunct of parents is *their.*

PARSING.—*Who* is a relative pronoun, because it represents the antecedent
word *children,* and connects the two clauses of the sentence ; it is of
the third person, because it represents the persons spoken of ; of the
plural number, because it denotes more than one ; of the masculine
gender, because it is a term equally applicable to both sexes (see
Obs. 3, page 51) ;* and in the nominative case, because it is the subject
of the verb *disobey;* its declension in both numbers is, Nom. *who;*
Poss. *whose ;* Obj. *whom.*

Their is a personal pronoun, because it shows by its form that it is of the

* It would be preferable, in the opinion of the editor of these exercises, to designate this the *common* gender, there being no reason to consider the masculine gender more "*worthy*" than the feminine.   Besides, gender is not a *distinction of objects
as to sex,* but a *distinction of words with respect to the sex which they denote;*
and therefore such words as belong, *in common,* to both sexes, are manifestly of the
common gender.

third person; it is of the plural number, masculine gender, and in the possessive case, because it denotes the possession of parents. Its declension is, Nom. *they*, Poss. *their*, or *theirs*, Obj. *them*.

(Parse the other words as in the preceding praxes.)

He who conquers his passions, overcomes his greatest enemies. Every teacher must love a pupil who evinces a love of study. Savages who have no settled abode, wander from place to place. Avoid rudeness of manners, which always hurts the feelings of others. A good reader will often make a pause, where no grammarian would place a point. He who, in nature, recognizes the Creator's hand, will ever survey its varied scenes with reverence. The poems of Homer celebrate the exploits of Achilles, who slew the Trojan prince, Hector. Prosperity gains many friends, but adversity tries them. I disregard their imputations, because I do not merit them. When he had sold his patrimony, he engaged in traffic.

CHAPTER VI.—OF VERBS.

A Verb is a word that signifies *to be, to act,* or *to be acted upon:* as, I *am,* I *rule,* I *am ruled;* I *love,* thou *lovest,* he *loves.*

CLASSES.

Verbs are divided, with respect to their *form,* into four classes; *regular, irregular, redundant,* and *defective.*

I. A *regular verb* is a verb that forms the preterit and the perfect participle by assuming *d* or *ed;* as, *love, lov*ED, *loving, lov*ED.

II. An *irregular verb* is a verb that does not form the preterit and the perfect participle by assuming *d* or *ed;* as, *see, saw, seeing, seen.*

III. A *redundant verb* is a verb that forms the preterit or the perfect participle in two or more ways, and so as to be both regular and irregular; as, *thrive, thrived* or *throve, thriving, thrived* or *thriven.*

IV. A *defective verb* is a verb that forms no participles, and is used in but few of the moods and tenses; as, *beware, ought, quoth.*

Obs.—Regular verbs form their preterit and perfect participle, by adding *d* to final *e*, and *ed* to all other terminations. The verb *hear, heard, hearing, heard,* adds *d* to *r*, and is therefore irregular.

Verbs are divided again, with respect to their *signification*, into four classes; *active-transitive, active-intransitive, passive,* and *neuter.*

I. An *active-transitive verb* is a verb that expresses an action which has some person or thing for its object; as, "Cain *slew Abel.*"

II. An *active-intransitive verb* is a verb that expresses an action which has no person or thing for its object; as, "John *walks.*"

III. A *passive verb* is a verb that represents its subject, or nominative, as being acted upon; as, "I *am compelled.*"

IV. A *neuter verb* is a verb that expresses neither action nor passion, but simply being, or a state of being; as, "Thou *art.*"—"He *sleeps.*"

Obs. 1.—In most grammars and dictionaries, verbs are divided into three classes only; *active, passive,* and *neuter.* In such a division, the class of *active* verbs includes those only which are *active-transitive,* and all the *active-intransitive* verbs are called *neuter.* But, in the division adopted above, *active-intransitive* verbs are made a distinct class; and those only are regarded as neuter, which imply a state of existence without action. When, therefore, we speak of verbs without reference to their regimen, we apply the simple term *active* to all those which express *action,* whether *transitive* or *intransitive.* "We *act* whenever we *do* any thing; but we *may act* without *doing* any thing."—*Crabb's Synonymes.*

Obs. 2.—Active-transitive verbs generally take the agent before them and the object after them; as, "Cæsar *conquered* Pompey." Passive verbs (which are derived from *active-transitive* verbs) reverse this order, and denote that the subject, or nominative, is affected by the action; and the agent follows, being introduced by the preposition *by:* as, "Pompey *was conquered* by Cæsar."

Obs. 3.—Most active verbs may be used either transitively or intransitively. Active verbs are transitive when there is any person or thing expressed or clearly implied, upon which the action terminates; when they do not govern such an object, they are intransitive.

Obs. 4.—Some verbs may be used either in an active or a neuter sense. In the sentence, "Here I rest," *rest* is a neuter verb; but in the sentence, "Here I rest my hopes," *rest* is an active-transitive verb, and governs *hopes.*

Obs. 5.—An active-intransitive verb, followed by a preposition and its object, will sometimes admit of being put into the passive form, the object of the preposition being assumed for the nominative, and the preposition being retained with the verb, as an adverb: as, (*Active,*) "They laughed at him."—(*Passive,*) "He was laughed at."

MODIFICATIONS.

Verbs have modifications of four kinds; namely, *Moods, Tenses, Persons,* and *Numbers.*

MOODS.

Moods are different forms of the verb, each of which

expresses the being, action, or passion, in some particular manner.

There are five moods; the *Infinitive*, the *Indicative*, the *Potential*, the *Subjunctive*, and the *Imperative*.

The *Infinitive mood* is that form of the verb, which expresses the being, action, or passion, in an unlimited manner, and without person or number: as, *To read, to speak.*

The *Indicative mood* is that form of the verb, which simply indicates, or declares a thing: as, I *write;* you *know:* or asks a question; as, *Do* you *know?*

The *Potential mood* is that form of the verb, which expresses the power, liberty, possibility, or necessity, of the being, action, or passion: as, I *can read;* we *must go.*

The *Subjunctive mood* is that form of the verb, which represents the being, action, or passion, as conditional, doubtful, and contingent: as, "If thou *go,* see that thou *offend* not."

The *Imperative mood* is that form of the verb, which is used in commanding, exhorting, entreating, or permitting: as, "*Depart* thou."—"*Be comforted.*"—"*Forgive* me."—"*Go* in peace."

Obs. 1.—The *infinitive* mood is distinguished by the preposition *to*, which, with a few exceptions, immediately precedes it. In dictionaries, *to* is generally prefixed to verbs, to distinguish them from other parts of speech. A verb in any other mood than the *infinitive*, is called, by way of distinction, a *finite* verb.

Obs. 2.—The *potential* mood is known by the signs *may, can, must, might, could, would*, and *should*. This mood as well as the indicative may be used in asking a question; as, *Must* we *go?*

Obs. 3.—The *subjunctive* mood is always connected with an other verb. Its dependence is usually denoted by a conjunction; as, *if, that, though, lest, unless.*

Obs. 4.—The *indicative* and *potential* moods, in all their tenses, may be used in the same dependent manner; but this seems not to be a sufficient reason for considering them as parts of the subjunctive mood.*

* In regard to the number and form of the tenses which should constitute the subjunctive mood in English, grammarians are greatly at variance; and some, supposing its distinctive parts to be but elliptical forms of the indicative or the potential, even deny the existence of such a mood altogether. On this point, the instructions published by Lindley Murray are exceedingly vague and inconsistent. The early editions of his Grammar gave to this mood *six tenses*, none of which had any of the personal inflections; consequently there was, in all the tenses, *some difference* between it and the indicative. His later editions make the subjunctive exactly like the indicative, except in the present tense, and in the choice of auxiliaries for the second-future. Both ways he goes too far. And while at last he restricts the *distinctive form* of the subjunctive to narrower bounds than he ought, and argues against, If thou *loved*, If thou *knew*, &c., he gives this mood not only the last five tenses of the indicative, but also all those of the potential; alleging, " that as the indicative mood is converted into the subjunctive, by the expression of a condition, motive, wish, supposition, &c. being superadded to it, so the potential mood may, in like manner, be turned into the subjunctive."— *Mur. Gram., Oct.,* p. 82. According to this, the subjunctive mood of every regular

TENSES.

Tenses are those modifications of the verb, which distinguish time.

There are six tenses; the *Present*, the *Imperfect*, the *Perfect*, the *Pluperfect*, the *First-future*, and the *Second-future*.

The *Present tense* is that which expresses what now *exists*, or *is taking* place: as, "I *hear* a noise; somebody *is coming*."

The *Imperfect tense* is that which expresses what *took* place, or *was occurring*, in time fully past: as, "I *saw* him yesterday; he *was walking* out."

The *Perfect tense* is that which expresses what *has taken* place, within some period of time not yet fully past: as, "I *have seen* him to-day."

The *Pluperfect tense* is that which expresses what *had taken* place, at some past time mentioned: as, "I *had seen* him, when I met you."

The *First-future* tense is that which expresses what *will take* place hereafter: as, "I *shall see* him again."

The *Second-future tense* is that which expresses what *will have taken* place, at some future time mentioned: as, "I *shall have seen* him by to-morrow noon."

Obs. 1.—The terms here defined are the names usually given to those parts of the verb to which they are in this work applied; and though some of them are not so strictly appropriate as scientific names ought to be, we think it inexpedient to change them.

Obs. 2.—The tenses do not all express time with equal precision. Those of the indicative mood, are the most definite. The time expressed by the same tenses (or what are called by the same names) in the other moods, is frequently relative, and sometimes indefinite.

Obs. 3.—The present tense, in the indicative mood, expresses general truths, and customary actions; as, "Vice *produces* misery."—"She often

verb embraces, in one voice, as many as one hundred and thirty-eight different expressions; and it may happen that in one single tense a verb shall have no fewer than fifteen different forms in each person and number. Six times fifteen are ninety; and so many are the several phrases which now compose Murray's pluperfect tense of the subjunctive mood of the verb *to strow*—a tense which most grammarians very properly reject as needless! But this is not all. The scheme not only confounds the moods, and overwhelms the learner with its multiplicity, but condemns as bad English what the author himself once adopted as the imperfect subjunctive, "If thou *loved*," &c., wherein he was sustained by Dr. Priestly and others of high authority. Dr. Johnson, indeed, made the preterit subjunctive like the indicative; and this may have induced the author to change his plan, and inflect this part of the verb with *st*. But Dr. Alexander Murray very positively declares this to be wrong: "When such words as *if, though, unless, except, whether*, and the like, are used before verbs, they lose their terminations of *est, eth*, and *s*, in those persons which commonly have them. No speaker of good English, expressing himself conditionally, says, Though thou *fallest*, or Though he *falls*, but, Though thou *fall*, and Though he *fall*; nor Though thou *camest*, but Though, or although, thou *came*."—*Hist. Europ. Lang.*, Vol. i. p. 55.

visits us." We also use it in speaking of persons who are dead, but whose works remain; as, "Seneca *reasons* well."

Obs. 4.—The present tense in the subjunctive mood, and in the other moods when preceded by *as soon as, after, before, till,* or *when,* is generally used with reference to future time; as, "If he *ask* a fish, will he give him a serpent?"—*Matt.,* vi, 10. "When he *arrives,* I will send for you."

Obs. 5.—In animated narrative, the present tense is sometimes substituted (by the figure *enallage*) for the imperfect; as, "As he lay indulging himself in state, he *sees* let down from the ceiling a glittering sword, hung by a single hair."—*Tr. of Cicero.* "Ulysses *wakes,* not knowing where he was."—*Pope.*

Obs. 6.—The present infinitive can scarcely be said to express any particular time. It is usually dependent on an other verb, and, therefore, relative in time. It may be connected with any tense of any mood; as, "I intend *to do* it, I intended *to do* it, I have intended *to do* it;" &c. It is often used to express futurity; as, "The time *to come.*"—"The world *to come.*"—"Rapture yet *to be.*"

Obs. 7.—The imperfect tense of the indicative mood, in its simple form, is called the *preterit;* as, *loved, saw, was.*

Obs. 8.—The perfect tense, like the present, is sometimes used with reference to future time; as, "He will be fatigued before he *has walked* a mile."

Obs. 9.—The pluperfect tense is often used conditionally, without a conjunction; as, "*Had* I *seen* you, I should have stopped."

PERSONS AND NUMBERS.

The person and number of a verb, are those modifications in which it agrees with its subject or nominative.

In each number, there are three persons; and in each person, two numbers: thus,

Singular.		*Plural.*	
1st per.	I love,	1st per.	We love,
2d per.	Thou lovest,	2d per.	You love,
3d per.	He loves;	3d per.	They love.

Obs. 1.—Thus the verb in some of its parts, varies its termination to distinguish, or agree with, the different persons and numbers. The change is, however, principally confined to the second and third persons singular of the present tense of the indicative mood, and to the auxiliaries *hast* and *has* of the perfect. In the ancient biblical style, now used only on solemn occasions, the second person singular is distinguished through all the tenses of the indicative and potential moods. And as the use of the pronoun *thou* is now mostly confined to the solemn style, the terminations of that style are retained in all our examples of the conjugation of verbs. In the plural number, there is no variation of ending, to denote the different persons; and the verb in the three persons plural, is the same as in the first person singular. As the verb is always attended by a noun or a pronoun, expressing the subject of the affirmation, no ambiguity arises from the want of particular terminations in the verb to distinguish the different persons and numbers.

Obs. 2.—Persons in high stations, being usually surrounded by attendants, it became, many centuries ago, a species of court flattery, to address individuals of this class, in the plural number. And the practice extended, in time, to all ranks of society: so that, at present the customary mode of familiar as well as complimentary address, is altogether plural; both the verb and the pronoun being used in that form. This practice, which confounds one of the most important distinctions of the language, affords a striking instance of the power of fashion. The society of *Friends,* or *Quakers,* however, continue to employ the singular number in familiar discourse ; and custom, which has now destroyed the compliment of the plural, has placed the appropriate form, (at least as regards them,) on an equality with the plural in point of respect. The singular is universally employed in reference to the Supreme Being ; and is generally preferred in poetry. It is the language of Scripture, and is consistently retained in all our grammars.

OBS. 3.—As most of the peculiar terminations by which the second person singular of verbs is properly distinguished in the solemn style, are not only difficult of utterance, but are quaint and formal in conversation ; the preterits and auxiliaries are seldom varied in familiar discourse, and the present is generally simplified by contraction. A distinction between the solemn and the familiar style, has long been admitted, in the pronunciation of the termination *ed*, and in the ending of the verb in the third person singular ; and it is evidently according to good taste and the best usage, to admit such a distinction in the second person singular. In the familiar use of the second person singular, the verb is usually varied only in the present tense of the indicative mood, and in the auxiliary *hast* of the perfect. This method of varying the verb renders the second person singular analogous to the third, and accords with the practice of the most intelligent of those who retain the common use of this distinctive and consistent mode of address. It disencumbers their familiar dialect of a multitude of harsh and useless terminations, which serve only, when uttered, to give an uncouth prominence to words not often emphatic ; and, without impairing the strength or perspicuity of the language, increases its harmony, and reduces the form of the verb in the second person singular nearly to the same simplicity as in the other persons and numbers.*

---

* The writings of the *Friends* being mostly of a grave cast, afford but few examples of their customary mode of forming the verb in connection with the pronoun *thou*, in familiar discourse. The following may serve to illustrate it : "To devote all thou *had* to his service;"—"If thou *should* come;"—"What thou *said ;*"—"Thou kindly *contributed ;*"—"The Epistle which thou *sent* me;"—"Thou *would* perhaps *allow ;*"—"If thou *submitted ;*"—"Since thou *left ;*"—"*Should* thou *act ;*"—"Thou *may* be ready;"—"That thou *had met ;*"—"That thou *had intimated ;*"—"Before thou *puts*" [putst] ;—"What thou *meets*" [meetst] ;—"If thou *had made ;*"—"I observed thou *was ;*"—"That thou *might put* thy trust;"—"Thou *had been* at my house."—J. KENDALL. "Thou *may be plundered ;*"—"That thou *may* feel;"—"Though thou *waited* long, and *sought* him;"—"I hope thou *will bear* my style;"—"Thou also *knows*" [knowst];—"Thou *grew* up;"—"I wish thou *would* yet *take* my counsel."—S. CRISP. "Thou *manifested* thy tender regard, *stretched* forth thy delivering hand, and *fed* and *sustained* us."—S. FOTHERGILL. The writer has met with thousands that use the second person singular in conversation, but never with one that employed, on ordinary occasions, all the regular endings of the solemn style. The simplification of the second person singular, which, to a greater or less extent, is everywhere adopted by the *Friends*, and which is here defined and explained, removes from each verb eighteen of these peculiar terminations ; and, (if the number of English verbs be, as stated by several grammarians, 8000,) disburdens their familiar dialect of 144,000 of these awkward and useless appendages. This simplification is supported by usage as extensive as the familiar use of the pronoun *thou ;* and is also in accordance with the canons of criticism. "All words and phrases which are remarkably harsh and unharmonious, and not absolutely necessary, should be rejected."—*Campbell's Philosophy of Rhetoric, B. II, Chap. ii, Sec. 2, Canon Sixth.* With the subject of this note, those who put *you* for *thou*, can have no concern ; and many may think it unworthy of notice, because *Murray* has said nothing about it. We write not for or against any sect, or any man ; but to teach all who desire to know the grammar of our tongue. And who is he that will pretend that the solemn style of the Bible may be used in familiar discourse, without a mouthing affectation ? In preaching, the ancient terminations of *est* for the second person singular and *eth* for the third, as well as *ed* pronounced as a separate syllable for the preterit, are admitted to be in better taste than the smoother forms of the familiar style ; because the latter, though now frequently heard in religious assemblies, are not so well suited to the dignity and gravity of a sermon or a prayer. In grave poetry also, especially when it treats of scriptural subjects, to which *you* put for *thou* is obviously unsuitable, the personal terminations of the verb, which from the earliest times to the present day have usually been contracted and often omitted by the poets, ought perhaps still to be insisted on, agreeably to the notion of our tuneless critics. The critical objection to their ellision, however, can have no very firm foundation while it is admitted by the objectors themselves, that,

Where the verb is varied, the second person singular is regularly formed by adding *st* or *est* to the first person; and the third person singular, in like manner, by adding *s* or *es:* as, I *see*, thou *seest*, he *sees ;* I *give*, thou *givest*, he *gives ;* I *go*, thou *goest*, he *goes ;* I *fly*, thou *fliest*, he *flies ;* I *vex*, thou *vexest*, he *vexes ;* I *lose*, thou *losest*, he *loses*.

OBS. 1.—In the solemn style, (except in Poetry, which usually contracts* these forms,) the second person singular of the present indicative, and that of the irregular preterits,† commonly end in *est*, pronounced as a separate

---

" *Writers generally have recourse to this mode of expression, that they may avoid harsh terminations.*"—*Irving's El. Eng. Composition*, p. 12. But if writers of good authority, such as Pope, Swift, and Pollok, have sometimes had recourse to this method of simplifying the verb even in the solemn style, the elision may, with tenfold stronger reason, be admitted in familiar writing or discourse, on the authority of general custom among those who choose to employ the pronoun *thou* in conversation. Some of the *Friends* (perhaps from an idea that it is less formal) misemploy *thee* for *thou*, and often join it to the third person of the verb in stead of the second. Such expressions as, *thee does, thee is, thee has, thee thinks*, &c., are double solecisms; they set all grammar at defiance. Many persons who are not ignorant of grammar, and who employ the pronoun aright, sometimes improperly sacrifice concord to a slight improvement in sound, and give to the verb the ending of the third person, for that of the second. Three instances of this occur in the examples quoted in the preceding paragraph. See also the following, and many more, in the works of the poet Burns; who says of himself, "Though it cost the schoolmaster some thrashings, I made an excellent English scholar; and, by the time I was ten or eleven years of age, I was a critic in substantives, *verbs*, and particles :"—"But when thou *pours ;*"—"There thou *shines* chief;"—"Thou *clears* the head;"—"Thou *strings* the nerves;"—"Thou *brightens* black despair;"—"Thou *comes ;*"—"Thou *travels* far;"—"Thou *paints ;*" "Unseen thou *lurks ;*"—"O thou pale orb that silent *shines*." This mode of simplifying the verb confounds the persons; and as it has little advantage in sound, over the regular contracted form of the second person, it ought to be avoided. It is too frequently used by the poets.

* The second person singular may be contracted, whenever the verb ends in a sound which will unite with that of *st*. The poets generally employ the contracted forms, but they seem not to have adopted a uniform and consistent method of writing them. Some insert the apostrophe, and, after a single vowel, double the final consonant before *st ;* as, *hold'st, bidd'st, said'st, ledd'st, may'st, might'st*, &c.: others add *st* only, and form permanent contractions; as, *holdst, bidst, saidst, ledst, mayst, mightst*, &c. Some retain the vowel in the termination of certain words, and suppress a preceding one; as, *quick'nest, happ'nest, scatt'rest, slumb'rest, slumb'redst :* others contract the termination of such words, and insert the apostrophe; as, *quicken'st, happen'st, scatter'st, slumber'st, slumber'dst*. The nature of our language, the accent and pronunciation of it, incline us to contract even all our regular verbs; so as to avoid, if possible, an increase of syllables in the inflection of them. Accordingly, several terminations which formerly constituted distinct syllables, have been either wholly dropped, or blended with the final syllables of the verbs to which they are added. Thus the plural termination *en* has become entirely obsolete; *th* or *eth* is no longer in common use; *ed* is contracted in pronunciation; the ancient *ys* or *is*, of the third person singular, is changed to *s* or *es*, and is usually added without increase of syllables; and *st* or *est* has, in part, adopted the analogy. So that the proper mode of forming these contractions of the second person singular, seems to be, to add *st* only, and to insert the apostrophe, when a vowel is suppressed from the verb to which this termination is added; as, *thinkst, sayst, bidst, lov'st, lov'dst, slumberst, slumber'dst*.

† Some grammarians say, that, whenever the preterit is like the present, it should take *edst* for the second person singular. This rule gives us such words as *cast-edst, cost-edst, bid-dedst, burst-edst, cut-tedst, hit-tedst, let-tedst, put-tedst, hurt-edst, rid-dedst, shed-dedst*, &c. The few examples which may be adduced from ancient writings, in suppor of this rule, are undoubtedly formed in the usual manner from regular preterits now obsolete; and if this were not the case, no person of taste could think of employing derivatives so uncouth. Dr. Johnson has justly remarked, that "the chief defect of our language is ruggedness and asperity." And this defect is peculiarly obvious, when even the regular termination of the second person singular is added to our preterits. Accordingly we find numerous instances among the poets, both ancient and modern, in which that termination is omitted.—[See *Percy's Reliques of Ancient Poetry everywhere.*

syllable. But as the termination *ed*, in solemn discourse, constitutes a syllable, the regular preterits form the second person singular, by adding *st*, without further increase of syllables; as, *loved, lovedst*—not *lovedest*. *Dost* and *hast*, and the irregular preterits *wast, didst*, and *hadst*, are permanently contracted. The auxiliaries *shall* and *will*, change the final *l* to *t*. To the auxiliaries *may, can, might, could, would*, and *should*, the termination *est* was formerly added; but they are now generally written with *st* only, and pronounced as monosyllables, even in solemn discourse.

Obs. 2.—The third person singular was anciently formed by adding *th* to verbs ending in *e*, and *eth* to all others. This method of forming the third person singular, almost always adds a syllable to the verb. It is now confined to the solemn style, and is little used. *Doth, hath*, and *saith*, are contractions of verbs thus formed.

Obs. 3.—When the second person singular is employed in familiar discourse, it is usually formed in a manner strictly analogous to that which is now adopted in the third person singular. When the verb ends in a sound which will unite with that of *st* or *s*, the second person singular is formed by adding *st* only, and the third, by adding *s* only; and the number of syllables is not increased: as, I *read*, thou *readst*, he *reads*; I *know*, thou *knowst*, he *knows*; I *take*, thou *takest*, he *takes*. For when the verb ends in mute *e*, no termination renders this *e* vocal in the familiar style, if a synæresis can take place.

Obs. 4.—But when the verb ends in a sound which will not unite with that of *st* or *s*, *st* and *s* are added to final *e*, and *est* and *es* to other terminations; and the verb acquires an additional syllable: as, I *trace*, thou *tracest*, he *traces*; I *pass*, thou *passest*, he *passes*; I *fix*, thou *fixest*, he *fixes*. But verbs ending in *o* or *y* preceded by a consonant, do not exactly follow this rule: in these, *y* is changed into *i*; and to both *o* and *i*, *est* and *es* are added without increase of syllables: as, I *go*, thou *goest*, he *goes*; I *undo*, thou *undoest*,* he *undoes*; I *fly*, thou *fliest*, he *flies*; I *pity*, thou *pitiest*, he *pities*.

Obs. 5.—The formation of the third person singular of verbs, is precisely the same as that of the plural number of nouns.

Obs. 6.—The auxiliaries *do, dost, does*, [pronounced *doo, dust, duz*,]—*am, art, is,—have, hast, has*,—being also in frequent use as principal verbs of the present tense, retain their peculiar form when joined to other verbs. The other auxiliaries are not varied, except in the solemn style.

Obs. 7.—The only regular terminations that are added to verbs, are *ing, d* or *ed, st* or *est, s* or *es, th* or *eth*. *Ing*, and *th* or *eth*, always add a syllable to the verb; except in *doth, hath, saith*. The rest, whenever their sound will unite with that of the final syllable of the verb, are added without increasing the number of syllables; otherwise, they are separately pronounced. In solemn discourse, however, *ed* and *est* are, by most speakers, uttered distinctly in all cases; except sometimes, when a vowel precedes.

CONJUGATION OF VERBS.

The conjugation of a verb is a regular arrangement of its moods, tenses, persons, numbers, and participles.

Obs.—The moods and tenses are formed partly by inflections, or changes made in the verb itself, and partly by the combination of the verb or its participle, with a few short verbs called *auxiliaries*, or *helping verbs*.

There are four PRINCIPAL PARTS in the conjugation of every simple and complete verb; namely, the *Present*, the *Preterit*, the *Imperfect Participle*, and the *Perfect Par-*

---

* The second person singular of the simple verb *do*, is now usually written *dost*, and read *dust*; being contracted in orthography, as well as pronunciation. And perhaps the compounds may follow; as, Thou *undost, outdost, misdost, overdost*, &c. But exceptions to exceptions are puzzling, even when they conform to the general rule.

ticiple. A verb which wants any of these parts is called *defective:* such are most of the auxiliaries.

Obs.—The present is radically the same in all the moods, and is the part from which all the rest are formed. The present infinitive is the *root*, or *simplest form*, of the verb. The preterit and the perfect participle are regularly formed by adding *d* or *ed*, and the imperfect participle by adding *ing*, to the present.

An *auxiliary* is a short verb prefixed to one of the principal parts of an other verb, to express some particular mode and time of the being, action, or passion. The auxiliaries are *do, be, have, shall, will, may, can*, and *must*, with their variations.

Obs. 1.—*Do, be*, and *have*, being also principal verbs, are complete: but the participles of *do* and *have*, are not used as auxiliaries; unless *having*, which forms the compound participle, may be considered as such. The other auxiliaries have no participles.

Obs. 2.—English verbs are principally conjugated by means of *auxiliaries;* the only tenses which can be formed by the simple verb, being the present and the imperfect; as, I *love*, I *loved*. And even here an auxiliary is usually preferred in questions and negations; as, *Do* you *love?* You *do* not *love.* All the other tenses, even in their simplest form, are compounds.

Obs. 3.—The form of conjugating the active verb is often called the *Active Voice;* and that of the passive verb, the *Passive Voice.* These terms are borrowed from the *Latin* and *Greek* grammars, and are of little or no use in *English.*

Obs. 4.—English verbs having few inflections, it is convenient to insert in the conjugations the preposition *to*, to mark the infinitive; *pronouns*, to distinguish the persons and numbers; the conjunction *if*, to denote the subjunctive; and the adverb *not*, to show the form of negation. With these additions, a verb may be conjugated in *four* ways:

1. *Affirmatively;* as, I *write*, I *do write*, or I *am writing.*
2. *Negatively;* as, I *write* not, I *do* not *write*, or, I *am* not *writing.*
3. *Interrogatively;* as, *Write* I? *Do* I *write?* or, *Am* I *writing?*
4. *Interrogatively and negatively;* as, *Write* I not? *Do* I not *write?* or, *Am* I not *writing?*

I. SIMPLE FORM, ACTIVE OR NEUTER.

The simplest form of an English conjugation, is that which makes the present and imperfect tenses without auxiliaries; but, even in these, auxiliaries are required for the potential mood, and are often preferred for the indicative.

FIRST EXAMPLE.

The regular active verb LOVE, conjugated affirmatively.

Principal Parts.

Present.	Preterit.	Imper. Participle.	Perfect Participle.
Love.	Loved.	Loving.	Loved.

INFINITIVE MOOD.

The infinitive mood is that form of the verb, which expresses the being, action, or passion, in an unlimited manner, and without person or number. It is used only in the present and perfect tenses.

Present Tense.

This tense is the *root*, or *radical verb;* and is usually preceded by the preposition *to,* which shows its relation to some other word: thus,—

To love.

Perfect Tense.

This tense prefixes the auxiliary *have* to the perfect participle, and is usually preceded by the preposition *to:* thus,—

To have loved.

INDICATIVE MOOD.

The indicative mood is that form of the verb, which simply indicates or declares a thing, or asks a question. It is used in all the tenses.

Present Tense.

The present indicative, in its simple form, is essentially the same as the present infinitive, or radical verb; except that the verb *be* has *am* in the indicative.

1. The simple form of the present tense is varied thus:—

Singular.	*Plural.*
1st per. I love,	1st per. We love,
2d per. Thou lovest,	2d per. You love,
3d per. He loves;	3d per. They love.

2. This tense may also be formed by prefixing the auxiliary *do* to the verb; thus,—

Singular.	*Plural.*
1. I do love,	1. We do love,
2. Thou dost love,	2. You do love,
3. He does love;	3. They do love.

Imperfect Tense.

This tense, in its simple form, is the *preterit;* which, in all regular verbs, adds *d* or *ed* to the present, but in others is formed variously.

1. The simple form of the imperfect tense is varied thus:—

Singular.	*Plural.*
1. I loved,	1. We loved,
2. Thou lovedst,	2. You loved,
3. He loved;	3. They loved.

2. This tense may also be formed by prefixing the auxiliary *did* to the present: thus,—

Singular.	*Plural.*
1. I did love,	1. We did love,
2. Thou didst love,	2. You did love,
3. He did love;	3. They did love.

Obs.—In a familiar question or negation, the auxiliary form is preferable to the simple. But in the solemn or the poetic style, the simple form is more dignified and graceful: as, "*Understandest* thou what thou readest?" —"Of whom *speaketh* the prophet this?"—*Acts*, viii, 30, 34. "Say, *heard* ye nought of lowland war?"—*Scott: L. of L.*, C. v, ¶ 5.

Perfect Tense.

This tense prefixes the auxiliary *have* to the perfect participle: thus,—

Singular.	*Plural.*
1. I have loved,	1. We have loved,
2. Thou hast loved,	2. You have loved,
3. He has loved;	3. They have loved.

Pluperfect Tense.

This tense prefixes the auxiliary *had* to the perfect participle: thus,—

Singular.	*Plural.*
1. I had loved,	1. We had loved,
2. Thou hadst loved,	2. You had loved,
3. He had loved;	3. They had loved.

First-future Tense.

This tense prefixes the auxiliary *shall* or *will* to the present: thus,—

1. Simply to express a future action or event :—

Singular.	*Plural.*
1. I shall love,	1. We shall love,
2. Thou wilt love,	2. You will love,
3. He will love;	3. They will love.

2. To express a promise, volition, command, or threat :—

Singular.	*Plural.*
1. I will love,	1. We will love,
2. Thou shalt love,	2. You shall love,
3. He shall love;	3. They shall love.

Obs.—In interrogative sentences, the meaning of these auxiliaries is reversed. When preceded by a conjunction implying condition or uncertainty, their import is somewhat varied.

Second-future Tense.

This tense prefixes the auxiliaries *shall have* or *will have* to the perfect participle: thus,—

Singular.	*Plural.*
1. I shall have loved,	1. We shall have loved,
2. Thou wilt have loved,	2. You will have loved,
3. He will have loved;	3. They will have loved.

Obs.—The auxiliary *shall* may also be used in the second and third persons of this tense, when preceded by a conjunction expressing condition or contingency; as, "If he *shall have finished* his work when I return." And perhaps *will* may here be used in the first person to express a promise or a determination, though such usage, I think, very seldom occurs.

7*

POTENTIAL MOOD.

The potential mood is that form of the verb, which expresses the power, liberty, possibility, or necessity, of the being, action, or passion. It is used in the first four tenses; but the potential *imperfect* is properly an *aorist*, and not necessarily a *past* tense. No definite time is usually implied in it.

Present Tense.

This tense prefixes the auxiliary *may*, *can*, or *must*, to the radical verb: thus,—

Singular.	Plural.
1. I may love,	1. We may love,
2. Thou mayst love,	2. You may love,
3. He may love;	3. They may love.

Imperfect Tense.

This tense prefixes the auxiliary *might, could, would,* or *should,* to the radical verb: thus,—

Singular.	Plural.
1. I might love,	1. We might love,
2. Thou mightst love,	2. You might love,
3. He might love;	3. They might love.

Perfect Tense.

This tense prefixes the auxiliaries, *may have, can have,* or *must have,* to the perfect participle: thus,—

Singular.	Plural.
1. I may have loved,	1. We may have loved,
2. Thou mayst have loved,	2. You may have loved,
3. He may have loved;	3. They may have loved.

Pluperfect Tense.

This tense prefixes the auxiliaries, *might have, could have, would have,* or *should have,* to the perfect participle: thus,—

Singular.	Plural.
1. I might have loved,	1. We might have loved,
2. Thou mightst have loved,	2. You might have loved,
3. He might have loved;	3. They might have loved.

SUBJUNCTIVE MOOD.

The subjunctive mood is that form of the verb, which represents the being, action, or passion, as conditional, doubtful, or contingent. This mood is generally preceded by a conjunction; as, *if, that, though, lest, unless,* &c. It does not vary its termination, in the different persons. It is used in the present, and sometimes in the imperfect tense; rarely in any other. As this mood can be used only in a dependent clause, the time implied in its tenses is always relative, and generally indefinite.

Present Tense.

This tense is generally used to express some condition on which a future action or event is affirmed. It is therefore considered by some grammarians, as an elliptical form of the future.

	Singular.		*Plural.*
1.	If I love,	1.	If we love,
2.	If thou love,	2.	If you love,
3.	If he love;	3.	If they love.

Obs.—In this tense the auxiliary *do* is sometimes employed; as, "If thou *do prosper* my way."—*Gen.*, xxiv, 42. "If he *do not utter* it."—*Lev.*, v, 1. This uninflected *do* proves the tense to be *present* and the mood *subjunctive;* for the word will come under no other mood or tense.

Imperfect Tense.

This tense, as well as the imperfect of the potential mood, with which it is frequently connected, is properly an aorist, or indefinite tense; and it may refer to time past, present, or future: as, "If therefore perfection *were* by the Levitical priesthood, what further need *was* there," &c.—*Heb.*, vii, 11. "If the whole body *were* an eye, where *were* the hearing ?"—1 *Cor.*, xii, 17. "If it *were* possible, they *shall deceive* the very elect."—*Matt.*, xxiv, 24.

	Singular.		*Plural.*
1.	If I loved,	1.	If we loved,
2.	If thou loved,	2.	If you loved,
3.	If he loved;	3.	If they loved.

IMPERATIVE MOOD.

The imperative mood is that form of the verb, which is used in commanding, exhorting, entreating, or permitting. It is commonly used only in the second person of the present tense.

Present Tense.

Singular. 2. Love [thou,]   *or* Do thou love ;
Plural.   2. Love [ye *or* you,]   *or* Do you love.

Obs.—In the *Greek* language, which has three numbers, the imperative mood is used in the *second* and *third persons* of them all; and has also several different tenses, some of which cannot be clearly rendered in *English.* In *Latin*, this mood has a distinct form for the *third person* both singular and plural. In *Italian, Spanish,* and *French,* the *first person plural* is also given it. *Imitations* of some of these forms are occasionally employed in *English,* particularly by the poets. Such imitations must be referred to this mood, unless by ellipsis and transposition we make them out to be something else. The following are examples: "*Blessed be he* that blesseth thee."—*Gen.*, xxvii, 29. "Thy *kingdom come.*"—*Matt.*, vi, 10.
"*Fall he* that must, beneath his rival's arms,
    And *live the rest*, secure of future harms."—*Pope.*
"My soul, turn from them—*turn we* to survey," &c.—*Goldsmith.*

PARTICIPLES.

1. *The Imperfect.*	2. *The Perfect.*	3. *The Preperfect.*
Loving.	Loved.	Having loved.

SYNOPSIS OF THE FIRST EXAMPLE.

First Person Singular.

Ind. I love, I loved, I have loved, I had loved, I shall love, I shall have loved. Pot. I may love, I might love, I may have loved, I might have loved. Subj. If I love, If I loved.

Second Person Singular.

IND. Thou lovest, Thou lovedst, Thou hast loved, Thou hadst loved, Thou wilt love, Thou wilt have loved. POT. Thou mayst love, Thou mightst love, Thou mayst have loved, Thou mightst have loved. SUBJ. If thou love, If thou loved. IMP. Love [thou,] or Do thou love.

Third Person Singular.

IND. He loves, He loved, He has loved, He had loved, He will love, He will have loved. POT. He may love, He might love, He may have loved, He might have loved. SUBJ. If he love, If he loved.

First Person Plural.

IND. We love, We loved, We have loved, We had loved, We shall love, We shall have loved. POT. We may love, We might love, We may have loved, We might have loved. SUBJ. If we love, If we loved.

Second Person Plural.

IND. You love, You loved, You have loved, You had loved, You will love, You will have loved. POT. You may love, You might love, You may have loved, You might have loved. SUBJ. If you love, If you loved. IMP. Love [ye or you,] or Do you love.

Third Person Plural.

IND. They love, They loved, They have loved, They had loved, They will love, They will have loved. POT. They may love, They might love, They may have loved, They might have loved. SUBJ. If they love, If they loved.

OBS.—In the familiar style, the second person singular of this verb, is usually formed thus: IND. Thou lov'st, Thou loved, Thou hast loved, Thou had loved, Thou will love, Thou will have loved. POT. Thou may love, Thou might love, Thou may have loved, Thou might have loved. SUBJ. If thou love, If thou loved. IMP. Love [thou,] or Do thou love.

SECOND EXAMPLE.

The irregular active verb SEE, conjugated affirmatively.

Principal Parts.

Present.	Preterit.	Imp. Participle.	Perf. Participle.
See.	Saw.	Seeing.	Seen.

INFINITIVE MOOD.
Present Tense.
To see.

Perfect Tense.
To have seen.

INDICATIVE MOOD.

Present Tense.

Singular.	*Plural.*
1. I see,	1. We see,
2. Thou seest,	2. You see,
3. He sees;	3. They see.

Imperfect Tense.

Singular.	*Plural.*
1. I saw,	1. We saw,
2. Thou sawest,	2. You saw,
3. He saw;	3. They saw.

Perfect Tense.

Singular.	*Plural.*
1. I have seen,	1. We have seen,
2. Thou hast seen,	2. You have seen,
3. He has seen;	3. They have seen.

Pluperfect Tense.

Singular.	*Plural.*
1. I had seen,	1. We had seen,
2. Thou hadst seen,	2. You had seen,
3. He had seen;	3. They had seen.

First-future Tense.

Singular.	*Plural.*
1. I shall see,	1. We shall see,
2. Thou wilt see,	2. You will see,
3. He will see;	3. They will see.

Second-future Tense.

Singular.	*Plural.*
1. I shall have seen,	1. We shall have seen,
2. Thou wilt have seen,	2. You will have seen,
3. He will have seen;	3. They will have seen.

POTENTIAL MOOD.

Present Tense.

Singular.	*Plural.*
1. I may see,	1. We may see,
2. Thou mayst see,	2. You may see,
He may see;	3. They may see.

4*

Imperfect Tense.

Singular.
1. I   might see,
2. Thou mightst see,
3. He   might see;

Plural.
1. We   might see,
2. You   might see,
3. They might see.

Perfect Tense.

Singular.
1. I   may have seen,
2. Thou mayst have seen,
3. He   may   have seen;

Plural.
1. We   may have seen,
2. You   may have seen,
3. They may have seen.

Pluperfect Tense.

Singular.
1. I   might   have seen,
2. Thou mightst have seen,
3. He   might   have seen;

Plural.
1. We   might have seen,
2. You   might have seen,
3. They might have seen.

SUBJUNCTIVE MOOD.

Present Tense.

Singular.
1. If I   see,
2. If thou see,
3. If he   see;

Pural.
1. If we   see,
2. If you   see,
3. If they see.

Imperfect Tense.

Singular.
1. If I   saw,
2. If thou saw,
3. If he   saw;

Plural.
1. If we   saw,
2. If you   saw,
3. If they saw.

IMPERATIVE MOOD.

Present Tense.

Singular. 2. See [thou,]   *or* Do thou see;
Plural.   2. See [ye *or* you,] *or* Do you see.

PARTICIPLES.

1. *The Imperfect.*   2. *The Perfect.*   3. *The Preperfect.*
Seeing.   Seen.   Having seen.

OBS.—In the familiar style, the second person singular of this verb, is usually formed thus: IND. Thou seest, Thou saw, Thou hast seen, Thou had seen, Thou will see, Thou will have seen. POT. Thou may see, Thou might see, Thou may have seen, Thou might have seen. SUBJ. If thou see, If thou saw. IMP. See [thou,] *or* Do thou see.

THIRD EXAMPLE.

The irregular neuter verb BE, conjugated affirmatively.

Principal Parts.

Present.	Preterit.	Imp. Participle.	Perf. Participle.
Be.	Was.	Being.	Been.

INFINITIVE MOOD.

Present Tense.

To be.

Perfect Tense.

To have been.

INDICATIVE MOOD.

Present Tense.

OBS.—*Be* was formerly used in the indicative present: as, "We *be* twelve brethren."—*Gen.*, xlii, 32. "What *be* these two olive branches?"—*Zech.*, iv, 12. But this construction is now obsolete.

Singular.	Plural.
1. I am,	1. We are,
2. Thou art,	2. You are,
3. He is;	3. They are.

Imperfect Tense.

Singular.	Plural.
1. I was,	1. We were,
2. Thou wast,*	2. You were,
3. He was;	3. They were.

Perfect Tense.

Singular.	Plural.
1. I have been,	1. We have been,
2. Thou hast been,	2. You have been,
3. He has been;	3. They have been.

Pluperfect Tense.

Singular.	Plural.
1. I had been,	1. We had been,
2. Thou hadst been,	2. You had been,
3. He had been;	3. They had been.

---

* *Wert* is sometimes used indicatively for *wast*; as, "Vainly *wert* thou wed."—*Byron.* "Whate'er thou art or *wert.*"—*Id.*

First-future Tense.

Singular.	Plural.
1. I shall be,	1. We shall be,
2. Thou wilt be,	2. You will be,
3. He will be;	3. They will be.

Second-future Tense.

Singular.	Plural.
1. I shall have been,	1. We shall have been,
2. Thou wilt have been,	2. You will have been,
3. He will have been;	3. They will have been.

POTENTIAL MOOD.

Present Tense.

Singular.	Plural.
1. I may be,	1. We may be,
2. Thou mayst be,	2. You may be,
3. He may be;	3. They may be.

Imperfect Tense.

Singular.	Plural.
1. I might be,	1. We might be,
2. Thou mightst be,	2. You might be,
3. He might be;	3. They might be.

Perfect Tense.

Singular.	Plural.
1. I may have been,	1. We may have been,
2. Thou mayst have been,	2. You may have been,
3. He may have been;	3. They may have been.

Pluperfect Tense.

Singular.	Plural.
1. I might have been,	1. We might have been,
2. Thou mightst have been,	2. You might have been,
3. He might have been;	3. They might have been.

SUBJUNCTIVE MOOD.

Present Tense.

Singular.	Plural.
1. If I be,	1. If we be,
2. If thou be,	2. If you be,
3. If he be;	3. If they be.

Imperfect Tense.

Singular.

1. If I were,
2. If thou wert, *or* were,
3. If he were ;

Plural.

1. If we were,
2. If you were,
3. If they were.

IMPERATIVE MOOD.

Present Tense.

Singular. 2. Be [thou,]   *or* Do thou be ;
Plural.   2. Be [ye *or* you,] *or* Do you be.

PARTICIPLES.

1. *The Imperfect.*   2. *The Perfect.*   3. *The Preperfect.*
   Being.   Been.   Having been.

Obs.—In the familiar style, the second person singular of this verb is usually formed thus : IND. Thou art, Thou was, Thou hast been, Thou had been, Thou will be, Thou will have been. POT. Thou may be, Thou might be, Thou may have been, Thou might have been. SUBJ. If thou be, If thou were. IMP. Be [thou,] *or* Do thou be.

II. COMPOUND FORM, ACTIVE OR NEUTER.

Active and neuter verbs may also be conjugated, by adding the Imperfect Participle to the auxiliary verb BE, through all its changes; as, I *am writing*—He *is sitting.* This form of the verb denotes a continuance* of the action or the state of being, and is, on many occasions, preferable to the simple form of the verb.

Obs.—Verbs of this form have sometimes a *passive* signification ; as, "The books *are* now *selling.*"—*Allen's Gram.*, p. 82. " It requires no motion in the organs whilst it *is forming.*"—*Murray's Gram.*, p. 8. " While the work of the temple *was carrying* on."—*Dr. J. Owen.* "The designs of Providence *are carrying* on."—*Bp. Butler.* " We are permitted to know nothing of what *is transacting* in the regions above us."—*Dr. Blair.* Expressions of this kind are condemned by some critics ; but the usage is unquestionably of far better authority, and (according to my apprehension) in far better taste, than the more complex phraseology which some late writers adopt in its stead ; as, "The books *are* now *being sold.*"

FOURTH EXAMPLE.

The irregular active verb READ, conjugated affirmatively in the Compound Form.

Principal Parts of the Simple Verb.

Present.	Preterit.	Imp. Participle.	Perf. Participle.
Read.	Read.	Reading.	Read.

---

* Those verbs which, in their simple form, imply continuance, do not admit the compound form ; thus we say, " I *respect* him ;" but not, " I *am respecting* him."

INFINITIVE MOOD.

Present Tense.

To be reading.

Perfect Tense.

To have been reading.

INDICATIVE MOOD.

Present Tense.

Singular.	Plural.
1. I am reading,	1. We are reading,
2. Thou art reading,	2. You are reading,
3. He is reading;	3. They are reading.

Imperfect Tense.

Singular.	Plural.
1. I was reading,	1. We were reading,
2. Thou wast reading,	2. You were reading,
3. He was reading;	3. They were reading.

Perfect Tense.

Singular.	Plural.
1. I have been reading,	1. We have been reading,
2. Thou hast been reading,	2. You have been reading,
3. He has been reading;	3. They have been reading.

Pluperfect Tense.

Singular.	Plural.
1. I had been reading,	1. We had been reading,
2. Thou hadst been reading,	2. You had been reading,
3. He had been reading;	3. They had been reading.

First-future Tense.

Singular.	Plural.
1. I shall be reading,	1. We shall be reading,
2. Thou wilt be reading,	2. You will be reading,
3. He will be reading;	3. They will be reading.

Second-future Tense.

Singular. 1. I   shall have been reading,
         2. Thou wilt have been reading,
         3. He   will have been reading;

Plural.   1. We   shall have been reading,
         2. You will have been reading,
         3 They will have been reading.

POTENTIAL MOOD.
Present Tense.

Singular.

1. I   may   be reading,
2. Thou mayst be reading,
3. He   may   be reading ;

Plural.

1. We may be reading,
2. You may be reading,
3. They may be reading.

Imperfect Tense.

Singular.

1. I   might be reading,
2. Thou mightst be reading,
3. He   might   be reading ;

Plural.

1. We   might be reading,
2. You might be reading,
3. They might be reading.

Perfect Tense.

Singular. 1. I   may   have been reading,
2. Thou mayst have been reading,
3. He   may   have been reading ;

Plural. 1. We may have been reading,
2. You may have been reading,
3. They may have been reading.

Pluperfect Tense.

Singular. 1. I   might   have been reading,
2. Thou mightst have been reading,
3. He   might   have been reading ;

Plural. 1. We   might have been reading,
2. You might have been reading,
3. They might have been reading.

SUBJUNCTIVE MOOD.
Present Tense.

Singular.

1. If I   be reading,
2. If thou be reading,
3. If he   be reading ;

Plural.

1. If we   be reading,
2. If you be reading,
3. If they be reading.

Imperfect Tense.

Singular.

1. If I   were reading,
2. If thou wert reading,
3. If he   were reading ;

Plural.

1. If we   were reading,
2. If you were reading,
3. If they were reading.

IMPERATIVE MOOD.
Present Tense.

Sing. 2. Be   [thou]   reading, *or* Do thou be reading ;
Plur. 2. Be [ye *or* you] reading, *or* Do you be reading.

PARTICIPLES.

1. *The Imperfect.*	2. *The Perfect.*	3. *The Preperfect.*
Being reading.	————	Having been reading.

Obs.—In the familiar style, the second person singular of this verb, is usually formed thus: Ind. Thou art reading, Thou was reading, Thou hast been reading, Thou had been reading, Thou will be reading, Thou will have been reading. Pot. Thou may be reading, Thou might be reading, Thou may have been reading, Thou might have been reading. Subj. If thou be reading, If thou were reading. Imp. Be [thou] reading, *or* Do thou be reading.

III. FORM OF PASSIVE VERBS.

Passive verbs, in English, are always of a compound form; being made from active-transitive verbs, by adding the Perfect Participle to the auxiliary verb BE, through all its changes: thus, from the active-transitive verb *love*, is formed the passive verb *be loved*.

Obs. 1.—A few active-intransitive verbs, that merely imply motion, or change of condition, may be put into this form, with a *neuter* signification; making not *passive* but *neuter* verbs, which express nothing more than the state which results from the change: as, I *am come;* He *is risen;* They *are fallen.* Our ancient writers, after the manner of the French, very frequently employed this mode of conjugation in a neuter sense; but, with a few exceptions, present usage is clearly in favour of the auxiliary *have* in preference to *be*, whenever the verb formed with the perfect participle is not passive; as, They *have* arrived—not, They *are* arrived.

Obs. 2.—Passive verbs may be distinguished from neuter verbs of the same form, by a reference to the agent or instrument; which frequently is, and always may be, expressed after *passive* verbs; but which never is, and never can be, expressed after *neuter* verbs: as, " The thief has been caught *by the officer.*"—" Pens are made *with a knife.*"

FIFTH EXAMPLE.

The regular passive verb BE LOVED, conjugated affirmatively.

Principal Parts of the Active Verb.

Present.	*Preterit.*	*Imper. Participle.*	*Perfect Participle.*
Love.	Loved.	Loving.	Loved.

INFINITIVE MOOD.

Present Tense.

To be loved.

Perfect Tense.

To have been loved.

INDICATIVE MOOD.

Present Tense.

Singular.	*Plural.*
1. I am loved,	1. We are loved,
2. Thou art loved,	2. You are loved,
3. He is loved;	3. They are loved.

Imperfect Tense.

Singular.	Plural.
1. I was loved,	1. We were loved,
2. Thou wast loved,	2. You were loved,
3. He was loved;	3. They were loved.

Perfect Tense.

Singular	Plural.
1. I have been loved,	1. We have been loved,
2. Thou hast been loved,	2. You have been loved,
3. He has been loved;	3. They have been loved.

Pluperfect Tense.

Singular.	Plural.
1. I had been loved,	1. We had been loved,
2. Thou hadst been loved,	2. You had been loved,
3. He had been loved;	3. They had been loved.

First-future Tense.

Singular.	Plural.
1. I shall be loved,	1. We shall be loved,
2. Thou wilt be loved,	2. You will be loved,
3. He will be loved;	3. They will be loved.

Second-future Tense.

Singular. 1. I shall have been loved,
2. Thou wilt have been loved,
3. He will have been loved;

Plural. 1. We shall have been loved,
2. You will have been loved,
3. They will have been loved.

POTENTIAL MOOD.

Present Tense.

Singular.	Plural.
1. I may be loved,	1. We may be loved,
2. Thou mayst be loved,	2. You may be loved,
3. He may be loved;	3. They may be loved.

Imperfect Tense.

Singular.	Plural.
1. I might be loved,	1. We might be loved,
2. Thou mightst be loved,	2. You might be loved,
3. He might be loved;	3. They might be loved.

8*

Perfect Tense.

Singular. 1. I   may   have been loved,
            2. Thou   mayst have been loved,
            3. He   may   have been loved;
Plural.   1. We   may have been loved,
            2. You   may have been loved,
            3. They   may have been loved.

Pluperfect Tense.

Singular. 1. I   might   have been loved,
            2. Thou   mightst have been loved,
            3. He   might   have been loved;
Plural.   1. We   might have been loved,
            2. You   might have been loved,
            3. They   might have been loved.

SUBJUNCTIVE MOOD.
Present Tense.

Singular.   *Plural.*
1. If I   be loved,   1. If we   be loved,
2. If thou be loved,   2. If you be loved,
3. If he   be loved;   3. If they be loved.

Imperfect Tense.

Singular.   *Plural.*
1. If I   were loved,   1. If we   were loved,
2. If thou wert loved,   2. If you   were loved,
3. If he   were loved;   3. If they were loved.

IMPERATIVE MOOD.
Present Tense.

Singular. 2. Be   [thou]   loved, *or* Do thou be loved;
Plural.   2. Be [ye *or* you] loved, *or* Do you be loved.

PARTICIPLES.

1. *The Imperfect.*   2. *The Perfect.*   3. *The Preperfect.*
Being loved.   Loved.   Having been loved.

Obs.—In the familiar style, the second person singular of this verb, is usually formed thus: Ind. Thou art loved, Thou was loved, Thou hast been loved, Thou had been loved, Thou will be loved, Thou will have been loved. Pot. Thou may be loved, Thou might be loved, Thou may have been loved, Thou might have been loved. Subj. If thou be loved, If thou were loved. Imp. Be [thou] loved, *or* Do thou be loved.

IV. FORM OF NEGATION.

A verb is conjugated *negatively*, by placing the adverb

not after it, or after the first auxiliary ; but the infinitive and participles take the negative first: as,

INF. Not to love, Not to have loved. IND. I love not, *or* I do not love, I loved not, *or* I did not love, I have not loved, I had not loved, I shall not love, I shall not have loved. POT. I may, can,* *or* must not love ; I might, could, would, *or* should not love ; I may, can, *or* must not have loved ; I might, could, would, *or* should not have loved. SUBJ. If I love not. If I loved not. PART. Not loving, Not loved, Not having loved.

V. FORM OF QUESTION.

A verb is conjugated *interrogatively,* in the indicative and potential moods, by placing the nominative after it, or after the first auxiliary : as,

IND. Do I love ? Did I love ? Have I loved ? Had I loved ? Shall I love ? Shall I have loved ? POT. May, can, *or* must I love ? Might, could, would, *or* should I love ? May, can, *or* must I have loved ? Might, could, would, *or* should I have loved ?

VI. FORM OF QUESTION WITH NEGATION.

A verb is conjugated *interrogatively* and *negatively,* in the indicative and potential moods, by placing the nominative and the adverb *not* after the verb, or after the first auxiliary : as,

IND. Do I not love ? Did I not love ? Have I not loved ? Had I not loved ? Shall I not love ? Shall I not have loved ? POT. May, can, *or* must I not love ? Might, could, would, *or* should I not love ? May, can, *or* must I not have loved ? Might, could, would, *or* should I not have loved ?

IRREGULAR VERBS.

An *irregular verb* is a verb that does not form the preterit and perfect participle by assuming *d* or *ed ;* as, *see, saw, seeing, seen.*

OBS. 1.—When the verb ends in a sharp consonant, *t* is sometimes improperly substituted for *ed,* making the preterit and the perfect participle irregular in spelling, when they are not so in sound: as, *distrest* for *distressed, tost* for *tossed. mixt* for *mixed, crackt* for *cracked.*

OBS. 2.—When the verb ends with a smooth consonant, the substitution of *t* for *ed* produces an irregularity in sound, as well as in writing. In some

---

* When power is denied, *can* and *not* are united to prevent ambiguity ; as, "I *cannot* go." But when the power is affirmed, and something else is denied, the words are written separately ; as, "The Christian apologist *can* not merely expose the utter baseness of the infidel assertion, but he has positive ground for erecting an opposite and confronting assertion in its place."—*Dr. Chalmers.*

such irregularities, the poets are indulged for the sake of rhyme; but the best speakers and writers of prose prefer the regular form wherever good use has sanctioned it: thus, *learned* is better than *learnt; burned*, than *burnt; penned*, than *pent; absorbed*, than *absorpt; spelled*, than *spelt; smelled*, than *smelt;* though both forms are allowable.

Obs. 3.—Several of the irregular verbs are variously used by the best authors; and many preterits and participles which were formerly in good use, are now obsolete, or becoming so.

Obs. 4.—The simple irregular verbs are about 110 in number, and are nearly all monosyllables. They are derived from the Saxon, in which language they are also, for the most part, irregular.

Obs. 5.—The following alphabetical list exhibits the simple irregular verbs, as they are now generally used. In this list, and also in that of the redundant verbs, those preterits and participles which are supposed to be preferable, and best supported by authorities, are placed first. Nearly all compounds that follow the form of their simple verbs, or derivatives that follow their primitives, are purposely omitted from both tables. *Welcome* and *behave*, unlike *come* and *have*, are always regular, and therefore belong not to either list. Some words which are obsolete, have also been omitted, that the learner might not mistake them for words in present use. Some of those which are placed last, are now little used.

LIST OF THE IRREGULAR VERBS.

Present.	Preterit.	Imp. Participle.	Perfect Participle.
Arise,	arose,	arising,	arisen.
Be,	was,	being,	been.
Bear,	bore *or* bare,	bearing,	borne *or* born.*
Beat,	beat,	beating,	beaten *or* beat.
Begin,	began *or* begun,	beginning,	begun.
Behold,	beheld,	beholding,	beheld.
Beset,	beset,	besetting,	beset.
Bestead,	bestead,	besteading,	bestead.†
Bid,	bid *or* bade,	bidding,	bidden *or* bid.
Bind,	bound,	binding,	bound.
Bite,	bit,	biting,	bitten *or* bit.
Bleed,	bled,	bleeding,	bled.
Break,	broke,	breaking,	broken.
Breed,	bred,	breeding,	bred.
Bring,	brought,	bringing,	brought.
Buy,	bought,	buying,	bought.
Cast,	cast,	casting,	cast.
Chide,	chid,	chiding,	chidden *or* chid.
Choose,	chose,	choosing,	chosen.
Cleave,‡	cleft *or* clove,	cleaving,	cleft *or* cloven.
Cling,	clung,	clinging,	clung.
Come,	came,	coming,	come.
Cost,	cost,	costing,	cost.
Cut,	cut,	cutting,	cut.

* *Borne* signifies *carried; born* signifies *brought forth.*
† "And they shall pass through it, hardly *bestead*, and hungry."—*Isaiah*, viii. 21.
‡ *Cleave* to split, is irregular as above; *cleave*, to stick, is regular, but *clave* was formerly used in the preterit, for *cleaved.*

Present.	Preterit.	Imp. Participle.	Perfect Participle.
Do,	did,	doing,	done.
Draw,	drew,	drawing,	drawn.
Drive,	drove,	driving,	driven.
Drink,	drank,	drinking,	drunk *or* drank.
Eat,	ate *or* ĕat,	eating,	eaten *or* eat.
Fall,	fell,	falling,	fallen.
Feed,	fed,	feeding,	fed.
Feel,	felt,	feeling,	felt.
Fight,	fought,	fighting,	fought.
Find,	found,	finding,	found.
Flee,	fled,	fleeing,	fled.
Fling,	flung,	flinging,	flung.
Fly,	flew,	flying,	flown.
Forbear,	forbore,	forbearing,	forborne.
Forsake,	forsook,	forsaking,	forsaken.
Get,	got,	getting,	got *or* gotten.
Give,	gave,	giving,	given.
Go,	went,	going,	gone.
Grow,	grew,	growing,	grown.
Have,	had,	having,	had.
Hear,	heard,	hearing,	heard.
Hide,	hid,	hiding,	hidden *or* hid.
Hit,	hit,	hitting,	hit,
Hold,	held,	holding,	held *or* holden.*
Hurt,	hurt,†	hurting,	hurt.
Keep,	kept,‡	keeping,	kept.
Know,	knew,	knowing,	known.
Lead,	led,	leading,	led.
Leave,	left,	leaving,	left.
Lend,	lent,	lending,	lent.
Let,	let,	letting,	let.
Lie, (to rest,)	lay,	lying,	lain.
Lose,	lost,	losing,	lost.
Make,	made,	making,	made.
Meet,	met,	meeting,	met.
Put,	put,	putting,	put.
Read,	rĕad,	reading,	rĕad.
Rend,	rent,	rending,	rent.§

* "*Holden* is not in general use; and is chiefly employed by attorneys."—*Crombie,* p. 196. Wells marks this word as "obsolescent."—*School Gram.,* p. 103. L. Murray rejected it; but Lowth gave it alone, as a participle, and *held* only as a preterit.
† "I have been found guilty of killing cats I never *hurted.*"—*Roderick Random.*
‡ "They *keeped* aloof as they passed her bye."—*J. Hogg, Pilgrims of the Sun,* p. 19.
§ Perhaps there is authority sufficient to place the verb *rend* among those which are redundant. See, in the Grammar of English Grammars, four examples of the regular form, "*rended.*"

Present.	Preterit.	Imp. Participle.	Perfect Participle.
Rid,	rid,	ridding,	rid.
Ride,	rode,	riding,	ridden *or* rode.
Ring,	rung *or* rang,	ringing,	rung.
Rise,	rose,	rising,	risen.
Run,	ran *or* run,	running,	run.
Say,	said,	saying,	said.
See,	saw,	seeing,	seen.
Seek,	sought,	seeking,	sought.
Sell,	sold,	selling,	sold.
Send,	sent,	sending,	sent.
Set,	set,	setting,	set.
Shed,	shed,	shedding,	shed.
Shoe,	shod,	shoeing,	shod.*
Shoot,	shot,	shooting,	shot.
Shut,	shut,	shutting,	shut.
Shred,	shred,	shredding,	shred.
Shrink,	shrunk *or* shrank,	shrinking,	shrunk *or* shrunken.
Sing,	sung *or* sang,	singing,	sung.
Sink,	sunk *or* sank,	sinking,	sunk.
Sit,	sat,	sitting,	sat.
Slay,	slew,	slaying,	slain.
Sling,	slung,	slinging,	slung.
Slink,	slunk *or* slank,	slinking,	slunk.
Smite,	smote,	smiting,	smitten *or* smit.
Speak,	spoke,	speaking,	spoken.
Spend,	spent,	spending,	spent.
Spin,	spun,	spinning,	spun.
Spit,	spit *or* spat,	spitting,	spit *or* spitten.
Spread,	spread,	spreading,	spread.
Spring,	sprung *or* sprang,	springing,	sprung.
Stand,	stood,	standing,	stood.
Steal,	stole,	stealing,	stolen.
Stick,	stuck,	sticking,	stuck.
Sting,	stung,	stinging,	stung.
Stink,	stunk *or* stank	stinking,	stunk.
Stride,	strode *or* strid,	striding,	stridden *or* strid.†
Strike,	struck,	striking,	struck *or* stricken.
Swear,	swore,	swearing,	sworn.

---

* "Shoe, *shoed* or shod, shoeing, *shoed* or shod."—*Old Gram.*, by *W. Ward*, p. 64; and *Fowle's True English Gram.*, p. 46.

† The verb *stride*, and its derivative *bestride*, each of which is used in two irregular forms, show also a tendency to become redundant. "He will find the political hobby which he has *bestrided* no child's nag."—*The Vanguard, a Newspaper.*

"Through the pressed nostril spectacle-*bestrid*."—*Cowper.*
"A lank haired hunter *strided*."—*Whittier's Sabbath Scene.*

Present.	Preterit.	Imp. Participle.	Perfect Participle.
Swim,	swum *or* swam,	swimming,	swum.
Swing,	swung *or* swang,	swinging,	swung.
Take,	took,	taking,	taken.
Teach,	taught,	teaching,	taught.
Tear,	tore,	tearing,	torn.
Tell,	told,	telling,	told.
Think,	thought,	thinking,	thought.
Thrust,	thrust,	thrusting,	thrust.
Tread,	trod,	treading,	trodden *or* trod.
Wear,	wore,	wearing,	worn.
Win,	won,	winning,	won.
Write,	wrote,	writing,	written.*

REDUNDANT VERBS.

A *redundant verb* is a verb that forms the preterit or the perfect participle in two or more ways, and so as to be both regular and irregular; as, *thrive, thrived* or *throve, thriving, thrived* or *thriven.* Of this class of verbs, there are about ninety-five, beside sundry derivatives and compounds.

Obs. 1.—Those irregular verbs which have more than one form for the preterit or for the perfect participle, are in some sense redundant; but, as there is no occasion to make a distinct class of such as have double forms that are never regular, these redundancies are either included in the preceding list of the simple irregular verbs, or omitted as being improper to be now recognized for good English. A few old preterits or participles may perhaps be accounted good English in the solemn style, which are not so in the familiar: as, "And none *spake* a word unto him."—*Job*, ii, 13. "When I *brake* the five loaves."—*Mark*, viii, 19. "Serve me till I have eaten and *drunken*."—*Luke*, xvii, 8. "It was not possible that he should be *holden* of it."—*Acts*, ii, 24. "Thou *castedst* them down into destruction."—*Psalms*, lxxiii, 18. "Behold I was *shapen* in iniquity."—*Ib.*, li, 5. "A meat-offering *baken* in the oven."—*Leviticus*, ii, 4.

"With *casted* slough, and fresh celerity."—*Shakspeare.*
"Thy dreadful vow, *loaden* with death."—*Addison.*

Obs. 2.—The list which is given below, (one that originated with G. B., and was prepared with great care,) exhibits the redundant verbs as they are now generally used, or as they may be used without grammatical impropriety. If the reader would see authorities for the forms admitted, he may find a great number cited in Brown's largest Grammar. No words are inserted in the following table, but such as some modern authors countenance. A word is not necessarily *ungrammatical* by reason of having a rival form that is more common; nor is every thing to be repudiated which some few grammarians condemn.

Obs. 3.—This school grammar, as now revised by the author in 1854, exhibits the several classes of verbs in the same manner as does the Grammar of English Grammars, which was first published in 1851. All former lists of our irregular and redundant verbs are, in many respects, defective and

* "*Writ* and *wrote* were formerly often used as participles, and *writ* also as a preterit, but they are now generally discontinued by good writers."—*Worcester's Dict.*

erroneous; nor is it claimed for those which are here presented, that they are absolutely perfect. I trust, however, they are much nearer to perfection, than are any earlier ones. Among the many individuals who have published schemes of these verbs, none have been more respected and followed than Lowth, Murray, and Crombie; yet are these authors' lists severally faulty in respect to as many as sixty or seventy of the words in question, though the whole number but little exceeds two hundred, and is commonly reckoned less than one hundred and eighty.

OBS. 4.—The grammatical points to be settled or taught by these tables, are very many. They are more numerous than all the preterits and perfect participles which the lists exhibit; because the mere *absence therefrom* of any form of preterit or perfect participle implies its condemnation, and the omission from both, of any entire verb, suggests that it is always regular.

LIST OF THE REDUNDANT VERBS.

Present.	*Preterit.*	*Imper. Participle.*	*Perfect Participle.*
Abide,	abode *or* abided,	abiding,	abode *or* abided.
Awake,	awaked *or* awoke,	awaking,	awaked *or* awoke.
Belay,	belayed *or* belaid,	belaying,	belayed *or* belaid.
Bend,	bent *or* bended,	bending,	bent *or* bended.
Bereave,	bereft *or* bereaved,	bereaving,	bereft *or* bereaved.
Beseech,	besought *or* beseeched,	beseeching,	besought *or* beseeched.
Bet,	betted *or* bet,	betting,	betted *or* bet.
Betide,	betided *or* betid,	betiding,	betided *or* betid.
Bide,	bode *or* bided,	biding,	bode *or* bided.
Blend,	blended *or* blent,	blending,	blended *or* blent.
Bless,	blessed *or* blest,	blessing,	blessed *or* blest.
Blow,	blew *or* blowed,	blowing,	blown *or* blowed.
Build,	built *or* builded,	building,	built *or* builded.
Burn,	burned *or* burnt,	burning,	burned *or* burnt.
Burst,	burst *or* bursted,	bursting,	burst *or* bursted.
Catch,	caught *or* catched,	catching,	caught *or* catched,
Clothe,	clothed *or* clad,	clothing,	clothed *or* clad.
Creep,	crept *or* creeped,	creeping,	crept *or* creeped.
Crow,	crowed *or* crew,	crowing,	crowed.
Curse,	cursed *or* curst,	cursing,	cursed *or* curst.
Dare,	dared *or* durst,	daring,	dared.
Deal,	dealt *or* dealed,	dealing,	dealt *or* dealed.
Dig,	dug *or* digged,	digging,	dug *or* digged.
Dive,	dived *or* dove,	diving,	dived *or* diven.
Dream,	dreamed *or* dreamt,	dreaming,	dreamed *or* dreamt.
Dress,	dressed *or* drest,	dressing,	dressed *or* drest.
Dwell,	dwelt *or* dwelled,	dwelling,	dwelt *or* dwelled.
Freeze,	froze *or* freezed,	freezing,	frozen *or* freezed.
Geld,	gelded *or* gelt,	gelding,	gelded *or* gelt.
Gild,	gilded *or* gilt,	gilding,	gilded *or* gilt.
Gird,	girded *or* girt,	girding,	girded *or* girt.
Grave,	graved,	graving,	graved *or* graven.
Grind,	ground *or* grinded,	grinding,	ground *or* grinded.
Hang,	hung *or* hanged,	hanging,	hung *or* hanged.
Heat,	heated *or* het,	heating,	heated *or* het.
Heave,	heaved *or* hove,	heaving,	heaved *or* hoven.
Hew,	hewed,	hewing,	hewed *or* hewn.
Kneel,	kneeled *or* knelt,	kneeling,	kneeled *or* knelt.
Knit,	knit *or* knitted,	knitting,	knit *or* knitted.
Lade,	laded,	lading,	laded *or* laden.
Lay,	laid *or* layed,	laying,	laid *or* layed.
Lean,	leaned *or* leant,	leaning,	leaned *or* leant.
Leap,	leaped *or* leapt,	leaping,	leaped *or* leapt.
Learn,	learned *or* learnt,	learning,	learned *or* learnt.
Light,	lighted *or* lit,	lighting,	lighted *or* lit.

Present.	Preterit.	Imper. Participle.	Perfect Participle.
Mean,	mĕant *or* meaned,	meaning,	mĕant *or* meaned.
Mow,	mowed,	mowing,	mowed *or* mown.
Mulct,	mulcted *or* mulct,	mulcting,	mulcted *or* mulct.
Pass,	passed *or* past,	passing,	passed *or* past.
Pay,	paid *or* payed,	paying,	paid *or* payed.
Pen, (to coop,)	penned *or* pent,	penning,	penned *or* pent.
Plead,	pleaded *or* pled,	pleading,	pleaded *or* pled.
Prove,	proved,	proving,	proved *or* proven.
Quit,	quitted *or* quit,	quitting,	quitted *or* quit.
Rap,	rapped *or* rapt,	rapping,	rapped *or* rapt.
Reave,	reft *or* reaved,	reaving,	reft *or* reaved.
Rive,	rived,	riving,	riven *or* rived.
Roast,	roasted *or* roast,	roasting,	roasted *or* roast.
Saw,	sawed,	sawing,	sawed *or* sawn.
Seethe,	seethed *or* sod,	seething,	seethed *or* sodden.
Shake,	shook *or* shaked,	shaking,	shaken *or* shaked.
Shape,	shaped,	shaping,	shaped *or* shapen.
Shave,	shaved,	shaving,	shaved *or* shaven.
Shear,	sheared *or* shore,	shearing,	sheared *or* shorn.
Shine,	shined *or* shone,	shining,	shined *or* shone.
Show,	showed,	showing,	showed *or* shown.
Sleep,	slept *or* sleeped,	sleeping,	slept *or* sleeped.
Slide,	slid *or* slided,	sliding,	slidden, slid *or* slided.
Slit,	slitted *or* slit,	slitting,	slitted *or* slit.
Smell,	smelled *or* smelt,	smelling,	smelled *or* smelt.
Sow,	sowed,	sowing,	sowed *or* sown.
Speed,	sped *or* speeded,	speeding,	sped *or* speeded.
Spell,	spelled *or* spelt,	spelling,	spelled *or* spelt.
Spill,	spilled *or* spilt,	spilling,	spilled *or* spilt.
Split,	split *or* splitted,	splitting,	split *or* splitted.
Spoil,	spoiled *or* spoilt,	spoiling,	spoiled *or* spoilt.
Stave,	stove *or* staved,	staving,	stove *or* staved.
Stay,	staid *or* stayed,	staying,	staid *or* stayed.
String,	strung *or* stringed,	stringing,	strung *or* stringed.
Strive,	strived *or* strove,	striving,	strived *or* striven.
Strow,	strowed,	strowing,	strowed *or* strown.
Sweat,	sweated *or* sweat,	sweating,	sweated *or* sweat.
Sweep,	swept *or* sweeped,	sweeping,	swept *or* sweeped.
Swell,	swelled,	swelling,	swelled *or* swollen.
Thrive,	thrived *or* throve,	thriving,	thrived *or* thriven.
Throw,	threw *or* throwed,	throwing,	thrown *or* throwed.
Wake,	waked *or* woke,	waking,	waked *or* woke.
Wax,	waxed,	waxing,	waxed *or* waxen.
Weave,	wove *or* weaved,	weaving,	woven *or* weaved.
Wed,	wedded *or* wed,	wedding,	wedded *or* wed.
Weep,	wept *or* weeped,	weeping,	wept *or* weeped.
Wet,	wet *or* wetted,	wetting,	wet *or* wetted.
Whet,	whetted *or* whet,	whetting,	whetted *or* whet.
Wind,	wound *or* winded,	winding,	wound *or* winded.
Wont,	wont *or* wonted,	wonting,	wont *or* wonted.
Work,	worked *or* wrought,	working,	worked *or* wrought.
Wring,	wringed *or* wrung,	wringing,	wringed *or* wrung.

DEFECTIVE VERBS.

A *defective verb* is a verb that forms no participles, and is used in but few of the moods and tenses; as, *beware,* *ought, quoth.*

OBs.—When any of the principal parts of a verb are wanting, the tenses usually derived from those parts are also, of course, wanting. All the auxiliaries, except *do, be*, and *have*, are defective; but, as auxiliaries, they become parts of other verbs, and do not *need* the parts which are technically said to be "*wanting*." The following brief catalogue contains all our defective verbs, except *methinks*, with its preterit *methought*, which is not only defective, but impersonal, irregular, and deservedly obsolescent.

LIST OF THE DEFECTIVE VERBS.

Present.	Preterit.	Present.	Preterit.
Beware,	——	Shall,	should.
Can,	could.	Will,	would.
May,	might.	Quoth,	quoth.
Must,	must.	Wis,	wist.
Ought,	ought.	Wit,	wot.

OBs. 1.—*Beware* is not used in the indicative present. *Must* is never varied in termination. *Ought* is invariable, except in the solemn style, where we find *oughtest*. *Will* is sometimes used as a principal verb, and as such is regular and complete. *Quoth* is used only in ludicrous language, and is not varied. It seems to be properly the third person singular of the present; for it ends in *th*, and *quod* was formerly used as the preterit: as,

"Yea, so sayst thou, (*quod* Tröylus,) alas!"—*Chaucer.*

OBs. 2.— *Wis*, preterit *wist*, to know, to think, to suppose, to imagine, appears to be now nearly or quite obsolete; but it seems proper to explain it, because it is found in the Bible: as, "I *wist* not, brethren, that he was the high priest."—*Acts*, xxiii, 5. "He himself '*wist* not that his face shone.'" —*Life of Schiller*, p. iv. *Wit*, to know, and *wot*, knew, are also obsolete except in the phrase *to wit ;* which, being taken abstractly, is equivalent to the adverb *namely*, or to the phrase, *that is to say.*

OBs. 3.—Some verbs from the nature of the subject to which they refer, can be used only in the third person singular; as, It *rains ;* it *snows ;* it *freezes ;* it *hails ;* it *lightens ;* it *thunders.* These have been called *impersonal* verbs. The neuter pronoun *it*, which is always used before them, does not seem to represent any noun, but, in connexion with the verb, merely to express a state of things.

CHAPTER VII.—OF PARTICIPLES.

A Participle is a word derived from a verb, participating the properties of a verb, and of an adjective or a noun; and is generally formed by adding *ing, d,* or *ed,* to the verb: thus, from the verb *rule*, are formed three participles, two simple and one compound; as, 1. *ruling,* 2. *ruled,* 3. *having ruled.*

OBs. 1.—Almost all verbs and participles seem to have their very essence in *motion*, or *the privation of motion*—in *acting*, or *ceasing to act.* And to all motion and rest, *time* and *place* are necessary concomitants; nor are the ideas of *degree* and *manner* often irrelevant. Hence the use of *tenses* and of *ad-*

verbs. For whatsoever comes to pass, must come to pass *sometime* and *some-where;* and, in every event, something must be affected *somewhat* and *some-how.* Hence it is evident that those grammarians are right, who say, that "*all participles imply time.*" But it does not follow that the *English* par-ticiples *divide* time, like the tenses of a verb, and *specify* the period of action; on the contrary, it is certain and manifest that they do not. The phrase, "*men labouring,*" conveys no other idea than that of *labourers at work;* it no more suggests the *time,* than the *place, degree,* or *manner* of their work. All these circumstances require other words to express them; as, "Men *now here awkwardly* labouring *much* to little purpose."

OBS. 2.—Participles retain the *essential meaning* of their verbs; and, *like verbs,* are either *active-transitive, active-intransitive, passive,* or *neuter,* in their signification. For this reason, many have classed them with the verbs. But their *formal meaning* is obviously different. They convey no affirma-tion, but usually relate to nouns or pronouns, *like adjectives,* except when they are joined with auxiliaries to form the compound tenses; or when they have in part the nature of substantives, like the Latin gerunds. Hence some have injudiciously ranked them with the adjectives. We have as-signed them a separate place among the parts of speech, because experience has shown that it is expedient to do so.

OBS. 3.—The English participles are all derived from the *roots* of their respective verbs, and do not, like those of some other languages, take their names from the *tenses.* They are reckoned among the principal parts in the conjugation of their verbs, and many of the tenses are formed from them. In the compound forms of conjugation, they are found alike *in all the tenses.* They do not therefore, of themselves, express *any particular time;* but they denote the state of the being, action, or passion, in regard to its progress or completion. [See *remarks on the Participles, in the Port-Royal Latin and Greek Grammars.*]

CLASSES.

English verbs have severally three participles; which have been very variously denominated, perhaps the most accurately thus: the *Imperfect,* the *Perfect,* and the *Pre-perfect.* Or, as their order is undisputed, they may be conveniently called the *First,* the *Second,* and the *Third.*

I. The *Imperfect Participle* is that which ends com-monly in *ing,* and implies a *continuance* of the being, action, or passion; as, *being, loving, seeing, writing—being loved, being seen, being writing.*

II. The *Perfect Participle* is that which ends commonly in *ed* or *en,* and implies a *completion* of the being, action, or passion; as, *been, loved, seen, written.*

III. The *Preperfect Participle* is that which takes the sign *having,* and implies a *previous completion* of the being, action, or passion; as, *having loved, having seen, having written—having been loved, having been writing, having been written.*

The *First* or *Imperfect* Participle, when simple, is al-ways formed by adding *ing* to the radical verb; as *look, looking:* when compound, it is formed by prefixing *being* to some other simple participle ; as, *being reading, being read, being completed.*

The *Second* or *Perfect* Participle is always simple, and is regularly formed by adding *d* or *ed* to the radical verb: those verbs from which it is formed otherwise, are inserted in the list as being irregular or redundant.

The *Third* or *Preperfect* Participle is always compound, and is formed by prefixing *having* to the perfect, when the compound is double, and *having been* to the perfect or the imperfect, when the compound is triple : as, *having spoken, having been spoken, having been speaking.*

OBS. 1.—Some have supposed that both the simple participles denote present *time;* some have supposed that the one denotes present, and the other, past time ; some have supposed that neither has any regard to time ; and some have supposed that both are of all times. In regard to the *manner* of their signification, some have supposed the one to be active and the other to be passive ; some have supposed the participle in *ing* to be active or neuter, and the other active or passive ; and some have supposed that either of them may be active, passive, or neuter. Nor is there any more unanimity among grammarians, in respect to the compounds. Hence several different names have been loosely given to each of the participles ; and sometimes with manifest impropriety ; as when Buchanan, in his conjugations, calls *being* Active—and *been, having been,* and *having had,* Passive. The *First* participle has been called the Present, the Imperfect, the Active, the Present active, the Present passive, the Present neuter ; the *Second* has been called the Perfect, the Past, the Passive, the Perfect active, the Perfect passive, the Perfect neuter ; and the *Third* has been called the Compound, the Compound active, the Compound passive, the Compound perfect, the Pluperfect, the Preterperfect, the Preperfect. But the application of a name is of little consequence, so that the thing itself be rightly understood by the learner. Grammar should be taught in a style at once neat and plain, clear and brief. Upon the choice of his terms the writer has bestowed much reflection ; yet he finds it impossible either to please everybody, or to explain all the reasons for preference.

OBS. 2.—The participle in *ing* represents the action or state as *continuing* and ever *incomplete;* it is therefore rightly termed the IMPERFECT participle : whereas the participle in *ed* always has reference to the action as *done* and *complete;* and is by proper contradistinction called the PERFECT participle. It is hardly necessary to add, that the terms *perfect* and *imperfect,* as thus applied to the *English* participles, have no reference to *time,* or to those *tenses* of the verb which are usually (but not very accurately) named by these epithets. The terms *present* and *past* do denote *time,* and are in a kind of oblique contradistinction ; but how well they apply to the participles may be seen by the following texts : "God *was* in Christ, *reconciling* the world unto himself."— "We pray you in Christ's stead, *be* ye *reconciled* to God."—*St. Paul.*

OBS. 3.—The participle in *ing* has, by many, been called the *Present* participle. But it is as applicable to past or future, as to present time ; otherwise such expressions as, "I had been *writing,*"—"I shall be *writing,*" would be solecisms. It has also been called the active participle. But it is not always active, even when derived from an active verb : for such expressions as, "The goods are *selling,*"—"The ships are now *building,*" are in use, and not without authority. The *distinguishing characteristic* of this participle is, that it denotes an unfinished and progressive state of the being, action, or passion ; it is therefore properly denominated the IMPERFECT participle. If the term were applied with reference to *time,* it would be no more objectionable than the word *present,* and would be equally supported by the usage of the *Greek* linguists. This name is approved by *Murray*,* and adopted by several of the more recent grammarians. See the works of *Dr. Cromtie, J. Grant, T. O. Churchill, R. Hiley, B. H. Smart, M. Harrison, W. G. Lewis, J. M. M'Culloch, E. Hazen, N. Butler, D. B. Tower, W. H. Wells, C. W. and J. C. Sanders.*

OBS. 4.—The participle in *ed*, as is mentioned above, denotes a *completion* of the being, action, or passion, and should therefore be denominated the PERFECT participle. But this completion may be spoken of as present, past, or future, for the participle itself has no *tenses*, and makes no distinction of time, nor should the name be supposed to refer to the perfect tense. The *perfect* participle of transitive verbs, being used in the formation of passive verbs, is sometimes called the *passive* participle. It has a passive signification, except when it is used in forming the compound tenses of the active verb. Hence the difference between the sentences, "I have written a letter," and, "I have a letter written;"—the former being equivalent to *Scripsi literas*, and the latter to *Sunt mihi literæ scriptæ.*

OBS. 5.—The third participle has most generally been called the *Compound* or the *Compound Perfect.* The latter of these terms seems to be rather objectionable on account of its length ; and against the former it may be urged that, in the compound forms of conjugation, the first or imperfect participle is a compound: as, *being writing, being seen.* Dr. Adam calls *having loved* the *perfect* participle *active,* which he says must be rendered in Latin by the *pluperfect* of the subjunctive, "as, he having loved, *quum amavisset ;*" but it is manifest that the perfect participle of the verb *to love*, whether active or passive, is the simple word *loved,* and not this compound. Many writers erroneously represent the participle in *ing* as always active, and the participle in *ed* as always passive; and some, among whom is Buchanan, making no distinction between the simple perfect *loved* and the compound *having loved,* place the latter with the former, and call it passive also. But if this participle is to be named with reference to its meaning, there is perhaps no better term for it than the epithet PREPERFECT,—a word which explains itself, like *prepaid* or *prerequisite.* Of the many other names, the most correct one is *Pluperfect,*—which is a term of very nearly the same meaning. Not because this compound is really of the pluperfect *tense*, but because it always denotes being, action, or passion, that is, or was, or will be, *completed before* the doing or being of something else; and, of course, when the latter thing is represented as past, the participle must correspond to the pluperfect tense of its verb; as, "*Having explained* her views, it was necessary she should expatiate on the vanity and futility of the enjoyments promised by Pleasure." *Jamieson's Rhet.*, p. 181. Here *having explained* is equivalent to *when she had explained.*

OBS. 6.—Participles often become *adjectives,* and are construed before nouns to denote quality. The terms so converted form the class of *participial adjectives.* Words of a participial form may be regarded as adjectives. 1. When they reject the idea of time, and denote something customary or habitual, rather than a transient act or state; as, A *lying* rogue, i. e., one addicted to lying. 2. When they admit adverbs of comparison; as, A *more learned* man. 3. When they are compounded with something that does not belong to the verb; as, un*feeling*, un*felt.* There is no verb *to unfeel ;* therefore, no participle *unfeeling* or *unfelt.* Adjectives are generally placed before their nouns; participles, after them.

OBS. 7.—Participles in *ing* often become *nouns.* When preceded by an article, an adjective, or a noun or pronoun of the possessive case, they are construed as nouns, and ought to have no regimen. A participle immedi-

---

* "The most unexceptionable distinction *which* grammarians make between the participles, is, that the one points to the continuation of the action, passion, or state denoted by the verb: and the other, to the completion of it. Thus, the present participle signifies *imperfect* action, or action begun and not ended: as, 'I am *writing* a letter.' The past participle signifies action *perfected,* or finished: 'I have *written* a letter.'—'The letter is *written.*'"—*Murray's Grammar,* 8vo, p. 65. "The first [participle] expresses a *continuation;* the others, a *completion.*"—*W. Allen's Gram.,* 12mo, *London,* 1813, p. 62.

ately preceded by a preposition, is not converted into a noun, and therefore retains its regimen; as, "I thank you *for helping him*." Participles in this construction correspond with the Latin gerund, and are sometimes called *gerundives*.

Obs. 8.—To distinguish the participle from the participial noun, the learner should observe the following *four* things: 1. *Nouns* take articles and adjectives before them; *participles*, as such, do not. 2. Nouns may govern the possessive case, but not the objective; *participles* may govern the objective case, but not the possessive. 3. *Nouns* may be the subjects or objects of verbs; *participles* cannot. 4. *Participial nouns* express actions as things; *participles* refer actions to their agents or recipients.

Obs. 9.—To distinguish the perfect participle from the preterit of the same form, observe the *sense*, and see which of the auxiliary forms will express it; thus, *loved* for *being loved*, is a participle; but *loved* for *did love*, is a preterit verb.

ANALYSIS.

An adjective, participle, noun, or pronoun, modifying or completing the predicate of a sentence, and relating to the subject, is called an *attribute ;* as, " Gold is *yellow*."—"The sun is *shining*."—"Honesty is the best *policy*."

Obs. 1.—All verbs except *to be* comprehend within themselves both the predicate and the attribute, into which they may generally be resolved. For example, in the sentence "The sun shines," the verb *shines* is equivalent to *is shining*, *is* being the affirmative or predicative word, and *shining*, the attribute.

Obs. 2.—The verb that connects the subject and the attribute, must be active-intransitive, passive, or neuter. It is sometimes called the *copula*, because it couples or unites the subject and the attribute.

Obs. 3.—The verb *to be*, in most cases, only affirms or indicates otherwise, the connection existing between the subject and the attribute. When the latter is a noun, it may express, 1. *Class ;* as, "Cain was a *murderer*." 2. *Identity ;* as, "Cain was *the* murderer of Abel." 3. *Name ;* as, "The child was called *John*." When *mere* existence is predicated, the verb *be* comprehends both the predicate and the attribute.

Obs. 4.—Class, identity, name, or quality may be attributed to the subject in various ways :

    1. By affirming directly a connection between it and the subject, as in the preceding examples.

    2. By affirming it to belong to the subject, in connection with a particular act or state of being; as, "She *looked* a goddess, and she *walked* a queen."—" The sun *stood* still."

    3. By affirming a connection, as the result of a change; as, "He *has become* a scholar."

    4. By affirming a connection, as the result of a process ; as, "He *was elected* President."—" The twig *has grown* a tree."

Obs. 5.—The attribute is often used *indefinitely*, that is, without reference to any particular subject; as, "To be *good* is to be *happy*."—" To be a *poet* requires genius." In analyzing, this may be called the *indefinite attribute*.

Obs. 6.—An attribute is sometimes *indirectly* affirmed of, or otherwise connected with, the *object* of a verb; as, "They elected him *president*."—" Vice has left him *without friends*" (i. e. *friendless*). This is to be considered as a modification of the predicate, and may be properly called the *indirect attribute*.

OBS. 7.—The conjunction *as* is often employed to express the connection of the attribute with the subject or object to which it refers; as, "She was known as *Curiosity*."—"They engaged her as a *governess*."

OBS. 8.—The attribute, when it is a noun or a pronoun, is in the same case as the subject to which it refers; as, "It is *I*, be not afraid."—"*Who* is she?"—"They believed it to be *me*."

In analyzing a sentence, the attribute should be considered one of the *principal parts*.

The principal parts of a sentence are, therefore, the SUBJECT, the PREDICATE, and the OBJECT or ATTRIBUTE, if there be either.

The other parts may be, 1. *Primary* or *secondary adjuncts*, 2. Words used to express *relation* or *connection*, 3. *Independent words*.

OBS.—Of the four principal parts of a sentence enumerated, the only two *essential* parts are the subject and the predicate; the other two being *accidental* or *occasional*, and used only to modify, limit, or complete the predicate. They, however, differ so widely from other adjuncts, and perform so important an office in every sentence in which they occur, that grammatical analysis is facilitated, and the exact nature of the sentence more clearly exhibited, by treating them as distinct, even though subordinate, elements of the sentence.

EXERCISES IN ANALYSIS AND PARSING.

PRAXIS V.—ETYMOLOGICAL.

In the Fifth Praxis, it is required of the pupil—to classify and analyze the sentence according to the preceding praxis; in addition, to point out the attributes and their adjuncts; and to parse the sentence as in the preceding praxes, distinguishing besides, the classes and modifications of the verbs. Thus :—

EXAMPLE ANALYZED AND PARSED.

"Can that be the man who deceived me?"

ANALYSIS.—This is a complex interrogative sentence, consisting of the two simple clauses, *Can that be the man?* and *Who deceived me*, connected by *who*.

The subject of the principal clause is *that;* the predicate is *can be;* and the attribute is *man.*

The subject and the predicate have no adjuncts; the adjuncts of the attribute are *the*, and the dependent clause.

The subject of the dependent clause is *who;* the predicate, *deceived;* and the object, *me.* Neither has any adjuncts.

PARSING.—*Can* is a verb auxiliary to the principal verb *be*, because it is added to the present infinitive to form the particular mood and tense in which the verb is found.

That is a pronominal adjective, representing *man* understood, in the third person, singular number, masculine gender, and is in the nominative case, because it is the subject of the verb *can be*, being used as a noun.

Can be is a verb, from *be, was, being, been ;* it is irregular, because it does not form its preterit and perfect participle by assuming *d* or *ed ;* neuter, because it expresses simply being ; it is found in the potential mood, because it expresses possibility ; in the present tense, because it has reference to what now exists ; it agrees with its subject *that* in the third person and singular number. (See Definition, page 71.)

The is the definite article.

Man is a common noun, of the third person, singular number, masculine gender, and in the nominative case, because it is an attribute relating to the subject *that.*

Who is a relative pronoun, because it represents the antecedent word *man*, and connects the principal and the dependent clause of the sentence. It is of the third person, singular number, masculine gender ; and is in the nominative case, because it is the subject of the verb *deceived.*

Deceived is a verb, from *deceive, deceived, deceiving, deceived ;* it is regular, because it forms its preterit and perfect participle by assuming *d ;* active-transitive, because it expresses action and has *me* for its object ; it is found in the indicative mood, because it simply declares ; in the imperfect tense, because it expresses time fully past ; and it agrees with its subject *who* in the third person and singular number.

Me is a personal pronoun, because it shows by its form that it is of the first person ; it is of the singular number, masculine gender ; and in the objective case, because it is the object of the verb, *deceived ;* it is declined, Nom. I, Poss. my, *or* mine, Obj. me.

LESSON I.

John has been very sick. William's brother, Henry, might have been a prosperous man. He has become a drunkard. Liberty is a great blessing. The leaves of roses are very fragrant. William rapidly became a good scholar. The project surely could not have been deemed a feasible one. The contract was pronounced fraudulent. Cool blows the summer breeze. He was born a lord. The princess was crowned queen. Washington could have been thrice elected president. The memory of mischief is no desirable fame. Art is long and time is fleeting. How wonderful is sleep! The soul of the diligent shall be made fat.

LESSON II.

The seed which was planted has become a large tree.

Whatever we do often, soon becomes easy to us.

They, who never were his favorites, did not expect so many kind attentions.

Columbus must indeed have been an extraordinary man.

The man who feels truly noble, will become so.

Thomas Jefferson, who wrote the Declaration of Independence, was elected the third president.

Who was it that made that great outcry?

Errors that originate in ignorance, are generally excusable.

He that loveth pleasure, will soon become a poor man.

When the atmosphere is clear, the distant hills look blue.

He might have been guilty, but no sufficient proof could be
found.

If you diligently cultivate your mind in youth, you will be
happy when you grow old.

A wicked messenger falleth into mischief; but a faithful
ambassador is health.

The liberal soul shall be made fat; and he that watereth
shall be watered also himself.

The fear of the Lord is the instruction of wisdom; and
before honor is humility.

If we do not carefully exercise our faculties, they will soon
become impaired.

It may have escaped his notice; but such was the fact.

Science may raise thee to eminence; but religion alone can
guide thee to felicity.

Soft is the strain when zephyr gently blows,
And the smooth stream in smoother numbers flows.

The shepherd of the Alps am I,
The castles far beneath me lie;
Here first the ruddy sunlight gleams,
Here linger last the parting beams.
The mountain boy am I.

CHAPTER VIII.—OF ADVERBS.

An Adverb is a word added to a verb, a participle, an
adjective, or an other adverb; and generally expresses
time, place, degree, or manner: as, They are *now here*,
studying *very diligently.*

OBS. 1.—Adverbs briefly express what would otherwise require several
words; as, *Now,* for *at this time—Here,* for *in this place—Very,* for *in a high
degree—Diligently,* for *in an industrious manner.*

OBS. 2.—There are several customary combinations of short words which
are used adverbially, and which some grammarians do not analyze in parsing; as, *Not at all, at length, in vain.* But all words that convey distinct
ideas, should be taken separately.

CLASSES.

Adverbs may be reduced to four general classes:
namely, adverbs of *time,* of *place,* of *degree,* and of
manner.

5*

I. Adverbs of *time* are those which answer to the question, *When? How long? How soon?* or *How often?* including these which ask.

Obs.—Adverbs of time may be subdivided as follows:—

1. Of time present; as, *Now, yet, to-day, presently, instantly, immediately.*
2. Of time past; as, *Already, yesterday, lately, recently, anciently, heretofore, hitherto, since, ago, erewhile.*
3. Of time to come; as, *To-morrow, hereafter, henceforth, by-and-by, soon, erelong.*
4. Of time relative; as, *When, then, before, after, while,* or *whilst, till, until, seasonably, betimes, early, late.*
5. Of time absolute; as, *Always, ever, never, aye, eternally, perpetually, continually.*
6. Of time repeated; as, *Often, oft, again, occasionally, frequently, sometimes, seldom, rarely, now-and-then, daily, weekly, monthly, yearly, once, twice, thrice,* or *three times,* &c.
7. Of the order of time; as, *First, secondly, thirdly, fourthly,* &c.

II. Adverbs of *place* are those which answer to the question, *Where? Whither? Whence?* or *Whereabout?* including these which ask.

Obs.—Adverbs of place may be subdivided as follows:—

1. Of place in which; as, *Where, here, there, yonder, above, below, about, around, somewhere, anywhere, elsewhere, everywhere, nowhere, wherever, within, without, whereabout, hereabout, thereabout.*
2. Of place to which; as, *Whither, hither, thither, in, up, down, back, forth, inwards, upwards, downwards, backwards, forwards.*
3. Of place from which; as, *Whence, hence, thence, away, out.*
4. Of the order of place; as, *First, secondly, thirdly, fourthly,* &c.

III. Adverbs of *degree* are those which answer to the question, *How much? How little?* or, to the idea of *more or less.*

Obs.—Adverbs of degree may be subdivided as follows:—

1. Of excess or abundance; as, *Much, too, very, greatly, far, besides; chiefly, principally, mainly, generally; entirely, full, fully, completely, perfectly, wholly, totally, altogether, all, quite, clear, stark; exceedingly, excessively, extravagantly, intolerably; immeasurably, inconceivably, infinitely.*
2. Of equality or sufficiency; as, *Enough, sufficiently, equally, so, as, even.*
3. Of deficiency or abatement; as, *Little, scarcely, hardly, merely, barely, only, but, partly, partially, nearly, almost.*
4. Of quantity in the abstract; as, *How,* (meaning, *in what degree,*) *however, howsoever, everso, something, nothing, anything,* and other nouns of quantity used adverbially.

IV. Adverbs of *manner* are those which answer to the question, *How?* or, by affirming, denying, or doubting, show *how* a subject is regarded.

Obs.—Adverbs of manner may be subdivided as follows:—

1. Of manner from quality; as, *Well, ill, wisely, foolishly, justly, quickly,* and many others formed by adding *ly* to adjectives of quality.
2. Of affirmation or assent; as, *Yes, yea, ay, verily, truly, indeed, surely, certainly, doubtless, undoubtedly, certes, forsooth, amen.*
3. Of negation; as, *No, nay, not, nowise.*
4. Of doubt; as, *Perhaps, haply, possibly, perchance, peradventure, may-be.*

5. Of mode or way; as, *Thus, so, how, somehow, however, howsoever, like, else, otherwise, across, together, apart, asunder, namely, particularly, necessarily.*
6. Of cause; as, *Why, wherefore, therefore.*

CONJUNCTIVE ADVERBS.

Adverbs sometimes perform the office of conjunctions, and serve to connect sentences, as well as to express some circumstance of time, place, degree, or manner : adverbs that are so used, are called *conjunctive adverbs.*

Obs. 1.—Conjunctive adverbs often relate equally to *two verbs* in different clauses, on which account it is the more necessary to distinguish them from others; as, " They feared *when* they heard that they were Romans."—*Acts,* xvi, 38.

Obs. 2.—The following words are the most frequently used as conjunctive adverbs : *after, again, also, as, before, besides, else, even, hence, however, moreover, nevertheless, otherwise, since, so, then, thence, therefore, till, until, when, where, wherefore, while* or *whilst.*

Obs. 3.—Adverbs of *time, place,* and *manner,* are generally connected with verbs or participles; those of *degree* are more frequently prefixed to adjectives or adverbs.

Obs. 4.—The adverbs *here, there,* and *where,* when prefixed to prepositions, have the force of pronouns: as, *Hereby,* for *by this ; thereby,* for *by that ; whereby,* for *by which.* Compounds of this kind are, however, commonly reckoned *adverbs.* They are now somewhat antiquated.

Obs. 5.—The adverbs *how, when, whence, where, whither, why,* and *wherefore,* are frequently used as *interrogatives ;* but, as such, they severally belong to the classes under which they are placed.

MODIFICATIONS.

Adverbs have no modifications, except that a few are compared after the manner of adjectives : as, *Soon, sooner, soonest ;—often, oftener, oftenest ;—long, longer, longest.*

The following are irregularly compared : *well, better, best ; badly* or *ill, worse, worst ; little, less, least ; much, more, most ; far, farther, farthest ; forth, further, furthest.*

Obs. 1.—Most adverbs of *quality,* will admit the comparative adverbs *more* and *most, less* and *least,* before them : as, *wisely, more wisely, most wisely ; culpably, less culpably least culpably.* But these should be parsed separately : the degree of comparison, as an inflection, belongs only to the adverb prefixed ; though the latter word also may be said to be compared *by means of* the former.

Obs. 2.—As comparison does not belong to adverbs in general, it should not be mentioned in parsing, except in the case of those few which are varied by it.

CHAPTER IX.—OF CONJUNCTIONS.

A Conjunction is a word used to connect words or sentences in construction, and to show the dependence of the terms so connected : as, " Thou *and* he are happy, *because* you are good."—*L. Murray.*

CLASSES.

Conjunctions are divided into two general classes, *copulative* and *disjunctive;* and some of each of these sorts are *corresponsive.*

I. A *copulative conjunction* is a conjunction that denotes an addition, a cause, or a supposition : as, "He *and* I shall not dispute; *for, if* he has any choice, I shall readily grant it."

II. A *disjunctive conjunction* is a conjunction that denotes opposition of meaning : as, "Be not overcome [by] evil, *but* overcome evil with good."—*Rom.,* xii, 21.

III. The *corresponsive conjunctions* are those which are used in pairs, so that one refers or answers to an other : as, "John came *neither* eating *nor* drinking."—*Matthew,* xi, 18.

LIST OF THE CONJUNCTIONS.

The following are the principal conjunctions :—

1. Copulative ; *And, as, both, because, even, for, if, that, then, since, seeing, so.*

2. Disjunctive ; *Or, nor, either, neither, than, though, although, yet, but, except, whether, lest, unless, save, notwithstanding.*

3. Corresponsive ; *Both—and ; as—as ; as—so ; if—then ; either—or ; neither—nor ; whether—or ; though,* or *although —yet.*

CHAPTER X.—OF PREPOSITIONS.

A Preposition is a word used to express some relation of different things or thoughts to each other, and is generally placed before a noun or a pronoun : as, The paper lies *before* me *on* the desk.

Obs.—Every *relation* of course implies more than one subject. In all correct language, the grammatical relation of the *words* corresponds exactly to the relation of the *things* or *ideas* expressed ; for the relation of words, is their dependence on each other *according to the sense.* To a preposition, the *antecedent* term of relation may be a noun, an adjective, a pronoun, a verb, a participle, or an adverb ; and the *subsequent* term may be a noun, a pronoun, an infinitive verb, or a participle. The learner must observe that the terms of relation are frequently transposed.

LIST OF THE PREPOSITIONS.

The following are the principal prepositions, arranged alphabetically : *Aboard, about, above, across, after, against, along, amid* or *amidst, among* or *amongst. around, at, athwart ;—Bating, before, behind, below, beneath, beside* or *besides, between* or *betwixt, beyond, by ;—Concerning ;—Down, during ;—Ere, except, excepting ;—For, from ;—In, into ;—Mid* or *midst ;—Notwithstanding ;—Of, off, on, out-of, over, overthwart ;—Past, pending ;—Regarding, respecting, round ;—Since ;—Through, throughout, till, to, touching, toward* or *towards ;—Under, underneath, until, unto, up, upon ;— With, within, without.*

Obs. 1.—The words in the preceding list are generally prepositions. But when any of them are employed without a subsequent term of relation, they are either adjectives or adverbs. *For,* when it signifies *because,* is a conjunction ; *without,* when used for unless, and *notwithstanding,* when placed before a nominative, are usually referred to the class of conjunctions also.

Obs. 2.—Several words besides those contained in the foregoing list, are (or have been) occasionally employed in English as prepositions: as, *A,* (chiefly used before participles,) *abaft, adown, afore, aloft, aloof, alongside, anear, aneath, anent, aslant, aslope, astride, atween, atwixt, besouth, bywest, cross, dehors, despite, inside, left-hand, maugre, minus, onto, opposite, outside, per, plus, sans, spite, thorough, traverse, versus, via, withal, withinside.*

CHAPTER XI.—OF INTERJECTIONS.

An Interjection is a word that is uttered merely to indicate some strong or sudden emotion of the mind: as, *Oh! alas! ah! poh! pshaw! avaunt!*

Obs.—Of pure interjections but few are ordinarily admitted into books. As words or sounds of this kind serve rather to indicate feeling than to express thought, they seldom have any truly definable signification. Their use also is so variable, that there can be no very accurate classification of them. Some significant words properly belonging to other classes, are ranked with interjections, when uttered with emotion and in an unconnected manner.

LIST OF THE INTERJECTIONS.

The following are the principal interjections, arranged according to the emotions which they are generally intended to indicate :—1. Of joy ; *eigh! hey! io!*—2. Of sorrow ; *oh! ah! hoo! alas! alack! lackaday! welladay!* or *welaway!*—3. Of wonder; *heigh! ha! strange! indeed!*—4. Of wishing, earnestness, or vocative address; (often with a noun or pronoun in the nominative absolute;) *O!*—5. Of praise; *well-done! good! bravo!*—6. Of surprise with disapproval ; *whew! hoity-toity! hoida! zounds! what!*—7. Of pain or fear; *oh! ooh! ah! eh! O dear!*—8. Of contempt; *fudge! pugh! poh!*

10

pshaw! pish! tush! tut! humph!—9. Of aversion; *foh! faugh! fie! fy! foy!*—10. Of expulsion; *out! off! shoo! whew! begone! avaunt! aroynt!*—11. Of calling aloud; *ho! soho! what-ho! hollo! holla! hallo! halloo! hoy! ahoy!*— 12. Of exultation; *ah! aha! huzza! hey! heyday! hurrah!* —13. Of laughter; *ha, ha, ha; he, he, he; te-hee, te-hee.*—14. Of salutation; *welcome! hail! all-hail!*—15. Of calling to attention; *ho! lo! la! law! look! see! behold! hark!*—16. Of calling to silence; *hush! hist! whist! 'st! aw! mum!* —17. Of dread or horror; *oh! ha! hah! what!*—18. Of languor or weariness; *heigh-ho! heigh-ho-hum!*—19. Of stopping; *hold! soft! avast! whoh!*—20. Of parting; *farewell! adieu! good-by! good-day!*—21. Of knowing or detecting; *oho! ahah! ay-ay!*—22. Of interrogating; *eh? ha? hey?*

Obs.—Besides these, there are several others, too often heard, which are unworthy to be considered as parts of a cultivated language. The frequent use of interjections, savours more of thoughtlessness than of sensibility.

ANALYSIS.

When two or more subjects, connected by a conjunction, belong to the same predicate, or two or more connected predicates have the same subject, the sentence should be considered *simple* with a *compound subject* or *predicate*.

A *phrase* is two or more words which express some relation of ideas, but no entire proposition; as, "Of a good disposition."—"To be plain with you."—"Having loved his own."

A phrase may be used in three ways; namely, 1. As one of the principal parts of a sentence; 2. As an adjunct; 3. It may be independent.

An adjunct phrase is *adjective, adverbial,* or *explanatory.*

A *substantive* phrase is one used in the place of a noun; as, "*To do good* is the duty of all."

An *independent* phrase is one, the principal part of which, is not related to, or connected with, any word in the rest of the sentence; as, "*He failing,* who shall meet success?"—"*To be plain with you,* I think you in fault."

The *principal part* of a phrase is that upon which all the others depend; as, "Under every *misfortune.*"— "*Having exhausted* every expedient."

Phrases are either *simple, complex,* or *compound.*

A *simple phrase* is one unconnected with any other; as, " Of an obliging disposition."

A *complex phrase* is one that contains a phrase or a clause, as an adjunct of its principal part; as, " By the bounty of Heaven."—" To be plain with you."

A *compound phrase* is one composed of two or more co-ordinate phrases; as, " Stooping down and looking in."

Phrases are also classified as to their form, depending upon the introducing word, or the principal part; thus,

1. A phrase, introduced by a preposition, is called a *prepositional phrase ;* as, " By doing good."—" Of an engaging disposition."

2. A phrase the principal part of which is a verb in the infinitive mood, is called an infinitive phrase; as, " *To be good* is *to be happy.*"

3. A phrase the principal word of which is a participle, is called a *participial phrase ;* as, " A measure *founded on justice.*"

Obs.—A preposition that introduces a phrase, serves only to express the relation between the principal part, and the word of the sentence, on which the phrase depends.

A phrase, used as the subject or the object of a verb, must be *substantive* in office, and, with a strict adherence to grammatical rules, can only be *infinitive* in form ; as, " *To disobey parents* is sinful."—" William loves *to study grammar.*" Participial phrases are, however, sometimes used by good writers in this way ; as, " *Hunting the buffalo,* is one of the sports of the West."—" John's father opposed *his going to sea.*" [See Obs. 8, page 102 ; and Note III., with Obs. 3, under it, Syntax, Rule XIV.]

A phrase, used as an attribute, may be substantive or adjective in office, and may have the following forms :

1. *Infinitive ;* as, " The object of punishment is *to reform the guilty.*"—" His conduct is *greatly to be admired.*" [In the latter example, the phrase is *adjective, to be admired* being equivalent to *admirable.*]

2. *Prepositional ;* as, " He is *in good health.*"—" The train was *behind time.*" [In each of these examples, the phrase is *adjective.*]

An adjective phrase may have the following forms :

1. *Prepositional ;* as, " Carelessness *in the use of money,* is a vice."

2. *Infinitive ;* as, "The desire *to do good* is praise-worthy."

3. *Participial ;* as, " *Seeing the danger*, he avoided it."

An adverbial phrase may have the following forms :

1. *Prepositional ;* as, " He was attentive *to his business*."

2. *Infinitive ;* as, " They were anxious *to ascertain the truth*."

3. *Idiomatic ;* as, " In vain."—" Day by day."—" By and by."—" As a general thing."

An explanatory phrase is always *substantive* in office, and infinitive in form ; as, " It is pleasant *to see the sun*."

The independent phrase is various in form and character. It may be distinguished as,

1. *Infinitive ;* as, " *To be candid*, I was in fault."

2. *Participial ;* as, " *Considering the circumstances*, much credit is due."

3. *Vocative ;* as, " Boast not, *my dear friend*, of to-morrow."

4. *Pleonastic ;* as, " *The blessing of the Lord*, it maketh rich."

5. *Absolute ;* as, " *The sun having risen*, the mists were dispersed."

OBS. 1.—The last form of this phrase is often adverbial in signification ; as in the example given, in which it is equivalent to the clause, *when the sun had risen.* It is, therefore, independent only in construction.

OBS. 2.—An adverbial phrase may be modified by an adverb; as, "It lasts *but for a moment ;*" i. e. *but* equivalent to *only*, and modifying the adverbial phrase, *for a moment.*

OBS. 3.—A phrase or a clause is sometimes used as the object of a preposition, and thus forms a prepositional phrase of a complex or anomalous character ; as, " Blows mildew *from between-his-shriveled-lips*."—" That depends *on who-can-run-the-fastest.*"

EXERCISES IN ANALYSIS AND PARSING.

PRAXIS VI.—ETYMOLOGICAL.

In the Sixth Praxis, it is required of the pupil—to classify and analyze the sentence as in the preceding praxis ; to classify and analyze each phrase ; and to parse the sentence, distinguishing the parts of speech, and all their classes and modifications. Thus :—

EXAMPLE ANALYZED AND PARSED.

" Ah ! who can tell the triumphs of the mind,
By truth illumined, and by taste refined ?"

ANALYSIS.—This is a simple interrogative sentence.

The subject is *who;* the predicate, *can tell ;* the object, *triumphs.*

The subject and predicate are unmodified ; the adjuncts of the object, are *the* and the complex adjective phrase, *of the mind illumined by truth, and refined by taste.*

The principal part of the phrase is *mind;* its adjuncts are *the* and the compound adjective phrase, *illumined by truth, and refined by taste,* which consists of the two coördinate participial phrases connected by *and.*

The principal part of the former is *illumined,* and its adjunct, the simple adverbial phrase, *by truth ;* the principal part of the latter is *refined,* and its adjunct, the simple adverbial phrase *by taste. Ah* is an independent word.

PARSING.—*Ah !* is an interjection, because it is a simple exclamation of wonder or admiration.

Who is an interrogative pronoun, of the third person, singular number, masculine gender ; and in the nominative case, because it is the subject of the verb *can tell.*

By is a preposition, because it shows the relation between *truth* and *illumined,* the phrase *by truth* being an adjunct of *illumined.*

Truth is a common noun, and abstract, because it is the name of a quality. It is of the third person, singular number, neuter gender ; and in the objective case, because it is the object of the preposition *by.*

Illumined is a perfect participle from the regular passive verb *be illumined.* It performs the office of a verb, by expressing passion ; and of an adjective, by modifying the noun *mind.*

And is a conjunction, because it connects the two phrases, *by truth illumined, by taste refined ;* it is copulative, because it expresses an addition.

☞ [Parse the other words as in the preceding praxes.]

LESSON I.

Frankness, suavity, and benevolence, were prominent traits in the character of Dr. Franklin.

Industry, good sense, and virtue, are essential to health, wealth, and happiness.

Rural employments are certainly natural, amusing, and healthful.

The study of natural history expands and elevates the mind.

Get justly, use soberly, distribute cheerfully, and live contentedly.

Junius Brutus, the son of Marcus Brutus, and Collatinus, the husband of Lucretia, were chosen the first consuls in Rome.

The son, bred in sloth, becomes a spendthrift and a profligate ; and goes out of the world a beggar.

In the varieties of life, we are inured to habits both of the active and the suffering virtues.

By disappointments and trials, the violence of our passions is tamed.

Having sold his patrimony he engaged in merchandise.

The bounty displayed in the earth, equals the grandeur manifested in the heavens.

10*

LESSON II.

He, stooping down and looking in, saw the linen clothes lying ; yet went he not in.

Cheerfulness keeps up a kind of day-light in the mind, and fills it with a steady and perpetual serenity.

Sitting is the best posture for deliberation ; standing for persuasion ; a judge, therefore, should speak sitting; a pleader, standing.

The pleasures of sense resemble a foaming torrent ; which, after a disorderly course, speedily runs out, and leaves an empty and offensive channel.

Most of the troubles which we meet with in the world, arise from an irritable temper, or from improper conduct.

The meeting was so respectable, that the propriety of its decision can hardly be questioned.

They who are moderate in their expectations, meet with few disappointments.

> The mighty tempest and the hoary waste,
> Abrupt and deep, stretch'd o'er the buried earth,
> Awake to solemn thought.

> Loose, then, from earth the grasp of fond desire,
> Weigh anchor, and some happier clime explore.

CHAPTER XII.—EXAMINATION.

QUESTIONS ON ETYMOLOGY.

LESSON I.—PARTS OF SPEECH.

Of what does Etymology treat ?
How many and what are the parts of speech ?
What is an article ?—What are the examples ?
What is a noun ?—What examples are given ?
What is an adjective ?—How is this exemplified ?
What is a pronoun ?—How is this exemplified ?
What is a verb ?—How is this exemplified ?
What is a participle ?—How is this exemplified ?
What is an adverb ?—How is this exemplified ?
What is a conjunction ?—How is this exemplified ?
What is a preposition ?—How is this exemplified ?
What is an interjection ?—What examples are given ?

LESSON II.—PARSING.

What is *Parsing ?*   What is a *sentence ?*
What a perfect *definition ?*—What is a *rule of grammar ?*
What is a *praxis ?* and what the literal meaning of the word ?
What is an *example ?*   What is an *exercise ?*
What is required of the pupil in the FIRST PRAXIS of parsing.

What is required in each of the three Exercises given ?
How is the following example parsed ? " The patient **ox** submits to the yoke, and meekly performs the labour required of him."
[Now parse, in like manner, the other examples under the *First Praxis*.]

LESSON III.—ARTICLES.

What is an ARTICLE ?—Mention the examples?
Are *an* and *a* different articles, or the same ?
When is *an* used ? and what are the examples?
When is *a* used ? and what are the examples?
What form of the article do the sounds of *w* and *y* require?
Repeat the alphabet, with *an* or *a* before the name of each letter.
Name the parts of speech, with *an* or *a* before each name.
How are the two articles distinguished in grammar ?
Which is the *definite* article, and what does it denote ?
Which is the *indefinite* article, and what does it denote ?
What modifications have the articles ?

LESSON IV.—NOUNS.

What is a NOUN ?—Can you give some examples ?
Into what general classes are nouns divided ?
What is a *proper* noun ?—a *common* noun ?
What particular classes are included among common nouns ?
What is a *collective* noun ?—an *abstract* noun ?—a *verbal* or *participial* noun ?
What is a thing *sui generis* ?
What modifications have nouns ?
What are Persons in grammar ?
How many persons are there, and what are they called ?
What is the *first* person ?—the *second* person ?—the *third* person ?
What are Numbers in grammar ?
How many numbers are there, and what are they called ?
What is the *singular* number ?—the *plural* number ?
How is the plural number of nouns regularly formed ?
What are the rules for adding *s* and *es* to form the plural ?

LESSON V.—NOUNS.

What are Genders in grammar ?
How many genders are there, and what are they called ?
What is the *masculine* gender ?—the *feminine* gender ?—the *neuter* gender ?
What are Cases in grammar ?
How many cases are there, and what are they called ?
What is the *nominative* case ?
What is the subject of a verb ?
What is the *possessive* case ?
How is the possessive case of nouns formed ?
What is the *objective* case ?
What is the object of a verb, participle, or preposition ?
What is the declension of a noun ?
How do you decline the nouns *friend, man, fox,* and *fly ?*

LESSON VI.—ANALYSIS AND PARSING.

What is *Analysis ?*—What is the *subject* of a sentence ?
What is a *predicate ?*—What is a *proposition ?*
What is a *simple sentence ?*
How are simple sentences divided ?—Define each.
What is required of the pupil in the *Second Praxis ?*

LESSON VII.—ADJECTIVES.

What is an ADJECTIVE ?—How is this exemplified ?
Into what classes may adjectives be divided ?
What is a *common* adjective ?—a *proper* adjective ?—a *numeral* adjective ?—a *pronominal* adjective ?—a *participial* adjective ?—a *compound* adjective ?

What modifications have adjectives?
What is Comparison in grammar?
How many, and what are the degrees of comparison?
What is the *positive* degree?—the *comparative* degree?—the *superlative* degree?
What adjectives cannot be compared?
What adjectives are compared by means of adverbs?
How are adjectives regularly compared?—Compare *great, wide,* and *hot.*
To what adjectives are *er* and *est* applicable?
Is there any other mode of expressing the degrees?
How are the degrees of diminution expressed?
How do you compare *good, bad,* or *ill, little, much,* and *many?*
How do you compare *far, near, fore, hind, in, out, up, low,* and *late?*

LESSON VIII.—ANALYSIS AND PARSING.

What are *Adjuncts?*—How are they divided?
What are *primary adjuncts?*—What are *secondary adjuncts?*
What is an *adjective adjunct?*—An *adverbial adjunct?*
What is an *explanatory adjunct?*
How may the subject, predicate, and object be modified?
What is required of the pupil in the *Third Praxis?*

LESSON IX.—PRONOUNS.

What is a PRONOUN?—Give the example.
How are pronouns divided?
What is a *personal* pronoun?—Tell the personal pronouns.
What is a *relative* pronoun?—Tell the relative pronouns.
What peculiarity has the relative *what?*
What is an *interrogative* pronoun?—Tell the interrogatives.
What modifications have pronouns?
What is the declension of a pronoun.
How do you decline the pronouns *I, thou, he, she,* and *it?*
What is said of the compound personal pronouns?
How do you decline *who, which, what,* and *that?*
How do you decline the compound relative pronouns?

LESSON X.—ANALYSIS AND PARSING.

What is a *Clause?*—How may clauses be connected?
What is a *dependent clause?*—A *principal clause?*
What is a *complex sentence?*—A *compound sentence?*
What is required of the pupil in the *Fourth Praxis?*

LESSON XI.—VERBS.

What is a VERB?—What are the examples?
How are verbs divided with respect to their form?
What is a *regular* verb?—an *irregular* verb?—a *redundant* verb?—a *defective* verb?
How are verbs divided with respect to their signification?
What is an *active-transitive* verb?—an *active-intransitive* verb?—a *passive* verb?—a *neuter* verb?
What modifications have verbs?
What are Moods in grammar?
How many moods are there, and what are they called?
What is the *infinitive* mood?—the *indicative* mood?—the *potential* mood?—the *subjunctive* mood?—the *imperative* mood?

LESSON XII.—VERBS.

What are Tenses in grammar?
How many tenses are there, and what are they called?
What is the *present* tense?—the *imperfect* tense?—the *perfect* tense?—the *pluperfect* tense?—the *first-future* tense?—the *second-future* tense?

What are the Person and Number of a verb?
How many persons and numbers belong to verbs?
How are the second and third persons singular formed?
What is the conjugation of a verb?
What are the *principal parts* in the conjugation of a verb?
What is a verb called which wants some of these parts?
What is an *auxiliary* in grammar?
What verbs are used as auxiliaries?

LESSON XIII.—CONJUGATION.

What is the simplest form of an English conjugation?
What is the first example of conjugation?
What are the principal parts of the verb LOVE?
How many and what tenses has the *infinitive* mood?—the *indicative?*—the *potential?*—the *subjunctive?*—the *imperative?*
What is the verb LOVE in the *Infinitive*, present?—perfect?—*Indicative*, present?—imperfect?—perfect?—pluperfect?—first-future?—second-future?—*Potential*, present?—imperfect?—perfect?—pluperfect?—*Subjunctive*, present?—imperfect?—*Imperative*, present?   What are its participles?

LESSON XIV.—SYNOPSIS.

What is the synopsis of the verb LOVE, in the first person singular?—second person singular?—third person singular?—first person plural?—second person plural?—third person plural?

LESSON XV.—THE VERB SEE.

What is the second example of conjugation?
How is the verb SEE conjugated throughout?
How do you form a synopsis of the verb *see*, with the pronoun *I? thou? he? we? you? they?*

LESSON XVI.—THE VERB BE.

What is the third example of conjugation?
How is the verb BE conjugated throughout?
How do you form a synopsis of the verb *be*, with the nominative *I? thou? he? we? you? they? the man? the men?*

LESSON XVII.—COMPOUND FORM.

How else may active and neuter verbs be conjugated?
What peculiar meaning does this form convey?
What is the fourth example of conjugation?
How is the verb READ conjugated in the compound form?
How do you form a synopsis of the verb *be reading*, with the nominative *I? thou? he? we? you? they? the boy? the boys?*

LESSON XVIII.—PASSIVE FORM.

How are passive verbs formed?
What is the fifth example of conjugation?
How is the passive verb BE LOVED, conjugated throughout?
How do you form a synopsis of the verb *be loved*, with the nominative *I? thou? he? we? you? they? the child? the children?*

LESSON XIX.—OTHER FORMS.

How is a verb conjugated *negatively?*
How is the form of negation exemplified?
How is a verb conjugated *interrogatively?*
How is the form of question exemplified?
How is a verb conjugated *interrogatively* and *negatively?*
How is the form of negative question exemplified?

LESSON XX.—IRREGULAR VERBS.

What is an *irregular* verb?
How many irregular verbs are there?—and whence are they derived?
How does the list exhibit the irregular verbs?
What are the principal parts of the following verbs :—Arise,—Be, bear, beat,
begin, behold, beset, bestead, bid, bind, bite, bleed, break, breed, bring,
buy,—Cast, chide, choose, cleave, cling, come, cost, cut,—Do, draw, drink,
drive,—Eat,—Fall, feed, feel, fight, find, flee, fling, fly, forbear, forsake,
—Get, give, go, grow,—Have, hear, hide, hit, hold, hurt,—Keep, know?

LESSON XXI.—IRREGULAR VERBS.

What are the principal parts of the following verbs :—Lead, leave, lend, let,
lie, lose,—Make, meet,—Put,—Read, rend, rid, ride, ring, rise, run,—Say,
see, seek, sell, send, set, shed, shoe, shoot, shut, shred, shrink, sing, sink,
sit, slay, sling, slink, choose, smite, speak, spend, spin, spit, spread, spring, stand,
steal, stick, sting, stink, stride, strike, swear, swim, swing,—Take, teach,
tear, tell, think, thrust, tread,—Wear, win, write?

LESSON XXII.—REDUNDANT VERBS.

What is a *redundant* verb?   How many redundant verbs are there?   What
are the principal parts of the following verbs :—Abide, awake,—Belay,
bend, bereave, beseech, bet, betide, bide, blend, bless, blow, build, burn,
burst,—Catch, clothe, creep, crow, curse,—Dare, deal, dig, dive, dream,
dress, dwell,—Freeze,—Geld, gild, gird, grave, grind,—Hang, heat, heave,
hew,—Kneel, knit,—Lade, lay, lean, leap, learn, light,—Mean, mow,
mulct?

LESSON XXIII.—REDUNDANT VERBS.

What are the principal parts of the following verbs :—Pass, pay, pen, plead,
prove,—Quit,—Rap, reave, rive, roast,—Saw, seethe, shake, shape, shave,
shear, shine, show, sleep, slide, slit, smell, sow, speed, spell, spill, split,
spoil, stave, stay, string, strive, strow, sweat, sweep, swell,—Thrive,
throw,—Wake, wax, weave, wed, weep, wet, whet, wind, wont, work,
wring?
What is a *defective* verb?—What tenses do such verbs lack?
What verbs are defective? and wherein are they so?

LESSON XXIV.—PARTICIPLES.

What is a Participle? and how is it generally formed?
How many kinds of participles are there? and what are they called?
How is the *imperfect* participle defined? and what are the examples?
How is the *perfect* participle defined? and what are the examples?
How is the *preperfect* participle defined? and what are the examples?
How is the first or imperfect participle formed?
How is the second or perfect participle formed?
How is the third or preperfect participle formed?
What are the participles of the following verbs, according to the simplest
form of conjugation :—Repeat, study, return, mourn, seem, rejoice, appear,
approach, suppose, think, set, come, rain, stand, know, deceive?

LESSON XXV.—ANALYSIS AND PARSING

What is an *Attribute?*
What are the *principal parts* of a sentence?
What may the other parts of a sentence be?
What may be *attributed* to the subject?—In what ways?
What is required of the pupil in the *Fifth Praxis?*

LESSON XXVI.—ADVERBS AND CONJUNCTIONS.

What is an Adverb?—What is the example?
To what classes may adverbs be reduced?

Which are adverbs of *time ?*—of *place ?*—of *degree ?*—of *manner ?*
What are *conjunctive* adverbs ?
Have adverbs any modifications ?
Compare *well, badly* or *ill, little, much, far* and *forth.*
What is a CONJUNCTION ?—How are conjunctions divided ?
What is a *copulative* conjunction ?—a *disjunctive* conjunction ?—a *corresponsive* conjunction ?
What are the copulative conjunctions ?—the disjunctive ?—the corresponsive ?

LESSON XXVII.—PREPOSITIONS AND INTERJECTIONS.

What is a PREPOSITION ?—How are the prepositions arranged ?
What are the prepositions beginning with *a ?*—with *b ?*—with *c ?*—with *d ?*—with *e ?*—with *f ?*—with *i ?*—with *m ?*—with *n ?*—with *o ?*—with *p ?*—with *r ?*—with *s ?*—with *t ?*—with *u ?*—with *w ?*
What is an INTERJECTION ?—How are the interjections arranged ?
What are the interjections of joy ?—of sorrow ?—of wonder?—of wishing or earnestness ?—of praise ?—of surprise ?—of pain or fear ?—of contempt?—of aversion ?—of expulsion ?—of calling aloud ?—of exultation ?—of laughter ?—of salutation ?—of calling to attention ?—of calling to silence ?—of surprise ?—of languor ?—of stopping ?—of parting ?—of knowing or detecting ?—of interrogating ?

LESSON XXVIII.—ANALYSIS AND PARSING.

What is a *compound subject or predicate ?*—What is a *phrase ?*
How may a phrase be used ?—What is a *substantive phrase ?*
What is an *independent phrase ?*—the *principal part* of a phrase ?
What is a *simple phrase ?*—What is a *complex phrase ?*
What is a *compound phrase ?*
What is required of the pupil in the *Sixth Praxis ?*

CHAPTER XIII.—FOR WRITING.

EXERCISES IN ETYMOLOGY.

☞ [When the pupil has become familiar with the different parts of speech, and their classes and modifications, and has been sufficiently exercised in *etymological parsing,* he should *write out* the following exercises.]

EXERCISE I.—ARTICLES.

1. Prefix the definite article to the following nouns : path, paths ; loss, losses ; name, names ; page, pages ; want, wants ; doubt, doubts ; votary, votaries.

2. Prefix the indefinite article to the following nouns : age, error, idea, omen, urn, arch, bird, cage, dream, empire, farm, grain, horse, idol, jay, king, lady, man, novice, opinion, pony, quail, raven, sample trade, uncle, vessel, window, youth, zone, whirlwind, union, onion, unit, eagle, house, honour, hour, herald, habitation, hospital, harper, harpoon, ewer, eye, humour.

3. Insert the definite article rightly in the following phrases : George second—fair appearance—part first—reasons most obvious—good man—wide circle—man of honour—man of world —old books—common people—same person—smaller piece— rich and poor—first and last—all time—great excess—nine

muses—how rich reward—so small number—all ancient writers—in nature of things—much better course.

4. Insert the indefinite article rightly in each of the following phrases : new name—very quick motion—other sheep—
such power—what instance—great weight—such worthy cause
—too great difference—high honour—humble station—universal law—what strange event—so deep interest—as firm hope
—so great wit—humorous story—such person—few dollars—
little reflection.

EXERCISE II.—NOUNS.

1. Write the plural of the following nouns : town, country,
case, pin, needle, harp, pen, sex, rush, arch, marsh, monarch,
blemish, distich, princess, gas, bias, stigma, wo, grotto, folio,
punctilio, ally, duty, toy, money, entry, valley, volley, half,
dwarf, strife, knife, roof, muff, staff, chief, sheaf, mouse, penny,
ox, foot, erratum, axis, thesis, criterion, bolus, rebus, son-in-
law, pailful, man-servant.

2. Write the feminines corresponding to the following
nouns : earl, friar, stag, lord, duke, marquis, hero, executor,
nephew, heir, actor, enchanter, hunter, prince, traitor, lion,
arbiter, tutor, songster, abbot, master, uncle, widower, son,
landgrave.

3. Write the possessive case singular of the following nouns:
table, leaf, boy, torch, park, porch, portico, lynx, calf, sheep,
wolf, echo, folly, cavern, father-in-law, court-martial.

4. Write the possessive case, plural, of the following nouns :
priest, tutor, scholar, mountain, city, courtier, judge, citizen,
woman, servant, writer, mother.

5. Write the possessive case, both singular and plural, of
the following nouns : body, fancy, lady, attorney, negro, nun-
cio, life, brother, deer, child, wife, goose, beau, envoy, distaff,
colloquy, hero, thief, wretch.

EXERCISE III.—ADJECTIVES.

1. Annex a suitable noun to each of the following adjectives,
without repeating any word : good, great, tall, wise, strong,
dark, dangerous, dismal, drowsy, twenty, true, difficult, pale,
livid, ripe, delicious, stormy, rainy, convenient, heavy. Thus
—good *pens*, &c.

2. Prefix a suitable adjective to each of the following nouns,
without repeating any word : man, son, merchant, work, fence,
fear, poverty, picture, prince, delay, suspense, devices, follies,
actions. Thus—*wise* man, &c.

3. Compare the following adjectives : black, bright, short,

white, old, high, wet, big, few, lovely, dry, fat, good, bad, little, much, many, far.

4. Express the degrees of the following qualities, by the comparative adverbs of increase: delightful, comfortable, agreeable, pleasant, fortunate, valuable, wretched, vivid, timid, poignant, excellent.

5. Express the degrees of the following qualities by the comparative adverbs of diminution; objectionable, formidable, forcible, comely, pleasing, obvious, censurable, prudent.

EXERCISE IV.—PRONOUNS.

1. Write the nominative plural of the following pronouns: I, thou, he, she, it, who, which, what, that.

2. Write the declension of the following pronouns: myself, thyself, himself, herself, itself, whosoever.

3. Write the following words in their customary form: her's, it's, our's, your's, their's, who's, meself, hisself, theirselves.

4. Write the objective singular of all the simple pronouns.

5. Write the objective plural of all the simple pronouns.

EXERCISE V.—VERBS.

1. Write the four principal parts of each of the following verbs: slip, thrill, caress, force, release, crop, try, die, obey, delay, destroy, deny, buy, come, do, feed, lie, say, huzza.

2. Write the following preterits in their appropriate form: exprest, stript, lispt, dropt, jumpt, prest, topt, whipt, soakt, propt, fixt, stopt, pluckt, crost, stept, distrest, gusht, confest, snapt, brusht, shipt, kist, discust, lackt.

3. Write the following verbs in the indicative mood, present tense, second person singular: move, strive, please, reach, confess, fix, deny, survive, know, go, outdo, close, lose, pursue.

4. Write the following verbs in the indicative mood, present tense, third person singular: leave, seem, search, impeach, fear, redress, comply, bestow, do, woo, sue, view, allure, rely, beset, release, be, bias.

5. Write the following verbs in the subjunctive mood, present tense, in the three persons singular: serve, shun, turn, learn, find, wish, throw, dream, possess, detest, disarm, allow, pretend.

EXERCISE VI.—VERBS.

1. Write a synopsis of the first person singular of the active verb *amuse*, conjugated affirmatively.

6

2. Write a synopsis of the second person singular of the neuter verb *sit*, conjugated affirmatively in the solemn style.

3. Write a synopsis of the third person singular of the active verb *speak*, conjugated affirmatively in the compound form.

4. Write a synopsis of the first person plural of the passive verb *be reduced*, conjugated affirmatively.

5. Write a synopsis of the second person plural of the active verb *lose*, conjugated negatively.

6. Write a synopsis of the third person plural of the neuter verb *stand*, conjugated interrogatively.

7. Write a synopsis of the first person singular of the active verb *derive*, conjugated interrogatively and negatively.

EXERCISE VII.—PARTICIPLES.

1. Write the simple imperfect participles of the following verbs: belong, provoke, degrade, impress, fly, do, survey, vie, coo, let, hit, put, defer, differ, remember.

2. Write the perfect participles of the following verbs: turn, burn, learn, deem, crowd, choose, draw, hear, lend, sweep, tear, thrust, steal, write, delay, imply, exist.

3. Write the pluperfect or preperfect participles of the following verbs: depend, dare, deny, value, forsake, bear, set, sit, lay, mix, speak, sleep, allot.

4. Write the following participles in their appropriate form: dipt, deckt, markt, equipt, ingulft, embarrast, astonisht, tost, embost, absorpt, attackt, gasht, soakt, hackt, blest, curst.

5. Write the regular participles which are now generally preferred to the following irregular ones: clad, graven, hoven, hewn, knelt, leant, lit, mown, quit, riven, sawn, sodden, shaven, shorn, sown, strown, swollen, thriven, wrought.

6. Write the irregular participles which are, or may be, preferred to the following regular ones: bended, builded, catched, creeped, dealed, digged, dreamed, dwelled, gilded, girded, hanged, knitted, laded, meaned, reaved, shined, slitted, splitted, stringed, strived, weeped, wonted, wringed.

EXERCISE VIII.—ADVERBS, &c.

1. Compare the following adverbs: soon, often, well, badly *or* ill, little, much, far, forth.

2. Prefix the comparative adverbs of increase to each of the following adverbs: purely, fairly, sweetly, earnestly, patiently, completely, fortunately, profitably.

3. Prefix the comparative adverbs of diminution to the following adverbs: secretly, slily, liberally, favourably, powerfully.

4. Insert suitable conjunctions in place of the following dashes: Love—fidelity are inseparable. Beware of parties—factions. Do well—boast not. Improve time—it flies. There would be few paupers—no time were lost. Be not proud—thou art human. I saw—it was necessary. Honesty is better—policy. Neither he—I can do it. It must be done—to day—to morrow. Take care—thou fall. Though I should boast—am I nothing.

5. Insert suitable prepositions in the place of the following dashes: Plead—the dumb. Qualify thyself—action—study. Think often—the worth—time. Live—peace—all men. Keep—compass. Jest not—serious subjects. Take no part—slander. Guilt starts—its own shadow. Grudge not—giving. Go not—sleep—malice. Debate not—temptation. Depend not—the stores—others. Contend not—trifles. Many fall—grasping—things—their reach. Be deaf—detraction.

6. Correct the following sentences, and adapt the interjections to the emotions expressed by the other words: Aha! aha! I am undone. Hey! io! I am tired. Ho! be still. Avaunt! this way. Ah! what nonsense. Heigh-ho! I am delighted. Hist! it is contemptible. Oh! for that sympathetic glow! Ah! what withering phantoms glare!

PART III.

SYNTAX.

SYNTAX treats of the relation, agreement, government, and arrangement, of words in sentences.

The *relation* of words, is their dependence, or connexion, according to the sense.

The *agreement* of words, is their similarity in person, number, gender, case, mood, tense, or form.

The *government* of words, is that power which one word has over an other, to cause it to assume some particular modification.

The *arrangement* of words, is their collocation, or relative position, in a sentence.

[OBS. 1.—*Syntax*, as the name indicates, has reference only to those principles and rules which serve to guide us in the construction of sentences. The principles of *analysis* lie much deeper in the subject of grammar—are much more fundamental, than the technical considerations which form the groundwork of syntactical rules.

Sentential analysis is founded upon the *general laws* of language; and, therefore, its principles are as applicable to one language as another; syntactical rules, on the other hand, can, as a general thing, have reference only to the particular language, the use of which they are designed to direct.

Analysis is generally introduced in connection only with syntax, as if it had a special and exclusive reference to that department of grammar; whereas it deals with principles that underlie almost all grammatical distinctions, and is quite as necessary to the proper elucidation of etymological relations as those which especially belong to syntax. The classification and definition of the different kinds of sentences, and their elements have therefore been removed from this part of the work (where they were originally placed by the author), and introduced progressively at intervals, in connection with the exercises of analysis and parsing, designed to illustrate, and practice the pupil in, each consecutive part of the subject studied. The definition of a *sentence* immediately follows that of *parsing ;* because up to that point, the term had been twice used; once, in the definition of a conjunction, and once, in that of parsing ; a fact which, of itself, demonstrates the elementary character of this definition, and to what extent even etymological distinctions depend upon it.

OBS. 2.—Syntactical rules are limited to the construction of *sentences*, as separate portions of discourse; the consideration of those principles and rules which regulate the combination of sentences into paragraphs, and these again into particular kinds of composition, is not comprised in the subject of *grammar*, but falls within the province of its kindred arts, *rhetoric* and *logic.*

OBS. 3.—Rules 1, 2, 4, 9, 14, 15, 16, 17, 18, 20, 22,—nearly one half of the twenty-six Rules of Syntax laid down in this work, are rather a repetition of the definitions comprehended in etymology, than separate rules necessary to guide us in the construction of sentences. For example, we need no rule to inform us that "the subject of a finite verb is in the nominative case," after learning that the "nominative case is that form or state of a noun or pronoun which denotes the subject of a finite verb." The case is different, however, when we have two or more connected subjects belonging to the same verb ; for here etymology gives us no *explicit* direction, although it still affords the *guiding principle.*

The rules, above enumerated, although without any directive utility, form, however, the basis for many subordinate rules, contained in the observations and notes, which should be attentively studied by the learner, and the exercises upon them be carefully performed.—EDITOR.]

OBS. 4.—Words that are omitted by ellipsis, and that are necessarily understood in order to complete the construction, must be supplied in analysis and parsing.

CHAPTER I.—THE RULES OF SYNTAX.

1. RULES OF RELATION AND AGREEMENT.

RULE I.—ARTICLES.

Articles relate to the nouns which they limit.

RULE II.—NOMINATIVES.

A Noun or a Pronoun which is the subject of a finite verb, must be in the nominative case.

RULE III.—APPOSITION.

A Noun or a personal Pronoun used to explain a preceding noun or pronoun, is put, by apposition, in the same case.

RULE IV.—ADJECTIVES.

Adjectives relate to nouns or pronouns.

RULE V.—PRONOUNS.

A Pronoun must agree with its antecedent, or the noun or pronoun which it represents, in person, number, and gender.

RULE VI.—PRONOUNS.

When the antecedent is a collective noun conveying the idea of plurality, the Pronoun must agree with it in the plural number.

RULE VII.—PRONOUNS.

When a Pronoun has two or more antecedents connected by *and*, it must agree with them in the plural number.

RULE VIII.—PRONOUNS.

When a Pronoun has two or more singular antecedents connected by *or* or *nor*, it must agree with them in the singular number.

RULE IX.—VERBS.

A finite Verb must agree with its subject, or nominative, in person and number.

RULE X.—VERBS.

When the nominative is a collective noun conveying the idea of plurality, the Verb must agree with it in the plural number.

RULE XI.—VERBS.

When a Verb has two or more nominatives connected by *and*, it must agree with them in the plural number.

RULE XII.—VERBS.

When a Verb has two or more singular nominatives connected by *or* or *nor*, it must agree with them in the singular number.

RULE XIII.—VERBS.

When Verbs are connected by a conjunction, they must either agree in mood, tense, and form, or have separate nominatives expressed.

RULE XIV.—PARTICIPLES.

Participles relate to nouns or pronouns, or else are governed by prepositions.

RULE XV.—ADVERBS.

Adverbs relate to verbs, participles, adjectives, or other adverbs.

RULE XVI.—CONJUNCTIONS.

Conjunctions connect either words or sentences.

RULE XVII.—PREPOSITIONS.

Prepositions show the relations of things.

RULE XVIII.—INTERJECTIONS.

Interjections have no dependent construction.

2. RULES OF GOVERNMENT.*

RULE XIX.—POSSESSIVES.

A noun or a pronoun in the Possessive case, is governed by the name of the thing possessed.

RULE XX.—OBJECTIVES.

Active-transitive verbs, and their imperfect and pre-perfect participles, govern the Objective case.

RULE XXI.—SAME CASES.

Active-intransitive, passive, and neuter verbs, and their participles, take the same case after as before them, when both words refer to the same thing.

RULE XXII.—OBJECTIVES.

Prepositions govern the Objective case.

RULE XXIII.—INFINITIVES.

The preposition TO governs the Infinitive mood, and commonly connects it to a finite verb.

RULE XXIV.—INFINITIVES.

The active verbs, *bid, dare, feel, hear, let, make, need, see*, and their participles, usually take the Infinitive after them, without the preposition TO.

RULE XXV.—NOM. ABSOLUTE.

A noun or a pronoun is put absolute in the Nominative, when its case depends on no other word.

RULE XXVI.—SUBJUNCTIVES.

A future contingency is best expressed by a verb in the Subjunctive, present; and a mere supposition, with indefinite time, by a verb in the Subjunctive, imperfect: but a conditional circumstance assumed as a fact, requires the Indicative mood.

---

* The *Arrangement* of words is treated of, in the Observations under the Rules of Syntax, in Chapters 2d and 3d.

EXERCISES IN ANALYSIS AND PARSING.

PRAXIS VII.—SYNTACTICAL.

In the Seventh Praxis, it is required of the pupil—to analyze the sentence according to the method indicated under each example ; to distinguish the parts of speech and their classes ; to mention their modifications in order ; to point out their relation, agreement, or government ; and to apply the Rule of Syntax.   Thus : —

EXAMPLE ANALYZED AND PARSED.

" To be continually subject to the breath of slander, will tarnish the purest reputation."

ANALYSIS.—This is a simple declarative sentence.

The subject is the complex infinitive phrase, *to be continually subject to the breath of slander ;* the predicate is *will tarnish ;* the object is *reputation.*

The principal part of the phrase is *to be,* and its adjuncts are *continually,* and the indefinite attribute, *subject,* which is modified by the complex adverbial phrase, *to the breath of slander ;* the principal part of this phrase is *breath,* which is modified by *the,* and the simple adjective phrase, *of slander.*

The predicate of the sentence has no adjuncts ; the adjuncts of the object are *the* and *purest.*

PARSING.—*To be* is an irregular neuter verb, from *be, was, being, been ;* found in the infinitive mood and present tense, and is, with the phrase of which it is the principal part, the subject of the verb *will tarnish ;* according to Note 11, under Rule IX., which says, " The infinitive mood, a phrase, or a sentence, is sometimes the subject to a verb."

Continually is an adverb of time, and relates to the verb *to be ;* according to Rule XV., which says, etc.

Subject is a common adjective, of the positive degree, compared only by means of the adverbs, *more* and *most,* and *less* and *least ;* it is taken abstractly with the infinitive *to be ;* according to Exception 2d, under Rule IV., which says, " With an infintive or a participle denoting being or action in the abstract, an adjective is sometimes also taken abstractly."

To is a preposition ; and shows the relation between *subject* and *breath ;* according to Rule XVII., which says, etc.

The is the definite article, and relates to *breath ;* according to Rule I., which says, etc.

Breath is a common noun, of the third person, singular number, neuter gender, and objective case ; and is governed by *to ;* according to Rule XXII., which says, etc.

Will tarnish is a regular active-transitive verb, from *tarnish, tarnished, tarnishing, tarnished ;* found in the indicative mood, first-future tense, third person, and singular number ; and agrees with its subject, the infinitive phrase *to be,* etc. ; according to Note 11, under Rule IX., which says, " The infinitive mood, a phrase, or a sentence, is sometimes the subject of a verb ; a subject of this kind, however composed, if it is taken as one whole, requires a verb in the third person singular."

Purest is a common adjective of the superlative degree, compared, *pure, purer, purest ;* it relates to *reputation ;* according to Rule IV., which says, etc.

Reputation is a common noun, of the third person, singular number, neuter gender, and objective case ; and is governed by *will tarnish ;* according to Rule XX., which says, etc.

EXERCISE I.—THE SUBJECT PHRASE.

To train* citizens is not the work of a day.

To be happy without the approval of conscience, is impossible.

To have remained calm under such provocation, was a proof of remarkable self-control.

To be at once a rake and glory in the character, discovers a bad disposition and a bad heart.

To meet danger boldly is better than to wait for it.

To be satisfied with the acquittal of one's own conscience, is the mark of a great mind.

To be totally indifferent to praise or censure, is a real defect of character.

To spring up from bed at the first moment of waking, is easy enough for people habituated to it.

To laugh were want of goodness and of grace,
And to be grave exceeds all power of face.

EXERCISE II.—THE OBJECT PHRASE.

EXAMPLE ANALYZED.

" Can a youth who refuses to yield obedience to his parents, expect to become a good or a wise man ?"

ANALYSIS.—This is a complex interrogative sentence.
The principal clause is, *Can a youth expect to become a good or wise man ?* The dependent clause is, *who refuses to yield obedience to his parents.* The connective is *who.*
The subject of the principal clause is *youth ;* the predicate is *expect ;* the object is the infinitive phrase, *to become a good or a wise man.*
The adjuncts of the subject are *a* and the dependent clause ; the predicate has no adjuncts ; the principal part of the phrase is *to become,* and its adjunct is the attribute *man,* which refers to the subject *youth,* and is modified by the adjuncts *a, good,* and *a, wise,* connected by *or.*

---

* The various usages of the infinitive mood, exhibited in these and the following classified phrases, might dictate some modification of Rule XXIII., which asserts that the infinitive mood is, in all cases, governed by the preposition *to*. The forms of expression, and their analysis, here given, show that this statement, if correct, explains scarcely at all the nature, and mode of use, of this form of the verb. We perceive that, with or without adjuncts, it may be used as the subject or the object of a verb, or as a substantive or adjective attribute, and that it may be independent. Moreover, when it introduces an adjective or adverbial phrase, it appears to be used as an adjective or adverb, although it may be considered to be the object of *to* (if a preposition), or of some preposition understood. In this case only, does Rule XXIII. appear to have any application whatever. A more general rule, and one more in consonance with the nature of this form of speech, would be, " The infinitive mood has the construction of a noun or an adjective."

6*

The subject of the dependent clause is *who ;* the predicate is *refuses ;* the object is the complex infinitive phrase, *to yield obedience to his parents.* The subject and the predicate have no adjuncts ; the principal part of the phrase is *to yield*, its adjunct is the object, *obedience*, which is modified by the simple adjective phrase, *to his parents ;* the principal part of this phrase is *parents*, and its adjunct is *his.*

☞ [*Man* is in the nominative case, after *become*, agreeing with *youth ;* according to Rule XXI.]

If you desire to be free from sin, avoid temptation.

By the faults of others, wise men learn how to correct their own.

In reasoning, avoid blending arguments confusedly together that are of a separate nature.

He who refuses to learn how to avoid evil, may properly be deemed guilty of it.

He did not oppose his son's going to sea, because he desired to remove him from the evil influence of bad company:

Never expect to be able to govern others, unless you have learned how to govern yourself.

He who loves to survey the works of nature, can anticipate, wherever he may be, finding sources of the purest enjoyment.

He who attempts to please every body, will soon become an object of general indifference or contempt.

None but the virtuous dare hope in bad circumstances.

If ever any author deserved to be called an *original*, it was Shakespeare.

EXERCISE III.—THE ATTRIBUTE PHRASE.

EXAMPLE ANALYZED.

" The predominant passion of Franklin seems to have been the love of the useful."

ANALYSIS.—This is a simple declarative sentence.

The subject is *passion ;* the predicate is *seems ;* the attribute is the infinitive phrase, *to have been the love of the useful.*

The adjuncts of the subject are *the, predominant,* and the simple adjective phrase, *of Franklin ;* the predicate has no adjuncts ; the principal part of the attribute phrase is *to have been,* and its adjunct is the attribute *love,* which refers to the subject *passion,* and is modified by *the,* and the simple adjective phrase, *of the useful.*

☞ [*To have been* is used as an adjective, and relates to *passion.*]

The fire of our minds is immortal, and not to be quenched.

Universal benevolence and patriotic zeal appear to have been the motives of all his actions.

Children should be permitted to be children, and not deprived of amusements proper for their age.

Was he not to live the best part of his life over again, and once more be all that he ever had been ?

Criminals are observed to grow more anxious as their trial approaches.

Knowledge is not to be received inertly like the influences of the atmosphere, by a mere residence at the place of instruction.

The great purpose of poetry is to carry the mind above and beyond the beaten, dusty, weary walks of ordinary life ; to lift it into a purer element; and to breathe into it more profound and generous emotion.

He seems to have made an injudicious choice, though he is esteemed a sensible man.

Integrity is of the greatest importance in every situation of life.

To be useful in some degree, is within the means of every one.

To discover the true nature of comets, has hitherto proved beyond the power of science.

His conduct was, under the circumstances, in very bad taste.

The merchant was to have sailed for Europe last week.

EXERCISE IV.—THE ADJECTIVE PHRASE.

EXAMPLE ANALYZED.

" Leaning my head upon my hand, I began to figure to myself the miseries of confinement."

ANALYSIS.—This is a simple declarative sentence.

The subject is *I;* the predicate is *began ;* the object is the complex infinitive phrase, *to figure to myself the miseries of confinement.* The principal part of the phrase is *to figure,* the adjuncts of which are the simple adverbial phrase, *to myself,* and the object *miseries,* which is modified by *the* and the simple adjective phrase, *of confinement.*

The adjunct of the subject is the complex adjective phrase *leaning my head upon my hand,* the principal part of which is *leaning,* and its adjuncts, the object *head* modified by *my,* and the simple adverbial phrase, *upon my hand,* the principal part of which is *hand,* and its adjunct, *my.*

Life bears us on like the stream of a mighty river.

Augustus had no lawful authority to make a change in the Roman constitution.

A habit of sincerity in acknowledging faults, is a guard against committing them.

The atrocious crime of being a young man, I shall attempt neither to palliate nor deny.

Envy, surrounded on all sides by the brightness of another's prosperity, like the scorpion, confined within the circle of fire, stings itself to death.

The requisites for a first-rate actor demand a combination of talents and accomplishments, not easily to be found.

The conflicts of the world were not to take place altogether* on the tented field; but ideas, leaping from the world's awakened intellect, and burning all over with indestructible life, were to be marshalled against principalities and powers.

EXERCISE V.—THE ADVERBIAL PHRASE.

EXAMPLE ANALYZED.

" We live in the past by a knowledge of its history, and in the future by hope and anticipation."

ANALYSIS.—This is a compound declarative sentence, abbreviated in form, and consisting of the two coördinate clauses, *We live in the past by a knowledge of its history*, and (*we live*) *in the future by hope and anticipation*, connected by *and*.

The subject of either clause is *we ;* and the predicate is *live*. Neither of the subjects is modified. The adjuncts of the first predicate are the simple adverbial phrase, *in the past*, and the complex adverbial phrase, *by a knowledge of its history ;* the principal part is *knowledge*, and its adjuncts are *a* and the simple adjective phrase, *of its history*. [The adjuncts of the second predicate are of the same character, and may be analyzed in the same manner.]

At that hour, O how vain was all sublunary happiness!

Abstain from injuring others, if you wish to be in safety.

The public are often deceived by false appearances and extravagant pretensions.

Day and night yield us contrary blessings ; and, at the same time, assist each other, by giving fresh lustre to the delights of both.

Man's happiness or misery is, in a great measure, put into his own hands.

Has not sloth, or pride, or ill temper, or sinful passion, misled you from the path of sound and wise conduct?

Man was created to search for truth, to love the beautiful, to desire the good, and to do the best.

Representation and taxation should always go hand in hand.

The statement which he made at first, he reiterated, again and again, without the least variation.

Jacob loved all his sons, but he loved Joseph the best.

We live in the past by a knowledge of its history, and in the future, by hope and anticipation.

---

* *Altogether* is here an adverb relating to the adverbial phrase, *on the tented field.* See Obs. 2, page 112.

EXERCISE VI.—THE EXPLANATORY PHRASE.

EXAMPLE ANALYZED.

"It is useless to expatiate upon the beauties of nature to one who is blind."

ANALYSIS.—This a complex declarative sentence.

The principal clause is, *It is useless to expatiate upon the beauties of nature to one*, and the dependent clause is, *who is blind*. The connective is *who*.

The subject of the principal clause is *it;* the predicate is *is;* and the attribute is *useless.*

The adjunct of the subject is the complex explanatory phrase, *to expatiate upon the beauties of nature to one.* The principal part of the phrase is *to expatiate*, the adjuncts of which are the complex adverbial phrase *upon the beauties of nature*, and the simple adverbial phrase *to one.* The principal part of the former is *beauties*, and its adjuncts are *the* and the simple adjective phrase *of nature;* the principal part of the latter is *one*, and its adjunct is the dependent adjectiv clause *who is blind.*

The subject of the dependent clause is *who;* the predicate, *is;* and the attribute, *blind;* each without adjuncts.

It is always profitable to know our own faults and infirmities.

It is the characteristic of a pedant to make an idle display of his learning.

If what I say be not true, it is easy to convict me of falsehood.

It is very often impossible to estimate the extent of injury which a careless word will produce.

How happy had it been for him to have died in that sickness, when all Italy was putting up vows and prayers for his safety!

It is certainly in the power of a sensible and well-educated mother to inspire such tastes and propensities in her son as shall nearly decide the destiny of the future man.

It is impossible to read a page in Plato, Tully, or any of the other eminent moralists of antiquity, without being a greater and better man for it.

If we would improve our minds by conversation, it is a great happiness to be acquainted with persons wiser than ourselves.

If we were base enough to desire it, it is now too late to retire from the contest.

It is a miserable state of mind to have few things to desire, and many things to fear.

> Death!   Great proprietor of all!   'tis thine
> To tread out empire, and to quench the stars.

> Through worlds unnumber'd though the God be known,
> 'Tis ours to trace him only in our own.

EXERCISE VII.—THE INDEPENDENT PHRASE.

EXAMPLE ANALYZED.

" This proposition being admitted, I now state my argument."

ANALYSIS.—This is a simple declarative sentence.

The subject is *I;* the predicate is *state ;* the object is *argument.*

The subject has no adjuncts ; the adjunct of the predicate is *now ;* the adjunct of the object is *my.*

This proposition being admitted is an independent phrase ; the principal part is *proposition*, and its adjuncts are *this* and *being admitted.*

EXAMPLE II.

" One day, I was guilty of an action, which, to say the least, was in very bad taste."

ANALYSIS.—This is a complex declarative sentence.

The principal clause is, *One day I was guilty of an action;* and the dependent clause is, *which, to say the least, was in very bad taste.* The connective is *which.*

The subject of the principal clause is *I;* the predicate is *was;* and the attribute is *guilty.*

The subject has no adjuncts ; the adjunct of the predicate is the adverbial phrase (prepositional in form), (*on*) *one day ;* the adjunct of the attribute is the adverbial phrase *of an action.* Of the latter phrase *action* is the principal part, and its adjuncts are *an* and the dependent clause.

The subject of the dependent clause is *which ;* the predicate is *was ;* and the attribute, the adjective phrase *in very bad taste.*

Neither has any adjuncts ; the principal part of the attribute phrase is *taste ; bad* being its primary, and *very* its secondary adjunct.

To say the least is an independent phrase of the infinitive form. The principal part is *to say*, and its adjunct, the object *least*, modified by *the.*

They being absent, we cannot come to a determination.

There being much obscurity in the case, he refuses to decide upon it.

To be plain with you, your conduct is very much to be censured.

Fathers ! Senators of Rome ! the arbiters of nations ! to you I fly for refuge.

The baptism of John ; was it from heaven, or of men ?

Generally speaking, the life of all truly great men has been a life of intense and incessant labor.

To give one instance more, and then I will have done with this rambling discourse.—*Hazlitt.*

The great utility of knowledge and religion being thus apparent, it is highly incumbent upon us to pay a studious attention to them in our youth.

A shoe coming loose from the fore-foot of the thill-horse, at the beginning of the ascent of Mount Taurina, the postillion

dismounted, twisted the shoe off, and put it in his pocket.—
Sterne.

> Want, and incurable disease, (fell pair !)
> On hopeless multitudes remorseless seize
> At once ; and make a refuge of the grave.

> Soldier, rest ! thy warfare o'er,
>   Sleep the sleep that knows not breaking :
> Dream of battle-fields no more,
>   Days of danger, nights of waking.

EXERCISE VIII.—THE SUBJECT CLAUSE.

EXAMPLE ANALYZED.

" That it is our duty to obey the laws of the country in
which we live, does not admit of question."

ANALYSIS.—This is a complex declarative sentence.
  The subject is the dependent clause, *That it is our duty to obey the laws of
    the country in which we live ;* the predicate is *does admit.* *That* is the
    connective.
  The adjuncts of the predicate are *not* and the phrase *of question.*
  The subject of the dependent clause is *it ;* the predicate is *is ;* and the at-
    tribute is *duty.*
  The adjunct of the subject is the complex explanatory phrase, *to obey the
    laws of the country in which we live ;* the adjunct of the attribute is *our.*
  The principal part of the explanatory phrase is *to obey,* which is modified
    by the object *laws,* the adjuncts of which are *the* and the complex
    phrase, *of the country in which we live.* The principal part of this
    phrase is *country,* and its adjuncts are *the* and the complex adjective
    clause, *in which we live.* The subject of the clause is *we ;* the predicate
    is *live,* which is modified by the simple adverbial phrase *in which.*

OBS.—It will be perceived from the example given in this exercise, that
a complex sentence may be analyzed by treating it as a whole, pointing out
the subject, predicate, etc., and analyzing the dependent clause in its proper
place, as one of the principal parts, or an adjunct to either ; instead of dividing the sentence immediately into the principal and dependent clauses,
explaining their connection, and then analyzing them separately, as in the
previous exercises. The latter method is preferable for beginners, but for
advanced scholars should give place to the other, which is more logical, and
easier for intricate sentences.

That the government of our desires is essential to the enjoyment of true liberty, is a truth never to be forgotten.

That it is glorious to die for one's country, is a sentiment
uniformly cherished by all good men.

At what period the poems of Homer were composed, has
not been positively ascertained.

Who was the author of the Letters of Phalaris, has been
the subject of very ingenious and learned discussion.

That an author's work is the mirror of his mind, is a position
that has led to very false conclusions.

Why a man with so excellent an education, and surrounded with so many inducements to a virtuous life, should have fallen into habits of vice and dissipation, is inexplicable.

That truth finally must prevail over error, and virtue be triumphant in a struggle with vice, are highly cherished sentiments among mankind.

How he was to extricate his army from so dangerous a position, baffled all conjecture.

Whether Columbus was the first discoverer of America or not, is a question among historians.

EXERCISE IX.—THE OBJECT CLAUSE.

EXAMPLE ANALYZED.

" Children should know that it is their duty to honor their parents, to ask advice of them, and to observe their wishes."

ANALYSIS.—This is a complex declarative sentence.
  The subject is *children ;* the predicate is *should know ;* the object is the dependent clause, *That it is their duty,* &c.   *That* is the connective.
  The subject of the dependent clause is *it ;* the predicate is *is ;* the attribute is *duty.*
  The adjuncts of the subject are the explanatory phrases, *to honor their parents, to ask advice of them,* and *to observe their wishes.*

He knew that solicitations or remonstrances would avail little with the companions of his enterprise.

Those who are skilled in the extraction and preparation of metals, declare that iron is everywhere to be found.

Columbus felt that there was a continent to be discovered ; and he discovered it.

The authors of the American Revolution believed that they were in the service of their own, and of all future generations.

It is interesting to notice how some minds seem almost to create themselves, springing up under every disadvantage, and working their solitary but irresistible way through a thousand obstacles.

Any man who attends to what passes within himself, may easily discern that the human character is a very complicated system.

How can he exalt his thoughts to any thing great or noble, who only believes that, after a short term on this stage of existence, he is to sink into oblivion, and to lose his consciousness forever ?

See, Aspasio, how all is calculated to administer the highest delight to mankind.

The majority of the assembly wisely considered that to decline a cessation, would be to refute all their professions of loyalty.

> Haply some hoary-headed swain may say,
> " Oft have we seen him at the peep of dawn,
> Brushing, with hasty steps, the dews away,
> To meet the sun upon the upland lawn."

EXERCISE X.—THE OBJECT CLAUSE.

INFINITIVE FORM.

Obs. 1.—In the infinitive form of this clause, the subject and predicate are connected *indirectly*. The predicate, instead of being a finite verb, is a verb in the infinitive mood, and its subject is in the objective case. Thus, in the sentence, " He commanded the army to march," *army* is the subject, and *to march*, the predicate; because it is indicated (although indirectly) that the act of marching is performed by the agent *army*, the sentence being equivalent to, " He commanded that the army should march."

Obs. 2.—The infinitive clause is also sometimes used as the *subject* of a sentence, and occasionally as an *explanatory adjunct*; as, " *For us to learn to die*, is the great business of life."—" It is the great business of life, *for us to learn to die*." [See Exception 2, Rule XVII.]

EXAMPLE ANALYZED.

"Let the child learn what is appropriate for his years."

ANALYSIS.—This is a complex imperative sentence. The subject is *thou* (understood); the predicate is *let*; the object is the infinitive clause, *the child learn*, &c.

The subject of the dependent clause is *child*; the predicate is *(to) learn*; the object is *that* (comprehended in the double relative *what*, equivalent to *that which*.)

The adjunct of the subject is *the*; the adjunct of the object is the simple adjective clause *which is appropriate for his years.*

The subject of this clause is *which*; the predicate, *is*; the attribute, *appropriate*, modified by the simple adverbial phrase, *for his years.*

Thou think'st it folly to be wise too soon.

In this melancholy state, he commanded messengers to recall his eldest son, Abouzaid, from the army.

Graves describes the steps by which Shenstone made the Leasowes become what it at last was.

Let us all, in our mourning attire, and accompanied by our children, go and entreat Veturia, the mother of Coriolanus, to intercede with her son for our common country.

Madam Roland heard herself sentenced to death with the air of one who saw in her condemnation merely her title to immortality.

Goldsmith said to Johnson very wittily and very justly, " If you were to write a fable about little fishes, doctor, you would make the little fishes talk like whales."

The fact of Shenstone's having written the School-mistress"
and the "Pastoral Ballad," alone entitles him to be ranked
amongst the classical poets of English literature.

The curiosity of the Caliph being awakened to know the
cause of his despair, he ordered Mezrour to knock at the door,
which being opened, they pleaded the privilege of strangers to
enter for rest and refreshment.

> See some strange comfort every state attend,
> And pride bestow'd on all, a common friend:
> See some fit passion every age supply;
> Hope travels through, nor quits us when we die.

> On what foundation stands the warrior's pride,
> How just his hopes, let Swedish Charles decide.

EXERCISE X.—THE ATTRIBUTE CLAUSE.

EXAMPLE ANALYZED.

" The truth is, that the most elaborate and manifold apparatus
of instruction can impart nothing of importance to the passive
and inert mind."

ANALYSIS.—This is a complex declarative sentence. The subject is *truth ;*
the predicate is *is ;* the attribute is the dependent clause, *The most
elaborate and manifold apparatus*, &c. The connective is *that.*

The subject of the dependent clause is *apparatus ;* the predicate is *can
impart ;* the object is *nothing.* The adjuncts of the subject are *the,
elaborate, manifold,* and *of instruction ; most* is an adjunct of *elaborate*
and *manifold ;* the adjunct of the predicate is the adverbial phrase
to the passive and inert mind ; the principal part of which is *mind,*
and its adjuncts *the,* and *passive and inert ;* the adjunct of the object
is the simple adjective phrase, *of importance.*

The crying sin of all governments is, that they meddle inju-
riously with human affairs, and obstruct the processes of nature
by excessive legislation.

One of the most useful effects of action is, that it renders
repose agreeable.

The only advantage which, in the voyage of life, the cautious had above the negligent, was, that they sunk later, and
more suddenly.

The characteristic peculiarity of the " Pilgrim's Progress" is,
that it is the only work of its kind which possesses a strong
human interest.

The proper end of instruction is, not that the scholar should
be able to repeat the thoughts of others, but that he should
have the power to think correctly for himself.

The physician's directions were, that the patient should
travel to the South, that he should avoid excitement, and that
he should be careful in diet.

EXERCISE XI.—THE ADJECTIVE CLAUSE.

EXAMPLE ANALYZED.

"Whoever yields to temptation, debases himself with a debasement from which he can never arise."

ANALYSIS.—This is a complex declarative sentence.
  The subject is *he* (comprehended in the double relative *whoever*); the predicate is *debases ;* the object is *himself.*
  The adjunct of the subject is the simple adjective clause, *who yields to temptation ;* the adjunct of the predicate is the complex phrase, *with a debasement from which he never can arise.* The principal part of the phrase is *debasement,* and its adjuncts are *a* and the simple adjective clause, *from which he never can arise.* The subject of this clause is *he ;* the predicate is *can arise.* The adjuncts of the predicate are *never,* and the simple adverbial phrase, *from which.*

The chief misfortunes that befall us in life, can be traced to some vices and follies which we have committed.

Every society has a right to prescribe for itself the terms on which its members shall be admitted.

There is no foundation for the popular doctrine, that a state may flourish by arts and crimes.

It is necessary to combat vigilantly that favorite idea of lively ignorance, that study is an enemy to originality.

Most of the troubles which we meet with in the world, arise from an irritable temper, or from improper conduct.

Neither his vote, his influence, nor his purse, was ever withheld from the cause in which he had engaged.

> He that has light within his own clear breast,
> May sit in the centre, and enjoy bright day ;
> But he that hides a dark soul and foul thoughts,
> Benighted walks under the mid-day sun.

> No flocks that range the valley, free,
>   To slaughter I condemn ;
> Taught by that power that pities me,
>   I learn to pity them.

EXERCISE XII.—THE ADVERBIAL CLAUSE.

EXAMPLE ANALYZED.

"Education, when it works upon a noble mind, draws out to view many latent virtues and perfections, which, without its aid, would never be able to make their appearance."

ANALYSIS.—This is a compound declarative sentence.
  The first clause is, *Education, when it works upon a noble mind, draws out to view many latent virtues and perfections ;* and the second is, *Which,*

without its aid, would never be able to make their appearance. The connective is *which.*

The first is a complex member ; the subject is *education ;* the predicate is *draws ;* the objects are *virtues* and *perfections.*

The subject has no adjuncts ; the adjuncts of the predicate are the adverbial clause, *when it works upon a noble mind,* out, and the simple adverbial phrase, *to view ;* the adjuncts of the objects are *many* and *latent.*

The subject of the dependent clause is *it ;* the predicate is *works.* The adjuncts of the predicate are *when,* and the adverbial phrase, *upon a noble mind.* The connective is *when.*

The subject of the second clause is *which ;* the predicate is *would be ;* the attribute is *able.*

The subject has no adjuncts ; the adjuncts of the predicate are the phrase, *without its aid,* and *never ;* the adjunct of the attribute is the simple adverbial phrase, *to make their appearance,* of which *to make* is the principal part, and its adjunct, the object *appearance,* modified by *their.*

When sickness, infirmity, or reverse of fortune, affects us, the sincerity of friendship is proved.

When the Creator had finished his labor on our planet, his last and noblest work being man, he conferred on him a partnership in his labors.

Loose conversation operates on the soul, as poison does on the body.

When Education had proceeded, in this manner, to the part of mountain where the declivity began to grow craggy, she resigned her charge to two powers of superior aspect.

While I was musing on this miserable scene, my protector called out to me, "Remember, Theodore, and be wise, and let not Habit prevail against thee."

While this thought passed over my mind, I lost sight of the remotest star, and the last glimmering of light was quenched in utter darkness. The agonies of despair every moment increased, as every moment augmented my distance from the last habitable world. I reflected with intolerable anguish, that, when ten thousand thousand years had carried me beyond the reach of all but that Power who fills infinitude, I should still look forward into an immense abyss of darkness, through which I should still drive without succor and without society, farther and farther still, forever and forever.

> Ages elapsed ere Homer's lamp appeared,
> And ages ere the Mantuan swan was heard.
> To carry nature lengths unknown before,
> To give a Milton birth, asked ages more.

EXERCISE XIII.—THE EXPLANATORY CLAUSE.

EXAMPLE ANALYZED.

" Why is it that to man have been given passions which he cannot tame, and which sink him below the brute ?"

ANALYSIS.—This is a complex interrogative sentence.
The subject is *it ;* the predicate is *is ;* the adjunct of the subject is the complex explanatory clause, *to man have been given passions which he cannot tame, and which sink him below ... brute ;* the connective is *that ;* the adjunct of the predicate is *u..y.*
The subject of the explanatory clause is *passions ;* the predicate is *have been given.* The adjuncts of the subject are the simple adjective clauses, *which he cannot tame,* and *which sink him below the brute.*
[Each to be analyzed as in previous exercises.]

It was the fate of Dr. Bentley, that every work, executed or projected by him, should be assailed.

It is surprising in what countless swarms the bees have overspread the far West, within but a moderate number of years.

To tell you the *why* and the *wherefore* would take too long ; suffice it to say, that they hate us with a deadly hatred.

Seeing these, I at length comprehended the meaning of those terrible words, " Must we kill them both ?"

It might be expected, that humanity itself would prevent them from breaking into the last retreat of the unfortunate.

It is an exquisite and beautiful thing in our nature, that when the heart is touched and softened by some tranquil happiness or affectionate feeling, the memory of the dead comes over it most powerfully and irresistibly.

Interesting it is to observe how certainly all deep feelings agree in this, that they seek for solitude, and are nursed by solitude.

Is it because foreigners are in a condition to set our malice at defiance, that we are willing to contract engagements of friendship ?

See ! and confess, one comfort still must rise ;
'Tis this, though man's a fool, yet God is wise.

Better for us, perhaps, it might appear,
Were there all harmony, all virtue here ;
That never air nor ocean felt the wind,
That never passion discompos'd the mind.

EXERCISE XIV.—THE PARENTHETICAL CLAUSE.

EXAMPLE ANALYZED.

" The virtuous man, it has been beautifully said, proceeds without constraint in the path of his duty."

ANALYSIS.—This is a compound declarative sentence ; composed of the simple clause, *The virtuous man proceeds without constraint in the path of his duty,* and the parenthetical clause, *It has been beautifully said.* [Let the pupil analyze each clause as in the preceding exercises.]

OBS.—Sentences of this form may often be analyzed by considering the parenthetical clause, the principal one, and the rest of the sentence depend-

ent upon it. The mode of analysis, indicated in the example, is, however,
preferable ; as, although the parenthetical clause is united in construction
with the other part of the sentence, it is not necessary to complete the sense.

How dangerous soever idleness may be, are there not pleasures, it may be said, which attend it ?

" I leave my second son, Andrew," said the expiring miser,
" my whole estate ; and desire him to be frugal."

" Go forth," it had been said to Elijah, " and stand upon the
mount before the Lord."

" I think, boys," said the schoolmaster, when the clock
struck twelve, " that I shall give you an extra half-holiday this
afternoon."

" You remember my garden, Henry," whispered the old
man, anxious to rouse him, for a dullness seemed gathering
upon the child, " and how pleasant it used to be in the evening-
time ?"

" Therefore," said he, " hath it in all confidence been ordered
by the Commons of Great Britain, that I impeach Warren
Hastings of high crimes and misdemeanors."

" Oh, no," said the Earth, " thou shalt not lie,
Neglected and lone, on my lap to die,
Thou fine and delicate child of the sky."

No further seek his merits to disclose,
Or draw his frailties from their dread abode,
(There they alike in trembling hope repose,)
The bosom of his Father, and his God.

EXERCISE XV.—COMPOUND SENTENCES.

Obs. 1.—In analyzing compound sentences, at this stage of the pupil's
progress, the *leading clause* should be distinguished from the *subordinate
clause.* It must, however, be understood that the dependence of the latter
upon the former, is *logical,* not *grammatical,* differing in this respect altogether from the relation of the *principal* and the *dependent* clause of a complex sentence, which is purely grammatical, since the latter is an adjunct,
or used as one of the principal parts, in the principal clause.

Obs. 2.—Some clauses are simply connected without logical or grammatical
dependence. They may then be called *coördinate clauses.*

[☞ In the following examples of analysis, for the purpose of abbreviation, and in order to furnish the pupil with a ready method of clearly representing, in written exercises, the parts of a sentence and their relations, the
compound clauses or *members* are marked by Capitals ; the *simple clauses,* by
numerals ; and the *phrases,* by small letters. When these are all written
out in the order in which they occur, care being taken to unite in brackets
dependent clauses contained in the same sentence or member, the character
and composition of the sentence analyzed will be exhibited.

According to this mode of representation, a simple sentence would, of
course, have no numerical or literal designation ; 1 would indicate a complex
sentence with a simple dependent clause ; 1, 2, a compound sentence consisting of two simple clauses, but if enclosed in brackets thus [1, 2], a com-

plex sentence containing two dependent clauses; A, 1, 2, B, 3, 4, a compound sentence composed of two compound members; but A, [1, 2], B, [3. 4], a compound sentence composed of two complex members, each containing two dependent clauses; A, 1, B, 2, a compound sentence composed of two complex members, each containing one dependent clause; A, 1, 2, B, 3, a compound sentence composed of a compound and a complex member; A, 1, B, 2, 3, a compound sentence containing a complex and a compound member; A, B, 1, a complex sentence containing a complex dependent member, which itself contains a complex dependent member; and so on.

This mode of presenting to the eye the general conformation of a sentence, its members, clauses, etc., in their order and, partially, their dependence, will be found easy after the previous practice, and cannot fail to be useful. In the forms of analysis given, S. stands for subject; P., for predicate; O., for object; Att., for attribute; Ad., for adjunct.]

EXAMPLES ANALYZED.

1. "Let him that hastens to be rich, take heed lest he suddenly become poor."

ANALYSIS.—Compound imperative sentence; consisting of
    A. (Leading) *Let him that hastens to be rich, take heed ;*
    1. (Subordinate) *He suddenly become poor.* Connective, *lest.*
  A. Complex imperative member.
    S. *Thou* (understood); P. *let ;* O. *him that hastens to be rich, take heed.* (B.)
  B. Complex infinitive member.
    S. *him ;* P. *take ;* O. *heed.*
    Ad. S. *that hastens to be rich.*   (2).
  2. Simple adjective clause.
    S. *that ;* P. *hastens ;* Ad. P. *to be rich.*   (a).
  a. Simple adverbial phrase.
    Prin. part, *to be ;* Ad. *rich* (indefinite attribute).
  1. Simple clause.
    S. *he ;* P. *become ;* Att. *poor ;* Ad. P. *suddenly.*

2. "Say not thou, ' I will recompense evil;' but wait on the Lord, and he shall save thee."

ANALYSIS.—Compound imperative sentence; consisting of two coördinate members:
    A. *Say not thou, " I will recompense evil."*
    B. *Wait on the Lord, and he shall save thee.* Con. *but.*
  A. Complex imperative member.
    S. *Thou ;* P. *say ;* O. *I will recompense evil* (1); Ad. P. *not.*
  1. Simple declarative clause.
    S. *I ;* P. *will recompense ;* O. *evil.*
  B. Compound imperative member.
    2. *Wait on the Lord.*
    3. *He shall save thee ;* connective, *and.*
  2. Simple imperative clause.
    S. *Thou* (understood); P. *wait ;* Ad. P. *on the Lord.*   (a).
  a. Simple adverbial phrase.
    Prin. part, *Lord ;* Ad. *the.*
  3. Simple declarative clause.
    S. *He ;* P. *shall save ;* O. *thee.*

If thine enemy be hungry, give him bread to eat ; if he be thirsty, give him water to drink.

If the mind were left uncultivated, though nothing else should find entrance, vice certainly would.

While riotous indulgence enervates both the body and the mind, purity and virtue heighten all the powers of human fruition.

If the King were present, Cleon, there would be no need of my answering to what thou hast just proposed.

He seems to have made an injudicious choice, though he is esteemed a sensible man.

The person he chanced to see, was, to appearance, an old, sordid, blind man ; but, upon his following him from place to place, he at last found, by his own confession, that he was Plutus, the god of riches.

I know not what course others may take, but as for me, give me liberty, or give me death.

Let any one resolve always to do right *now*, leaving *then* to do as it can, and if he were to live to the age of Methuselah, he would never do wrong ; but the common error is to resolve to act right after breakfast, or after dinner, or to-morrow morning, or *next time ;* but *now, just now, this once,* we must go on the same as ever.

It seems easier to do right to-morrow than to-day, merely because we forget, that when to-morrow comes, *then* will be *now.*

> The lamb thy riot dooms to bleed to-day,
> Had he thy reason, would he skip and play ?

> Inspiring thought of rapture yet to be !
> The tears of love were hopeless but for thee !
> If in that frame no deathless spirit dwell,
> If that faint murmur be the last farewell,
> If fate unite the faithful but to part,
> Why is their memory sacred to the heart ?

EXERCISE XVI.—MISCELLANEOUS SENTENCES.

EXAMPLES ANALYZED.

1. "Rasselas could not catch the fugitives, with his utmost efforts ; but, resolving to weary, by perseverance, him whom he could not surpass in speed, he pressed on till the foot of the mountain stopped his course."—*Johnson.*

ANALYSIS.—Compound declarative sentence :
1. *Rasselas could not catch the fugitive with his utmost efforts ;*
A. *Resolving to weary . . . . course.* Connective, *but.*
1. Simple declarative clause.
S. *Rasselas ;* P. *could catch ;* O. *fugitive.*
Ad. P. *not, with his utmost efforts* (a); Ad. O. *the.*
a. Simple adverbial phrase.
Prin. part, *efforts ;* Ad. *his* and *utmost.*
A. Complex declarative member.

S. *He ;* P. *pressed.*
Ad. S. *resolving to weary, by perseverance, him . . . . speed* (b) ;
Ad. P. *on,* and *till the foot of the mountain stopped his course* (2).
b. Complex adjective phrase.
Prin. part, *resolving ;* Ad. *to weary . . . . speed* (c).
c. Complex objective phrase.
Prin. part, *to weary ;* Ad. *him* (obj.) and *by perseverance ;* Ad. of
him, whom . . . . speed (8).
3. Simple adjective clause.
S. *He ;* P. *could surpass ;* O. *whom ;* Ad. P. *not* and *in speed.*
2. Simple adverbial clause.
S. *foot ;* P. *stopped ;* O. *course.*
Ad. S. *the, of the mountain ;* Ad. P. *till ;* Ad. O. *his ;* Connective, *till.*

2. " There is strong reason to suspect that some able Whig
politicians, who thought it dangerous to relax, at that moment,
the laws against political offences, but who could not, without
incurring the charge of inconsistency, declare themselves adverse to relaxation, had conceived a hope that they might, by
fomenting the dispute about the court of the lord high steward,
defer for at least a year the passing of a bill which they dis-
liked, and yet could not decently oppose."—*Macauley.*

ANALYSIS.—Complex, declarative sentence :
S. *Reason ;* P. *is.*
Ad. S. *strong, to suspect . . . . oppose ;* (a) Ad. P. *there.*
a. Complex adjective phrase.
Prin. part, *to suspect ;* Ad. (object), *Some able . . . . oppose ;* (A)
Con. *that.*
A. Complex object clause.
S. *Politicians ;* P. *had conceived ;* O. *hope.*
Ad. S. *Some, able, Whig,* and the two coördinate clauses, connected
by *but, Who thought . . . . offences,* (B), *Who could . . . . re-
laxation* (C) ; Ad. O. *They might . . . . oppose* (D). Con. *that.*
B. Complex adjective clause.
S. *who ;* P. *thought ;* O. *It (to be) dangerous . . . . offences* (1).
1. Simple object clause, of the infinitive form.
S. *It ;* P. *to be* (und.) ; At. *dangerous.*
Ad. S. *to relax . . . . offences.* (b)
b. Complex explanatory phrase.
Prin. part, *to relax ;* Ad. (primary), *at that moment,* (c) and *laws ;*
(Secondary), *the,* and *against political offences.* (d)
c. Simple adverbial phrase.
d. Simple adjective phrase, modifying *laws.*
C. Complex adjective clause.
S. *Who ;* P. *could declare ;* O. *themselves (to be) adverse to relaxa-
tion* (2).
Ad. P. *not, without incurring the charge of inconsistency* (e).
e. Complex adverbial phrase.
Prin. part, *incurring ;* Ad. (primary), *charge ;* (secondary), *the,* and
of inconsistency.
2. Simple object clause, infinitive form.
S. *themselves ;* P. *to be* (und.) ; Att. *adverse ;* Ad. Att. *to relaxation.*
D. Complex adjective clause.
S. *they ;* P. *might defer ;* O. *passing.*
Ad. P. *by fomenting . . . . steward* (f), *for at least a year* (g) ;
Ad. O. *the,* and *of a bill which . . . . oppose* (h).
f. Complex adverbial phrase.
Prin. part, *fomenting ;* Ad. (primary), *dispute,* (secondary), *the,* and
about . . . . steward (i).

7

    i. Complex adjective phrase.
      Prin. part, *court ;* Ad. *the,* and *of the lord high steward* (k).
    k. Simple adjective phrase.
    g. Simple adverbial phrase.
      Prin. part, *year ;* Ad. *a. At least,* independent phrase.
    h. Complex adjective phrase.
      Prin. part, *bill ;* Ad. *a,* and *which . . . . oppose* (3).
    3. Simple adjective clause, with a compound predicate.
      S. *they ;* P. (compound), *disliked,* and *could oppose*; Con. *and ;* O. *which.*
      Ad. P. (second), *not* and *decently.*

3.   What wonder, when
    Millions of fierce encount'ring Angels fought
    On either side, the least of whom could wield
    These elements, and arm him with the force
    Of all their regions? How much more of pow'r
    Army 'gainst army numberless, to raise
    Dreadful combustion warring, and disturb,
    Though not destroy, their happy native seat ;
    Had not th' Eternal King omnipotent
    From his strong hold of Heav'n high over-ruled
    And limited their might ; though number'd such
    As each divided legion might have seem'd
    A num'rous host, in strength each armed band
    A legion, led in fight yet leader seem'd
    Each warrior single as in chief, expert
    When to advance, or stand, or turn the sway
    Of battle, open when, and when to close
    The ridges of grim war.—*Paradise Lost,* VI., 219.

ANALYSIS.—The first period which terminates at *regions,* is a compound interrogative sentence.
    1. *What wonder (should there be)?* A. *When . . . . regions ;* Con. *when* (used as a conjunction).
    1. Simple interrogative clause.
    A. Compound declarative member.
    2. *When millions . . . . side ;* 3. *The least . . . . regions*; Con. *whom.*
The second period, comprising the remainder of the passage, is a compound exclamatory sentence.
    1. *How . . . . seat ;* A. *Had . . . . grim war ;* Con. *if* (understood).
    1. Simple exclamatory clause.
      S. *army ;* P. *would have wielded* (understood) ; O. *power.*
      Ad. S. *numberless,* and *warring against (numberless) army ;* Ad. O. *to raise dreadful combustion, and disturb, though not destroy their happy native seat.*
    A. Compound member.
    2. *Had . . . . might ;* B. *Though . . . . war ;* Con. *though.*
    2. Simple clause, with a compound predicate.
    B. Compound declarative member.
    3. *(They were) number'd such ;*
    C. *Each divided legion . . . . war ;* Con. *as* (for *that*).
    3. Simple declarative clause.
    C. Compound declarative member.
    4. *Each divided legion . . . . host ;*
    5. *In strength . . . . legion ;*

D. *Led in fight* . . . . *war.* No connective.
4. 5. Simple declarative clauses.
    D. Compound delarative member.
      E. *Each single warrior seemed as a leader in chief, expert* . . . . *war ;*
      6. (*He was*) *led in fight.* Connectives (correspond.), *though* and *yet.*
    E. Complex declarative member.
      S. *Warrior ;* P. *seemed ;* Att. *leader* (connected to the subject by *as*).
      Ad. S. *each, single ;* Ad. Att. *a, in chief,* and *expert ;* Ad. of *expert,*
      When to advance . . . . *war* (a).
    a. Compound adverbial phrase.
      b. *When to advance ;* c. *when to stand ;* d. *when to turn the sway of battle ;* e. *when to open and when to close the ridges of grim war.*

☞ [*Let the pupil be required to analyze and parse orally, according to the Praxis, the sentences in the following paragraphs, or to prepare a written analysis of each, according to the method, indicated in the examples, and explained in the Remark on page* 142.]

1. Let the ambitious, whether soldiers, tribunes, or kings, reflect, that if there are mercenary soldiers to serve them, and flatterers to excuse them while they reign, there is the conscience of humanity afterwards to judge them, and pity to detest them.—*Lamartine.*

2. Some, in their discourse, desire rather commendation of wit, in being able to hold all arguments, than of judgment in discerning what is true ; as if it were a praise to know what might be said, and not what should be thought.—*Bacon.*

3. If all the means of education which are scattered over the world, and if all the philosophers and teachers of ancient and modern times, were to be collected together, and made to bring their combined efforts to bear upon an individual, all they could do would be to afford the opportunity of improvement.—*Degerando.*

4. Dreams are the bright creatures of poem and legend, who sport on earth in the night-season, and melt away in the first beams of the sun, which lights grim Care and stern Reality in their daily pilgrimage through the world.—*Dickens.*

5. Montaigne saith prettily, when he inquired the reason, why the word of the lie should be such a disgrace and such an odious charge. Saith he, " If it be well weighed, to say that a man lieth, is as much to say, as that he is brave towards God, and a coward towards men."—*Bacon.*

6. Dear sensibility ! source inexhausted of all that is precious in our joys, or costly in our sorrows, thou chainest thy martyr down upon his bed of straw, and 'tis thou who lift'st

him up to heaven! Eternal fountain of our feeling! 'tis here
I trace thee, and this is thy "*divinity which stirs within me ;*"
not that, in some sad and sickening moments, "*my soul shrinks
back upon herself, and startles at destruction!*" (mere pomp
of words!) but that I feel some generous cares beyond myself.
All comes from thee, great—great Sensorium of the world!
which vibrates, if a hair of our heads but falls to the ground,
in the remotest desert of thy creation.—*Sterne.*

7. On the fourth day of creation, when the sun after a glorious, but solitary course, went down in the evening, and darkness began to gather over the face of the uninhabited globe,
already arrayed in the exuberance of vegetation, and prepared
by the diversity of land and water, for the abode of uncreated
animals and man,—a star, single and beautiful, stepped forth
into the firmament. Trembling with wonder and delight in
new-found existence, she looked abroad, and beheld nothing, in
heaven or on earth, resembling herself. But she was not long
alone; now one, then another, here a third, there a fourth
resplendent companion had joined her, till, light after light
stealing through the gloom, in the lapse of an hour, the whole
hemisphere was brilliantly bespangled.—*Montgomery.*

8. To learn A, B, C, is felt to be extremely irksome by the
infant, who cannot comprehend what it is for. The boy, forced
to school, cons over his dull lesson because he must, but feels
no amusement or satisfaction in it. The labor he is obliged to
undergo is not small; the privations of pleasure and activity,
he regrets still more; and all for what? To learn what he
does not like; to force into his mind words to which he at-
taches no ideas, or ideas which appear to him to be of no value;
[because] he cannot put them to any proper use. Youth is
not aware, that not for present use is all this designed. The
dull, laborious, but necessary routine, like plowing and sowing
the land, is in hopes of reaping abundance, at some not very
distant season. Education is not the end, but only the means.
—*Taylor.*

9. Fired with a perusal of the Abyssinian pilgrim's explora-
tory ramblings after the cradle of the infant Nilus, we well
remember, on one fine summer holiday (a "whole day's leave"
we called it at Christ's Hospital), sallying forth at rise of sun,
not very well provisioned either for such an undertaking, to
trace the current of the New River—Middletonian stream!—
to its scaturient source, as we had read, in meadows by fair
Amwell.—*Lamb.*

10. The voice of the world had whispered to Columbus that

the world is one; and as he went forth toward the west, ploughing a wave which no European keel had entered, it was his high purpose not merely to open new paths to islands or to continents, but to bring together the ends of the earth, and join all nations in commerce and spiritual life.—*Bancroft.*

11. To a limited apprehension, it would seem as if the greater part of the existence here allotted us, were little more than an apprenticeship to the business of living; and that, if ever we come to understand our authentic position and relations in the world, and how our time and talents might have been wisely and most effectually employed, it is at a stage of life, when the journey is drawing to a close, and hardly an opportunity is left us to turn what we have been learning to account.—*R. Chambers.*

12. We never, in a moral way, applaud or blame either ourselves or others for what we enjoy or what we suffer; or for having impressions made upon us, which we consider as being altogether out of our power: but only for what we do, or would have done had it been in our power; or for what we leave undone which we might have done, or would have left undone though we could have done it.—*Bp. Butler.*

13. Resisting or not, however, we are doomed to suffer a bitter pang as often as the irrecoverable flight of our time is brought home with keenness to our hearts. The spectacle of a lady floating over the sea in a boat, and waking suddenly from sleep to find her magnificent ropes of pearl necklace, by some accident detached at one end from its fastenings, the loose string hanging down into the water, and pearl after pearl slipping off forever into the abyss, brings before us the sadness of the case.—*De Quincey.*

14. Glowing with a vivid conception of these truths, so wonderful and so indisputable, let me ask, whether, among all the spectacles which earth presents, and which angels might look down upon with an ecstasy too deep for utterance, is there one fairer and more enrapturing to the sight than that of a young man, just fresh from the Creator's hands, and with the unspent energies of the coming eternity wrapped up in his bosom, surveying and recounting, in the solitude of his closet, or in the darkness of midnight, the mighty gifts with which he has been endowed, and the magnificent career of usefulness and of blessedness, which has been opened before him; and resolving, with one all-concentrating and all-hallowing vow, that he will live, true to the noblest capacities of his being, and in obedience to the highest law of his nature!—*Horace Mann.*

13*

15. Could every man apply himself to [the] employments which are most suited to his capabilities, and, in his appointed calling, work only with a view to serviceable, sincere, and ennobling results, the measure of his achievements might still, perchance, fall short of his original aspirations; but, being commensurate with his powers, and conformable to the eternal laws, it could not fail to yield him that assurance of security and contentment which, by necessity, proceeds from all faithfulness of action.—*Chambers.*

16. By the immortal gods, I wish (pardon me, O my country! for I fear what I shall say out of a pious regard for Milo may be deemed impiety against thee) that Clodius not only lived, but were prætor, consul, dictator, rather than [that I should] be witness to such a scene as this. Immortal gods! how brave a man is that, and how worthy of being preserved by you! By no means, he cries; the ruffian met with the punishment he deserved; and let me, if it must be so, suffer the punishment I have not deserved.—*Duncan's Cicero.*

17. Where American liberty raised its first voice, and where its youth was nurtured and sustained, there it still lives, in the strength of its manhood, and full of its original spirit. If discord and disunion shall wound it; if party strife and blind ambition shall hawk at and tear it; if folly and madness, if uneasiness under salutary restraint, shall succeed to separate it from that Union, by which alone its existence is made sure, it will stand, in the end, by the side of that cradle in which its infancy was rocked; it will stretch forth its arm with whatever of vigor it may still retain, over the friends who gathered around it; and it will fall at last, if fall it must, amid the proudest monuments of its glory, and on the very spot of its origin.—*Webster.*

18. So live, that when thy summons comes to join
The innumerable caravan, that moves
To the pale realms of shade, where each shall take
His chamber in the silent halls of death,
Thou go not like the quarry-slave at night,
Scourged to his dungeon, but, sustained and soothed
By an unfaltering trust, approach thy grave,
Like one who wraps the drapery of his couch
About him, and lies down to pleasant dreams.—*Bryant.*

19. Of chance or change, O let not man complain,
Else shall he never, never cease to wail;
For, from the imperial dome, to where the swain
Rears the lone cottage in the silent dale,

All feel th' assaults of Fortune's fickle gale;
Art, empire, Earth itself, to change are doom'd;
Earthquakes have raised to heaven the humble vale,
And gulfs the mountain's mighty mass entomb'd;
And where th' Atlantic rolls, wide continents have bloom'd.
Beattie.

20. The One remains, the many change and pass;
Heaven's light forever shines, Earth's shadows fly;
Life, like a dome of many-colored glass,
Stains the white radiance of Eternity,
Until Death tramples it to fragments.—Die,
If thou wouldst be with that which thou dost seek!
Follow where all is fled!—Rome's azure sky,
Flowers, ruins, statues, music,—words are weak
The glory they transfuse, with fitting truth to speak.
Shelley.

21.   The honey-bee, that wanders all day long
The field, the woodland, and the garden o'er,
To gather in his fragrant winter store,
Humming in calm content his quiet song,
Seeks not alone the rose's glowing breast,
The lily's dainty cup, the violet's lips;
But from all rank and noisome weeds he sips
The single drop of sweetness ever pressed
Within the poisoned chalice.   Thus, if we
Seek only to draw forth the hidden sweet
In all the varied human flowers we meet
In the wide garden of humanity,
And, like the bee, if home the spoil we bear,
Hived in our hearts, it turns to nectar there.
A. C. Lynch.

22. And Ardennes waves above them her green leaves,
Dewy with Nature's tear-drops, as they pass,
Grieving, if aught inanimate ere grieves,
Over the unreturning brave,—alas!
Ere evening to be trodden like the grass,
Which now beneath them, but above shall grow
In its next verdure, when the fiery mass
Of living valor, rolling on the foe,
And burning with high hope, shall moulder cold and low.
Byron.

23. Heaven from all creatures hides the book of fate,
All but the page prescribed, their present state;

From brutes what men, from men what spirits know ;
Or who could suffer being here below ?
The lamb thy riot dooms to bleed to-day,
Had he thy reason, would he skip and play ?
Pleas'd to the last, he crops the flowery food,
And licks the hand just rais'd to shed his blood.
Oh blindness to the future ! kindly given
That each may fill the circle mark'd by Heaven,
Who sees with equal eye, as God of all,
A hero perish, or a sparrow fall,
Atoms or systems into ruin hurl'd,
And now a bubble burst, and now a world.—*Pope.*

24. As thus the snows arise ; and, foul and fierce,
All Winter drives along the darkened air ;
In his own loose-revolving fields, the swain
Disaster'd stands ; sees other hills ascend,
Of unknown joyless brow ; and other scenes,
Of horrid prospect, shag the trackless plain ;
Nor finds the river, nor the forest, hid
Beneath the formless wild ; but wanders on
From hill to dale, still more and more astray ;
Impatient flouncing through the drifted heaps,
Stung with the thoughts of home ; the thoughts of home
Rush on his nerves, and call their vigor forth
In many a vain attempt.— *Thomson.*

25. O treacherous conscience ! while she seems to sleep
On rose and myrtle, lull'd with syren song ;
While she seems, nodding o'er her charge, to drop
On headlong appetite the slacken'd reign,
And give us up to license, unrecall'd,
Unmark'd ;—see, from behind her secret stand,*
The sly informer minutes every fault,
And her dread diary with horror fills.
Not the gross act alone employs her pen :
She reconnoitres fancy's airy band,
A watchful foe ! the formidable spy,
Listening, o'erhears the whispers of our camp ;
Our dawning purposes of heart explores,
And steals our embryos of iniquity.— *Young.*

26. The pulpit, therefore, (and I name it, filled
With solemn awe, that bids me well beware
With what intent I touch that holy thing,)—

---

* See Obs. 3, page 112.

The pulpit (when the satirist has, at last,
Strutting and vaporing in an empty school,
Spent all his force and made no proselyte)—
I say the pulpit (in the sober use
Of its legitimate, peculiar powers)
Must stand acknowledged, while the world shall stand,
The most important and effectual guard,
Support, and ornament of virtue's cause.
There stands the messenger of truth; there, stands
The legate of the skies; his theme, divine;
His office, sacred; his credentials, clear.
By him the violated law speaks out
Its thunders; and, by him, in strains as sweet
As angels use, the Gospel whispers peace.—*Cowper.*

27.   Look, as I blow this feather from my face,
And as the air blows it to me again,
Obeying with my wind when I do blow,
And yielding to another when it blows,
Commanded always by the greater gust;
Such is the lightness of you common men.
                                        Shakspeare.

28.   Nature never did betray
The heart that loved her; 'tis her privilege
Through all the years of this our life, to lead
From joy to joy; for she can so inform
The mind that is within us, so impress
With quietness and beauty, and so feed
With lofty thoughts, that neither evil tongues,
Rash judgments, nor the sneers of selfish men
Shall e'er prevail against us, or distrust
Our cheerful faith that all which we behold
Is full of blessings.— *Wordsworth.*

29.   O, Adam, one Almighty is, from whom
All things proceed, and up to him return,
If not depraved from good, created all
Such to perfection, one first matter all,
Endued with various forms, various degrees
Of substance, and in things that live, of life;
But more refined, more spirituous, and pure,
As nearer to him placed, or nearer tending
Each in their sev'ral active spheres assign'd,
Till body up to spirit work, in bounds
Proportion'd to each kind.—*Milton.*

7*

CHAPTER II.—RELATION AND AGREEMENT.

In this chapter and the next, the Rules of Syntax are again exhibited, in their former order, with Examples, Exceptions, Observations, Notes, and False Syntax. The Notes are all of them, in form and character, subordinate rules of syntax, designed for the detection of errors. The correction of the False Syntax placed under the rules and notes, will form an *oral exercise*, somewhat similar to that of parsing, and perhaps more useful.

Obs.—*Relation* and *Agreement* are taken together that the rules may stand in the order of the parts of speech. The latter is moreover naturally allied to the former. Seven of the ten parts of speech are, with a few exceptions, incapable of any agreement; of these, the *relation and use* must be explained in parsing; and all *necessary agreement* between any of the rest, is confined to words that *relate* to each other.

RULE I.—ARTICLES.

Articles relate to the nouns which they limit: as, " At *a* little distance from *the* ruins of *the* abbey, stands *an* aged elm."

EXCEPTION FIRST.

The definite article, used intensively, may relate to an *adjective* or *adverb* of the comparative or the superlative degree; as, " A land which was *the mightiest.*"—*Byron.* " *The farther* they proceeded, *the greater* appeared their alacrity."—*Dr. Johnson.* " He chooses it *the rather.*"—*Cowper.* [See Obs. 7th, next page.]

EXCEPTION SECOND.

The indefinite article is sometimes used to give a collective meaning to an *adjective of number;* as, " Thou hast *a few* names, even in Sardis."—*Rev.* " There are *a thousand* things which crowd into my memory."—*Spectator*, No. 468. [See Obs. 12th, next page.]

OBSERVATIONS ON RULE I.

Obs. 1.—Articles often relate to nouns *understood;* as, " The [*river*] Thames,"—" Pliny the younger" [*man*],—" The honourable [*body*], the Legislature,"—" The animal [*world*] and the vegetable world,"—" Neither to the right [*hand*] nor to the left" [*hand*].—*Bible.* " He was a good man, and a just" [*man*].—*Ib.* " The pride of swains Palemon was, the generous [*man*], and the rich" [*man*].—*Thomson.*

Obs. 2.—It is not always necessary *to repeat* the article before several nouns in the same construction : the same article serves sometimes to limit the signification of more than one noun ; but we doubt the propriety of ever construing two articles as relating to one and the same noun.

Obs. 3.—The article *precedes* its noun, and is never, by itself, placed after it ; as, " Passion is *the* drunkenness of *the* mind."—*Southey.*

Obs. 4.—When an *adjective* precedes the noun, the article is placed before the adjective, that its power may extend over that also ; as,

" *The* private path, *the* secret acts of men,
If noble, far *the* noblest of their lives."—*Young.*

Except the adjectives *all, such, many, what, both,* and those which are preceded by the adverbs *too, so, as,* or *how ;* as, *" All the* materials were bought
at *too dear a* rate."—" Like *many an* other poor wretch, I now suffer *all the*
ill consequences of *so foolish an* indulgence."

Obs. 5.—When the adjective is placed *after* the noun, the article generally
retains its place *before* the noun, and is not repeated before the adjective;
as, "*A* man ignorant of astronomy,"—" *The* primrose pale." In *Greek,* when
an adjective is placed after its noun, if the article is prefixed to the noun, it
is repeated before the adjective; as, 'Η πόλις ἡ μεγάλη, *The* city *the* great ; i. e.,
The great city.

Obs. 6.—Articles, according to their own definition, belong *before* their
nouns ; but the definite article and an adjective seem sometimes to be placed
after the noun to which they both relate: as, "Section *the* Fourth,"—" Henry
the Eighth." Such examples, however, may be supposed elliptical; and, if
they are so, the article, in *English,* can never be placed after its noun, nor
can two articles ever properly relate to one noun, in any particular construction of it.

Obs. 7.—The definite article is often prefixed to *comparatives* and *superlatives;* and its effect is, as *Murray* observes, (in the words of *Lowth,)* "to
mark the degree more strongly, and to define it *the* more precisely:" as,
" *The* oftener I see him, *the* more I respect him."—" A constitution *the* most
fit."—"A claim, *the* strongest, and *the* most easily comprehended."—" The
men *the* most difficult to be replaced." In these instances, the article seems
to be used *adverbially,* and to relate only to the *adjective* or *adverb* following
it; but after the *adjective,* the noun may be supplied.

Obs. 8.—The article *the* is applied to nouns of both numbers ; as, *The* man,
the men ;—*The* good boy, *the* good boys.

Obs. 9.—The article *the* is generally prefixed to adjectives that are used, by
ellipsis, as nouns ; as,

> " *The* great, *the* gay, shall they partake
> The heav'n that thou alone canst make ?"—*Cowper.*

Obs. 10.—The article *the* is sometimes elegantly used in stead of a possessive pronoun; as, " Men who have not bowed *the* knee to the image of
Baal."—*Rom.,* xi, 4.

Obs. 11.—*An* or *a* implies one, and belongs to nouns of the singular number only; as, *A* man, *a* good boy.

Obs. 12.—*An* or *a* is sometimes put before an adjective of number, when
the noun following is plural; as, "*A* few days,"—"*A* hundred sheep,"—
"There are *a* great many adjectives."—*Dr. Adam.* In these cases, the article seems to relate only to the *adjective.* Some grammarians however call
these words of number *nouns,* and suppose an ellipsis of the preposition *of.*
Murray and many others call them *adjectives,* and suppose a peculiarity of
construction in the *article.*

Obs. 13.—*An* or *a* has sometimes the import of *each* or *every ;* as, "He
came twice *a* year." The article in this sense with a preposition understood,
is preferable to the mercantile *per,* so frequently used ; as, " Fifty cents [for]
a bushel,"—rather than, "*per* bushel."

Obs. 14.—*A,* as prefixed to participles in *ing,* or used in composition, is a
preposition ; being, probably, the French *a,* signifying *to, at, on, in,* or *of ;* as,
"They burst out *a* laughing."—*M. Edgeworth.* " He is gone *a* hunting."—
"She lies *a*-bed all day."—" He stays out *a*-nights."—"They ride out *a*-
Sundays." *Shakspeare* often uses the prefix *a,* and sometimes in a manner
peculiar to himself; as, " Tom's *a* cold,"—"*a* weary."

Obs. 15.—*An* is sometimes a *conjunction,* signifying *if ;* as,

> " Nay, *an* thou'lt mouthe, I'll rant as well as thou."—*Shak.*

NOTES TO RULE I.

Note I.—When the indefinite article is required, *a* should
always be used before the sound of a consonant, and *an,* before

that of a vowel; as, "With the talents of *an* angel, *a* man
may be *a* fool."—*Young.*

Obs.—*An* was formerly used before all words beginning with *h*, and before
several other words which are now pronounced in such a manner as to require *a*: thus, we read in the Bible, "*An* house,"—"*an* hundred,"—"*an*
one,"—"*an* ewer,"—"*an* usurer."

Note II.—When nouns are joined in construction, without
a close connexion and common dependence, the article must
be repeated. The following sentence is therefore inaccurate:
"She never considered the quality, but merit of her visitors."
—*Wm. Penn. The* should be inserted before *merit.*

Note III.—When adjectives are connected, and the qualities belong to things individually different, though of the same
name, the article should be repeated: as, "*A* black and *a*
white horse;"—i. e., *two* horses, one black and the other white.

Note IV.—When adjectives are connected, and the qualities
all belong to the same thing or things, the article should not
be repeated: as, "*A* black and white horse;"—i. e., *one* horse,
piebald.

Obs. 1.—The reason of the two preceding notes is this: by a repetition of
the article before several adjectives in the same construction, a repetition of
the noun is implied; but without a repetition of the article, the adjectives
are confined to one and the same noun.

Obs. 2.—To avoid repetition, we sometimes, with one article, join inconsistent qualities to a *plural* noun; as, "The Old and New Testaments,"—
for, "*The* Old and *the* New Testament." But the phrases, "The Old and
New *Testament,*" and, "*The* Old and *the* New *Testaments,*" are both obviously incorrect.

Note V.—The article should not be used before the names
of virtues, vices, passions, arts, or sciences; before simple
proper names; or before any noun whose signification is sufficiently definite without it: as, "*Falsehood* is odious."—"*Iron*
is useful."—"*Beauty* is vain."

Note VI.—When titles are mentioned merely as titles, or
names of things merely as names or words, the article should
not be used; as, "He is styled *Marquis.*"—"Ought a teacher
to call his pupil *Master?*"

Note VII.—In expressing a comparison, if both nouns refer
to the same subject, the article should not be inserted; if to
different subjects, it should not be omitted: thus, if we say,
"He is a better teacher than poet," we compare different
qualifications of the same man; but if we say, "He is a better
teacher than *a* poet," we refer to different men.

Note VIII.—The definite article, or some other definitive,
is generally required before the antecedent to the pronoun *who*
or *which* in a restrictive clause; as, "*The* men who were present, consented."

NOTE IX.—The article is generally required in that construction which converts a participle into a verbal noun; as, *"The completing* of this, by *the working-out* of sin inherent, must be by the power and spirit of Christ, in the heart."— *Wm. Penn.* " They shall be *an abhorring* unto all flesh."— *Isaiah,* lxvi, 24.

NOTE X.—The article should not be prefixed to a participle that is not taken in all respects as a noun; as, " He made a mistake in *the* giving out the text." Expunge *the.*

FALSE SYNTAX UNDER RULE I.—ARTICLES.

[The Examples of False Syntax placed under the rules, are to be corrected *orally* by the pupil, according to the formules given, or according to others framed in like manner, and adapted to the several notes.]

Examples under Note 1.—*AN or A.*

He went into an house.

[FORMULE.—Not proper, because the article *an* is used before *house,* which begins with the sound of the consonant *h.* But, according to Note 1st under Rule 1st, " When the indefinite article is required, *a* should always be used before the sound of a consonant, and *an* before that of a vowel." Therefore, *an* should be *a;* thus, He went into *a* house.]

This is an hard saying.
A humble heart shall find favour.
Passing from an earthly to an heavenly diadem.
Few have the happiness of living with such an one.
She evinced an uniform adherence to the truth.
A hospital is an asylum for the sick.
This is truly an wonderful invention.
He is an younger man than we supposed.
An humorsome child is never long pleased.
A careless man is unfit for a hostler.

Under Note 2.—*Nouns Connected.*

Avoid rude sports : an eye is soon lost, or bone broken.
As the drop of the bucket and dust of the balance.
Not a word was uttered, nor sign given.
I despise not the doer, but deed.

Under Note 3.—*Adjectives Connected.*

What is the difference between the old and new method?
The sixth and tenth have a close resemblance.
Is Paris on the right hand or left?
Does Peru join the Atlantic or Pacific ocean?
He was influenced both by a just and generous principle.
The book was read by the old and young.
I have both the large and small grammar.
Are both the north and south line measured?

Are the north line and south both measured?
Are both the north and south lines measured?
Are both the north lines and south measured?

Under Note 4.—*Adjectives Connected.*

Is the north and the south line measured?
Are the two north and the south lines both measured?
A great and a good man looks beyond time.
They made but a weak and an ineffectual resistance.
The Allegany and the Monongahela rivers form the Ohio.
I rejoice that there is an other and a better world.
Were God to raise up an other such a man as Moses.
The light and the worthless kernels will float.

Under Note 5.—*Articles not Requisite.*

Cleon was an other sort of a man.
There is a species of an animal called a seal.
Let us wait in the patience and the quietness.
The contemplative mind delights in the silence.
Arithmetic is a branch of the mathematics.
You will never have an other such a chance.
I expected some such an answer.
And I persecuted this way unto the death.

Under Note 6.—*Titles and Names.*

He is entitled to the appellation of a gentleman.
Cromwell assumed the title of a Protector.
Her father is honoured with the title of an Earl.
The chief magistrate is styled a President.
The highest title in the state is that of the Governor.
"For the oak, the pine, and the ash, were names of whole
    classes of objects."—*Blair's Rhetoric*, p. 73.

Under Note 7.—*Comparisons.*

He is a better writer than a reader.
He was an abler mathematician than a linguist.
I should rather have an orange than apple.

Under Note 8.—*Nouns with Who or Which.*

Words which are signs of complex ideas, are liable to be mis-
    understood.
Carriages which were formerly in use, were very clumsy.
The place is not mentioned by geographers who wrote at that
    time.

Under Note 9.—Participial Nouns.

Means are always necessary to accomplishing of ends.
By seeing of the eye, and hearing of the ear, learn wisdom.
In keeping of his commandments, there is great reward.
For revealing of a secret, there is no remedy.
Have you no repugnance to torturing of animals?

Under Note 10.—Participles, not Nouns.

By the breaking the law, you dishonour the lawgiver.
An argument so weak is not worth the mentioning.
In the letting go our hope, we let all go.
Avoid the talking too much of your ancestors.
The cuckoo keeps the repeating her unvaried notes.
Forbear the boasting of what you can do.

RULE II.--NOMINATIVES.

A Noun or a Pronoun which is the subject of a finite
verb, must be in the nominative case: as,

"I know *thou* sayst it: says thy *life* the same?"—*Young.*

OBSERVATIONS ON RULE II.

Obs. 1.—To this rule there are *no exceptions.* And in connected language,
every nominative stands as the subject of some verb expressed or understood; except such as are put *in apposition* with other nominatives, according to Rule 3d—*after a verb,* according to Rule 21st—or *absolute,* according
to Rule 25th.

Obs. 2.—The subject, or nominative, is generally placed *before* the verb;
as, "*Peace dawned* upon his mind."—*Johnson.* "*What is written* in the
law?"—*Bible.*

Obs. 3.—But, in the following nine cases, the subject is usually placed
after the verb, or after the first auxiliary:—

1. When a question is asked, without an interrogative pronoun in the
nominative case; as, "*Shall mortals be* implacable?"—"What *art thou
doing?*"—*Hooke.*

2. When the verb is in the imperative mood; as, "*Go thou.*"

3. When an earnest wish, or other strong feeling is expressed; as, "*May
she be* happy!"—"How *were we struck!*"—*Young.*

4. When a supposition is made without a conjunction; as, "*Were it* true,
it would not injure us."

5. When *neither* or *nor,* signifying *and not,* precedes the verb; as, "This
was his fear; *nor was* his *apprehension* groundless."

6. When, for the sake of emphasis, some word or words are placed before
the verb, which more naturally come after it; as, "Here *am I.*"—"Narrow
is the *way.*"—"Silver and gold *have I* none; but such as I have, *give I* thee."
—*Bible.*

7. When the verb has no regimen, and is itself emphatical; as, "*Echo* the
mountains round."—*Thomson.*

8. When the verbs *say, think, reply,* and the like, introduce the parts of a
dialogue; as, "'Son of affliction,' *said Omar,* 'who art thou?' 'My name,'
replied the *stranger,* 'is Hassan.'"—*Johnson.*

9. When the adverb *there* precedes the verb; as, "There *lived* a *man.*"—
Montg. "In all worldly joys, there *is* a secret *wound.*"—*Owen.*

FALSE SYNTAX UNDER RULE II.—NOMINATIVES.

Thee must have been idle.

[FORMULE.—Not proper, because the objective pronoun *thee* is made the subject of the verb *must have been*. But, according to Rule 2d, "A noun or a pronoun which is the subject of a finite verb, must be in the nominative case." Therefore, *thee* should be *thou;* thus, *Thou* must have been idle.]

Him that is studious, will improve.

Them that seek wisdom, will be wise.

She and me are of the same age.

You are two or three years older than us.

Are not John and thee cousins?

I can write as handsomely as thee.

Nobody said so but him.

Whom dost thou think was there?

Who broke this slate? Me.

We are alone; here's none but thee and I.—*Shak.*

Them that honour me, I will honour; and them that despise me, shall be lightly esteemed.

He whom in that instance was deceived, is a man of sound judgement.

RULE III.—APPOSITION.

A Noun or a personal Pronoun used to explain a preceding noun or pronoun, is put, by apposition, in the same case: as,

"But *he*, our gracious *Master*, kind as just,
    Knowing our frame, remembers we are dust."—*Barbauld.*

OBSERVATIONS ON RULE III.

OBS. 1.—*Apposition* is the using of different words or appellations, to designate the same thing. *Apposition* also denotes the relation which exists between the words which are so employed. In parsing, rule third should be applied only to the *explanatory term;* because the case of the *principal term* depends on its relation to the rest of the sentence, and comes under some other rule.

OBS. 2.—To this rule, there are properly *no exceptions*. But there are many puzzling examples under it, which the following observations are designed to explain. The rule supposes the first word to be the principal term, with which the other is in apposition; and it generally is so: but the explanatory word is sometimes placed first, especially among the poets; as,

"From bright'ning fields of ether fair disclos'd,
    Child of the sun, refulgent *Summer* comes."—*Thomson.*

OBS. 3.—The pronouns of the *first* and *second* persons are often prefixed to nouns, merely to distinguish their person; as, "*I John* saw these things."—"This is the stone which was set at nought of *you builders*."—*Bible.* "His praise, *ye brooks*, attune."—*Thomson.* In this case of apposition, the words are closely united, and either of them may be taken as the explanatory term: the learner will find it easier to parse the *noun* by rule third.

OBS. 4.—When two or more nouns of the *possessive case* are put in apposition, the possessive termination added to one, denotes the case of both or all: as, "His *brother Philip's* wife;"—"*John* the *Baptist's* head;"—"At my *friend Johnson's,* the *bookseller."* By a repetition of the possessive sign, a distinct governing noun is implied, and the apposition is destroyed.

OBS. 5.—In like manner, a noun without the possessive sign, is sometimes put in apposition with a *pronoun of the possessive case;* as, "As an *author,* his ' Adventurer' is *his* capital work."—*Murray.*

> " Thus shall mankind *his* guardian care engage,
> The promised *father* of the future age."—*Pope.*

OBS. 6.—When a noun or a pronoun *is repeated* for the sake of emphasis, the word which is repeated, may properly be said to be in apposition with that which is first introduced ; as, "They have forsaken *me,* the *Fountain* of living waters, and hewed them out *cisterns,* broken *cisterns,* that can hold no water."—*Jer.,* ii, 13.

OBS. 7.—A noun is sometimes put in apposition to a *sentence ;* as, " He permitted me to consult his library—a *kindness* which I shall not forget."— *W. Allen.*

OBS. 8.—A *distributive term* in the singular number, is frequently construed in apposition with a comprehensive plural ; as, " *They* reap vanity, *every one* with his neighbour."—*Bible.* " Go ye *every man* unto his city."— *Ibid.* And sometimes a *plural word* is emphatically put after a series of particulars comprehended under it ; as, " Ambition, interest, honour, *all* concurred."—*Murray.* " Royalists, republicans, churchmen, sectaries, courtiers, patriots, *all parties* concurred in the illusion."—*Hume.*

OBS. 9.—To express a reciprocal action or relation, the pronominal adjectives *each other* and *one* an *other* are employed : as, " They love *each other ;*" —" They love *one* an *other."* The words, separately considered, are singular ; but, taken together, they imply plurality ; and they can be properly construed only after plurals, or singulars taken conjointly. *Each other* is usually applied to two objects ; and *one an other,* to more than two. The terms, though reciprocal, and closely united, are never in the same construction. If such expressions be analyzed, *each* and *one* will generally appear to be in the nominative case, and *other* in the objective ; as, " They love *each other ;*" i. e., *each* loves *the other. Each* is properly in apposition with *they,* and *other* is governed by the verb. The terms, however, admit of other constructions ; as, " Be ye helpers *one* of an *other."*—*Bible.* Here *one* is in apposition with *ye,* and *other* is governed by *of.* " Ye are *one* an *other's* joy."—*Ib.* Here *one* is in apposition with *ye,* and *other's* is in the possessive case, being governed by *joy.* " Love will make you *one* an *other's* joy." Here *one* is in the objective case, being in apposition with *you,* and *other's* is governed as before. The *Latin* terms *alius alium, alii alios,* &c., sufficiently confirm this doctrine.

OBS. 10.—The *common* and the *proper name* of an object are often associated, and put in apposition ; as, The river Thames,—The ship Albion,—The poet Cowper,—Lake Erie,—Cape May,—Mount Atlas. But the proper name of a *place,* when accompanied by the common name, is generally put in the objective case, and preceded by *of ;* as, The city *of* New York,—The land *of* Canaan.

OBS. 11.—The *several proper names* which distinguish an individual, are always in apposition, and should be taken together in parsing ; as, *William Pitt,*—*Marcus Tullius Cicero.*

OBS. 12.—When an object *acquires* a new name or character from the action of a verb, the new appellation is put in apposition with the object of the active verb, and in the nominative after the passive : as, " They named the *child John ;*"—" The *child* was named *John."*—" They elected *him president ;*" —"*He* was elected *president."* After the active verb, the acquired name must be parsed by Rule 3d ; after the passive, by Rule 21st.

FALSE SYNTAX UNDER RULE III.—APPOSITION.

I have received a letter from my cousin, she that was here last week.

[FORMULE.—Not proper, because the nominative pronoun *she* is used to explain the objective noun *cousin.* But, according to Rule 3d, "A noun or a personal pronoun

used to explain a preceding noun or pronoun, is put, by apposition, in the same case."
Therefore, *she* should be *her ;* thus, I have received a letter from my cousin, *her* that
was here last week.]

The book is a present from my brother Richard, he that keeps
the bookstore.

I am going to see my friends in the country, they that we met
at the ferry.

This dress was made by Catharine, the milliner, she that we
saw at work.

Dennis, the gardener, him that gave me the tulips, has promised me a piony.

Resolve me, why the cottager and king,
Him whom sea-sever'd realms obey, and him
Who steals his whole dominion from the waste,
Repelling winter blasts with mud and straw,
Disquieted alike, draw sigh for sigh.

RULE IV.—ADJECTIVES.

Adjectives relate to nouns or pronouns: as, "He is a
wise man, though *he* is *young.*"

EXCEPTION FIRST.

An adjective sometimes relates to a *phrase* or *sentence* which is made the
subject of an intervening verb; as, "*To insult the afflicted,* is *impious.*"—
Dillwyn. "*That he should refuse,* is not *strange.*"

EXCEPTION SECOND.

With an infinitive or a participle denoting being or action in the abstract,
an adjective is sometimes also taken *abstractly ;* (that is, without reference
to any particular noun, pronoun, or other subject;) as, "To be *sincere,* is to
be *wise, innocent,* and *safe.*"—*Hawkesworth.* "*Capacity* marks the abstract
quality of being *able* to receive or hold."—*Crabb's Synonymes.*

OBSERVATIONS ON RULE IV.

Obs. 1.—Adjectives often relate to nouns understood; as, "The nine"
[*muses*].—" Philip was one of the seven" [*deacons*].—*Acts,* xxi, 8. " He came
unto his own [*possessions*], and his own [*men*] received him not."—*John,* i,
11. " The Lord your God is God of gods, and Lord of lords, a great God, a
mighty [*God*], and a terrible" [*God*].—*Deut.,* x, 17.

Obs. 2.—In as much as *qualities* belong only to *things,* most grammarians
teach that every adjective belongs to some *noun* expressed or understood ;
and suppose a countless number of unnecessary ellipses. But it is evident
that in the construction of sentences, adjectives often relate immediately to
pronouns, and, through them, to the nouns they represent. This is still
more obviously the case, in some other languages, as may be seen by the
following examples, which retain something of the *Greek* idiom : "*All ye* are
brethren."—*Matt.,* xxiii, 8. " Whether of *them twain* did the will of his
father ?"—*Matt.,* xxi, 31.

Obs. 3.—When an adjective follows a finite verb, and is not followed by a
noun, it generally relates to the *subject* of the verb; as, "*I* am *glad* that the
door is made *wide.*"—" Every thing which is *false, vicious,* or *unworthy,* is
despicable to him, though all the world should approve it."—*Spectator,* No.

520.   Here *false*, *vicious*, and *unworthy*, relate to *which;* and *despicable* relates to *thing.*

OBS. 4.—When an adjective follows an infinitive or a participle, the noun or pronoun to which it relates, is sometimes before it, and sometimes after it, and often considerably remote; as, " A real gentleman cannot but practise those virtues *which*, by an intimate knowledge of mankind, he has found to be *useful* to them."—" He [a melancholy enthusiast] thinks *himself* obliged in duty to be *sad* and *disconsolate.*"—*Addison.* " He is scandalized at *youth* for being *lively*, and at *childhood* for being *playful.*"—*Id.* "But growing *weary* of one who almost walked him out of breath, *he* left him for Horace and Anacreon."—*Steele.*

OBS. 5.—Adjectives preceded by the definite article, are often used, by ellipsis, as having the force of *nouns.* They designate those classes of objects which are characterized by the qualities they express; and, in parsing, the noun may be supplied. They are most commonly of the plural number, and refer to *persons, places,* or *things*, understood; as, " The *careless* [persons] and the *imprudent*, the *giddy* and the *fickle*, the *ungrateful* and the *interested* everywhere meet us."—*Blair.*

> "Together let us beat this ample field,
>   Try what the *open* [places], what the *covert*, yield."—*Pope.*

OBS. 6.—The adjective is generally placed immediately *before its noun ;* as, " *Vain* man ! is grandeur given to *gay* attire ?"—*Beattie.*

OBS. 7.—Those adjectives which relate to *pronouns* most commonly *follow them ;* as, "They left *me weary* on a grassy turf."—*Milton.*

OBS. 8.—In the following instances, the adjective is placed *after the noun* to which it relates :

1. When other words depend on the adjective; as, " A mind *conscious of right*,"—" A wall *three feet thick.*"

2. When the quality results from the action of a verb; as, " Virtue renders life *happy.*"

3. When the adjective would thus be more clearly distinctive; as, " Goodness *infinite*,"—" Wisdom *unsearchable.*"

4. When a verb comes between the adjective and the noun; as, " Truth stands *independent* of all external things."—*Burgh.*

OBS. 9.—In some cases, the adjective may *either precede or follow* the noun; as,

1. In poetry; as,

> " Wilt thou to the *isles*
> *Atlantic*, to the *rich Hesperian clime*,
> Fly in the train of Autumn ?"—*Akenside.*

2. In some technical expressions; as, " A notary public," or, " A public notary."

3. When an adverb precedes the adjective; as, " A Being infinitely wise," or, " An infinitely wise Being."

4. When several adjectives belong to the same noun; as, " A woman, modest, sensible, and virtuous," or, " A modest, sensible, and virtuous woman."

OBS. 10.—An emphatic adjective *may be placed first* in the sentence, though it belong after the verb; as, " *Weighty* is the anger of the righteous."—*Bible.*

OBS. 11.—By an ellipsis of the noun, an adjective with a preposition before it, is sometimes *equivalent to an adverb ;* as, "*In particular ;*" that is, *in a particular manner ;* equivalent to "*particularly.*" In parsing, supply the ellipsis. [See *Obs.* 2*d, under Rule* xxii.]

NOTES TO RULE IV.

NOTE I.—Adjectives that imply unity or plurality, must agree with their nouns in number; as, *That* sort, *those* sorts.

NOTE II.—When the adjective is necessarily plural, or necessarily singular, the noun should be made so too; as, "*Twenty pounds*,"—not, "Twenty *pound ;*"—"*One session*,"—not, "One *sessions.*"

Obs. 1.—In some peculiar phrases, this rule appears to be disregarded; as, "*Two hundred pennyworth* of bread is not sufficient."—*John*, vi, 7. "*Twenty sail* of vessels ;"—"A *hundred head* of cattle."

Obs. 2.—To denote a collective number, a singular adjective may precede a plural one; as, "*One* hundred men,"—"*Every* six weeks,"—"*One* seven times."—*Dan.*, iii, 19.

Obs. 3.—To denote plurality, the adjective *many* may, in like manner, precede *an* or *a* with a *singular* noun; as,

"Full *many a flower is born* to blush unseen,
And waste *its* sweetness on the desert air."—*Gray.*

Note III —The reciprocal expression, *one an other*, should not be applied to *two* objects, nor *each other*, or *one the other*, to *more* than two : because reciprocity between two is some act or relation of each or one to *the other*, an object definite, and not of one to *an other*, which is indefinite; but reciprocity among three or more is of one, each, or every one, not to *one other* solely, or *the other* definitely, but to *others*, a plurality, or to *an other*, taken indefinitely and implying this plurality.

Note IV.—The comparative degree can only be used in reference to *two objects*, or classes of objects; the superlative compares one or more things with *all others* of the same class, whether few or many : as, "Edward is *taller* than James; he is the *largest* of my scholars."

Note V.—When the comparative degree is employed, the latter term of comparison should never *include* the former; as, "*Iron* is more useful than *all the metals.*"   It should be, "than *all the other metals.*"

Note VI.—When the superlative degree is employed, the latter term of comparison should never *exclude* the former; as, "A fondness for show, is, of all *other* follies, the most vain." The word *other* should be expunged.

Note VII.—Comparative terminations, and adverbs of degree, should not be applied to adjectives that are not susceptible of comparison; and all double comparatives and double superlatives should be avoided : as, "*So universal* a complaint :" say, "*So general.*"—"Some *less nobler* plunder :" say, "*less noble.*"—"The *most straitest* sect :" expunge *most.*

Note VIII.—When adjectives are connected by *and, or,* or *nor*, the shortest and simplest should in general be placed first; as, "He is *older* and *more respectable* than his brother."

Note IX.—An adjective and its noun may be taken as a compound term, to which other adjectives may be prefixed. The most distinguishing quality should be expressed next to the noun : as, "A fine young man,"—not, "A young fine man."

Note X.—In prose, the use of adjectives for adverbs, is improper: as, "He writes *elegant;*"—say, "*elegantly.*"

Obs. 1.—In *poetry*, an adjective relating to the noun or pronoun, is sometimes elegantly used in stead of an adverb qualifying the verb or participle; as,

> "To thee I bend the knee; to thee my thoughts
> *Continual* climb."—*Thomson.*

Obs. 2.—In order to determine, in difficult cases, whether an adjective or an adverb is required, the learner should carefully attend to the definitions of these parts of speech, and consider whether, in the case in question, *quality* or *manner* is to be expressed: if the former, an adjective is proper; if the latter, an adverb. The following examples will illustrate this point: "She looks *cold;*—she looks *coldly* on him."—" I sat *silent;*—I sat *silently* musing."—" Stand *firm;*—maintain your cause *firmly.*"

Note XI.—The pronoun *them* should never be used as an adjective in lieu of *those:* say, "I bought *those* books,"—not, "*them* books." This is a vulgar error.

Note XII.—When the pronominal adjectives, *this* and *that,* or *these* and *those,* are contrasted; *this* or *these* should represent the latter of the antecedent terms, and *that* or *those,* the former; as,

> "And, reason raise o'er instinct as you can,
> In *this* 'tis God directs, in *that* 'tis man."—*Pope.*

> "Farewell my friends! farewell my foes!
> My peace with *these,* my love with *those!*"—*Burns.*

Note XIII.—The pronominal adjectives *each, one, either,* and *neither,* are always in the third person singular; and, when they are the leading words in their clauses, they require verbs and pronouns, to agree with them accordingly: as, "*Each* of you *is* entitled to *his* share."—" Let no *one* deceive *himself.*"

Note XIV.—The pronominal adjectives *either* and *neither* relate to two things only; when more are referred to, *any* and *none* should be used in stead of them: as, "*Any* of the three;" —not, "*Either* of the three."—"*None* of the four;"—not, "*Neither* of the four."

Note XV.—Participial adjectives retain the termination, but not the government, of participles; when, therefore, they are followed by the objective case, a preposition must be inserted to govern it: as, "The man who is most *sparing of* his words, is generally most *deserving of* attention."

FALSE SYNTAX UNDER RULE IV.—ADJECTIVES.

Examples under Note 1.—Of Agreement.

Those sort of people you will find to be troublesome.

[FORMULE.—Not proper, because the adjective *those* is in the plural number, and does not agree with its noun *sort,* which is singular. But, according to Note 1st under Rule 4th, "Adjectives that imply unity or plurality, must agree with their nouns in number." Therefore, *those* should be *that;* thus, *That* sort of people you will find to be troublesome.]

Things of these sort are easily understood.
Who broke that tongs?
Where did I drop this scissors?
Bring out that oats.
Extinguish that embers.
I disregard this minutiæ.
Those kind of injuries we need not fear.
What was the height of those gallows which Haman erected?

Under Note 2.—Of Fixed Numbers.

We rode about ten mile an hour.
'Tis for a thousand pound.—*Cowper.*
How deep is the water? About six fathom.
The lot is twenty-five foot wide.
I have bought eight load of wood.

Under Note 3.—Of Reciprocals.

Two negatives in English destroy one another.—*Lowth.*
That the heathens tolerated each other, is allowed.
David and Jonathan loved one an other tenderly.
Words are derived from each other in various ways.
Teachers like to see their pupils polite to each other.
The Graces always hold the one the other by the hand.

Under Note 4.—Of Degrees.

He chose the latter of these three.
Trissyllables are often accented on the former syllable.
Which are the two more remarkable isthmuses in the world?

Under Note 5.—Of Comparatives.

The Scriptures are more valuable than any writings.
The Russian empire is more extensive than any government
    in the world.
Israel loved Joseph more than all his children, because he was
    the son of his old age.—*Gen.,* xxxvii, 3.

Under Note 6.—Of Superlatives.

Of all other ill habits idleness is the most incorrigible.
Eve was the fairest of all her daughters.
Hope is the most constant of all the other passions.

Under Note 7.—Extra Comparisons.

That opinion is too universal to be easily corrected.
Virtue confers the supremest dignity upon man.
How much more are ye better than the fowls!—*Luke,* xii.

Do not thou hasten above the Most Highest.—*Esdras*, iv.
This was the most unkindest cut of all.—*Shakspeare.*
The waters are more sooner and harder frozen.—*Verstegan.*
A more healthier place cannot be found.
The best and the most wisest men often meet with discouragements.

Under Note 8.—Adjectives Connected.

He showed us a more agreeable and easier way.
This was the most convincing and plainest argument.
Some of the most moderate and wisest of the senators.
This is an honourable and ancient fraternity.
There vice shall meet an irrevocable and fatal doom.

Under Note 9.—Adjectives Prefixed.

He is a young industrious man.
She has a new elegant house.
The two first classes have read.
The oldest two sons have removed to the westward.
England had not seen such an other king.—*Goldsmith.*

Under Note 10.—Adjectives for Adverbs.

She reads well and writes neat.
He was extreme prodigal.
They went, conformable to their engagement.
He speaks very fluent, and reasons justly.
The deepest streams run the most silent.
These appear to be finished the neatest.
He was scarce gone when you arrived.
I am exceeding sorry to hear of your misfortunes.
The work was uncommon well executed.
This is not such a large cargo as the last.
Thou knowst what a good horse mine is.
I cannot think so mean of him.
He acted much wiser than the others.

Under Note 11.—Them for Those.

I bought them books at a very low price.
Go and tell them boys to be still.
I have several copies: thou art welcome to them two.
Which of them three men is the most useful?

Under Note 12.—This and That.

Hope is as strong an incentive to action, as fear: this is the anticipation of good, that of evil.

The poor want some advantages which the rich enjoy; but we should not therefore account those happy, and these miserable.

> Memory and forecast just returns engage,
> This pointing back to youth, that on to age,

Under Note 13.—*Each, One, &c.*

Let each of them be heard in their turn.

On the Lord's day every one of us Christians keep the sabbath.—*Irenæus.*

Are either of these men known?

No: neither of them have any connexions here.

Under Note 14.—*Either and Neither.*

Did either of the company stop to assist you?

Here are six; but neither of them will answer.

Under Note 15.—*Participial Adjectives.*

Some crimes are thought deserving death.

Rudeness of speech is very unbecoming a gentleman.

To eat with unwashen hands, was disgusting a Jew.

> Leave then thy joys, unsuiting such an age,
> To a fresh comer, and resign the stage.—*Dryden.*

RULE V.—PRONOUNS.

A Pronoun must agree with its antecedent, or the noun or pronoun which it represents, in person, number, and gender: as, "This is the friend of *whom* I spoke; *he* has just arrived."—"This is the book *which* I bought; *it* is an excellent work."—"*Ye*, therefore, *who* love mercy, teach *your* sons to love *it* too."—*Cowper.*

EXCEPTION FIRST.

When a pronoun stands for some person or thing *indefinite* or *unknown* to the speaker, this rule is not strictly applicable; because the person, number, and gender, are rather assumed than regulated by an antecedent: as, "I do not care *who* knows it."—*Steele.* "*Who* touched me? Tell me *who* it was."

EXCEPTION SECOND.

The neuter pronoun *it* may be applied to a young child, or to other creatures masculine or feminine by nature, when they are not obviously distinguishable with regard to sex; as, "Which is the real friend to the *child*, the person who gives *it* the sweetmeats, or the person who, considering only *its* health, resists *its* importunities?"—*Opie.* "He loads the *animal*, he is showing me, with so many trappings and collars, that I cannot distinctly view *it*."—*Murray.* "The *nightingale* sings most sweetly when *it* sings in the night."—*Burke.*

EXCEPTION THIRD.

The pronoun *it* is often used without a definite reference to any antecedent, and is sometimes a mere expletive; as, "Whether she grapple *it* with the pride of philosophy."—*Chalmers.*

> "Come, and trip *it* as you go
> On the light fantastic toe."—*Milton.*

EXCEPTION FOURTH.

A singular antecedent with the adjective *many*, sometimes admits a plural pronoun, but never in the same clause; as,

> "In Hawick twinkled *many a light*,
> Behind him soon *they* set in night."—*W, Scott,*

EXCEPTION FIFTH.

When a plural pronoun is put by enallage for the singular, it does not agree with its noun in number, because it still requires a plural verb; as, "*We* [Lindley Murray] *have followed* those authors."—*Murray's Gram.*, 8vo, p. 29. "*We shall close our* remarks on this subject."—*Ib.* "My lord, *you* know I love *you*."—*Shakspeare.*

OBSERVATIONS ON RULE V.

Obs. 1.—The pronoun *we* is used by the speaker to represent himself and others, and is therefore plural. But it is sometimes used, by a sort of fiction, in stead of the singular, to intimate that the speaker is not alone in his opinions. Monarchs sometimes join it to a singular noun; as, "*We* Alexander, Autocrat of all the Russias." They also employ the compound *ourself*, which is not used by other people.

Obs. 2.—The pronoun *you*, though originally and properly plural, is now generally applied alike to one person or to more. [See *Obs. 2d*, page 71.] This usage, however it may seem to involve a solecism, is established by that authority against which the mere grammarian has scarcely a right to remonstrate. We do not, however, think it necessary or advisable, to encumber the conjugations, as some have done, by introducing this pronoun and the corresponding form of the verb, as singular. It is manifestly better to say that the plural is used *for* the singular, by the figure *Enallage*. This change has introduced the compound *yourself*, which is used in stead of *thyself*.

Obs. 3.—The general usage of the *French* is like that of the *English*, *you* for *thou;* but *Spanish, Portuguese,* and *German* politeness requires that the *third* person be substituted for the second. And, when they would be very courteous, the *Germans* use also the plural for the singular, as *they* for *thou*. Thus they have a fourfold method of addressing a person: as, *they*, denoting the highest degree of respect; *he*, a less degree; *you*, a degree still less; and *thou*, none at all, or absolute reproach. Yet, even among them, the last is used as a term of endearment to children, and of veneration to God!

Obs 4.—Such perversions of the original and proper use of language, are doubtless matters of considerable moment. These changes in the use of the pronouns being evidently a sort of *complimentary fictions*, some have made it a matter of conscience to abstain from them, and have published their reasons for so doing. But the *moral objections* which may lie against such or any other applications of words, do not come within the grammarian's province. Let every one consider for himself the moral bearing of what he utters. [See *Matthew*, xii, 36 and 37.]

Obs. 5.—When a pronoun represents the name of an inanimate object *personified*, it agrees with its antecedent in the figurative, and not in the literal sense; [See the figure *Syllepsis*, in PART IV;] as,

> "*Penance* dreams *her* life away."—*Rogers.*
> "Grim *Darkness* furls *his* leaden shroud."—*Id.*

Obs. 6.—When the antecedent is applied *metaphorically*, the pronoun agrees with it in its literal, and not in its figurative sense; as, "Pitt was the *pillar* which upheld the state."—"The *monarch* of mountains rears *his* snowy head." [See *Figures*, in PART IV.]

Obs. 7.—When the antecedent is put by *me'onymy* for a noun of different properties, the pronoun sometimes agrees with it in the figurative, and sometimes in the literal sense ; as,

> "The wolf, who [that] from the nightly fold,
> Fierce drags the bleating *prey*, ne'er drunk *her* milk,
> Nor wore *her* warming fleece."—*Thomson.*

> "That each may fill the circle mark'd by *Heaven*,
> *Who* sees with equal eye, as God of all,
> A hero perish or a sparrow fall."—*Pope.*

> "And *heaven* beholds *its* image in his breast."—*Id.*

Obs. 8.—When the antecedent is put by *synecdoche* for more or less than it literally signifies, the pronoun agrees with it in the figurative, and not in the literal sense ; as,

> "A dauntless *soul* erect, *who* smiled on death."—*Thomson.*

> "But, to the generous still improving *mind*,
> *That* gives the hopeless heart to sing for joy,
> To *him* the long review of ordered life
> Is inward rapture only to be felt."—*Id.*

Obs. 9.—Pronouns usually *follow* the words which they represent; but this order is sometimes reversed : as, "*Whom* the cap fits, let *him* put it on." —"Hark ! *they* whisper," *angels* say," &c.

Obs. 10.—A pronoun sometimes represents a *phrase* or *sentence;* and in this case, the pronoun is always in the third person singular neuter: as, "*She is very handsome;* and she has the misfortune to know *it*."—"Yet men can go on to vilify or disregard Christianity ; *which* is to talk and act as if they had a demonstration of its falsehood."—*Bp. Butler.*

Obs. 11.—When a pronoun follows two words, having a neuter verb between them, and both referring to the same thing, it may represent either of them, *but not with the same meaning;* as, 1. "I am the man who command :" here, *who command* belongs to the subject *I*, and the meaning is, "I who command, am the man." (The latter expression places the relative nearer to its antecedent, and is therefore preferable.) 2. "I am the man who commands :" here, *who commands* belongs to the predicate *man*, and the meaning is, "I am the commander."

Obs. 12.—After the expletive *it*, which may be employed to introduce a noun or pronoun of any person, number, or gender, the above-mentioned distinction is generally disregarded ; and the relative is made to agree with the latter word : as, "*It* is not I *that do* it." The propriety of this construction is questionable.

Obs. 13.—The pronoun *it* frequently refers to something mentioned in the subsequent part of the sentence. This pronoun is a necessary expletive at the commencement of a sentence in which the verb is followed by a clause which, by transposition, may be made the subject of the verb; as, "*It* is impossible *to please every one*."—"*It* was requisite *that the papers should be sent*."

Obs. 14.—*Relative* and *interrogative* pronouns are placed at or near the *beginning* of their own clauses ; and the learner must observe that, through all their cases, they almost invariably retain this situation in the sentence, and are often found before their verbs when the order of construction would reverse this arrangement : as, "He *who* preserves me, to *whom* I owe my being, *whose* I am, and *whom* I serve, is eternal."—*Murray.* "*Who* but God can tell us *who* they are ?"—*Pope.* "He *whom* you seek."—*Lowth.*

Obs. 15.—Every *relative pronoun*, being the representative of some antecedent word or phrase, derives from this relation its person, number, and gender, but not its case. By taking an other relation of case, it helps to form an other clause; and, by retaining the essential meaning of its antecedent, serves to connect this clause to that in which the antecedent is found. Relatives, therefore, cannot be used in an independent simple sentence, nor with a subjunctive verb; but, like other connectives, they belong at the head of a clause in a compound sentence, and they exclude conjunctions, except when two such clauses are to be joined together : as, "Blessed is the man, *who* feareth the Lord, *and who* keepeth his commandments."

OBS. 16.—The *special rules* commonly given by the grammarians, for the construction of relatives, are both unnecessary and faulty. It usually takes two rules to parse a pronoun; one for its agreement with the noun or nouns which it represents, and the other for its case. But neither relatives nor interrogatives require any special rules for the construction of their *cases*, because the general rules for the cases apply to pronouns as well as to nouns. And both relatives and interrogatives generally admit every construction common to nouns, except apposition. Let the learner parse the following examples:—

1. *Nominatives by Rule 2d:* "I *who* write;—Thou *who* writest;—He *who* writes;—the animal *which* runs."—*Dr. Adam.* "He *that spareth* his rod, hateth his son."—*Solomon.* "He *who* does any thing *which* he knows *is* wrong, is a sinner."—"*What* will become of us without religion?"—*Blair.* "Here I determined to wait the hand of death; *which*, I hope, when at last it comes, *will fall* lightly upon me."—*Dr. Johnson.* "*What is* sudden and unaccountable, *serves* to confound."—*Crabb.* "They only are wise, *who are* wise to salvation."—*Goodwin.*

2. *Nominatives by Rule 21st:* "*Who* art thou?"—"*What* were we?"—*Bible.* "Do not tell them *who* I am."—"Let him be *who* he may, he is not the honest fellow *that* he seemed."—"The general conduct of mankind is neither *what* it was designed, nor *what* it ought to be."

3. *Nominatives absolute by Rule 25th:* "There are certain bounds to imprudence and misbehaviour, *which being transgressed*, there remains no place for repentance in the natural course of things."—*Bp. Butler.* This construction of the relative is a *Latinism*, and very seldom used by the best *English* writers.

4. *Possessives by Rule 19th:* "The chief man of the island, *whose* name was Publius."—*Acts.* "Despair, a cruel tyrant, from *whose* prisons none can escape."—*Dr. Johnson.* "To contemplate on Him *whose* yoke is easy and *whose* burden is light."—*Steele.*

5. *Objectives by Rule 20th:* "Those *whom* she persuaded."—*Dr. Johnson.* "The cloak *that* I left at Troas."—*St. Paul.* "By the things *which* he suffered."—*Id.* "A man *whom* there is reason to suspect."—"*What* are we to do?"—*Burke.* "Love refuseth nothing *that* love sends."—*Gurnall.* "*Whomsoever* you please to appoint."—*Lowth.* "*Whatsoever* he doeth, shall prosper."—*Bible.* "*What* we are afraid to do before men, we should be afraid to think before God."—*Sibs.* "Shall I hide from Abraham that thing *which* I do?"—*Gen.*, xviii, 32. "Shall I hide from Abraham *what* I do?"— "Call imperfection *what* thou fanciest such."—*Pope.*

6. *Objectives by Rule 21st:* "He is not the man *that* I took him to be."— "*Whom* did you suppose me to be?"—"Let the lad become *what* you wish him to be."

7. *Objectives by Rule 22d:* "To *whom* shall we go?"—*Bible.* "The laws by *which* the world is governed, are general."—*Butler.* "*Whom* he looks upon as his defender."—*Addison.* "That secret heaviness of heart *which* unthinking men are subject to."—*Id.* "I cannot but think the loss of such talents *as* the man of *whom* I am speaking was master of, a more melancholy instance."—*Steele.*

OBS. 17.—In familiar language, the relative in the *objective* case is frequently understood; as, "Here is the letter [*which*] I received." The omission of the relative in the *nominative* case, is inelegant; as, "This is the worst thing [*that*] could happen." The latter ellipsis sometimes occurs in poetry; as,

"In this 'tis God—directs, in that 'tis man."—*Pope.*

OBS. 18.—The *antecedent* is sometimes suppressed, especially in poetry; as, "How shall I curse [*him* or *them*] whom God hath not cursed."— *Numb.*, xxiii, 8.

[*He*] "Who lives to nature, rarely can be poor;
[*He*] Who lives to fancy, never can be rich."—*Young.*

OBS. 19.—*What* is sometimes used *adverbially;* as, "Though I forbear, *what* am I eased?"—*Job*, xvi, 6.—That is, *how much?* or *wherein?* "The enemy having his country wasted, *what* by himself and *what* by the soldiers, findeth succour in no place."—*Spenser.* Here *what* means *partly,*—" wasted *partly* by himself and *partly* by the soldiers."

Obs. 20.— *What* is sometimes used as a mere *interjection ;* as,

" *What!* this a sleeve ? 'tis like a demi-cannon."—*Shakspeare.*
" *What!* can you lull the winged winds asleep ?—*Campbell.*

NOTES TO RULE V.

Note I.—A pronoun should not be introduced in connexion with words that belong more properly to the antecedent, or to an other pronoun ; as,

" My banks *they* are furnished with bees."—*Shenstone.*

Obs.—This is only an example of *pleonasm ;* which is allowable and frequent in animated discourse, but inelegant in any other. [See *Pleonasm,* in PART IV.]

Note II.—A change of number in the second person, is inelegant and improper ; as, " *You* wept, and I for *thee.*"

Obs.—Poets have sometimes adopted this *solecism,* to avoid the harshness of the verb in the second person singular ; as,

" As, in that lov'd Athenian bower,
You learn'd an all commanding power,
Thy mimic soul, O nymph endear'd !
Can well recall what then it heard."—*Collins.*

Note III.—The relative *who* is applied only to persons, and to animals personified ; and *which,* to brute animals and inanimate things : as, " The *judge who* presided ;"—" The old *crab who* advised the young one ;"—" The *horse which* ran ;"—" The *book which* was given me."

Obs.— *Which,* as well as *who,* was formerly applied to persons ; as, " Our *Father which* art in heaven."—*Bible.* It may still be applied to a young child ; as, " The child *which* died."—Or even to adults, when they are spoken of without regard to a distinct personality or identity ; as, " *Which* of you will go ?"—" Crabb knoweth not *which* is *which,* himself or his parodist." —*Leigh Hunt.*

Note IV.—Nouns of multitude, unless they express persons directly as such, should not be represented by the relative *who :* to say, " The *family whom* I visited," would hardly be proper ; *that* would here be better. When such nouns are strictly of the neuter gender, *which* may represent them ; as, " The committees *which* were appointed."

Note V.—A proper name taken merely as a name, or an appellative taken in any sense not strictly personal, must be represented by *which,* and not by *who ;* as, " Herod—*which* is but another name for cruelty."—" In every prescription of duty, God proposeth himself as a rewarder ; *which* he is only to those that please him."—*Dr. J. Owen.*

Note VI.—The relative *that* may be applied either to persons or to things. In the following cases, it is generally preferable to *who* or *which,* unless it be necessary to use a prepo-

sition before the relative :—1. After an adjective of the superlative degree, when the relative clause is *restrictive ;* as, " He
was the *first that* came."—2. After the adjective *same*, to explain its import; as, " This is the *same* person *that* I met before."—3. After the antecedent *who ;* as, " *Who that* has common sense, can think so ?"—4. After a joint reference to persons and things ; as, " He spoke of the *men* and *things that* he
had seen."—5. After an unlimited antecedent, which the relative and its verb are to restrict; as, " *Thoughts that* breathe,
and *words that* burn."—6. After an antecedent introduced by
the expletive *it ;* as, " *It is you that* command."—" *It was I
that* did it."—7. And, in general, where the propriety of *who*
or *which* is doubtful ; as, " The little child *that* was placed in
the midst."

NOTE VII.—When several relative clauses come in succession, and have a similar dependence in respect to the antecedent, the same pronoun must be employed in each; as, " O
thou *who* art, and *who* wast, and *who* art to come !"—" And
they shall spread them before the sun, and the moon, and all
the host of heaven, *whom* they have loved, and *whom* they have
served, and after *whom* they have walked, and *whom* they have
sought, and *whom* they have worshipped."—*Jer.*, viii, 2.

NOTE VIII.—The relative, and the preposition governing it,
should not be omitted, when they are necessary to give connexion to the sentence ; as, " He is still in the situation [*in
which*] you saw him."

NOTE IX.—An adverb should not be used where a preposition and a relative pronoun would better express the relation
of the terms ; as, " A cause *where* [for *in which*] justice is so
much concerned."

NOTE X.—Where a pronoun or a pronominal adjective will
not express the meaning clearly, the noun must be repeated,
or inserted in stead of it.   Example : " We see the beautiful
variety of colour in the rainbow, and are led to consider the
cause of *it*" [—that variety].

NOTE XI.—To prevent ambiguity or obscurity, the relative
should be placed as near as possible to the antecedent.   The
following sentence is therefore faulty : " He is like a beast of
prey, that is void of compassion."   Better : " He that is void
of compassion, is like a beast of prey."

NOTE XII.—The pronoun *what* should never be used in
stead of the conjunction *that ;* as, " He will not believe but
what I am to blame."   *What* should be *that.*

NOTE XIII.—A pronoun should not be used to represent an
adjective ; because it can neither express a concrete quality as
15*

such, nor convert it properly into an abstract.   Example:
"Be *attentive ;* without *which* you will learn nothing."   Better:
" Be attentive ; *for* without *attention* you will learn nothing."

FALSE SYNTAX UNDER RULE V.—PRONOUNS.

No person should be censured for being careful of their reputation.

[FORMULE.—Not proper, because the pronoun *their* is of the plural number, and
does not correctly represent its antecedent noun *person*, which is of the third person,
singular, masculine. But, according to Rule 5th, "A pronoun must agree with its
antecedent, or the noun or pronoun which it represents, in person, number, and gender." Therefore, *their* should be *his :* thus, No person should be censured for being
careful of *his* reputation.]

Every one must judge of their own feelings.—*Byron.*
Can any person, on their entrance into the world, be fully se-
cure that they shall not be deceived?
He cannot see one in prosperity without envying them.
I gave him oats, but he would not eat it.
Rebecca took goodly raiment, and put them on Jacob.
Take up the tongs, and put it in its place.
Let each esteem others better than themselves.
A person may make themselves happy without riches.
Every man should try to provide for themselves.
The mind of man should not be left without something on
which to employ his energies.

> An idler is a watch that wants both hands,
> As useless if he goes, as when he stands.

Under Note 1.—Pronouns Wrong or Needless.

Many words they darken speech.
These praises he then seemed inclined to retract them.
These people they are all very ignorant.
Asa his heart was perfect with the Lord.
Who, in stead of going about doing good, they are perpetually
intent upon doing mischief.—*Tillotson.*
Whom ye delivered up, and denied him in the presence of
Pontius Pilate.—*Acts*, iii, 13.
Whom, when they had washed, they laid her in an upper
chamber.—*Acts*, ix, 37.
What I have mentioned, there are witnesses of the fact.
What he said, he is now sorry for it.
The empress, approving these conditions, she immediately
ratified them.
This incident, though it appears improbable, yet I cannot doubt
the author's veracity.

Under Note 2.—Change of Number.

Thou art my father's brother, else would I reprove you.

Your weakness is excusable, but thy wickedness is not.
Now, my son, I forgive thee, and freely pardon your fault.

> You draw the inspiring breath of ancient song,
> Till nobly rises emulous thy own.—*Thomson.*

Under Note 3.—*Of Who and Which.*

This is the horse whom my father imported.
Those are the birds whom we call gregarious.
He has two brothers, one of which I am acquainted with.
What was that creature whom Job called leviathan?
Those which desire to be safe, should be careful to do that
    which is right.
A butterfly which thought himself an accomplished traveller,
    happened to light upon a bee-hive.
There was a certain householder which planted a vineyard.

Under Note 4.—*Nouns of Multitude.*

He instructed and fed the crowds who surrounded him.
The court, who has great influence upon the public manners,
    ought to be very exemplary.
The wild tribes who inhabit the wilderness, contemplate the
    ocean with astonishment, and gaze upon the starry heavens
    with delight.

Under Note 5.—*Mere Names.*

Judas (who is now another name for treachery) betrayed his
    master with a kiss.
He alluded to Phalaris,—who is a name for all that is cruel.

Under Note 6.—*That Preferable.*

He was the first who entered.
He was the drollest fellow whom I ever saw.
This is the same man whom we saw before.
Who is she who comes clothed in a robe of green?
The wife and fortune whom he gained, did not aid him.
Men who are avaricious, never have enough.
All which I have, is thine.
Was it thou, or the wind, who shut the door?
It was not I who shut it.
The babe who was in the cradle, appeared to be healthy.

Under Note 7.—*Relative Clauses Connected.*

He is a man that knows what belongs to good manners, and
    who will not do a dishonourable act.
The friend who was here, and that entertained us so much, will
    never be able to visit us again.

The curiosities which he has brought home, and that we shall have the pleasure of seeing, are said to be very rare.

Under Note 8.—*Relative and Preposition.*

Observe them in the order they stand.
We proceeded immediately to the place we were directed.
My companion remained a week in the state I left him.
The way I do it, is this.

Under Note 9.—*Adverbs for Relatives.*

Remember the condition whence thou art rescued.
I know of no rule how it may be done.
He drew up a petition, where he too freely represented his own merits.
The hour is hastening, when whatever praise or censure I have acquired, will be remembered with equal indifference.

Under Note 10.—*Repeat the Noun.*

Many will acknowledge the excellence of religion, who cannot tell wherein it consists.
Every difference of opinion is not that of principle.
Next to the knowledge of God, this of ourselves seems most worthy of our endeavour.

Under Note 11.—*Place of the Relative.*

Thou art thyself the man that committed the act, who hast thus condemned it.
There is a certain majesty in simplicity, which is far above the quaintness of wit.
Thou hast no right to judge who art a party concerned.
It is impossible for such men as those, ever to determine this question, who are likely to get the appointment.
There are millions of people in the empire of China, whose support is derived almost entirely from rice.

Under Note 12.—*What for That.*

I had no idea but what the story was true.
The post-boy is not so weary but what he can whistle.
He had no intimation but what the men were honest.

Under Note 13.—*Adjectives for Antecedents.*

Some men are too ignorant to be humble; without which there can be no docility.—*Berkley.*
Judas declared him innocent; which he could not be, had he in any respect deceived the disciples.—*Porteus.*

Be accurate in all you say or do; for it is important in all the concerns of life.

Every law supposes the transgressor to be wicked; which indeed he is, if the law is just.

RULE VI.—PRONOUNS.

When the antecedent is a collective noun conveying the idea of plurality, the Pronoun must agree with it in the plural number; as, "The *council* were divided in *their* sentiments."

OBSERVATION ON RULE VI.

Most collective nouns of the neuter gender, may take the regular *plural form*, and be represented by a pronoun in the third person, plural, neuter; as, "The *nations* will enforce *their* laws." This construction comes under Rule 5th. To Rule 6th there are *no exceptions*.

NOTE TO RULE VI.

A collective noun conveying the idea of unity, requires a pronoun in the third person, singular, neuter, agreeably to Rule 5th; as, "The *nation* will enforce *its* laws."

FALSE SYNTAX UNDER RULE VI.—PRONOUNS.

The jury will be confined till it agrees on a verdict.

[FORMULE.—Not proper, because the pronoun *it* is of the singular number, and does not correctly represent its antecedent *jury*, which is a collective noun, conveying the idea of plurality. But, according to Rule 6th, "When the antecedent is a collective noun conveying the idea of plurality, the pronoun must agree with it in the plural number." Therefore, *it* should be *they*; thus, The jury will be confined till *they* agree on a verdict.]

In youth, the multitude eagerly pursue pleasure, as if it were its chief good.

The council were not unanimous, and it separated without coming to any determination.

The committee were divided in sentiment, and it referred the business to the general meeting.

There happened to the army a very strange accident, which put it in great consternation.

The enemy were not able to support the charge, and he dispersed and fled.

The defendant's counsel had a difficult task imposed on it.

The board of health publish its proceedings.

I saw all the species thus delivered from its sorrows.

Under Note to Rule 6th.—The Idea of Unity.

I saw the whole species thus delivered from their sorrows.

This court is famous for the justice of their decisions.

8*

The convention then resolved themselves into a committee of the whole.

The crowd was so great that the judges with difficulty made their way through them.

RULE VII.—PRONOUNS.

When a Pronoun has two or more antecedents con-nected by *and*, it must agree with them in the plural number; as, *"James and John* will favour us with *their* company."

EXCEPTION FIRST.

When two or more antecedents connected by *and*, serve merely to describe one person or thing; they are in apposition, and do not require a plural pronoun: as, " This great *philosopher* and *statesman* continued in public life till *his* eighty-second year."—" The same *Spirit, light,* and *life, which en-lighteneth,* also sanctifieth, and there is not an other."—*Penington.*

EXCEPTION SECOND.

When two antecedents connected by *and,* are emphatically distinguished; they belong to different propositions, and (if singular) do not require a plu-ral pronoun: as, " The *butler,* and *not* the *baker,* was restored to *his* office." —" The *good man,* and the *sinner too,* shall have *his* reward."—" *Truth,* and *truth only,* is worth seeking for *its* own sake."

EXCEPTION THIRD.

When two or more antecedents connected by *and,* are preceded by the adjective *each, every,* or *no;* they are taken separately, and do not require a plural pronoun: as, "*Every plant* and *every tree* produces others after *its* kind."—" It is the original cause of *every reproach* and *distress which has at-tended* the government."—*Junius.*

OBSERVATIONS ON RULE VII.

Obs. 1.—When the antecedents are of *different persons,* the first person is preferred to the second, and the second to the third: as, " John, and thou, and I, are attached to *our* country."—" John and thou are attached to *your* country."

Obs. 2.—The *gender* of pronouns, except in the third person singular, is distinguished only by their antecedents. In expressing that of a pronoun which has antecedents of *different genders,* the masculine should be preferred to the feminine, and the feminine to the neuter.

FALSE SYNTAX UNDER RULE VII.—PRONOUNS.

Discontent and sorrow manifested itself in his countenance.

[FORMULE.—Not proper, because the pronoun *itself* is of the singular number, and does not correctly represent its two antecedents *discontent* and *sorrow,* which are connected by *and,* and taken conjointly. But, according to Rule 7th, " When a pro-noun has two or more antecedents connected by *and,* it must agree with them in the plural number." Therefore, *itself* should be *themselves;* thus, Discontent and sorrow manifested *themselves* in his countenance.]

Your levity and heedlessness if it continue, will prevent all substantial improvement.

Poverty and obscurity will oppress him only who esteems it oppressive.

Good sense and refined policy are obvious to few, because it cannot be discovered but by a train of reflection.

Avoid haughtiness of behaviour, and affectation of manners: it implies a want of solid merit.

If love and unity continue, it will make you partakers of one an other's joy.

Suffer not jealousy and distrust to enter: it will destroy, like a canker, every germ of friendship.

Hatred and animosity are inconsistent with Christian charity: guard, therefore, against the slightest indulgence of it.

Every man is entitled to liberty of conscience, and freedom of opinion, if he does not pervert it to the injury of others.

RULE VIII.—PRONOUNS.

When a Pronoun has two or more singular antecedents connected by *or* or *nor*, it must agree with them in the singular number: as, "*James or John* will favour us with *his* company."

OBSERVATIONS ON RULE VIII.

Obs. 1.—When a pronoun has two or more *plural* antecedents connected by *or* or *nor*, it is of course plural, and agrees with them severally. To the foregoing rule, there are properly *no exceptions.*

Obs. 2.—When antecedents of different persons, numbers, or genders, are connected by *or* or *nor*, they cannot be represented by a pronoun that is not applicable to each of them. The following sentence is therefore inaccurate: "Either *thou* or *I* am greatly mistaken in our judgement on this subject."—*Murray's Key.* But different pronouns may be so connected as to refer to such antecedents taken separately; as, "By requiring greater labour from such *slave or slaves*, than *he or she or they* are able to perform."—*Prince's Digest.* Or, if the gender only be different, the masculine may involve the feminine by implication; as, "If a man smite the eye of his *servant* or the eye of his *maid* that it perish, he shall let *him* go free for *his* eye's sake."—*Exodus*, xxi, 26.

FALSE SYNTAX UNDER RULE VIII.—PRONOUNS.

Neither wealth nor honour can secure the happiness of their votaries.

[FORMULE.—Not proper, because the pronoun *their* is of the plural number, and does not correctly represent its two antecedents *wealth* and *honour*, which are connected by *nor*, and taken disjunctively. But, according to Rule 6th, "When a pronoun has two or more singular antecedents connected by *or* or *nor*, it must agree with them in the singular number." Therefore, *their* should be *its;* thus, Neither wealth nor honour can secure the happiness of *its* votaries.]

Neither Sarah, Ann, nor Jane, has performed their task.

One or the other must relinquish their claim.

A man is not such a machine as a clock or a watch, which will move only as they are moved.

Rye or barley, when they are scorched, may supply the place of coffee.

A man may see a metaphor or an allegory in a picture, as well
as read them in a description.
Despise no infirmity of mind or body, nor any condition of
life, for they may be thy own lot.

RULE IX.—VERBS.

A finite Verb must agree with its subject, or nominative, in person and number: as, " I *know;* thou *knowst,*
or *knowest;* he *knows,* or *knoweth.*"—" The bird *flies;* the
birds *fly.*"

OBSERVATIONS ON RULE IX.

Obs. 1.—To this general rule for the verb, there are properly *no exceptions.*
The *infinitive mood,* having no relation to a nominative, is of course exempt
from such agreement; and all the special rules which follow, virtually accord
with this.

Obs. 2.—Every *finite* verb (that is, every verb not in the *infinitive* mood)
must have some noun, pronoun, or phrase equivalent, known as the subject
of the being, action, or passion; and with this subject the verb must agree
in person and number.

Obs. 3.—Different verbs always *have* different subjects, expressed or understood; except when two or more verbs are connected in the same construction, or when the same verb is repeated for the sake of emphasis.

Obs. 4.—Verbs in the *imperative mood,* commonly agree with the pronoun
thou, ye, or *you,* understood; as, "*Do [thou]* as thou list."—*Shak.* "*Trust*
God and *be doing,* and *leave* the rest with him."—*Dr. Sibs.*

Obs. 5.—The *place* of a verb can have reference only to that of the subject
with which it agrees, and that of the object which it governs; this matter is
therefore sufficiently explained in the observations under Rule 2d and Rule
20th.

NOTES TO RULE IX.

Note I.—" The adjuncts of the nominative do not control
its agreement with the verb: as, Six months' *interest was* due."
—*W. Allen.* " The *propriety* of these rules *is* evident."—*Id.*
" The *mill,* with all its appurtenances, *was destroyed.*"

Note II.—The infinitive mood, a phrase, or a sentence, is
sometimes the subject to a verb: a subject of this kind, however composed, if it is taken as one whole, requires a verb in
the third person singular; as, "*To lie* is base."—"*To see the
sun* is pleasant."—"*That you have violated the law,* is evident."
—"*For what purpose they embarked,* is not yet known."—"*How
far the change would contribute to his welfare,* comes to be considered."—*Blair.*

Obs. 1.—The same meaning will be expressed, if the pronoun *it* be placed
before the verb, and the infinitive, phrase, or sentence, after it; as, "*It* is
base *to lie.*"—"*It* is evident *that you have violated the law.*" The construction
of the following sentences is rendered defective by the omission of the pronoun: " Why do ye that which [*it*] is not lawful to do on the sabbath days?"
—*Luke,* vi, 2. " The show-bread which [*it*] is not lawful to eat, but for the
priests only."—*Luke,* vi, 4.

Obs. 2.—When the infinitive mood is made the subject of a finite verb, it is used to express some action or state in the abstract; as, "*To be* contents his natural desire."—*Pope.* Here *to be* stands for simple *existence.* In connexion with the infinitive, a concrete quality may also be taken as an abstract; as, "*To be good* is *to be happy.*" Here *good* and *happy* express the quality of *goodness* and the state of *happiness*, considered abstractly; and therefore these adjectives do not relate to any particular noun. So also the passive infinitive, or a perfect participle taken in a passive sense; as, "*To be satisfied with a little,* is the greatest wisdom."—"*To appear discouraged,* is the way to become so.*" Here the *satisfaction* and the *discouragement* are considered abstractly, and without reference to any particular person.

Obs. 3.—When the action or state is to be limited to a particular person or thing, the noun or pronoun may be introduced before the infinitive, by the preposition *for;* as, "*For a prince to be reduced* by villany to my distressful circumstances, is calamity enough."—*Tr. of Sallust.*

NOTE III.—A neuter or a passive verb between two nominatives should be made to agree with that which precedes it; as, "Words are wind:" except when the terms are transposed, and the proper subject is put after the verb by *question* or *hyperbaton;* as, "His pavilion *were* dark *waters* and thick *clouds* of the sky."—*Bible.* "Who *art thou?*"—*Ib.* "The wages of sin *is death.*"—*Ib.*

NOTE IV.—When the verb has different forms, that form should be adopted, which is the most consistent with present and reputable usage in the style employed: thus, to say familiarly, "The clock *hath stricken,*"—"Thou *laughedst* and *talkedst,* when thou *oughtest* to have been silent,"—"He *readeth* and *writeth,* but he *doth* not cipher,"—would be no better, than to use *don't, won't, can't, shan't,* and *didn't,* in preaching.

NOTE V.—Every finite verb not in the imperative mood, should have a separate nominative expressed; as, "*I came, I saw, I conquered:*" except when the verb is repeated for the sake of emphasis, or connected to an other in the same construction; as,

"They bud, *blow, wither, fall,* and *die.*"—*Watts.*

FALSE SYNTAX UNDER RULE IX.—VERBS.

You was kindly received.

[FORMULE.—Not proper, because the passive verb *was received* is of the singular number, and does not agree with its nominative *you,* which is of the second person, plural. But, according to Rule 9th, "A finite verb must agree with its subject, or nominative, in person and number." Therefore, *was received* should be *were received;* thus, You *were* kindly *received.*]

We was disappointed.
She dare not oppose it.
His pulse are too quick.
Circumstances alters cases.
He need not trouble himself.
Twenty-four pence is two shillings.
On one side was beautiful meadows.
He may pursue what studies he please.

What have become of our cousins ?
There was more impostors than one.
What says his friends on this subject?
Thou knows the urgency of the case.
What avails good sentiments with a bad life ?
Has those books been sent to the school ?
There is many occasions for the exercise of patience.
What sounds have each of the vowels ?
There were a great number of spectators.
There are an abundance of treatises on this easy science.

> While ever and anon there falls
> Huge heaps of hoary moulder'd walls.—*Dyer.*

He that trust in the Lord, will never be without a friend.
Errors that originates in ignorance, is generally excusable.
Be ye not as the horse, or as the mule, which have no under-
standing.
Not one of the authors who mentions this incident, is entitled
to credit.
The man and woman that was present, being strangers to him,
wondered at his conduct.
There necessarily follows from thence these plain and unques-
tionable consequences.

> O thou, for ever present in my way,
> Who all my motives and my toils survey.

Under Note 1.—*Nominatives with Adjuncts.*

The derivation of these words are uncertain.
Four years' interest were demanded.
One added to nineteen, make twenty.
The increase of orphans render the addition necessary.
The road to virtue and happiness, are open to all.
The ship, with all her crew, were lost.
A round of vain and foolish pursuits, delight some folks.

Under Note 2.—*Composite Subjects.*

To obtain the praise of men, were their only object.
To steal and then deny it, are a double sin.
To copy and claim the writings of others, are plagiarism.
To live soberly, righteously, and piously, are required of all
men.
That it is our duty to promote peace and harmony among
men, admit of no dispute.

Under Note 3.—*Verb between Nominatives.*

The reproofs of instruction is the way of life.
A diphthong are two vowels joined in one syllable.

So great an affliction to him was his wicked sons.
What is the latitude and longitude of that island?
He churlishly said to me, "Who is you?"

Under Note 4.—Adapt Form to Style.

1. For the Familiar Style.

Was it thou that buildedst that house?
That boy writeth very elegantly.
Couldest not thou write without blotting thy book?
Thinkest thou not it will rain to-day?
Doth not your cousin intend to visit you?
That boy hath torn my book.
Was it thou that spreadest the hay?
Was it James or thou that didst let him in?
He dareth not say a word.
Thou stoodest in my way and hinderedst me.

2. For the Solemn Style.

The Lord has prepar'd his throne in the heavens; and his king-dom rules over all.
Thou answer'd them, O Lord our God: thou was a God that forgave them, though thou took vengeance of their inventions.
Then thou spoke in vision to thy Holy One, and said—
So then it is not of him that wills, nor of him that runs, but of God that shows mercy.

Under Note 5.—Express the Nominative.

New York, Fifthmonth 3d, 1823.

Dear friend, Am sorry to hear of thy loss; but hope it may be retrieved. Should be happy to render thee any assist-ance in my power. Shall call to see thee to-morrow morn-ing. Accept assurances of my regard.   A. B.

New York, May 3d, P. M., 1823.

Dear sir, Have just received the kind note favoured me with this morning; and cannot forbear to express my gratitude to you. On further information, find have not lost so much as at first supposed; and believe shall still be able to meet all my engagements. Should, however, be happy to see you. Accept, dear sir, my most cordial thanks.   C. D.

> Will martial flames forever fire thy mind,
> And never, never be to Heaven resign'd?—*Pope.*

RULE X.—VERBS.

When the nominative is a collective noun conveying

the idea of plurality, the Verb must agree with it in the plural number; as, " The council *were divided.*"

OBSERVATION ON RULE X.

To this rule there are *no exceptions.* Whenever the collective noun conveys the idea of plurality without the form, the verb is to be parsed by Rule 10th; but if the nominative conveys the idea of unity or takes the plural form, the verb is to be parsed by Rule 9th. The only difficulty is, to determine in what sense the noun should be taken. In modern usage, a plural verb is commonly adopted wherever it is admissible; as, " The public *are informed,*"—" The plaintiff's counsel *are* of opinion,"—" The committee *were instructed.*"

NOTE TO RULE X.

A collective noun conveying the idea of unity, requires a verb in the third person, singular ; and generally admits also the regular plural construction : as, " His *army was defeated.*" " His *armies were defeated.*"

FALSE SYNTAX UNDER RULE X.—VERBS.

The people rejoices in that which should cause sorrow.

[FORMULE.—Not proper, because the verb *rejoices* is of the singular number, and does not correctly agree with its nominative *people,* which is a collective noun conveying the idea of plurality. But, according to Rule 10th, " When the nominative is a collective noun conveying the idea of plurality, the verb must agree with it in the plural number." Therefore, *rejoices* should be *rejoice;* thus, The people *rejoice* in that which should cause sorrow.]

The nobility was assured that he would not interpose.
The committee has attended to their appointment.
Mankind was not united by the bonds of civil society.
The majority was disposed to adopt the measure.
The peasantry goes barefoot, and the middle sort makes use of wooden shoes.
All the world is spectators of your conduct.
Blessed is the people that know the joyful sound.

Under Note to Rule 10.— The Idea of Unity.

The church have no power to inflict corporal punishments.
The fleet were seen sailing up the channel.
The meeting have established several salutary regulations.
The regiment consist of a thousand men.
A detachment of two hundred men were immediately sent.
Every auditory take this in good part.
In this business, the house of commons were of no weight.
Are the senate considered as a separate body ?
There are a flock of birds.
No society are chargeable with the disapproved conduct of particular members.

RULE XI.—VERBS.

When a Verb has two or more nominatives connected by *and*, it must agree with them in the plural number: as,

"Judges *and* senates *have been bought* for gold,
Esteem *and* love *were* never to be sold."—*Pope.*

EXCEPTION FIRST.

When two or more nominatives connected by *and*, serve merely to describe one person or thing; they are in apposition, and do not require a plural verb: as, "This *philosopher* and *poet was banished* from his country."—"*Toll, tribute,* and *custom, was paid* unto them."—*Ezra,* iv, 20.

"Whose icy *current* and compulsive *course*
Ne'er *feels* retiring ebb, but *keeps* due on."—*Shakspeare.*

EXCEPTION SECOND.

When two nominatives connected by *and*, are emphatically distinguished; they belong to different propositions, and (if singular) do not require a plural verb: as, "*Ambition,* and *not the safety* of the state, *was concerned.*"—*Goldsmith.*

"*Ay,* and *no too, was* no good divinity."—*Shakspeare.*
"*Love,* and *love only, is* the loan for love."—*Young.*

EXCEPTION THIRD.

When two or more nominatives connected by *and*, are preceded by the adjective *each, every,* or *no;* they are taken separately, and do not require a plural verb: as, "When *no part* of their substance, and *no one* of their properties, *is* the same."—*Butler.* "Every limb and feature *appears* with *its* respective grace."—*Steele.*

EXCEPTION FOURTH.

When the verb separates its nominatives, it agrees with that which precedes it, and is understood to the rest; as,

"———————Forth in the pleasing spring,
Thy *beauty walks,* thy *tenderness,* and love."—*Thomson.*

OBSERVATIONS ON RULE XI.

Obs. 1.—The conjunction is sometimes *understood;* as,
"Art, empire, earth itself, to change are doomed."—*Beattie.*

Obs. 2.—In *Greek* and *Latin,* the verb frequently agrees with the nearest nominative, and is understood to the rest; and this construction is sometimes improperly imitated in *English:* as, "Νυνὶ δὲ ΜΕΝΕΙ πίστις, ἐλπὶς, ἀγάπη, τὰ τρία ταῦτα."—"Nunc verò *manet* fides, spes, charitas; tria hæc."—"Now *abideth* faith, hope, charity; these three."—1 *Cor.,* xiii, 13.

Obs. 3.—When the nominatives are of *different persons,* the verb agrees with the first person in preference to the second, and with the second in preference to the third; for *thou* and *I* (or *he, thou,* and *I*) are equivalent to *we;* and *thou* and *he* are equivalent to *you:* as, "Why speakest thou any more of thy matters? I have said, *thou and Ziba divide* the land."—2 *Sam.,* xix, 29. I. e., "*divide ye* the land."

NOTES TO RULE XI.

Note I.—When two subjects or antecedents are connected, one of which is taken affirmatively, and the other negatively,

16*

they belong to different propositions; and the verb or pronoun must agree with the affirmative subject, and be understood to the other : as, "Diligent *industry*, and not mean savings, *produces* honourable competence."—" Not a loud voice, but strong *proofs bring* conviction."

NOTE II.—When two subjects or antecedents are connected by *as-well-as*, *but*, or *save*, they belong to different propositions; and, (unless one of them is preceded by the adverb *not*,) the verb and pronoun must agree with the former and be understood to the latter : as, "*Veracity*, as well as justice, *is* to be our rule of life."—*Butler.* "*Nothing*, but wailings, *was heard.*—"*None*, but thou, *can aid* us."—"No mortal *man*, save he, &c., *had* e'er *survived* to say he saw."— *W. Scott.*

OBS. 1.—The conjunction *as*, when it connects nominatives that are in *apposition*, is commonly placed at the beginning of the sentence, so that the verb agrees with its proper nominative following the explanatory word; thus, "*As a poet, he holds* a high rank."—*Murray.* But when this conjunction denotes a *comparison* between two nominatives, there must be two verbs expressed or understood, each agreeing with its own subject; as, "Such *writers* as he [is] *have* no reputation among the learned."

OBS. 2.—Some grammarians say that *but* and *save*, when they denote exception, should govern the objective case, as *prepositions;* but this is not according to the usage of the best authors. The objective case of *nouns* being like the nominative, the point can be proved only by the *pronouns;* as, "There is none *but he* alone."—*Perkins's Theology*, 1608. "There is none other *but he.*"—*Mark*, xii, 32. (This text is good authority as regards the *case*, though it is incorrect in an other respect : it should have been, "There is *none but he*," or, "There is *no other than he.*") "No man hath ascended up to heaven, *but he* that came down from heaven."—*John*, iii, 13. "Not that any man hath seen the Father, *save he* which is of God."—*John*, vi, 46. "Few can, *save he and I.*"—*Byron's Werner.* "There is none justified, *but he* that is in measure sanctified."—*Penington.* *Save*, as a conjunction, is nearly obsolete. In *Rev.*, ii, 17, we read, "Which no man knoweth, *saving he* that receiveth it."

NOTE III.—When two or more subjects or antecedents are preceded by the adjective *each*, *every* or *no*, they are taken separately, and require a verb and pronoun in the singular number : as,

"And every sense, and every heart *is* joy."—*Thomson.*
"Each beast, each insect, happy in *its* own."—*Pope.*

NOTE IV.—When words are to be taken conjointly as subjects or antecedents, the conjunction *and* must connect them.

OBS.—In *Latin*, *cum* with an ablative, sometimes has the force of the conjunction *et* with a nominative; as, "Dux *cum* aliquot principibus capiuntur." —*Livy.* In imitation of this construction, some *English* writers have substituted *with* for *and*, and varied the verb accordingly; as, "A long course of time, *with* a variety of accidents and circumstances, *are* requisite to produce these revolutions."—*Hume.* But, as the preposition makes its object only an adjunct of the preceding noun, this construction cannot be justified.

NOTE V.—Two or more distinct subject phrases connected by *and*, require a plural verb: as, "*To be wise in our own eyes, to be wise in the opinion of the world,* and *to be wise in the sight of our Creator,* are three things so very different, as rarely to coincide."—*Blair.*

FALSE SYNTAX UNDER RULE XI.—VERBS.

Industry and frugality leads to wealth.

[FORMULE.—Not proper, because the verb *leads* is in the singular number, and does not correctly agree with its two nominatives, *industry* and *frugality,* which are connected by *and,* and taken conjointly. But, according to Rule 11th. "When a verb has two or more nominatives connected by *and,* it must agree with them in the plural number." Therefore *leads* should be *lead ;* thus, Industry and frugality *lead* to wealth.]

Temperance and exercise preserves health.
Time and tide waits for no man.
My love and affection towards thee remains unaltered.
Wealth, honour, and happiness, forsakes the indolent.
My flesh and my heart faileth.
In all his works, there is sprightliness and vigour.
Elizabeth's meekness and humility was extraordinary.
In unity consists the security and welfare of every society.
High pleasures and luxurious living begets satiety.
Much does human pride and folly require correction.
Our conversation and intercourse with the world is, in several respects, an education for vice.
Occasional release from toil, and indulgence of ease, is what nature demands, and virtue allows.
What generosity, and what humanity, was then displayed !
—————————————————What thou desir'st,
And what thou fearst, alike destroys all hope.

Under Note 1.—*Affirmation with Negation.*

Wisdom, and not wealth, procure esteem.
Prudence, and not pomp, are the basis of his fame.
Not fear, but labour have overcome him.
The decency, and not the abstinence, make the difference.
Not her beauty, but her talents attracts attention.
It is her talents, and not her beauty, that attracts attention.
It is her beauty, and not her talents, that attract attention.

Under Note 2.—*As Well As, But, or Save.*

His constitution, as well as his fortune, require care.
Their religion, as well as their manners, were ridiculed.
Every one, but thou, hadst been legally discharged.
The buyer, as well as the seller, render themselves liable.
All songsters, save the hooting owl, was mute.
None, but thou, O mighty prince ! canst avert the blow.
Nothing, but frivolous amusements, please the indolent.
Cæsar, as well as Cicero, were admired for their eloquence.

Under Note 3.—*Each, Every, or No.*

Each day, and each hour, bring their portion of duty.
Every house, and even every cottage, were plundered.
Every thought, every word, and every action, will be brought
  into judgement, whether they be good or evil.
The time will come, when no oppressor, no unjust man, will
  be able to screen themselves from punishment.

> No bandit fierce, no tyrant mad with pride,
> No cavern'd hermit, rest self-satisfied.

Under Note 4.—*And Required.*

In this affair, perseverance with dexterity were requisite.
Town or country are equally agreeable to me.
Sobriety with humility lead to honour.
The king, with the lords, and the commons, compose the
  British parliament.
The man with his whole family are dead.
A small house in addition to a trifling annuity, are still granted
  him.

Under Note 5.—*Distinct Subject Phrases.*

To profess, and to possess, is very different things.
To do justly, to love mercy, and to walk humbly with God, is
  duties of universal obligation.
To be round or square, to be solid or fluid, to be large or
  small, and to be moved swiftly or slowly, is all equally
  alien from the nature of thought.

RULE XII.—VERBS.

When a Verb has two or more *singular* nominatives
connected by *or* or *nor*, it must agree with them in the
singular number: as, "Fear *or* jealousy *affects* him."

OBSERVATION ON RULE XII.

To this rule there are properly *no exceptions*.   But in the learned languages,
a *plural verb* is often employed with singular nominatives thus connected;
as,

> "Tunc nec mens mihi, nec color
> Certa sede *manent*."—*Horace.*

And the best scholars have sometimes *improperly* imitated this construction in *English ;* as,

> "He comes—nor want nor cold his course *delay ;*
> Hide, blushing Glory! hide Pultowa's day."—*Dr. Johnson.*

NOTES TO RULE XII.

Note I.—When a verb has nominatives of different persons
or numbers, connected by *or* or *nor*, it must agree with that

which is placed next to it, and be understood to the rest, in the person and number required; as, "Neither he nor his brothers *were* there."—"Neither you nor I *am* concerned."— "That neither they nor ye also die."—*Numb*, xviii, 3.

Obs. 1.—When the latter nominative is parenthetical, the verb agrees with the former only; as, "One example (or ten) *says* nothing against the universal opinion."—*Leigh Hunt.* "And we (or future ages) *may* possibly *have* a proof of it."—*Bp. Butler.*

Obs. 2.—When the alternative is merely in the *words*, not in the *thought*, the terms are virtually in apposition, and the principal nominative alone controls the verb; but there is always a harshness in this mixture of different numbers: as, "A *parathesis*, or brackets, *consists* of two angular strokes, or hooks, enclosing one or more words."—*Whiting.* "To show us that our own *schemes*, or prudence, *have* no share in our advancements."—*Addison.* "The Mexican *figures*, or picture-writing, *represent* things, not words; *they* exhibit images to the eye, not ideas to the understanding."—*Murray's Gram.*, p. 243.

Note II.—But when the nominatives require different forms of the verb, it is in general more elegant to express the verb, or its auxiliary, in connexion with each of them; as, "Either thou *art* to blame, or I *am*."—"Neither *were* their numbers, nor *was* their destination known."

Note III.—The speaker should generally mention himself last; as, "Thou or *I* must go."—"He then addressed his discourse to my father and *me*." But in confessing a fault he may assume the first place; as, "*I* and Robert did it."—*M. Edgeworth.*

Note IV.—Two or more distinct subject phrases connected by *or* or *nor*, require a singular verb; as, "*That a drunkard should be poor*, or *that a fop should be ignorant*, is not strange."

FALSE SYNTAX UNDER RULE XII.—VERBS.

Ignorance or negligence have caused this mistake.

[FORMULE.—Not proper, because the verb *have caused* is of the plural number, and does not correctly agree with its two nominatives, *ignorance* and *negligence*, which are connected by *or*, and taken disjunctively. But, according to Rule 12th, "When a verb has two or more singular nominatives connected by *or* or *nor*, it must agree with them in the singular number." Therefore, *have caused* should be *has caused*; thus, Ignorance or negligence *has caused* this mistake.]

Neither imprudence, credulity, nor vanity, have ever been imputed to him.

What the heart or the imagination dictate, flows readily.

Neither authority nor analogy support such an opinion.

Either ability or inclination were wanting.

Redundant grass or heath afford abundance to their cattle.

The returns of kindness are sweet; and there are neither honour, nor virtue, nor utility, in repelling them.

The sense or drift of a proposition, often depend upon a single letter.

Under Note 1.—*Nominatives that Disagree.*

Neither he nor you was there.
Either the boys or I were in fault.
Neither he nor I intends to be present.
Neither the captain nor the sailors was saved.
Whether one person or more was concerned in the business, does not yet appear.

Under Note 2.—*Complete the Concord.*

Are they or I expected to be there?
Neither he, nor am I, capable of it.
Either he has been imprudent, or his associates vindictive.
Neither were their riches, nor their influence great.

Under Note 3.—*Place of the First Person.*

I and my father were riding out.
The premiums were given to me and George.
I and Jane are invited.
They ought to invite me and my sister.
We dreamed a dream in one night, I and he.

Under Note 4.—*Distinct Subject Phrases.*

To practise tale-bearing, or even to countenance it, are great injustice.
To reveal secrets, or to betray one's friends, are contemptible perfidy.

RULE XIII.—VERBS.

When Verbs are connected by a conjunction, they must either agree in mood, tense, and form, or have separate nominatives expressed: as, "He himself *held* the plough, *sowed* the grain, and *attended* the reapers."— "She *was* proud, but she *is* now humble."

EXCEPTION.

Verbs differing in mood, tense, or form, may sometimes agree with the same nominative, especially if the simplest verbs be placed first; as,

"What nothing earthly *gives* or *can destroy*."—*Pope.*
"Some *are*, and *must be*, greater than the rest."—*Id.*

OBSERVATIONS ON RULE XIII.

Obs. 1.—When separate nominatives are expressed, distinct sentences are formed, and the verbs have not a common construction. Those examples which require a repetition of the nominative might be corrected equally well by Note 5th to Rule 9th.

Obs. 2.—Those parts which are common to several verbs, are generally expressed to the first, and understood to the rest: as, "Every sincere endeavour to amend shall be assisted, [*shall be*] accepted, and [*shall be*] rewarded."

"Honourably do the best you can" [*do*].—"He thought as I did" [*think*].—
"You have seen it, but I have not" [*seen it*].—"If you will go, I will" [*go*].

NOTES TO RULE XIII.

NOTE I.—The preterit should not be employed to form the compound tenses, nor should the perfect participle be used for the preterit. Thus: say, "To have *gone*,"—not, "To have *went;*" and, "I *did* it,"—not, "I *done* it."

NOTE II.—Care should be taken, to give every verb its appropriate form and signification. Thus: say, "He *lay* by the fire,"—not, "He *laid* by the fire;"—" He *had entered* into the connexion,"—not, " He *was entered* into the connexion ;"—"I *would* rather *stay*,"—not, " I *had* rather *stay*."

OBS.—Several verbs which resemble each other in form, are frequently confounded: as, to *flee*, to *fly;* to *lay*, to *lie;* to *sit*, to *set ;* to *fall*, to *fell ;* to *rend*, to *rent ;* to *ride*, to *rid ;* &c. Some others are often misapplied; as, *learn*, for *teach*. There are also erroneous forms of some of the compound tenses: as, " We *will be convinced*," for, " We *shall be convinced ;*"—" If I *had have seen* him," for, " If I *had seen* him." All such errors are to be corrected by the foregoing note.

FALSE SYNTAX UNDER RULE XIII.—VERBS.

They would neither go in themselves, nor suffered others to enter.

[FORMULE.—Not proper, because the two verbs *would go* and *suffered*, which are connected without separate nominatives, do not agree in mood. But according to Rule 13th, "When verbs are connected by a conjunction, they must either agree in mood, tense, and form, or have separate nominatives expressed." The sentence is best* corrected by changing *suffered* to *would suffer ;* (*would* understood ;) thus, They *would* neither *go* in themselves, nor *suffer* others to enter.]

Doth he not leave the ninety and nine, and goeth into the mountains, and seeketh that which is gone astray ?

Did he not tell thee his fault, and entreated thee to forgive him ?

If he understands the business, and attend to it, wherein is he deficient ?

The day is approaching, and hastens upon us, in which we must give an account of our stewardship.

If thou dost not turn unto the Lord, but forget him who remembered thee in thy distress, great will be thy condemnation.—*Barclay*.

There are a few who have kept their integrity to the Lord, and prefer his truth to all other enjoyments.

This report was current yesterday, and agrees with what we heard before.

Virtue is generally praised, and would be generally practised also, if men were wise.

---

* Errors under this rule may generally be corrected in *three* ways: 1. By changing the first verb, to agree with the second—2. By changing the second verb, to agree with the first—3. By inserting the nominative. The form preferred, is in the Key.

Under Note 1.—Preterits and Participles.

IIe would have went with us, if we had invited him.
They have chose the part of honour and virtue.
He soon begun to be weary of having nothing to do.
Somebody has broke my slate.
I seen him when he done it.

Under Note 2.—Adapt Form to Sense.

He was entered into the conspiracy.
The American planters grow cotton and rice.
The report is predicated on truth.
I entered the room and set down.
Go and lay down, my son.
With such books, it will always be difficult to learn children to
read.

RULE XIV.—PARTICIPLES.

Participles relate to nouns or pronouns, or else are
governed by prepositions: as, Elizabeth's tutor, at one
time *paying* her a visit, found her *employed* in *reading*
Plato."—*Hume.*

EXCEPTION FIRST.

A participle sometimes relates to a preceding *phrase* or *sentence*, of which
it forms no part; as,

"But *ever to do ill* our sole delight,
As *being* the contrary to his high will."—*Milton.*

EXCEPTION SECOND.

With an infinitive denoting being or action in the abstract, a participle is
sometimes also taken *abstractly ;* (that is, without reference to any particular
noun, pronoun, or other subject;) as, "To seem *compelled*, is disagreeable."
—"To keep always *praying* aloud, is plainly impossible."

OBSERVATIONS ON RULE XIV.

Obs. 1.—To this rule there are properly *no other exceptions ;* for we cannot
agree with *Murray* that it is strictly correct to make participles in *ing* the
subjects or *objects* of verbs, while they retain the government and adjuncts of
participles ; as, "Not *attending* to this rule, is the cause of a very common
error."—*Murray's Key.* "He abhorred *being* in debt."—*Ibid.* "*Cavilling*
and *objecting* upon any subject, is much easier than *clearing* up difficulties."
—*Bp. Butler.* This mixed and erroneous construction of the participle, is a
great blemish in the style of several English authors. It is at best a useless
anomaly, which it is always easy to avoid; as, "*Inattention* to this rule is
the cause of a very common error."—"He abhorred *debt*."—"*To cavil* and
object upon any subject is much easier than *to clear* up difficulties."
Obs. 2.—The word to which the participle relates, is sometimes *understood ;* as, "*Granting* this to be true, what is to be inferred from it ?"—*Murray.* That is, "*I granting* this to be true, *ask* what is to be inferred from
it ?"—"The very chin was, [*I*,] modestly *speaking*, [*say*,] as long as my whole
face."—*Addison.* Some grammarians have erroneously taught that such
participles are *put absolute.*

Obs. 3.—Participles are almost always *placed after* the words on which their construction depends, but sometimes they are introduced before them; as,

"*Immur'd* in cypress shades, a sorcerer dwells."—*Milton.*

NOTES TO RULE XIV.

Note I.—Active Participles have the same government as the verbs from which they are derived; the preposition *of,* therefore, should never be used after the participle, when the verb does not require it. Thus, in phrases like the following, *of* is improper: " Keeping *of* one day in seven,"—"By preaching *of* repentance,"—"They left beating *of* Paul."

Obs.—When participles are compounded with something that does not belong to the verb, they become *adjectives;* and, as such, they cannot govern an object after them. The following sentence is therefore inaccurate: "When Caius did any thing *unbecoming* his dignity."—*Jones's Church History.* Such errors are to be corrected either by Note 15th to Rule 4th, or by changing the particle prefixed; as, "Unbecoming *to* his dignity," or, "*Not* becoming his dignity."

Note II.—When a transitive participle is converted into a noun, *of* must be inserted to govern the object following.

Obs. 1.—An imperfect or a compound participle, preceded by an article, an adjective, or a noun or pronoun of the possessive case, becomes a *verbal noun;* and, as such, it cannot govern an object after it. A word which may be the object of the *participle* in its proper construction, requires the preposition *of,* to connect it with the *verbal noun ;* as, 1. The Participle: " *Worshiping* idols, the Jews sinned."—" *Thus worshiping* idols,—*In worshiping* idols,—or, *By worshiping* idols, they sinned." 2. The Verbal Noun: " *The worshiping of* idols,—Such *worshiping of* idols,—or, *Their worshiping of* idols, was sinful."—' *In the worshiping of* idols, there is sin."

Obs. 2.—When the use of the preposition produces ambiguity or harshness, the expression must be varied. Thus, the sentence, "He mentions *Newton's writing of* a commentary," is both ambiguous and awkward. If the preposition be omitted, the word *writing* will have a double construction, which is inadmissible. Some would say, "He mentions *Newton writing* a commentary." This is still worse ; because it makes the leading word in sense the adjunct in construction. The meaning may be correctly expressed thus : "He mentions *that Newton wrote* a commentary." "By *his* studying the Scriptures, he became wise." Here *his* serves only to render the sentence incorrect: all such possessives are to be expunged by Note 5th to Rule 19th.

Obs. 3.—We sometimes find a participle that takes the same case after as before it, converted into a verbal noun, and the latter word retained unchanged in connexion with it; as, "I have some recollection of his *father's* being a *judge.*"—" To prevent *its* being a dry *detail* of terms."—*Buck.* The noun after the verbal, is in apposition with the possessive going before. Nouns that are in apposition with the possessive case, *do not admit the possessive sign.* But the above-mentioned construction is anomalous, and perhaps it would be better to avoid it; thus: "I have some recollection *that his father was* a judge."—" To prevent it *from* being a dry detail of terms."

Obs. 4.—The verbal noun should not be accompanied by any adjuncts of the verb or participle, unless they be taken into composition; as, "The hypocrite's hope is like the *giving up* of the ghost." The following phrase is therefore inaccurate: "For the *more easily* reading of large numbers." Yet if we say, "For reading large numbers *the more easily,*" the construction is different, and not inaccurate.

Note III.—A participle should not be used where the infinitive mood, the verbal noun, a common substantive, or a phrase equivalent, will better express the meaning.

Obs. 1.—Participles that have become nouns, may be used as such with or without the article; as, *spelling, reading, writing, drawing*. But we sometimes find those which retain the government and the adjuncts of participles, used as nouns before or after verbs; as, "*Exciting* such disturbances, is unlawful."—"Rebellion is *rising* against government." This mongrel construction is liable to ambiguity, and ought to be avoided. The infinitive mood, the verbal or some other noun, or a clause introduced by the conjunction *that*, will generally express the idea in a better manner; as, "*To excite* such disturbances,—*The exciting of* such disturbances,—*The excitation of* such disturbances,—or, *That one should excite* such disturbances, is unlawful."

Obs. 2.—After verbs signifying *to persevere* or *to desist*, the participle in *ing*, relating to the nominative, may be used in stead of the infinitive connected to the verb; as, "So when they continued *asking* him."—*John*, viii, 7. Here *continued* is intransitive, and *asking* relates to *they*. Greek, Ὡς δὲ ἐπέμενον ἐρωτῶντες αὐτόν. Latin, "Cùm ergo perseverarent *interrogantes* eum." But in sentences like the following, the participle seems to be improperly made the *object* of the verb: "I intend *doing* it."—"I remember *meeting* him." Better, "I intend *to do* it."—"I remember to *have met* him." Verbs do not govern participles.

Obs. 3.—After verbs of *beginning, omitting*, and *avoiding*, some writers employ the participle in *English*, though the analogy of general grammar evidently requires in such cases the infinitive or a noun; as, "It is now above three years since he began *printing*."—*Dr. Adam's Pref. to Rom. Antiquities.* "He omits *giving* an account of them."—*Tooke's Div. of Purley*, Vol. i, p. 251. "He studied to avoid *expressing* himself too severely."—*Murray's Gram., 8vo*, Vol. i, p. 194. If these examples are good *English*, (for the point is questionable,) the verbs are all *intransitive*, and the participles relate to the nominatives going before, as in the text quoted in the preceding observation. But *Murray*, not understanding this construction, or not observing what verbs admit of it, has very unskillfully laid it down as a rule, that, "The participle with its adjuncts, may be considered as a *substantive phrase* in the objective case, governed by the preposition or *verb*;" whereas he himself, on the preceding page, had adopted from *Lowth* a different doctrine, and cautioned the learner against treating words in *ing*, "as if they were of an *amphibious* species, partly *nouns* and partly *verbs*;" that is, "partly *nouns* and partly *participles*;" for, according to Murray, participles are verbs. The term "*substantive phrase*" is a solecism, invented merely to designate this anomalous construction. Copying *Lowth* again, he defines a phrase to be "two or more words rightly put together;" and whatsoever words are rightly put together, may be regularly parsed. But how can one indivisible word be made two different parts of speech at once? And is not this the situation of every transitive participle that is made either the *subject* or the *object* of a verb? Adjuncts never alter either the nature or the construction of the words on which they depend; and participial nouns always differ from participles in both. The former express *actions as things*; the latter attribute them *to their agents or recipients*.

Note IV.—In the use of participles and of verbal nouns, the leading word in sense, should always be made the leading or governing word in the construction.

Obs.—A participle construed after the nominative or the objective case, is not equivalent to a verbal noun governing the possessive. There is sometimes a nice distinction to be observed in the application of these two constructions. For the leading word in sense should not be made the adjunct in construction. The following sentences exhibit a disregard to this principle, and are both inaccurate: "He felt his *strength's* declining."—"He was sensible of his *strength* declining." In the former sentence the noun *strength* should be in the objective case, governed by *felt;* and in the latter, in the possessive, governed by *declining.*

Note V.—Participles, in general, however construed, should have a clear reference to the proper subject of the being, action, or passion. The following sentence is therefore faulty : "By *giving* way to sin, trouble is encountered." This suggests that *trouble gives way to sin.* It should be, "By *giving* way to sin, *we* encounter trouble."

Note VI.—The preterit of irregular verbs should not be used for the perfect participle : as, "A certificate *wrote* on parchment"—for, "A certificate *written* on parchment." This error should be carefully avoided.

Note VII.—Perfect participles being variously formed, care should be taken to express them agreeably to the best usage : thus, *earnt, snatcht, checkt, snapt, mixt, tost,* are erroneously written for *earned, snatched, checked, snapped, mixed, tossed;* and *holden, foughten, proven,* are now mostly superseded by *held, fought, proved.*

FALSE SYNTAX UNDER RULE XIV.—PARTICIPLES.

Examples under Note 1.—Expunge Of.

In forming of his sentences, he was very exact.

[Formule.—Not proper, because the preposition *of* is used after the participle *forming*, whose verb does not require it. But, according to Note 1st under Rule 14th, "Participles have the same government as the verbs from which they are derived; the preposition *of*, therefore, should not be used after the participle, when the verb does not require it." Therefore, *of* should be omitted; thus, In forming his sentences, he was very exact.]

By observing of truth, you will command respect.
I could not, for my heart, forbear pitying of him.
I heard them discussing of this subject.
By consulting of the best authors, he became learned.
Here are rules, by observing of which, you may avoid error.

Under Note 2.—Insert Of.

Their consent was necessary for the raising any supplies.
Thus the saving a great nation devolved on a husbandman.
It is an overvaluing ourselves, to decide upon every thing.
The teacher does not allow any calling ill names.
That burning the capitol was a wanton outrage.
May nothing hinder our receiving so great a good.
My admitting the fact will not affect the argument.
Cain's killing his brother, originated in envy.

Under Note 3.—Change the Expression.

Cæsar carried off the treasures, which his opponent had neglected taking with him.—*Goldsmith.*

It is dangerous playing with edge tools.
I intend returning in a few days.
Suffering needlessly is never a duty.
Nor is it wise complaining.—*Cowper.*
I well remember telling you so.
Doing good is a Christian's vocation.—*H. More.*
Piety is constantly endeavouring to live to God.   It is earnestly desiring to do his will, and not our own.—*Id.*

Under Note 4.—The Leading Word.

There is no harm in women knowing about these things.
They did not give notice of the pupil leaving.
The sun's darting his beams through my window, awoke me.
The maturity of the sago tree is known by the leaves being covered with a delicate white powder.

Under Note 5.—Reference of Participles.

Sailing up the river, the whole town may be seen.
Being conscious of guilt, death becomes terrible.
By yielding to temptation, our peace is sacrificed.
In loving our enemies, no man's blood is shed.
By teaching the young, they are prepared for usefulness.

Under Note 6.—Preterits for Participles.

A nail well drove will support a great weight.
See here a hundred sentences stole from my work.
I found the water entirely froze, and the pitcher broke.
Being forsook by my friends, I had no other resource.

Under Note 7.—Form of Participles.

Till by barbarian deluges o'erflown.
Like the lustre of diamonds sat in gold.
A beam ethereal, sullied and absorpt.
With powerless wings around them wrapt.
Error learnt from preaching, is held as sacred truth.

RULE XV.—ADVERBS.

Adverbs relate to verbs, participles, adjectives, or other adverbs : as, "Any passion that *habitually* discomposes our temper, or unfits us for *properly* discharging the duties of life, has *most certainly* gained a *very* dangerous ascendency."—*Blair.*

EXCEPTION FIRST.

The adverbs *yes* and *yea*, expressing a simple affirmation, and the adverbs *no* and *nay*, expressing a simple negation, are always independent. They generally answer a question, and are equivalent to a whole sentence. Is it clear, that they ought to be called adverbs? *No*

EXCEPTION SECOND.

The word *amen*, which is commonly called an adverb, is often used independently at the beginning or end of a declaration or prayer; and is itself a prayer, meaning, *so let it be.*

OBSERVATIONS ON RULE XV.

OBS. 1.—On this rule *Dr. Adam* remarks, "Adverbs sometimes likewise qualify *substantives ;*" and gives Latin examples of the following import: "Homer *plainly* an orator ;"—"*Truly* Metellus ;"—"*To-morrow* morning ;"—"*Yesterday* morning." But this doctrine is not well proved by such imperfect phrases, nor can it ever be consistently admitted; because it destroys the characteristic difference between an *adjective* and an *adverb.*

OBS. 2.—Whenever any of those words which are commonly used adverbially, are made to relate directly to nouns or pronouns, they must be reckoned *adjectives*, and parsed by Rule 4th; as, "The *above** verbs."—*Dr. Adam.* "God *only*."—*Bible.* "He *alone*."—*Id.* "A *far* country."—*Id.* "*No* wine, —*No* new thing,—*No* greater joy."—*Id.* "Nothing *else*."—*Blair.* "*To-morrow* noon."—*Scott.* "This *beneath* world."—*Shak.* "Calamity *enough*." —*Tr. of Sallust.* "My *hither* way."

OBS. 3.—When words of an adverbial character are used after the manner of nouns, they must be parsed *as nouns* and *not as adverbs:* as, "The Son of God—was not *yea* and *nay*, but in him was *yea*."—*Bible.* "For a great *while* to come."—*Id.* "On this *perhaps*, this *peradventure* infamous for lies." —*Young.* "From the extremest *upward* of thine head."—*Shak.* "Prate of my *whereabout*."—*Id.* "An eternal *now* does always last."—*Cowley.* "Discourse requires an animated *no*."—*Cowper.*

OBS. 4.—Adverbs sometimes relate to verbs *understood ;* as, "The former has written correctly; but the latter, *elegantly*." "And, [*I say*] *truly*, if they had been mindful of that country from whence they came out, they might have had opportunity to have returned."—*Heb.*, xi, 15.

OBS. 5.—To abbreviate expressions, and give them vivacity, verbs of self-motion (as *go, come, rise, get*, &c.) are sometimes suppressed, being suggested to the mind by an emphatic adverb; as,

"I'll *hence* to London on a serious matter."—*Shakspeare.*
"I'll *in*. I'll *in*. Follow your friend's counsel. I'll *in*."—*Id.*
"*Away* old man; give me thy hand; *away*."—*Id.*
"Would you youth and beauty stay,
Love hath wings, and will *away*."—*Waller.*
"*Up, up*, Glentarkin! rouse thee, ho!"—*W. Scott.*

OBS. 6.—Most *conjunctive adverbs* relate to two verbs at the same time, and thus connect the two clauses; as, "And the rest will I set in order *when* I come."—1 *Cor.*, xi, 34. Here *when* is an adverb of time, relating to the two verbs, *will set* and *come ;* the meaning being, "And the rest will I set in order *at the time at which* I come."

NOTES TO RULE XV.

NOTE I.—Adverbs must be placed in that position which will render the sentence the most perspicuous and agreeable.

---

* *Murray* and *his copyists* strongly condemn this use of *above*, and we do not contend for it; but, both he and they, (as well as others,) have repeatedly employed the word in this manner: as, "The *above* construction."—*Murray's Gram.*, 8vo, p. 149. "The *above* instances."—p. 202. "The *above* rule."—p. 270. "In such instances as the *above*."—p. 24. "The same as the *above*."—p. 66.

Ons.—For the placing of adverbs, no definite general rule can be given. Those which relate to adjectives, immediately precede them; and those which belong to compound verbs, are commonly placed after the first auxiliary.

NOTE II.—Adverbs should not be used as adjectives; nor should they be employed, when *quality* is to be expressed, and not *manner*: as, "The *soonest* time;"—"Thine *often* infirmities;"—"It seems *strangely*." All these are wrong.

NOTE III.—With a verb of motion, most grammarians prefer *hither, thither*, and *whither*, to *here, there*, and *where*, which are in common use, and perhaps allowable, though not so good; as, "Come *hither* Charles,"—or, "Come *here*."

NOTE IV.—To the adverbs *hence, thence*, and *whence*, the preposition *from* is frequently (though not with strict propriety) prefixed. It is well to omit all needless words.

NOTE V.—The adverb *how* should not be used before the conjunction *that*, nor in stead of it; as, "He said *how* he would go." Expunge *how*. This is a vulgar error.

NOTE VI.—The adverb *no* should not be used with reference to a *verb* or a *participle*. Such expressions as, "Tell me whether you will go or *no*," are therefore improper: *no* should be *not;* for "*go*" is understood after it.

Ons.—*No* is sometimes an adverb of *degree;* and as such it has this peculiarity, that it can relate only to comparatives: as, "*No* more,"—"*No* better," —"*No* greater,"—"*No* sooner." When this word is prefixed to a noun, it is clearly an *adjective*, corresponding to the Latin *nullus;* as, "*No* clouds, *no* vapours intervene."—*Dyer*.

NOTE VII.—A negation, in English, admits but one negative word: as, "I could not wait any longer,"—not, "*no* longer." Double negatives are vulgar.

Ons. 1.—The repetition of a negative word or clause, strengthens the negation; as, "No, no, no." But two negatives in the same clause, destroy the negation, and render the meaning affirmative; as, "*Nor* did they *not* perceive their evil plight."—*Milton*. That is, they *did* perceive it.

Obs. 2.—*Ever* and *never* are directly opposite in sense, and yet they are frequently confounded and misapplied even by respectable writers; as "Seldom, or *never*, can we expect," &c.—*Blair's Lectures*, p. 305. "Seldom, or *ever*, did any one rise," &c.—*Ibid.*, p. 272. Here *never* is right, and *ever* is wrong. But as the negative adverb applies only to *time*, *ever* is preferable to *never*, in *sentences* like the following: "Now let man reflect but *never* so little on himself."—*Burlamaqui*, p. 29. "Which will not hearken to the voice of charmers, charming *never* so wisely."—*Ps.*, lviii, 5. For the phrase *ever so*, (which ought perhaps to be written as one word,) is a very common expression, denoting *degree*, however great or small; as, "*ever* so little"— "*ever* so wisely." And it seems to be this, and not time, that is intended in the last two examples.

Ons. 3.— By the customary (but faulty) omission of the negative before *but*, that conjunction has acquired the adverbial sense of *only;* and it may, when used with that signification, be called an *adverb*. Thus, the text, "He hath *not* grieved me but in part," [2 *Chr.*, ii, 5,] might drop the negative, and still convey the same meaning: "He hath grieved me *but* in part,"

"Reason itself, *but* gives it edge and power."—*Pope*.
"Born *but* to die, and reasoning *but* to err."—*Id*.

FALSE SYNTAX UNDER RULE XV.—ADVERBS.

Examples under Note 1.—The Placing of Adverbs.

We were received kindly.

[FORMULE.—Not proper, because the adverb *kindly* is not in the most suitable place. But, according to Note 1st under Rule 15th, " Adverbs must be placed in that position which will render the sentence the most perspicuous and agreeable." The sentence will be improved by placing *kindly* before *received ;* thus, We were kindly received.]

The work will be never completed.
We always should prefer our duty to our pleasure.
It is impossible continually to be at work.
He impertinently behaved to his master.
The heavenly bodies are in motion perpetually.
Not only he found her busy, but pleased and happy even.

Under Note 2.—Adverbs for Adjectives.

Give him a soon and decisive answer.
When a substantive is put absolutely.
Such expressions sound harshly.
Such events are of seldom occurrence.
Velvet feels very smoothly.

Under Note 3.—Here for Hither, &c.

Bring him here to me.
I shall go there again in a few days.
Where are they all riding in so great haste ?

Under Note 4.—From Hence, &c.

From hence it appears that the statement is incorrect.
From thence arose the misunderstanding.
Do you know from whence it proceeds ?

Under Note 5.—The Adverb How.

You see how that not many are required.
I knew how that they had heard of his misfortunes.
He remarked, how time was valuable.

Under Note 6.—The Adverb No.

Know now, whether this be thy son's coat or no.
Whether he is in fault or no, I cannot tell.
I will ascertain whether it is so or no.

Under Note 7.—Double Negatives.

I will not by no means entertain a spy.
Nobody never invented nor discovered nothing, in no way to
  be compared with this.

Be honest, nor take no shape nor semblance of disguise.
I did not like neither his temper nor his principles.
Nothing never can justify ingratitude.

RULE XVI.—CONJUNCTIONS.

Conjunctions connect either words or sentences: as,
"Let there be no strife, I pray thee, between me *and*
thee, *and* between my herdmen *and* thy herdmen; *for*
we are brethren."—*Gen.*, xiii, 8.

EXCEPTION FIRST.

The conjunction *that* sometimes serves merely to introduce a sentence which is made the subject of a verb; as, "*That* mind is not matter, is certain."

EXCEPTION SECOND.

When two corresponding conjunctions occur, in their usual order, the former should be parsed as referring to the latter, which is more properly the connecting word; as, "*Neither* sun *nor* stars in many days appeared."—*Acts*, xxvii, 20.

EXCEPTION THIRD.

Either, corresponding to *or*, and *neither*, corresponding to *nor* or *not*, are sometimes transposed, so as to repeat the disjunction or negation at the end of the sentence; as, "Where then was their capacity of standing, *or* his *either?*"—*Barclay.* "It is *not* dangerous *neither.*"—*Bolingbroke.* "He is very tall, but *not* too tall *neither.*"—*Spectator.*

OBSERVATIONS ON RULE XVI.

Obs. 1.—Conjunctions that connect *particular words*, generally join similar parts of speech in a common dependence on some other term. Those which connect *sentences* or *clauses*, commonly unite one to an other, either as an additional affirmation, or as a condition, a cause, or an end. They are *placed between* the terms which they connect, except there is a transposition, and then they stand *before* the dependent term.

Obs. 2.—Two or three conjunctions sometimes come together; as,
"What rests, *but that* the mortal sentence pass?"—*Milton.*

Obs. 3.—Conjunctions should not be unnecessarily accumulated; as, "*But* AND *if* that evil servant say in his heart."—*Matthew*, xxiv, 48. Greek, "Ἐὰν δὲ εἴπῃ ὁ κακὸς δοῦλος ἐκείνος," &c. Here is no *and.*

Obs. 4.—The conjunction *as* often unites words that are in *apposition;* as, "He offered *himself* as a *journeyman.*" [See *Obs.* 5, *Rule* xx.] So, likewise, when an intransitive verb takes the same case after as before it, by Rule xxi; as, "*Johnson* soon after engaged *as usher* in a school."—*Murray.* "*He* was employed *as usher.*" This also is a virtual *apposition.* If after the verb "*engaged*" we supply *himself, usher* becomes objective, and is in apposition with the pronoun.

Obs. 5.—*As* frequently has the force of a relative pronoun; as, "Avoid such *as are* vicious." "But to as many *as received* him," &c. "He then read the conditions *as follow.*" Here *as* represents a noun, and is the subject of a verb. [See *Tooke's Diversions of Purley.*] But when a clause, or sentence, is the antecedent, it is better to consider *as* a conjunction, and to supply the pronoun *it;* as, "He is angry, as [it] appears by this letter."

Obs. 6.—The conjunction *that* is frequently understood; as,
"Thou warnst me [*that*] I have done amiss."—*Scott.*

Obs. 7.—After *than* or *as* expressing a comparison, there is usually an ellipsis of some word or words. The construction of the words employed may be known by supplying the ellipsis; as, "She is younger than I" [*am*].— "He does nothing who endeavours to do more than [*what*] is allowed to humanity."—*Johnson.* "My punishment is greater than [*what*] I can bear."—*Bible.*

NOTES TO RULE XVI.

NOTE I.—When two terms connected refer jointly to a third, they must be adapted to it and to each other, both in sense and in form. Thus: in stead of, "It always *has*, and always will be laudable," say, "It always *has been*, and *it* always will be laudable."

NOTE II.—The disjunctive conjunction *lest* or *but*, should not be employed where the copulative *that*, would be more proper: as, "I feared *that* I should be deserted;" not, "*lest* I should be deserted."

NOTE III.—After *else, other, rather*, and *all comparatives*, the latter term of comparison should be introduced by the conjunction *than*: as, "Can there be any *other than* this?"— *Harris.* "Is not the life *more than* meat?"—*Bible.*

NOTE IV.—The words in each of the following pairs, are the proper *correspondents* to each other; and care should be taken, to give them their right place in the sentence.

1. *Though—yet;* as, "*Though* he were dead, *yet* shall he live."—*John,* xi, 25.

2. *Whether—or;* as, "*Whether* there be few *or* many."

3. *Either—or;* as, "He was *either* ashamed *or* afraid."

4. *Neither—nor;* as, "John the Baptist came *neither* eating bread *nor* drinking wine."—*Luke,* vii, 33.

5. *Both—and;* as, "I am debtor *both* to the Greeks *and* to the Barbarians."—*Rom.,* i, 14.

6. *Such—as;* as, "An assembly *such as* earth saw never." —*Cowper.*

7. *Such—that;* with a finite verb following, to express a consequence: as, "My health is *such that* I cannot go."

8. *As—as;* with an adjective or an adverb, to express equality: as, "The peasant is *as* gay *as* he."—*Cowper.*

9. *As—so;* with two verbs, to express equality or proportion: as, "*As* two are to four, *so* are six to twelve."

10. *So—as;* with an adjective or an adverb, to limit the degree by comparison: as, "How can you descend to a thing *so* base *as* falsehood?"

11. *So—as;* with a negative preceding, to deny equality: as, "No lamb was e'er *so* mild *as* he."—*Langhorne.*

12. *So—as;* with an infinitive following, to express a consequence: as, "These difficulties were *so* great *as* to discourage age him."

9*

13. *So—that ;* with a finite verb following, to express a consequence : as, " He was *so* much injured, *that* he could not walk."

FALSE SYNTAX UNDER RULE XVI.—CONJUNCTIONS.

Examples under Note 1.—*Two Terms with One.*

The first proposal was essentially different and inferior to the second.

[FORMULE.—Not proper, because the preposition *to,* is used with joint reference to the two adjectives *different* and *inferior,* which require different prepositions. But, according to Note 1st under Rule 16th, " When two terms connected refer jointly to a third, they must be adapted to it and to each other, both in sense and in form." The sentence may be corrected thus; The first proposal was essentially different *from* the second, and inferior *to* it.]

He has made alterations and additions to the work.

He is more bold, but not so wise, as his companion.

Sincerity is as valuable, and even more so, than knowledge.

I always have, and I always shall be, of this opinion.

What is now kept secret, shall be hereafter displayed and heard in the clearest light.

We pervert the noble faculty of speech, when we use it to the defaming or to disquiet our neighbours.

Be more anxious to acquire knowledge than of showing it.

The court of chancery frequently mitigates and breaks the teeth of the common law.

Under Note 2.—*Lest or But for That.*

We were apprehensive lest some accident had happened.

I do not deny but he has merit.

Are you afraid lest he will forget you?

These paths and bow'rs, doubt not but our joint hands,
Will keep from wilderness.—*Milton.*

Under Note 3.—*Prefer Than.*

It was no other but his own father.

Have you no other proof except this?

I expected something more besides this.

He no sooner retires but his heart burns with devotion.

Such literary filching is nothing else but robbery.

Under Note 4 — *Of Correspondents.*

Neither despise or oppose what you do not understand.

He would not either do it himself nor let me do it.

The majesty of good things is such, as the confines of them are reverend.

Whether he intends to do so, I cannot tell.

Send me such articles only, that are adapted to this market.

As far as I am able to judge, the book is well written.

No errors are so trivial but they deserve correction.

It will improve neither the mind, nor delight the fancy.

The one is equally deserving as the other.

There is no condition so secure as cannot admit of change.

Do you think this is so good as that?

The relations are so obscure as they require much thought.

None is so fierce that dare stir him up.

There was no man so sanguine who did not apprehend some ill consequence.

I must be so candid to own that I do not understand it.

The book is not as well printed as it ought to be.

> So still he sat as those who wait
> Till judgment speak the doom of fate.—*Scott.*

RULE XVII.—PREPOSITIONS.

Prepositions show the relations of things: as, "He came *from* Rome *to* Paris, *in* the company *of* many eminent men, and passed *with* them *through* many cities."—*Analectic Magazine.*

EXCEPTION FIRST.

The preposition *to*, before an abstract infinitive, and at the head of a phrase which is made the subject of a verb, has no proper antecedent term of relation; as, "*To* learn to die, is the great business of life."—*Dillwyn.* "Nevertheless, *to* abide in the flesh, is more needful for you."—*St. Paul.* "*To* be reduced to poverty, is a great affliction."

EXCEPTION SECOND.

The preposition *for*, when it introduces its object before an infinitive, and the whole phrase is made the subject of a verb, has properly no antecedent term of relation; as, "*For* us to learn to die, is the great business of life."—"Nevertheless, *for* me to abide in the flesh, is more needful for you."—"*For* an old man to be reduced to poverty, is a very great affliction."

OBSERVATIONS ON RULE XVII.

OBS. 1.—In parsing any ordinary *preposition*, the learner should name the *two terms of the relation*, and apply the foregoing rule. The principle is simple and etymological, yet not the less important as a rule of syntax. Among tolerable writers, the prepositions exhibit more errors than any other equal number of words. This is probably owing to the careless manner in which they are usually slurred over in parsing.

OBS. 2.—If the learner be at any loss to discover the two terms of relation, let him ask and answer *two questions;* first, with the interrogative *what* before the preposition, to find the antecedent; and then, with the same pronoun after the preposition, to find the subsequent term. These questions answered according to the sense, will always give the true terms. If one term is obvious, find the other in this way; as, "Day unto day uttereth speech, and night unto night showeth knowledge."—*Psal.* *What* unto day? Ans. "*Uttereth unto day.*" *What* unto night? Ans. "*Showeth unto night.*" To parse rightly is to understand rightly; and what is well expressed, it is a shame to misunderstand or misinterpret.

Obs. 3.—When a preposition *begins* or *ends* a sentence or clause, the terms of relation are transposed; as, "To a studious *man*, action is a *relief*."— *Burgh.* "*Science* they [the ladies] do not *pretend* to."—*Id.* "Until 1 have done that *which I have spoken* to thee of."—*Gen.*, xxviii, 15.

Obs. 4.—The *former* or *antecedent* term of relation may be a noun, an adjective, a pronoun, a verb, a participle, or an adverb: the *latter* or *subsequent* term may be a noun, a pronoun, a pronominal adjective, an infinitive verb, or an imperfect or preperfect participle. The word governed by the preposition, is always the *subsequent* term, however placed.

Obs. 5.—Both the terms of relation are usually expressed; though either of them *may be understood*; as, 1. *The former*—"All shall know me, [reckoning] FROM the least to the greatest."—*Heb.*, viii, 11. [I *say*] "IN a word, it would entirely defeat the purpose."—*Blair.* 2. *The latter*—"Opinions and ceremonies [*which*] they would die FOR."—*Locke.* "IN [*those*] who obtain defence, or who defend."—*Pope.*

Obs. 6.—The only proper exceptions to the foregoing rule, are those which are inserted above, unless the abstract infinitive used as a predicate is also to be excepted; as, "To reason right, is *to* submit."—*Pope.* But here most if not all grammarians would say, the verb *is*, is the antecedent or governing term. The relation, however, is not such as when we say, "He is *to* submit;" but, perhaps, to insist on a different mode of parsing these two infinitives, would be a needless refinement. In relation to the infinitive, *Dr. Adam* remarks, that the preposition *to* is often taken *absolutely*; as, "*To* confess the truth."—"*To* proceed." But the assertion is not entirely true; nor are his examples appropriate; for what he and many other grammarians call the *infinitive absolute*, evidently depends on something *understood*; and the preposition is surely in no instance independent of what follows it, and is therefore never entirely absolute. Prepositions are not to be supposed to have no antecedent term, merely because they stand at the head of a sentence which is made the subject of a verb; for the sentence itself often contains that term, as in the following example: "*In* what way mind acts upon matter, is unknown." Here *in* shows the relation between *acts* and *way*; because it is suggested, that mind *acts* IN *some way*."

Obs. 7.—The preposition (as its name implies) *precedes* the word which it governs. But, in poetry, the preposition is sometimes placed after its object; as,

> "Wild Carron's lonely *woods among*."—*Langhorne.*

Obs. 8.—In the familiar style, a preposition governing a relative or an interrogative pronoun, is often separated from its object, and connected with the other term of relation; as, "*Whom* did he speak *to?*" But it is more dignified, and in general more graceful, to place the preposition before the pronoun; as, "*To whom* did he speak?"

Obs. 9.—Two prepositions sometimes come together; as, "Lambeth is *over against* Westminster-abbey."—*Murray.*

> "And *from before* the lustre of her face."—*Thomson.*
> "Blows mildew *from between* his shrivel'd lips.—*Cowper.*

These should be written as compounds, and taken together in parsing; for if we parse them separately, we must either call the first an *adverb*, or suppose some very awkward ellipsis.

Obs. 10.—Two separate prepositions have sometimes a joint reference to the same noun: as, "He boasted *of*, and contended *for*, the privilege." This construction is formal, and scarcely allowable, except in the law style. It is better to say, "He boasted of the privilege, and contended for it."

Obs. 11.—The preposition *into*, expresses a relation produced by motion or change; and *in*, the same relation, without reference to motion: hence, "to walk *into* the garden," and, "to walk *in* the garden," are very different.

Obs. 12.—*Between* or *betwixt* is used in reference to two things or parties: *among* or *amidst*, in reference to a greater number, or to something by which an other may be surrounded; as,

> "Thou pendulum *betwixt* a smile and tear."—*Byron.*
> "The host *between* the mountain and the shore."—*Id.*

" To meditate *amongst* decay, and stand
A ruin *amidst* ruins."—*Id.*

NOTES TO RULE XVII

Note I.—Prepositions must be chosen and employed agreeably to the usage and idiom of the language, so as rightly to express the relations intended.

Note II.—An *ellipsis* or *omission* of prepositions is inelegant, except in those phrases in which long and general use has sanctioned it. In the following sentence, *of* is needed.

" ———— I will not flatter you,
That all I see in you is *worthy love.*"— *Shak.*

FALSE SYNTAX UNDER RULE XVII.—PREPOSITIONS.

Examples under Note 1.— *Choice of Prepositions.*

Her sobriety is no derogation to her understanding.

[Formule.—Not proper. because the relation between *derogation* and *understanding* is not correctly expressed by the preposition *to*. But, according to Note 1st under Rule 17th. "Prepositions must be chosen and employed agreeably to the usage and idiom of the language. so as rightly to express the relations intended." This relation would be better expressed by *from;* thus, Her sobriety is no derogation *from* her understanding.]

She finds a difficulty of fixing her mind.
This affair did not fall into his cognizance.
He was accused for betraying his trust.
There was no water, and he died for thirst.
I have no occasion of his services.
You may safely confide on him.
I entertain no prejudice to him.
You may rely in what I tell you.
Virtue and vice differ widely with each other.
This remark is founded in truth.
After many toils, we arrived to our journey's end.
I will tell you a story very different to that.
Their conduct is agreeable with their profession.
Excessive pleasures pass from satiety in disgust.
I turned into disgust from the spectacle.
They are gone in the meadow.
Let this be divided between the three.
The shells were broken in pieces.
The deception has passed among every one.
They never quarrel among each other.
Amidst every difficulty, he persevered.
Let us go above stairs.
I was at London, when this happened.
We were detained to home, and disappointed in our walk.
This originated from mistake.

18

The Bridewell is situated to the west of the City-Hall, and it
has no communication to the other buildings.

I am disappointed of the work; it is very inferior from what
I expected.

Under Note 2.—Omission of Prepositions.

Be worthy me, as I am worthy you.—*Dryden.*
They cannot but he unworthy the care of others.
Thou shalt have no portion on this side the river.
Sestos and Abydos were exactly opposite each other.
Ovid was banished Rome by his patron Augustus.

RULE XVIII.—INTERJECTIONS.

Interjections have no dependent construction: as, "*O!*
let not thy heart despise me."—*Johnson.*

OBSERVATIONS ON RULE XVIII.

Obs. 1.—To this rule there are properly *no exceptions.* Though interjections are sometimes uttered in close connexion with other words, yet, being
mere signs of passion and feeling, they cannot have any strict grammatical
relation, or dependence according to the sense. Being destitute alike of relation, agreement, and government, they must be used independently, if
used at all.

Obs. 2.—The interjection *O* is common to many languages, and is frequently prefixed to nouns or pronouns put absolute by direct address; as,
"Arise, *O Lord; O God,* lift up thine hand."—*Psalms,* x, 12. "*O ye* of
little faith!"—*Mat.,* vi, 30. The *Latin* and *Greek* grammarians, therefore,
made this interjection the sign of the *vocative case;* which is the same as the
nominative put absolute by address in *English.*

Obs. 3.—"Interjections in English have no government."—*Lowth.* When
a word not in the nominative absolute, follows an interjection, as part of an
imperfect exclamation, its construction depends on something *understood;*
as, "Ah *me!*"—that is, "Ah! *pity* me."—"Alas *for* them!"—that is, "Alas!
I *sigh* for them."—"O *for* that warning voice!"—that is, "O! *how I long* for
that warning voice!"—"O! *that* they were wise!"—that is, "O! *how I wish*
that they were wise!" Such expressions, however, lose much of their vivacity, when the ellipsis is supplied.

Obs. 4.—Interjections may be placed *before* or *after* a simple sentence, and
sometimes *between* its parts; but they are seldom allowed to interrupt the
connexion of words closely united in sense. Murray's definition of an interjection is faulty, and directly contradicted by his example: "O virtue! how
amiable thou art!"

CHAPTER III.—GOVERNMENT.

Government has respect only to nouns, pronouns, verbs,
participles, and prepositions; the other five parts of
speech neither govern nor are governed. The *governing*
words, may be either nouns, pronouns, verbs, participles,

or prepositions; the words *governed* are either nouns, pronouns, verbs, or participles. In parsing, the learner must remember that the rules of government are not to be applied to the *governing* words, but to those which *are governed;* and which, for the sake of brevity, are often technically named after the particular form or modification assumed; as, *possessives, objectives, same cases, infinitives, gerundives.* Taken in this way, none of the following rules can have any exceptions.

Obs.—The *Arrangement* of words, (which is treated of in the observations on the rules of construction,) is an important part of syntax, in which not only the beauty but the propriety of language is intimately concerned, and to which particular attention should therefore be paid in composition. But it is to be remembered, that the mere collocation of words in a sentence never affects the method of parsing them; on the contrary, the same words, however placed, are always to be parsed in precisely the same way, so long as they express precisely the same meaning. In order to show that we have parsed any part of an inverted or difficult sentence rightly, we are at liberty to declare the meaning by any arrangement which will make the construction more obvious, provided we retain both the sense and all the words unaltered; but to drop or alter any word, is to pervert the text and to make a mockery of parsing. Grammar rightly learned, enables one to understand both the sense and the construction of whatsoever is rightly written; and he who reads what he does not understand, reads to little purpose. With great indignity to the muses, several pretenders to grammar have foolishly taught, that, "in parsing poetry, in order to *come at the meaning* of the author, the learner will find it necessary to transpose his language."—*Kirkham's Gr.,* p. 166. See also *Merchant, Wilcox, Hull,* and others, to the same effect. To what purpose can he *transpose* a sentence, who does not first see what it means, and how to explain or parse it as it stands?

RULE XIX.—POSSESSIVES.

A noun or a pronoun in the Possessive case, is governed by the name of the thing possessed; as,

"*Theirs* is the vanity, the learning *thine;*
"Touch'd by *thy* hand, again *Rome's* glories shine."

OBSERVATIONS ON RULE XIX.

Obs. 1.—Every possessive is governed by some *noun* expressed or understood, except such as (without the possessive sign) are put in apposition with others so governed; and for every possessive termination there must be a separate governing word. The possessive sign *may* and *must* be omitted in certain cases; but it is never omitted *by ellipsis,* as *Murray* erroneously teaches. The four lines of Note 2d below, are sufficient to show, in every instance, when it must be used, and when omitted; but *Murray,* after as many octavo pages on the point, still leaves it undetermined. If a person knows what he means to say, let him express it according to the note, and he shall not err.

Obs. 2.—The possessive case generally comes *immediately before* the governing noun; as, "All *nature's* difference keeps all *nature's* peace."—*Pope.* "Lady! be *thine* [i. e. thy walk] the *Christian's* walk."—*Ch. Observer.* But to this general principle there are some exceptions: as,

₁. When an adjective intervenes; as, "*Flora's* earliest *smells.*"—*Milton.* "Of *Will's* last night's *lecture.*"—*Spectator.*

2. When the possession is affirmed or denied; as, "The book is *mine*, and not *John's.*" But here the governing noun *may be supplied* in its proper place; and, in some such sentences, it *must be*, else a pronoun will be the only governing word: as, "Ye are Christ's [disciples], and Christ is God's" [son].—*St. Paul.*

3. When the case occurs without the sign; as, "In her *brother* Absalom's house."—*Bible.* "David and Jonathan's friendship."—"Adam and Eve's morning hymn."—*Dr. Ash.* "Behold, the heaven, and the heaven of heavens, is the Lord's thy *God.*"—*Deut.*, x, 14.

Obs. 3.—Where the governing noun cannot be easily mistaken, it is often omitted by ellipsis; as, "At the alderman's" [house]—"A book of my brother's" [*books*]—"A subject of the emperor's" [*subjects*]. This is the true explanation of all *Murray's* "double genitives;" for the first noun, being partitive, naturally suggests a plurality of the same kind.

Obs. 4.—When two or more nouns of the possessive form are in any way connected, they usually refer to things individually different, but of the same name; and, when such is the meaning, the governing noun is *understood* wherever the sign is added without it: as,

"From Stiles's pocket into *Nokes's*" [*pocket*].—*S. Butler.*
"Add *Nature's, Custom's, Reason's,* Passion's strife."—*Pope.*

Obs. 5.—The possessive sign is sometimes annexed to that part of a compound name, which is, of itself, in the objective case; as, "The *captain-of-the-guard's* house."—*Bible.* "The *Bard-of-Lomond's* lay is done."—*Hogg.* "Of the *Children-of-Israel's* half thou shalt take one portion."—*Num.*, xxxi, 30. Such compounds ought always to be written with hyphens, and parsed together as *possessives* governed in the usual way. The words cannot be explained separately.

Obs. 6.—In the following phrase, the possessive sign is awkwardly added to a distinct *adjective:* "In Henry the *Eighth's* time."—*Walker's Key, Introd.* p. 11. Better, "In the time *of* Henry the Eighth." But, in the following line, the adjective elegantly takes the sign; because there is an ellipsis of both nouns:

"The rich *man's joys* increase, the *poor's* decay."—*Goldsmith.*

Obs. 7.—To avoid a concurrence of hissing sounds, the *s* is sometimes omitted, and the apostrophe alone retained to mark the possessive singular; as, "For *conscience'* sake."—*Bible.* "*Moses'* minister."—*Ibid.* "*Felix'* room."—*Ibid.* "*Achilles'* wrath."—*Pope.* But the elision should be sparingly indulged. It is in general less agreeable than the regular form; as, *Hicks'* for *Hicks's,*—*Barnes'* for *Barnes's.*

Obs. 8.—Whatever word or term gives rise to the direct relation of property, and is rightly made to govern the possessive case, must be a *noun*—must be the *name* of some substance, quality, state, or action. When therefore other parts of speech assume this relation, they become nouns; as, "Against the day of *my burying.*"—*John*, xii, 7. "Of *my whereabout.*"—*Shak.* "The very head and front of *my offending.*"—*Id.*

Obs 9.—Some grammarians say, that a *participle* may govern the possessive case before it, and yet retain the government and adjuncts of a *participle;* as. "We also *properly* say, 'This will be the effect of the *pupil's composing* frequently.'"—*Murray's Gram.* "What can be the reason of the *committee's having delayed* this business?"—*Murray's Key.* This construction is *faulty*, because it confounds the properties of different parts of speech, and produces a hybridous class between the participle and the noun; "but this," says *Lowth*, "is inconsistent; let it be either the one or the other, and abide by its proper construction." It is also *unnecessary*, because the same idea may be otherwise expressed more elegantly; as, "This will be the effect, *if the pupil compose* frequently."—"*Why have the committee* delayed this business?"

NOTES TO RULE XIX.

NOTE I.—In the use of the possessive case, its appropriate

form should be observed: thus, write *men's, hers, its, ours, yours, theirs;* and not, *mens', her's, it's, our's, your's, their's.*

NOTE II.—When nouns of the possessive case, are connected by conjunctions, or put in apposition, the sign of possession must always be annexed to such, and such only, as immediately precede the governing noun, expressed or understood; as, "*John* and *Eliza's* teacher is a man of more learning than *James's* or *Andrew's.*"—"For *David* my *servant's* sake."—*Bible.* "Lost in *love's* and *friendship's* smile."—*Scott.*

NOTE III.—The relation of property may also be expressed by the preposition *of* and the objective: as, "The will *of man;*" for, "*man's* will." Of these forms, we should adopt that which will render the sentence the most perspicuous and agreeable; and, by the use of both, avoid an unpleasant repetition of either.

NOTE IV.—A noun governing the possessive plural, should not be made plural, unless the sense requires it. Thus: say, "We have changed our *mind,*" if only one purpose or opinion is meant.

OBS.—A noun taken figuratively may be singular, when the literal meaning would require the plural: such expressions as, "their *face*,"—"their *neck*,"—"their *hand*,"—"their *head*,"—"their *heart*,"—"our *mouth*,"—"our *life*,"—are frequent in the Scriptures, and are not improper.

NOTE V.—The possessive case should not be prefixed to a participle that is not taken in all respects as a noun. The following phrase is therefore wrong: "Adopted by the Goths in *their* pronouncing the Greek."—*Walker's Key*, p. 17. Expunge *their.*

FALSE SYNTAX UNDER RULE XIX.—POSSESSIVES.

Examples under Note 1.—*The Possessive Form.*

Thy ancestors virtue is not thine.

[FORMULE.—Not proper, because the noun *ancestors*, which is intended for the possessive plural, has not the appropriate form of that case. But, according to Note 1st under Rule 19th, "In the use of the possessive case, its appropriate form should be observed." An apostrophe is required after *ancestors*; thus, Thy *ancestors'* virtue is not thine."]

Mans chief good is an upright mind.
I will not destroy the city for ten sake.
Moses rod was turned into a serpent.
They are wolves in sheeps clothing.
The tree is known by it's fruit.
The privilege is not their's, any more than it is your's.

Yet he was gentle as soft summer airs,
Had grace for others sins, but none for theirs'.

18*

Under Note 2.—*Possessives Connected.*

There is but little difference between the Earth and Venus's diameter.

This hat is John, or James's.

The store is opposite to Morris's and Company's.

This palace had been the grand Sultan's Mahomet's.

This was the Apostle's Paul's advice.

Were Cain's occupation and Abel the same?

Were Cain and Abel's occupation the same?

Were Cain's and Abel's occupations the same?

Were Cain and Abel's parents the same?

Were Cain's parents and Abel the same?

Was Cain's and Abel's father there?

Were Cain's and Abel's parents there?

> Thy Maker's will has placed thee here,
> A Maker's wise and good.

Under Note 3.—*Choice of Forms.*

The world's government is not left to chance.

He was Louis the Sixteenth's son's heir.

The throne we honour is the choice of the people.

We met at my brother's partner's house.

An account of the proceedings of the court of Alexander.

Here is a copy of the Constitution of the Society of Teachers of the city of New York.

Under Note 4.—*Nouns with Possessives Plural.*

Their healths perhaps may be pretty well secured.—*Locke.*

We all have talents committed to our charges.

For your sakes forgave I it, in the sight of Christ.

We are, for our parts, well satisfied.

The pious cheerfully submit to their lots.

Fools think it not worth their whiles to be wise.

Under Note 5.—*Possessives with Participles.*

I rewarded the boy for his studying so diligently.

Have you a rule for your thus parsing the participle?

He errs in his giving the word a double construction.

By our offending others, we expose ourselves.

They deserve our thanks, for their quickly relieving us.

RULE XX.—OBJECTIVES.

Active-transitive verbs, and their imperfect and pre-perfect participles, govern the objective case; as "I found *her* assisting *him*."—"Having finished the *work*, I submit *it*."

OBSERVATIONS ON RULE XX.

Obs. 1.—Every objective is governed by some *verb* or *participle*, according to this Rule, or by some *preposition*, according to Rule 22d; except such as are put *in apposition* with others according to Rule 3d, or *after an infinitive or participle* according to Rule 21st; as, "Like him of Gath, *Goliath*."—"They took him to be *me*."

Obs. 2.—The objective case generally follows the governing word: but when it is emphatic, it often precedes the nominative; as, "*Me* he restored to mine office, and *him* he hanged."—*Gen.*, xli, 13. "*Home* he had not."—*Thomson.* "This *point* they have gained." In poetry it is sometimes placed between the nominative and the verb; as, "His daring foe securely *him* defied."—*Milton.* "The broom its yellow *leaf* hath shed."—*Langhorne.* A relative or an interrogative pronoun is commonly placed at the head of its clause, and of course it precedes the verb which governs it; as, "I am Jesus, *whom* thou persecutest."—*Acts.* "*Whom* will the meeting appoint?"

Obs. 3.—All active-transitive verbs have some *noun* or *pronoun* for their object. Though verbs are often followed by the infinitive mood, or a dependent clause, forming a part of the logical predicate; yet these terms, being commonly introduced by a connecting particle, do not constitute *such an object* as is contemplated in our definition of a transitive verb. If, in the sentence, "Boys *love* to play," the verb is transitive, as several grammarians affirm; why not also in "Boys *like* to play," "Boys *delight* to play," "Boys *seem* to play," "Boys *cease* to play," and the like? The construction is precisely the same. It must, however, be confessed, that some verbs which thus take the infinitive after them, cannot otherwise be intransitive.

Obs. 4.—The word *that*, which is often employed to introduce a clause, is, by some grammarians, considered as a pronoun, representing the clause which follows it. And their opinion seems to be warranted both by the origin and the general import of the particle. But in conformity to general custom, and to his own views of the practical purposes of grammatical analysis, the author has ranked it with the conjunctions. And he thinks it better, to call those verbs intransitive, which are followed by *that* and a dependent clause, than to supply the very frequent ellipses which the other explanation supposes. To explain it as a conjunction, *connecting an active-transitive verb and its object*, (as several respectable grammarians do,) appears to involve some inconsistency.

Obs. 5.—Active-transitive verbs are often followed by two objectives in apposition: as, "Thy saints proclaim *thee king*."—*Cowper.* "The Author of my being formed *me man*."—*Murray.* "And God called the *firmament Heaven*."—*Bible.* And, in such a construction, the direct object is sometimes placed before the verb; as, "And *Simon* he surnamed Peter."—*Mark*, iii, 15.

Obs. 6.—When a verb is followed by two words in the objective case, which are neither in apposition nor connected by a conjunction, one of them is governed by a preposition understood; as, "I paid [to] *him* the money."—"They offered [to] *me* a *seat*."—"He asked [of] *them* the *question*."—"I yielded, and unlock'd [to] *her* all my *heart*."—*Milton.*

Obs. 7.—In expressing such sentences passively, the object of the preposition is sometimes erroneously assumed for the nominative; as, "*He* was paid *the money*," in stead of, "*The money* was paid [to] *him*."

NOTES TO RULE XX.

Note I.—Those verbs and participles which require an object, should not be used intransitively; as, "She *affects* [*kindness*,] in order to *ingratiate* [*herself*] with you."—"I will not *allow of* it." Expunge *of*, that *allow* may govern the pronoun *it.*

Note II.—Those verbs and participles which do not admit an object, should not be used transitively; as, " The planters *grow* cotton." Say *raise*, or *cultivate.*

Obs.—Some verbs will govern a kindred noun, or its pronoun, but no other; as, " He *lived* a virtuous *life.*"—" Hear, I pray you, this *dream which* I *have dreamed.*"—*Gen.*, xxxvii, 6.

Note III.—The passive verb should always take for its subject the direct object of the active-transitive verb from which it is derived; as, (*Active*) " They denied me this privilege."— (*Passive*,) " This *privilege* was denied me,"—not, "*I* was denied this privilege."

FALSE SYNTAX UNDER RULE XX.—OBJECTIVES.

She I shall more readily forgive.

[Formule.—Not proper, because the pronoun *she* is in the nominative case, and is used as the object of the active-transitive verb *shall forgive.* But according to Rule 20th, " Active-transitive verbs, and their imperfect and preperfect participles, govern the objective case."—Therefore, *she* should be *her;* thus, *Her* I shall more readily forgive.]

Thou only have I chosen.
Who shall we send on this errand?
My father allowed my brother and I to accompany him.
He that is idle and mischievous, reprove sharply.
Who should I meet but my old friend!
He accosts whoever he meets.
Whosoever the court favours, is safe.
They that honour me I will honour.
Who do you think I saw the other day?

Under Note 1.—An Object Required.

The ambitious are always seeking to aggrandize.
I must premise with three circumstances.
This society does not allow of personal reflections.
False accusation cannot diminish from real merit.
His servants ye are to whom ye obey.

Under Note 2.—False Transitives.

Good keeping thrives the herd.
We endeavoured to agree the parties.
Being weary, he sat him down.
Go, flee thee away into the land of Judah.
The popular lords did not fail to enlarge themselves on the subject.

Under Note 3.—Passive Verbs.

They were refused the benefit of their recantation.
Believers are not promised temporal riches.
We were shown several beautiful pictures.
But, unfortunately, I was denied the favour.
You were paid a high compliment.
I have never been asked the question.

RULE XXI.—SAME CASES.

Active-intransitive, passive, and neuter verbs, and their participles, take the same case *after* as *before* them, when both words refer to the same thing: as, "*He* returned a *friend, who* came a *foe.*"—*Pope.* "The *child* was named *John.*"—"*It* could not be *he.*"

OBSERVATIONS ON RULE XXI.

Obs. 1.—The verbs described in this rule do not, like active-transitive verbs, require a regimen, or case after them; but their finite tenses may be followed by a nominative, and their infinitives and participles by a nominative or an objective, explanatory of a noun or pronoun which precedes them. And as these cases belong after the verb or participle, they may in a certain sense be said to be *governed* by it. But the rule is perhaps more properly a rule of agreement; the word which follows the verb or participle, may be said to form a simple concord with that which precedes it, as if the two were *in apposition.* [See Rule 3d.]

Obs. 2.—In this rule the terms *after* and *before* refer rather to the order of the sense and construction, than to the placing of the words. The proper subject of the verb is the nominative *to* it, or *before* it, by Rule 2d; and the other nominative, however placed, belongs after it, by Rule 21st. In general, however, the proper subject *precedes* the verb, and the other word *follows* it, agreeably to the literal sense of the rule. But when the proper subject is placed after the verb, as in the nine instances specified under Rule 2d, the explanatory nominative, is commonly introduced still later; as, "But be *thou* an *example* of the believers."—1 *Tim.*, iv, 12.

Obs. 3.—In interrogative sentences, the terms are usually transposed, or both are placed after the verb; as,

"Whence, and *what* art *thou*, execrable shape?"—*Milton.*
"Art *thou* that traitor *angel?* art *thou he?*"—*Idem.*

Obs. 4.—In a declarative sentence, there may be a rhetorical or poetical transposition of the terms; as, "I was eyes to the blind, and *feet* was *I* to the lame."—*Job*, xxix, 15.

"Far other *scene* is *Thrasymenè* now."—*Byron.*

Obs. 5.—In some peculiar constructions, both words naturally come before the verb; as, "I know not *who she* is."—"Inquire thou whose *son the stripling* is."—1 *Sam.*, xvii, 56. "Man would not be the creature *which he* now is."—*Blair.* "I could not guess *who it* should be."—*Addison.* And they are sometimes placed in this manner by *hyperbaton*, or transposition; as, "Yet *He it* is."—*Young.* "No contemptible *orator he* was."—*Dr. Blair.*

Obs. 6.—As infinitives and participles have no nominatives of their own, such as are not transitive in themselves, may take different cases after them; and, in order to determine what case it is that follows them, the learner must carefully observe what preceding word denotes the same person or thing. This word being often remote and sometimes understood, the sense is the only clew to the construction. Examples: "*Who* then can bear the thought of *being* an *outcast* from his presence?"—*Addison.* "*I* cannot help *being* so passionate an *admirer* as I am."—*Steele.* "To recommend *what* the soberer part of mankind look upon to *be* a *trifle.*"—*Id.* "*It* would be a romantic *madness*, for a *man* to be a *lord* in his closet."—*Id.* "To affect to be a *lord* in one's closet, would be a romantic *madness.*" In this last sentence, *lord* is in the objective after *to be;* and *madness*, in the nominative after *would be.*

FALSE SYNTAX UNDER RULE XXI.—SAME CASES.

We did not know that it was him.

[FORMULE.—Not proper, because the pronoun *him*, which belongs after the neuter verb *was*, is in the objective case, and does not agree with the pronoun *it*, which belongs before it as the nominative; both words referring to the same thing. But, according to Rule 21st, "Active-intransitive, passive, and neuter verbs, and their participles, take the same case after as before them, when both words refer to the same thing." Therefore, *him* should be *he;* thus, We did not know that it was *he.*]

We thought it was thee.
I would act the same part, if I were him.
It could not have been her.
It is not me, that he is angry with.
They believed it to be I.
It was thought to be him.
If it had been her, she would have told us.
We know it to be they.
Whom do you think it is?
Who do you suppose it to be?
We did not know whom they were.
Thou art him whom they described.
Impossible! it can't be me.
Whom did he think you were?
Whom say ye that I am?

RULE XXII.—OBJECTIVES.

Prepositions govern the Objective case: as,
"Truth and good are one:
And beauty dwells *in them*, and they *in her*,
With like *participation.*"—*Akenside.*

OBSERVATIONS ON RULE XXII.

OBS. 1.—Most of the prepositions may take the *imperfect participle* for their object; and some, the *preperfect*, or *pluperfect:* as, "*On opening* the trial, they accused him *of having defrauded* them."—"A quick wit, a nice judgement, &c., could not raise this man *above being received* only upon the foot *of contributing* to mirth and diversion."—*Steele.* And the preposition *to* is often followed by an *infinitive.* But, as prepositions, when they introduce declinable words, or words that have cases, always govern the *objective*, there are properly *no exceptions* to the foregoing rule.—Let not the learner suppose, that infinitives or participles, when they are governed by prepositions, are therefore in the *objective case;* for case is no attribute of either of them. They are governed *as participles* or *as infinitives*, and not *as cases.* The mere fact of government is so far from creating the modification governed, that it necessarily presupposes it to exist.

OBS. 2.—Prepositions are sometimes *elliptically* construed with *adjectives;* as, *in vain, in secret, at first, on high ;* i. e., *in a vain manner, in secret places, at the first time, on high places.* Such phrases imply time, place, degree, or manner, and are equivalent to adverbs. In parsing, the learner may supply the ellipsis.

OBS. 3.—In a few instances prepositions precede *adverbs ;* as, *at once, from above, for ever.* These should be united, and parsed as *adverbs,* or else the adverb must be parsed as a noun, according to observation 3d on Rule 15th.

OBS. 4.—When nouns of *time* or *measure* are connected with verbs or adjectives, the prepositions which govern them, are generally suppressed: as, "We rode sixty miles that day;" that is, "*through* sixty miles *on* that day." —"The wall is ten feet high;" that is, "high *to* ten feet." In parsing, supply the ellipsis; or else you must take the time or measure *adverbially,* as relating to the verb or adjective qualified by it. Such expressions as, "A board of six feet long,"—"A boy of twelve years old," are wrong. Strike out *of;* or say, "A board of six feet *in length,*"—"A boy of twelve years *of age.*"

OBS. 5.—After the adjectives *like, near,* and *nigh,* the preposition *to* or *unto* is often understood; as, "It is *like* [*to* or *unto*] silver."—*Allen.* "How *like* the former!"—*Dryden.* "*Near* yonder copse."—*Goldsmith.* "*Nigh* this recess."—*Garth.* As similarity and proximity are *relations,* and not *qualities,* it might seem proper to call *like, near,* and *nigh,* prepositions; and some grammarians have so classed the last two. *Dr. Johnson* seems to be inconsistent in calling *near* a preposition in the phrase, "*So near* thy heart," and an adjective, in the phrase, "Being *near* their master !" We have not placed them with the prepositions for *four* reasons: (1.) Because they are sometimes *compared ;* (2.) Because they sometimes have *adverbs* evidently relating to them; (3.) Because the preposition *to* or *unto* is sometimes expressed after them; and, (4.) Because the words which *usually* stand for them in the learned languages, are clearly *adjectives.* *Like,* when it expresses similarity of *manner,* and *near* and *nigh,* when they express proximity of *degree,* are *adverbs.*

OBS. 6.—The word *worth* is often followed by an adjective, or a participle, which it appears to *govern ;* as, "If your arguments produce no conviction, they are *worth* nothing to me."—*Beattie.* "To reign is *worth* ambition."— *Milton.* "This is life indeed, life *worth* preserving."—*Addison.* It is not easy to determine to what part of speech *worth* here belongs. *Dr. Johnson* calls it an *adjective,* but says nothing of the *object* after it, which some suppose to be governed by *of* understood. In this supposition, it is gratuitously assumed, that *worth* is equivalent to *worthy,* after which *of* should be expressed; as, "Whatsoever is *worthy of* their love, is *worth* their anger."— *Denham.* But, as *worth* appears to have no *certain* characteristic of an *adjective,* some call it a *noun,* and suppose a double ellipsis; as, "The book is [of the] worth [of] a dollar." This is still less satisfactory; and, as the whole appears to be mere guess-work, we see no good reason why *worth* is not a *preposition,* governing the noun or participle. If an *adverb* precede *worth,* it may as well be referred to the foregoing verb, as when it occurs before any other preposition.

OBS. 7.—Both *Dr. Johnson* and *Horne Tooke,* (who never agreed if they could help it,) unite in saying that *worth,* in the phrases, "Wo *worth* the man,"—"Wo *worth* the day," &c., is from the imperative of the *Saxon* verb *wrythan* or *weorthan, to be;* i. e., "Wo *be* [*to*] the man," or, "Wo *betide* the man," &c. And the latter affirms, that, as *by* is from the imperative of *beon, to be,* so *with* (though admitted to be sometimes from *withan, to* join) is often no other than this same imperative verb *wyrth* or *worth :* if so, the words *by, with,* and *worth,* were originally synonymous, and should now be referred to one and the same class. The *dative case,* or oblique object, which they governed as *Saxon verbs,* becomes their proper object, when taken as *English prepositions ;* and in this also they appear to be alike.

OBS. 8.—After verbs of *giving, procuring,* and some others, there is usually an ellipsis of *to* or *for* before the objective of the person; as, "Give [*to*] him water to drink."—"Buy [*for*] me a knife." So in the exclamation, "Wo is *me!*"—meaning, "Wo is *to* me!"

FALSE SYNTAX UNDER RULE XXII.—OBJECTIVES.

It rests with thou and me to decide.

[FORMULE.—Not proper, because the pronoun *thou* is in the nominative case, and is governed by the preposition *with.* But, according to Rule 22d, "Prepositions govern the objective case." Therefore, *thou* should be *thee;* thus, It rests with *thee* and me to decide.]

Let that remain a secret between you and I.
I lent the book to some one, I know not who.
Who did he inquire for? Thou.
From he that is needy, turn not away.
We are all accountable, each for his own act's.
Does that boy know who he is speaking to?
I bestow my favours on whosoever I will.

RULE XXIII.—INFINITIVES.

The preposition TO governs the Infinitive mood, and commonly connects it to a finite verb; "I desire TO learn."—*Dr. Adam.*

OBSERVATIONS ON RULE XXIII.

OBS. 1.—No word is more variously explained by grammarians, than this word TO, which is prefixed to the verb in the infinitive mood. *Johnson, Walker, Scott, Todd,* and other lexicographers, call it an *adverb;* but, in explaining its use, they say it denotes certain *relations,* which it is not the office of an *adverb,* to express. [See *Johnson' Dictionary,* 4to.] *Lowth, Murray, Webster, Coar, Comly,* and others, call it a *preposition ;* and some of these ascribe it to the *government* of the verb, and others do not. *Lowth* says, "The *preposition* TO placed before the verb, *makes* the infinitive mood." *Skinner,* in his *Canones Etymologici,* calls it an *equivocal article. Horne Tooke,* who shows that most of our conjunctions and prepositions may be traced back to ancient verbs and nouns, says that *to* has the same origin as *do,* and he seems to consider it an *auxiliary verb.* Many are content to call it a *prefix,* a *particle,* a *sign of the infinitive,* &c., without telling us *why* or *how* it is so, or to *what part of speech* it belongs. If it be a *part of the infinitive,* it is a *verb,* and must be classed with the *auxiliaries. Dr. Ash* placed it among the auxiliaries; but he says, the auxiliaries "seem to have the nature of *adverbs.*" We have given in the preceding rule that explanation which we consider to be the most correct and the most simple. Who first parsed the infinitive in this manner we know not; the doctrine is found in several English grammars, one of which, written by a *classical teacher,* was published in London in 1796.—See *Coar's Grammar,* 12mo, p. 263.

OBS. 2.—Most English grammarians have considered the word *to* as a *part of the infinitive ;* and, like the teachers of Latin, have referred the government of this mood to a preceding verb. But the rule which they give is partial, and often inapplicable; and their exceptions to it are numerous and puzzling. They teach that at least half the different parts of speech *frequently* govern the infinitive: if so, there should be a distinct rule for each; for why should the government of one part of speech be made an exception to that of an other? and, if this be done, with respect to the infinitive, why not also with respect to the objective case? In all instances to which their rule is applicable, the rule here given amounts to the same thing; and it obviates the necessity for their numerous exceptions, and the embarrassment arising from other constructions of the infinitive not noticed in them.

Obs. 3.—The infinitive thus admits a simpler solution in *English*, than in most other languages. In *French*, the infinitive, though frequently placed in immediate dependence on an other verb, may also be governed by several different prepositions, (as *à, de, pour, sans, après,*) according to the sense.* In *Spanish* and *Italian*, the construction is similar. In *Latin* and *Greek*, the infinitive is, for the most part, dependent on an other verb. But, according to the grammars, it may stand for a noun in all the six cases; and many have called it an *indeclinable noun*. See the *Port-Royal Latin and Greek Grammars;* in which several peculiar constructions of the infinitive, are referred to the government of a *preposition*.

Obs. 4.—Though the infinitive is commonly made an adjunct to some finite verb, yet it may be joined to almost all the other parts of speech, or to an other infinitive; as,

1. To a *noun;* as, "He had *leave to go.*"
2. To an *adjective;* as, "We were *anxious to see* you."
3. To a *pronoun;* as, "I discovered *him to be* a scholar."
4. To a *verb in the infinitive;* as, "*To cease to do* evil."
5. To a *participle;* as, "*Endeavouring to escape,* he fell."
6. To an *adverb;* as, "She is old *enough to go* to school."
7. To a *conjunction;* as, "He knows better *than to trust* you."
8. To a *preposition;* as, "I was *about to write.*"—*Rev.,* x, 4.
9. To an *interjection;* (by ellipsis;) as, "*O to forget* her!"—*Young.*

Obs. 5.—The infinitive is the mere verb, without affirmation; and, in some respect, resembles a noun. It may stand for—

1. A *subject;* as, "*To steal* is sinful."
2. A *predicate;* as, "To enjoy is *to obey.*"—*Pope.*
3. A *purpose*, or an *end;* as, "He's gone *to do* it."—*Edgeworth.*
4. An *employment;* as, "He loves *to ride.*"
5. A *cause;* as, "I rejoice *to hear* it."
6. A *coming event;* as, "A structure soon *to fall.*"—*Cowper.*
7. A *term of comparison;* as, "He was so much affected as *to weep.*"

Obs. 6.—Anciently, the infinitive was sometimes preceded by *for* as well as *to;* as, "I went up to Jerusalem *for to* worship."—*Acts,* xxiv, 11. "What went ye out *for to* see?"—*Luke,* vii, 26.

> ————————"Learn skilfullie how
> Each grain *for to* laie by itself on a mow."—*Tusser.*

Modern usage rejects the former preposition.

Obs. 7.—The infinitive sometimes depends on a verb *understood;* as, "*To be* candid with you, [*I confess*] I was in fault." Some grammarians have erroneously taught that the infinitive in such sentences is *put absolute.*

Obs. 8.—The infinitive, or a phrase of which the infinitive is a part, being introduced apparently as the subject of a verb, but superseded by some other word, *is put absolute,* or left unconnected, *by pleonasm;* as,

> "*To be,* or *not to be;—that* is the question."—*Shakspeare.*

Obs. 9.—The infinitive of the *verb be,* is often understood; as, "I suppose it [*to be*] necessary." [See *Obs. 2d on Rule* xxiv.]

Obs. 10.—The infinitive usually *follows* the word on which it depends; but this order is sometimes reversed; as,

> "*To catch* your vivid scenes, *too gross* her hand."—*Thomson.*

---

* "La préposition, est un mot indéclinable, placé devant les noms, les pronoms, et les *verbes*, qu'elle régit.—The preposition is an indéclinable word placed before the nouns, pronouns, and *verbs*, which it *governs.*"—*Perrin's Grammar,* p. 152

"Every verb placed immediately after an other verb, or after a preposition, ought to be put in the *infinitive;* because it is then *the regimen* of the verb or preposition which precedes."—*Gram. des Gram. par Girault Du Vivier,* p. 774.

FALSE SYNTAX UNDER RULE XXIII.—INFINITIVES.

Ought these things be tolerated?

[FORMULE.—Not proper, because the infinitive *be tolerated*, is not preceded by the preposition *to*. But, according to Rule 23d, "The preposition *to* governs the infinitive mood, and commonly connects it to a finite verb." Therefore, *to* should be inserted; thus, Ought these things *to* be tolerated?]

Please excuse my son's absence.
Cause every man go out from me.
Forbid them enter the garden.
Do you not perceive it move?
Allow others discover your merit.
He was seen go in at that gate.
Permit me pass this way.

RULE XXIV.—INFINITIVES.

The active verbs, *bid, dare, feel, hear, let, make, need, see,* and their participles, usually take the Infinitive after them, without the preposition TO: as, "If he bade thee *depart,* how darest thou *stay?*"

OBSERVATIONS ON RULE XXIV.

OBS. 1.—The preposition is almost always employed after the passive form of these verbs, and in some instances after the active: as, "He was heard *to* say."—"I cannot see *to* do it."—"What would dare *to* molest him who might call, on every side, to thousands enriched by his bounty?"—*Dr. Johnson.*

OBS. 2.—The auxiliary *be* of the passive infinitive is also suppressed, after *feel, hear, make,* and *see;* as, "I heard the letter *read,*"—not, "*be read.*"

OBS. 3.—A few other verbs, besides the eight which are mentioned in the foregoing rule, *sometimes* have the infinitive after them without *to;* such as, *behold, find, have, help, mark, observe,* and other equivalents of *see.* Example: "Certainly it is heaven upon earth, to *have* a man's mind *move* in charity, *rest* in Providence, and turn upon the poles of truth."—*Ld. Bacon.*

FALSE SYNTAX UNDER RULE XXIV.—INFINITIVES.

They need not to call upon her.

[FORMULE.—Not proper, because the preposition *to* is inserted before *call,* which follows the active verb *need.* But, according to Rule 24th, "The active verbs *bid, dare, feel, hear, let, make, need, see,* and their participles, usually take the infinitive after them, without the preposition *to.*" Therefore, *to* should be omitted; thus, They need not call upon her.]

I felt a chilling sensation to creep over me.
I have heard him to mention the subject.
Bid the boys to come in immediately.
I dare to say he has not got home yet.
Let no rash promise to be made.
We sometimes see bad men to be honoured.
A good reader will make himself to be distinctly heard.

RULE XXV.—NOM. ABSOLUTE.

A noun or a pronoun is put absolute in the Nominative, when its case depends on no other word: as, "*He failing*, who shall meet success?"—"Your *fathers*, where are they? and the *prophets*, do they live forever?"—*Zech.*, i, 5.

"*This said*, he form'd thee, *Adam!* thee, O *man! Dust* of the ground!"—*Milton.*

OBSERVATIONS ON RULE XXV.

OBS. 1.—In parsing the nominative absolute, tell *how* it is put so, whether with a *participle*, by direct *address*, by *pleonasm*, or by *exclamation;* for a noun or a pronoun is put absolute in the nominative, under the following *four circumstances:*

1. When, *with a participle*, it is used to express a cause, or a concomitant fact; as,

—— ——"*Thou looking on,* Shame to be overcome or overreach'd, Would utmost vigor raise."—*Milton.*

2. When, *by direct address*, it is put in the second person, and set off from the verb by a comma; as, "At length, *Seged*, reflect and be wise."—*Dr. Johnson.*

3. When, *by pleonasm*, it is introduced abruptly for the sake of emphasis; as, "*He* that is in the city, famine and pestilence shall devour him." "*Gad*, a troop shall overcome him."—*Gen.*, xlix, 19. "The *north* and the *south*, thou hast created them."—*Psalms*, lxxxix, 12. [See the figure *Pleonasm*, in PART IV.]

4. When, *by mere exclamation*, it is used without address, and without other words expressed or implied to give it construction; as,

"Oh! deep enchanting *prelude* to repose, The *dawn* of bliss, the *twilight* of our woes!"—*Campbell.*

OBS. 2.—The nominative *put absolute, with a participle*, is equivalent to a dependent clause, commencing with *when, while, if, since,* or *because;* as, "I being a child,"—equal to, "When I was a child."

OBS. 3.—The participle *being* is often understood after nouns or pronouns put absolute; as,

"Alike in ignorance, his reason [——] such, Whether he thinks too little or too much."—*Pope.*

OBS. 4.—All *nouns in the second person* are either put absolute, according to Rule 25th, or in apposition with their own pronouns placed before them, according to Rule 3d: as, "This is the stone which was set at nought of *you builders.*"—*Acts.*

"Peace! *minion*, peace! it boots not me to hear The selfish counsel of *you hangers-on.*"—*Author.*

OBS. 5.—Nouns preceded by an article, are almost always in the *third person;* and, in exclamatory phrases, such nouns sometimes appear to have no determinable construction; as, "O *the depth* of the riches both of the wisdom and knowledge of God."—*Rom.*, xi, 33.

OBS. 6.—The case of nouns used in exclamations, or in mottoes and abbreviated sayings, often depends, or may be conceived to depend, on something *understood;* and, when their construction can be satisfactorily explained on the principle of ellipsis, *they are not put absolute.* The following examples may perhaps be resolved in this manner, though the expressions will lose much of their vivacity: "A *horse!* a *horse!* my *kingdom* for a horse!"—

INSTITUTES OF ENGLISH GRAMMAR. [PART III.

Shak. "*Heaps* upon heaps," —"*Skin* for skin,"—" An *eye* for an eye, and a *tooth* for a tooth,"—"*Day* after day,"—" *World* without end."—*Bible.*

FALSE SYNTAX UNDER RULE XXV.—NOM. ABSOLUTE.

Him having ended his discourse, the assembly dispersed.

[Formule.—Not proper, because the pronoun *him*, whose case depends on no other word, is in the objective case. But, according to Rule 25th, "A noun or a pronoun is put absolute in the nominative, when its case depends on no other word. Therefore, *him* should be *he ;* thus, *He* having ended his discourse, the assembly dispersed.]

Me being young, they deceived me.
Them refusing to comply, I withdrew.
Thee being present, he would not tell what he knew.
The child is lost ; and me, whither shall I go?
Oh happy us! surrounded thus with blessings !—*Murray.*
"Thee too! Brutus, my son !" cried Cæsar overcome.

> But him, the chieftain of them all,
> His sword hangs rusting on the wall.

> Her quick relapsing to her former state,
> With boding fears approach the serving train.

> There all thy gifts and graces we display,
> Thee, only thee, directing all our way.

RULE XXVI.—SUBJUNCTIVES.

A future contingency is best expressed by a verb in the Subjunctive present; and a mere supposition with indefinite time, by a verb in the Subjunctive imperfect: but a conditional circumstance assumed as a fact, requires the Indicative mood: as, "If thou *forsake* him, he will cast thee off forever."—"If it *were* not so, I would have told you."—"If thou *went,* nothing would be gained."—"Though he *is* poor, he is contented."

NOTES TO RULE XXVI.

NOTE I.—In connecting words that express time, the order and fitness of time should be observed. Thus: in stead of, "I *have seen* him *last week*," say, "I *saw* him *last week ;*" and in stead of, "I *saw* him *this week*," say, "I *have seen* him *this week.*"

NOTE II.—Verbs of *commanding, desiring, expecting, hoping, intending, permitting,* and some others, in all their tenses, refer to actions or events, relatively present or future : one should therefore say, "I hoped you *would come*,"—not, "*would have come ;*" and, "I intended *to do* it,"—not, "*to have done* it;" &c.

NOTE III.—Propositions that are at all times equally true

or false, should generally be expressed in the present tense; as, "He seemed hardly to know, that two and two *make* four," —not, "*made*."

FALSE SYNTAX UNDER RULE XXVI.—MOODS.

Under the First Clause of Rule 26.—Future Contingencies.

He will not be pardoned, unless he repents.

[FORMULE.—Not proper, because the verb *repents*, which is used to express a future contingency, is in the indicative mood. But, according to the first clause of Rule 26th, "A future contingency is best expressed by a verb in the subjunctive present." Therefore, *repents*, should be *repent;* thus, He will not be pardoned, unless he *repeat*.

He will maintain his cause, though he loses his estate.
They will fine thee, unless thou offerest an excuse.
I shall walk out in the afternoon, unless it rains.
Let him take heed lest he falls.
On condition that he comes, I consent to stay.
If he is but discreet, he will succeed.
Take heed that thou speakest not to Jacob.
If thou castest me off, I shall be miserable.
Send them to me, if thou pleasest.
Watch the door of thy lips, lest thou utterest folly.

Under the Second Clause of Rule 26.—Mere Suppositions.

And so would I, if I was he.

[FORMULE.—Not proper, because the verb *was*, which is used to express a mere supposition, with indefinite time, is in the indicative mood. But, according to the second clause of Rule 26th, "A mere supposition, with indefinite time, is best expressed by a verb in the subjunctive imperfect." Therefore *was* should be *were;* thus, And so would I, if I *were* he.]

If I was to write, he would not regard it.
If thou feltest as I do, we should soon decide.
Though thou sheddest thy blood in the cause, it would but
  prove thee sincerely a fool.
If thou lovedst him, there would be more evidence of it.
I believed, whatever was the issue, all would be well.
If love was never feigned, it would appear to be scarce.
There fell from his eyes as it had been scales.
If he was an impostor, he must have been detected.
Was death denied, all men would wish to die.
O that there was yet a day to redress thy wrongs!
Though thou wast huge as Atlas, thy efforts would be vain.

Under the Last Clause of Rule 26.—Assumed Facts.

If he know the way, he does not need a guide.

[FORMULE.—Not proper, because the verb *know*, which is used to express a conditional circumstance assumed as a fact, is in the subjunctive mood. But, according to the last clause of Rule 26th, "A conditional circumstance assumed as a fact, requires the indicative mood." Therefore, *know* should be *knows;* thus, If he *knows* the way, he does not need a guide.]

Though he seem to be artless, he has deceived us.

If he think as he speaks, he may be safely trusted.

Though this event be strange, it certainly did happen.

If thou love tranquillity of mind, seek it not abroad.

If seasons of idleness be dangerous, what must a continued
. habit of it prove ?—*Blair.*

Though he were a son, yet learned he obedience by the things
which he suffered.

I knew thou wert not slow to hear.

Under Note 1.— Words of Time.

The work has been finished last week.

He was out of employment this fortnight.

This mode of expression has been formerly in use.

I should be much obliged to him if he will attend to it.

I will pay the vows which my lips have uttered when I was in
trouble.

I have compassion on the multitude, because they continue
with me now three days.

I thought, by the accent, that he had been speaking to his
child.

And he that was dead sat up and began to speak.

Thou hast borne, and hast patience, and for my name's sake
hast laboured, and hast not fainted.—*Rev.*, ii, 3.

Ye will not come unto me that ye might have life.

At the end of this quarter, I shall be at school two years.

We have done no more than it was our duty to have done.

Under Note 2.—Relative Tenses.

We expected that he would have arrived last night.

Our friends intended to have met us.

We hoped to have seen you.

He would not have been allowed to have entered.

Under Note 3.—Permanent Propositions.

The doctor affirmed, that fever always produced thirst.

The ancients asserted, that virtue was it own reward.

PROMISCUOUS EXAMPLES OF FALSE SYNTAX.

LESSON I.

[It is here expected that the learner will ascertain for himself the proper form of
correcting each example, according to the particular Rule or Note under which it belongs.]

There is a spirit in man ; and the inspiration of the Almighty
giveth them understanding.

My people doth not consider.

I have never heard who they invited.

> Then hasten thy return; for, thee away,
> Nor lustre has the sun, nor joy the day.

I am as well as when you was here.

That elderly man, he that came in late, I supposed to be the superintendent.

All the virtues of mankind are to be counted upon a few fingers, but his follies and vices are innumerable.

It must indeed be confessed that a lampoon or a satire do not carry in them robbery or murder.

There was more persons than one engaged in this affair.

A man who lacks ceremony, has need for great merit.

A wise man avoids the showing any excellence in trifles.

The most important and first female quality is sweetness of temper.

We choose rather lead than follow.

Ignorance is the mother of fear, as well as admiration.

He must fear many, who many fear.

Every one partake of honour bestowed on the worthy.

The king nor the queen were not at all deceived.

Was there no difference, there would be no choice.

I had rather have been informed.

Must thee return this evening?

Life and death is in the power of the tongue.

I saw a person that I took to be she.

Let him be whom he may, I shall not stop.

This is certainly an useful invention.

That such a spirit as thou dost not understand me.

'It is no more but justice,' quoth the farmer.

LESSON II.

Great improvements has been made.

It is undoubtedly true what I have heard.

The nation is torn by feuds which threaten their ruin.

The account of these transactions were incorrect.

Godliness with contentment are great gain.

The number of sufferers have not been ascertained.

There are one or more of them yet in confinement.

They have chose the wisest part.

He spent his whole life in doing of good.

They know scarcely that temperance is a virtue.

I am afraid lest I have laboured in vain.

Mischief to itself doth back recoil.

This construction sounds rather harshly.

What is the cause of the leaves curling?

Was it thee, that made the noise?
Let thy flock clothe upon the naked.
Wisdom and knowledge is granted unto thee.
His conduct was surprising strange.
This woman taught my brother and I to read.
Let your promises be such that you can perform.
We shall sell them in the state they now are.
We may add this observation, however.
This came in fashion when I was young.
I did not use the leaves, but root of the plant.
We have used every mean in our power continually.
Pass ye away, thou inhabitant of Saphir.—*Micah*, i, 11.
Give every syllable and every letter their proper sound.

LESSON III.

To know exactly how much mischief may be ventured upon
  with impunity, are knowledge enough for some folks.
Every leaf and every twig teem with life.
I was rejoiced at this intelligence.
At this stage of advancement, there is little difficulty in the
  pupil's understanding the passive and neuter verbs.
I was afraid that I should have lost the parcel.
Which of all these patterns is the prettier?
They which despise instruction shall not be wise.
Both thou and thy advisers have mistaken their interest.
A idle soul shall suffer hunger.
The lips of knowledge is a precious jewel.
I and my cousin are requested to attend.
Can only say that such is my belief.
This is different from the conscience being made to feel.
Here is ground for their leaving the world with peace.
Where are you all running so fast?
A man is the noblest work of creation.
Of all other crimes willful murder is the most atrocious.
The tribes whom I visited, are partially civilized.
From hence I conclude they are in error.
The girls' books are neater than the boys.
I intended to have transcribed it.
Shall a character made up of the very worst passions, pass
  under the name of a gentleman?
Rhoda ran in, and told how Peter stood before the gate.
What is latitude and longitude?
Cicero was more eloquent than any Roman.
Who dares apologize for Pizarro?—who is but another name
  for rapacity?

LESSON IV.

Tell me whether you will do it or no.

After the most straitest sect, I lived a Pharisee.

We have no more but five loaves and two fishes.

I know not who it was who did it.

> Doubt not, little though there be,
> But I'll cast a crumb to thee.—*Langhorne.*

This rule is the best which can be given.

I have never seen no other way.

These are poor amends for the men and treasures which we have lost.

Dost thou know them boys?

This is a part of my uncle's father's estate.

Many people never learn to speak correct.

Some people are rash, and others timid : those apprehend too much, these too little.

Is it lawful for us to give tribute to Cæsar or no?

It was not worth while preserving any permanent enmity.

I no sooner saw my face in it, but I was startled at the shortness of it.

Every person is answerable for their own conduct.

They are men that scorn a mean action, and who will exert themselves to serve you.

I do not recollect ever having paid it.

The stoics taught that all crimes were equal.

Every one of these theories are now exploded.

Either of these four will answer.

There is no situation where he would be happy.

The boy has been detected in stealing, that you thought so clever.

I will meet thee there if thee please.

He is not so sick, but what he can laugh.

These clothes does not fit me.

The audience was all very attentive.

> Wert thou some star, which from the ruin'd roof
> Of shak'd Olympus by mischance didst fall!—*Milton.*

LESSON V.

Was the master, or many of the scholars, in the room?

His father's and mother's consent was asked.

Whom is he supposed to be?

He is an old venerable man.

It was then my purpose to have visited Sicily.

It is to the learner only, and he that is in doubt, that this assistance is recommended.

10*

There are not the least hope of his recovery.

Anger and impatience is always unreasonable.

In his letters, there are not only correctness, but elegance.

Opportunity to do good is the highest preferment which a noble mind desires.

The year when he died, is not mentioned.

Had I knew it, I should not have went.

Was it thee, that spoke to me?

The house is situated pleasantly.

He did it as private as he possibly could.

Subduing our passions is the noblest of conquests.

James is more diligent than thee.

Words interwove with sighs found out their way.

He appears to be diffident excessively.

The number of our days are with thee.

Like a father pitieth his children, so the Lord pitieth them that fear him.—*Psalms*, ciii, 13.

The circumstances of this case, is different.

Well for us, if some such other men should rise!

A man that is young in years, may be old in hours, if he have lost no time.

The chief captain, fearing lest Paul should have been pulled in pieces of them, commanded the soldiers to go down, and to take them by force from among them.—*Acts*, xxiii, 10.

> Nay, weep not, gentle Eros; there is left us
> Ourselves to end ourselves.—*Shakspeare.*

CHAPTER IV.—GENERAL ITEMS.

The following comprehensive canon for the correction of all sorts of nondescript errors in syntax, a few general observations on the foregoing code of instructions, some examples of false syntax to be corrected by the General Rule, and a series of parsing lessons, illustrative of the Exceptions and Observations previously presented, constitute the present chapter.

GENERAL RULE OF SYNTAX.

In the formation of sentences, the consistency and adaptation of all the words should be carefully observed; and a regular, clear, and correspondent construction should be preserved throughout.

GENERAL OBSERVATIONS ON THE SYNTAX.

OBS. 1.—In proportion as the rules of Syntax are made few and general, they must be either vague or liable to exceptions. The number of the principles which deserve to be placed in the rules, is not fixed by any obvious distinction; hence the diversity in the number of the rules as given by different grammarians. In this matter a middle course seems to be best. We have therefore taken the parts of speech in their order, and comprised all the general principles of relation, agreement, and government, in *twenty-six leading Rules*. Of these rules, *eight* (namely, the 1st, the 4th, the 14th, the 15th, the 16th, the 17th, the 18th, and the 19th,) are used only in *parsing*; *two* (namely, the 13th and the 26th,) are necessary only for the *correction of false syntax*; the remaining *sixteen* answer the double purpose of *parsing* and *correction*. The *Exceptions*, of which there are *twenty-six*, belong to ten different rules. The *Notes*, of which there are *eighty-seven*, are subordinate rules of syntax, formed for the detection of errors. The *Observations*, of which there are about *two hundred*, are chiefly designed to explain the arrangement of words, and whatever is difficult or peculiar in construction.

OBS. 2.—The *General Rule of Syntax*, being designed to meet every possible form of error in construction, necessarily includes all the particular rules and notes. It is too broad to convey very definite instruction, and ought not to be applied were a special rule or note is applicable. A few examples, not properly coming under any other head, will serve to show its use and application: such examples are given in the *false syntax* below.

OBS. 3.—In the foregoing pages, the principles of *syntax* or *construction*, are supposed to be pretty fully developed; but there may be in composition many errors of such a nature that no rule of grammar can show *what should be substituted*. The greater the inaccuracy, the more difficult the correction; because the sentence may require a change throughout. Thus, the following definition, though very short, is a fourfold solecism: "*Number* is the *consideration* of *an* object, as *one* or *more*."—*Murray*. This sentence, though written by one grammarian, and copied by twenty others, cannot be corrected but by changing every word in it: but this will of course destroy its *identity*, and form an *other sentence*, not an *amendment*. It is unfortunate for youth, that a volume of these incorrigible sentences might be culled from our *grammars!* Examples of false syntax cannot embrace what is either utterly wrong in thought, or utterly unintelligible in language; for the writer's meaning must be preserved in the correction, and where no sense is discovered, particular improprieties can never be detected and proved. The sentence above is one which we cannot correct; but we can say of it—*first*, that *number* in grammar never can be defined, because unity and plurality have no common property—*secondly*, that number is not *consideration*, in any sense of the word—*thirdly*, that *an* object is known to be *one* object, by mere intuition, and not by consideration—and, *fourthly*, that he who considers *an* object as *more* than one, misconceives it!!!!

OBS. 4.—In the first eighteen rules, we have given the *syntax* of all the parts of speech in regard to *relation and agreement*. And, by placing the rules in the order of the parts of speech, we hope to have relieved the pupil from all difficulty in recollecting the numbers by which they are distinguished; for, in the exercise of parsing, it is very important that the Rules be distinctly and accurately quoted by the pupil. Relation and agreement have been taken together, because they could not properly be separated. One word may *relate* to an other and *not agree* with it; but there is never any *necessary agreement* between words that have not a *relation*, or a dependence on each other according to the sense.

OBS. 5.—The *English* language having few inflections, has also few concords or agreements. Articles, adjectives, and participles, which in many other languages *agree* with their nouns in gender, number, and case, have usually in English, no modifications in which they can agree with their nouns. *Lowth* says, "The adjective in English, having no variation of gender and number, *cannot but agree* with the substantive in these respects." What then is the *agreement* of words? Can it be any thing else than their *similarity* in some common property or modification?   And is it not obvious, that no two things in nature can any wise *agree* or *be alike*, except in some qual- ity or accident which belongs to each of them?   Yet how often have *Murray* and others, as well as *Lowth*, forgotten this!   To give one instance out of many: "*Gender* has respect only to the third person singular of the pro- nouns, *he, she, it.*"—*Murray, Pierce, Flint, Lyon, Bacon, Russell, Fisk, Maltby, Alger, Miller, Merchant, Kirkham*, and other idle copyists.   Yet, ac- cording to these same gentlemen, "Gender is *the distinction of nouns*, with regard to sex;" and, "Pronouns *must always agree* with their antecedents, *and* the nouns for which they stand, *in gender.*"   Now, not one of these three careless assertions can possibly be reconciled with either of the others ! ! !

FALSE SYNTAX UNDER THE GENERAL RULE.

If I can contribute to your and my country's glory.— *Goldsmith.*

[FORMULE.—Not proper, because the pronoun *your* has not a clear and regular con- struction. But, according to the General Rule of Syntax, "In the formation of sen- tences, the consistency and adaptation of all the words should be carefully observed; and a regular, clear, and correspondent construction should be preserved throughout." The sentence having a double meaning, may be corrected in two ways: thus, If I can contribute to *our* country's glory—or, If I can contribute to your glory and that of my country.]

Is there, then, more than one true religion?

The laws of Lycurgus but substituted insensibility to enjoy- ment.— *Goldsmith.*

Rain is seldom or ever seen at Lima.

The young bird raising its open mouth for food, is a natural indication of corporeal want.— *Cardell.*

There is much of truth in the observation of Ascham.— *Id.*

Adopting the doctrine which he had been taught.— *Id.*

This library exceeded half a million volumes.— *Id.*

The Coptic alphabet was one of the latest formed of any.— *Id.*

Many evidences exist of the proneness of men to vice.— *Id.*

To perceive nothing, or not to perceive, is the same.

The king of France or England was to be the umpire.

He may be said to have saved the life of a citizen ; and, con- sequently, entitled to the reward.

The men had made inquiry for Simon's house, and stood be- fore the gate.— *Acts*, x, 17.

Give no more trouble than you can possibly help.

The art of printing being then unknown, was a circumstance in some respects favourable to freedom of the pen.

Another passion which the present age is apt to run into, is to make children learn all things.— *Goldsmith.*

It requires few talents to which most men are not born, or, at least, may not acquire.

Nor was Philip wanting in his endeavours to corrupt Demos- thenes, as he had most of the leading men in Greece.— *Goldsmith.*

The Greeks, fearing to be surrounded on all sides wheeled
about and halted, with the river on their backs.—*Id.*

Poverty turns our thoughts too much upon the supplying of
our wants ; and riches, upon enjoying our superfluities.

> That brother should not war with brother,
> And worry and devour each other.—*Cowper.*

> Such is the refuge of our youth and age ;
> The first from hope, the last from vacancy.—*Byron.*

> Triumphant Sylla! couldst thou then divine,
> By aught than Romans Rome should thus be laid?—*Id.*

EXAMPLES FOR ANALYSIS AND PARSING.

SENTENCES OF PECULIAR OR IRREGULAR CONSTRUCTION.

*The examples here given, with the subjoined references and anno-
tations, are designed to illustrate, and exercise the pupil in,
the various Observations, Exceptions, and Notes under the
Sections upon Analysis, and the Rules of Syntax. The
Praxis is the same as in the preceding Syntactical Exercises.*

I. PROSE.

The philosopher, the saint, or the hero—the wise, the good,
or the great man—very often lies hid and concealed in a ple-
beian, *which*[a] a proper education might have disinterred and
brought to light.—*Addison.*

Knowest thou not this of old, since man was placed upon
the earth, that the triumphing of the wicked is short, and the
joy of the hypocrite *but*[b] for a moment?—*Job,* xx., 4, 5.

Wherefore ye *needs*[c] must be subject, not only for wrath, but
also for *conscience'd* sake.—*Rom.,* xiii., 5.

For now I see through a glass darkly ; but then, *face to
face*[e] : now I know in part; but then shall I know even as
also I am known.—1 *Cor.,* xiii., 12.

Ye have heard that it hath been said, '*An eye for an eye,
and a tooth for a tooth*'[f].—*Matt.,* v., 37.

Every man should let his man-servant, and every man his
maid-servant, being a Hebrew or an Hebrewess, go free ; that

---

a Note V., Rule V.
b Obs. 3, Note VII., Rule XV.; and Obs. 2, page 112.
c Adverb. Contraction of *need is.*
d Obs. 7, Rule XIX.
e Adverbial phrase, *idiomatic ;* or independent phrase, *absolute.* [See page 112.]
f Explanatory clause, predicate being understood. Obs. 6, Rule XXV.

none should serve himself of them, *to wit*[g], of a Jew his brother.—*Jer.*, xxxiv., 9.

The beautiful forest in which we were encamped, abounded in bee-trees; *that is to say*[h], trees in the decayed trunks of which, wild bees had established their hives.—*Irving.*

And this is the record of John, when the Jews sent priests and Levites from Jerusalem *to ask him*[i], 'Who art thou?' And he confessed, and denied not, but confessed, 'I am not the Christ.' And they asked him, 'What then? Art thou Elias?' and he saith, 'I am not.'—'Art thou that prophet?' and he answered, '*No.*'[k]—*John*, i., 19.

The rudiments of every language, therefore, must be given *as*[l] a task, not as an amusement.—*Goldsmith.*

Time we ought to consider *as*[l] a sacred trust committed to us by God, of which we are now the depositories, and [of which] we are *to render an account at the last*[m].—*Blair.*

True generosity is a duty as indispensably necessary as *those*[n] imposed upon us by law.—*Goldsmith.*

To teach men to be orators, is little less than *to teach them to be poets.*—*Id.*

Lysippus is told *that his banker asks a debt of forty pounds*[o], and that a distressed acquaintance petitions for the same sum. He gives it, without hesitating, to the latter; for he demands as a favor what the former requires as a debt.—*Id.*

The laws of eastern hospitality allowed them to enter, and the master welcomed them, *like*[p] a man liberal and wealthy. He was skilful enough in appearances soon *to discern*[q] that they were no common guests, and spread his table with magnificence.—*Dr. Johnson.*

The year before, he had so used the matter, that, *what*[r] by force, *what* by policy, he had taken from the Christians above thirty small castles.—*Knolles.*

We exhorted them *to trust in God,*[s] and to love *one an other*[t].—*J. Campbell.*

With all due respect for the calculations of men of science, *I*

[g] An infinitive used as a conjunction.
[h] A clause used as a conjunction.
[i] Verbs of asking and teaching and some others are followed by two objects, one a person, the other a thing; here, *him*, and the following object clause. See Obs. 6 and 7, Rule XX.
[k] Exception 1, Rule XV.
[l] Obs. 7, page 102.
[m] Infinitive phrase, used as an adjective attribute.
[n] Subject of *are* understood. Obs. 7, Rule XVI.
[o] Obs. 7, Rule XX. This clause is a modification of the predicate.
[p] An adjective followed by *to* understood. Obs. 5, Rule XXII.
[q] *To discern* with its adjunct clause, modifies *enough.*
[r] Obs. 19, Rule V.
[s] Obs. 6, Rule XX.
[t] Obs. 9, Rule III.

cannot but remember[u] that when most confident, they have sometimes erred.

I could not do a better thing than *to commend*[v] this habit to my brethren as one closely connected with their own personal piety, and their usefulness in the world.—*A. Barnes.*

It is a good practical rule to keep one's reading well *proportioned*[w] in the two great divisions, prose and poetry.—*H. Reid.*

For a prince to be reduced by villany to my distressful circumstances[x], is calamity enough.—*Sallust.*

Who knows *but*[y] that God, who made the world, may cause that giant Despair may die.—*Bunyan.*

What can be more strange than, that an ounce weight should balance hundreds of pounds, by the intervention of a few bars of thin iron?[z]

This lovely land, this glorious liberty, these benign institutions, the dear purchase of our fathers, are ours ; ours *to enjoy,* ours *to preserve,* ours *to transmit*[a].— *Webster.*

The knowledge of *why they so exist*[b], must be the last act of favor which time and toil will bestow.—*Rush.*

To do what is right, with unperverted faculties, is *ten times*[c] easier than to undo what is wrong.—*Porter.*

And he charged *them that they should tell no man*[d] ; but *the* more he charged them, so much *the*[e] more *a great deal*[f] they published it.—*Mark,* vii., 36.

For in *that he himself hath suffered being tempted*[g], he is able to succour them that are tempted.—*Hebrews,* xi., 18.

It is not to inflate national vanity, nor to swell a light and empty feeling of self-importance ; but it is, *that we may judge justly of our situation and of our duties*[h], *that I earnestly urge this consideration of our position and our character among the nations of the earth*[i].— *Webster.*

I had rather believe all the fables in the Legend, and the

[u] *Remember* is here infinitive and the object of *but,* a preposition equivalent to *except; can* auxiliary to *do* understood.
[v] *To commend* with its adjuncts, subject of a verb understood.   Obs. 7, Rule XVI.
[w] Indirect attribute.   Obs. 6, page 102.
[x] Subject infinitive clause.   Obs. 2, page 137.   Exception 2, Rule XVII.
[y] *But,* a preposition governing the following clause.
[z] The clause introduced by *that,* is the subject of *is* understood.   Obs. 7, Rule XVI.
[a] Infinitives used as adjectives in the active, instead of the passive, voice.
[b] A clause used as the object of a preposition.   Obs. 3, page 112.
[c] Adverbial modification of *easier ;*—a prepositional phrase, *by* being understood.
[d] Double object.
[e] Adverbial modification of *more,* itself modified by *so much.*   Exception 1, Rule I.
[f] Adverbial modification of *more ; deal* governed by *by* understood.
[g] Clause used as the object of *in.*   Obs. 3, page 112.
[h] An adjective attribute clause.
[i] Explanatory clause; adjunct of *it.*

Talmud, and the Alcoran, than *that this universal frame is without a mind*[k].—*Bacon.*

Nevertheless there being others, besides the first supposed author, men not unread nor unlearned in antiquity, who admit that for approved story, which the former explode for fiction; and seeing that ofttimes relations heretofore accounted fabulous, have been often found to contain in them many footsteps and reliques of something true, as what we read in poets of the flood, and giants little believed, till undoubted witnesses taught us, that all was not feigned[l]; I have therefore determined to bestow the telling over *even*[m] of these repeated tales; be it for nothing else but in favour of our English poets and rhetoricians, who by their art will know how to use them judiciously.—*Milton.*

That a nation should be so valorous and courageous to win their liberty in the field, and when they have won it, should be so heartless and unwise in their counsels, as not to know how to use it, value it, what to do with it, or with themselves; but after ten or twelve years' prosperous war and contestation with tyranny, basely and besottedly to run their necks again into the yoke which they have broken, and prostrate all the fruits of their victory for nought at the feet of the vanquished, besides our loss of glory and such an example as kings or tyrants never yet had the like to boast of, will be an ignominy, if it befall us, that never yet befell any nation possessed of their liberty.—*Id.*

II. POETRY.

See the sole bliss Heaven could on all bestow,
Which who but feels, can taste, but thinks can know;
Yet, poor with fortune, and with learning blind,
The bad must miss, the good, untaught, will find.—*Pope.*

Shame to mankind! Philander had his foes;
He felt the truths I sing, and I, in him;
But *he, nor I feel*[a] more.—*Young.*

---

[k] Object clause, *believe* being understood. *Without a mind* is an adjective attribute referring to *frame.*

[l] The part of this sentence ending with *feigned* consists of two very complex independent phrases, connected by *and*, one *absolute*, introduced by *then*, and the other participial, introduced by *seeing.* The other part of the sentence which comes first in analysis, may be resolved into, 1, A. a. b, c, d, 2, c, f, B, 3; and the independent phrases in continuation, into, g, C, h, D, i, k, E, 4, omitting the very simple phrases.

[m] The word *even*, as very frequently used, seems to perform the office of no part of speech, but to be employed merely to give *emphasis* to the particular word or phrase which it precedes. Here it simply makes the phrase *of these reputed tales* emphatic. It has been designated by one author a "word of *euphony*;" but with no apparent propriety since *euphony* and *emphasis* seem not to be necessarily identical. It might perhaps be called a *word of emphasis.*

[a] Obs. 2, Rule VIII.

So reads he nature, whom the lamp of truth
Illuminates :—thy lamp, mysterious Word!
Which whoso sees, no longer wanders lost,
With intellect bemaz'd in endless doubt,
But runs the *road*[b] of wisdom.—*Cowper.*

Yet O the thought, *that thou art safe*[c], and he!
That thought is joy, arrive what may to me.—*Id.*

The *bless'd to-day*[d] is as completely so,
As who began a[e] thousand years ago[f].—*Pope.*

Full *many a gem*[g] of purest ray serene
The dark unfathom'd caves of ocean bear ;
Full many a flower *is* born to blush unseen,
And waste its sweetness on the desert air.—*Gray.*

Then kneeling down to heaven's eternal King,
The saint, the father, and the husband prays[h] ;
Hope ' springs exulting on triumphant wing,'
That thus they all shall meet in future days.—*Burns.*

He can't flatter, he!
An honest mind and plain ; he must speak truth ;
An[i] they will hear it, so ; if not, he's plain.—*Shak.*

What[k]! canst thou not forbear me *half an hour*[l]?
Then get thee *gone*[m], and dig my grave thyself.—*Id.*

If still she loves thee, hoard that gem ;
'Tis *worth*[n] thy vanish'd diadem.—*Byron.*

He calls for Famine, and the meagre fiend
Blows mildew *from between his shrivel'd lips*[o],
And taints the golden ear.—*Cowper.*

Here he had need
All circumspection ; and we now, no less,
Choice in our suffrage ; for on *whom we send*[o],
The weight of all, and our last hope relies.—*Milton.*

---

b Obs., Note II., Rule XX.
c Adjective clause modifying *thought.*
d *Blessed-to-day*, is used here as a noun, equivalent to, *The man who is blessed to-day.*
e Obs. 12. Rule I.
f *A thousand years ago* is an independent phrase (absolute); *ago* being used for *agone, gone,* or *past.*
g Obs. 3. Note II., Rule IV.
h Exception 1, Rule XI.
i Obs. 15. Rule I.
k Obs. 15. Rule V.
l Obs 4. Rule XXII.
m Indirect attribute. Obs. 6, page 102.
n Obs. 6. Rule XXII.
o Obs. 3, page 112.

Who wickedly is wise, or madly brave,
Is but the[p] more a fool, *the* more a knave.—*Pope.*

O God! *methinks*[q] it were a happy life
To be no better than a homely swain;
To sit upon a hill, as I do now,
To carve out dials quaintly, point by point,
Thereby to see the minutes how they run.—*Shak.*

Poor guiltless I! and can I choose *but smile*[r],
When every coxcomb knows me by my style.—*Pope.*

Me[s] miserable! which way shall I fly
Infinite wrath, and infinite despair?—*Milton.*

Ay, but *to die*[t], and we *go* we know not where;
To lie in cold abstraction, and *to rot*;
This sensible warm motion *to become*
A kneaded clod;
        'tis too horrible.—*Shak.*

My soul, turn from them—*turn we*[u] to survey
Where roughest climes a nobler race display.—*Goldsmith.*

Cursed *be I*[u] that did so! All the *charms*
Of Sycorax, toads, beetles, bats, *light*[v] on you?—*Shak.*

Then thus my guide, in accent higher raised
Than I before had heard him: 'Capaneus!
Thou art more punish'd, in *that this thy pride
Lives yet unquench'd*[w]; no torment, save thy rage,
Were[x] to thy fury pain proportion'd full.'—*Cary's Dante.*

    Yet a few days[y], and thee,
The all-beholding sun shall see no more
In all his course; nor yet, in the cold ground,
Where thy pale form was laid with many tears,
Nor in the embrace of ocean, shall exist
Thy image.—*Bryant.*

Nor then the solemn nightingale ceas'd *warbling*[z].—*Milton.*

---

p Exception 1, Rule I.
q Impersonal verb. Contracted from *it thinks me*, a Latin idiom. Obs., page 98.
r *Smile*, an infinitive governed by preposition *but*.
s Exception to Rule XXV. See Obs. 3, Rule XVIII.
t Infinitive absolute. Obs. 8, Rule XXIII.
u Imperative, first person. See Obs., page 79.
v Imperative, third person, plural.
w Obs. 3, page 112.
x Subjunctive mood used for the potential.
y Independent phrase, days being absolute with *being* or *passing* understood.
z Attribute. See Obs. 2, Rule XIV.

CHAPTER V.—EXAMINATION.

QUESTIONS ON SYNTAX.

LESSON I.—DEFINITIONS.

Of what does syntax treat?
What is the *relation* of words?—the *agreement* of words?—the *government* of words?—the *arrangement* of words?

LESSON II.—THE RULES.

How many special rules of syntax are there?
Of what do the first eighteen rules of syntax treat?
Of what do the last eight rules principally treat?
Where is the *arrangement* of words treated of?
To what do articles relate?
What case is employed as the subject of a verb?
What agreement is required between words in apposition?
To what do adjectives relate?
How does a pronoun agree with its antecedent?
How does a pronoun agree with a collective noun?
How does a pronoun agree with joint antecedents?
How does a pronoun agree with disjunct antecedents?

LESSON III.—THE RULES.

How does a verb agree with its subject or nominative?
How does a verb agree with a collective noun?
How does a verb agree with joint nominatives?
How does a verb agree with disjunct nominatives?
What agreement is required, when verbs are connected?
How are participles employed?
To what do adverbs relate?
What is the use of conjunctions?
What is the use of prepositions?
To what do interjections relate?

LESSON IV.—THE RULES.

By what is the possessive case governed?
What case do active-transitive verbs govern?
What case is put after other verbs?
What case do prepositions govern?
What governs the infinitive mood?
What verbs take the infinitive after them without the preposition *to*?
When is a noun or pronoun put absolute?
When should the subjunctive mood be employed?

LESSON V.—THE RULES.

What are the several titles, or subjects, of the twenty-six rules?
What says Rule 1st?—Rule 2d?—Rule 3d?—Rule 4th?—Rule 5th?—Rule 6th?—Rule 7th?—Rule 8th?—Rule 9th?—Rule 10th?—Rule 11th?—Rule 12th?—Rule 13th?—Rule 14th?—Rule 15th?—Rule 16th?—Rule 17th?—Rule 18th?—Rule 19th?—Rule 20th?—Rule 21st?—Rule 22d?—Rule 23d?—Rule 24th?—Rule 25th?—Rule 26th?

LESSON VI.—EXCEPTIONS.

What are the general contents of chapters second and third of this code of syntax?
What are the nature and purpose of the notes to the rules?
What is said of the correction of false syntax.
How many and what exceptions are there to Rule 1st?—to Rule 2d?—to Rule 3d?—to Rule 4th?—to Rule 5th?—to Rule 6th?—to Rule 7th?—to Rule 8th?—to Rule 9th?—to Rule 10th?—to Rule 11th?—to Rule 12th?—

to Rule 13th?—to Rule 14th?—to Rule 15th?—to Rule 16th?—to Rule 17th?—to Rule 18th.

[Now explain and correct orally all the false syntax placed under the Rules and Notes; learning for each lesson about thirty examples, and reciting them without recurrence to the Key during the exercise.]

LESSON VII.—OBSERVATIONS.

What is observed of the *placing* of Articles?—Nominatives?—Words in Apposition?—Adjectives?—Pronouns?—Verbs?—Participles?—Adverbs?—Conjunctions?—Prepositions?—Interjections?—Possessives?—Objectives?—Same Cases?—Infinitives?

Under how many and what circumstances are nouns put absolute?

[Now read all the other observations, so as to be able to refer to them if necessary; and then parse the five lessons of the *Eighth Praxis*.]

CHAPTER VI.—FOR WRITING.

EXERCISES IN SYNTAX.

☞ [When the pupil has been sufficiently exercised in *syntactical parsing*, and has corrected *orally*, according to the formules given, all the examples of false syntax designed for oral exercises; he should *write out* the following exercises, correcting them according to the principles of syntax given in the rules and notes.]

EXERCISE I.—ARTICLES.

Christianity claims an heavenly origin.
An useless excellence is a contradiction in terms.
It would have an happy influence on genius.
Part not with a old friend for an new acquaintance.
Justice eyes not the parties, but cause.
I found in him a friend, and not mere promiser.
These fathers lived in the fourth and following century.
The rich and poor are seldom intimate.
The Bible contains the Old and the New Testaments.
An elegant and florid style are very different.
The humility is a deep which no man can fathom.
The true cheerfulness is the privilege of the innocence.
A devotion is a refuge from a human frailty.
The duplicity and the friendship are not congenial.
The familiarity with the vicious fosters a vice.
A forced happiness is a solecism in the terms.
The favourites are generally the objects of the envy.
An equivocation is a mean and a sneaking vice.
He sent an other and rather a more modest letter.
The flatterers are put to a flight by an adversity.
An obstinacy is unfavourable to the discovery of the truth.
The conic sections are a part of the geometry.
What is the proper meaning of a Landgrave?
Sensuality is one kind of pleasure, such an one as it is.
What sovereign assumes the title of an Autocrat?

Believe me, the man is less a fool than a knave.
He is a much deeper deceiver than a sufferer.
Laziness is a greater thief than pickpocket.
Heroes who then flourished, have passed away.
Time which is to come, may not come to us.

EXERCISE II.—NOUNS.

A friend should bear a friends infirmities'.
Deviations' from rectitude are approaches to sin.
Crafty person's often entrap themselves.
Mens mind's seem to be somewhat variously constituted.
The great doctors, adept's in science, often disagree.
The two men were ready to cut each others' throats.
We went at the rate of five mile an hour.
His income is a thousand pound a year.
Five bushel of wheat are worth forty shilling.
Reading is one mean's of acquiring knowledge.
The well is at least ten fathom deep.
I shall be a hundred mile off by that time.
Wisdom and Folly's votaries travel different roads.
The true philanthropist is all mankind's friend.
He desires the whole human race's happiness.
The idler and the spendthrift's faults are similar.
A good mans words inflict no injury.
Be not generous at other peoples expense.
True hope is swift, and flies with swallows wings.
Lifes current holds its course, and never returns.
Many assume Virtues livery, who shun her service.
I left the parcel at Richardson's, the bookseller's.
The books are for sale at Samuel Wood's & Sons'.
Where shall we find friendship like David's and Jonathan's?
Acquiesce for peace's and harmony's sake.
The moons disk often appears larger than the sun.
Consult Sheridan, Johnson, and Walker's Dictionary.
Such was my uncle's agent's wife's economy.
A frugal plenty marks the wise mans board.
This mob, for honesty sake, broke open all the prisons.
Our sacks shall be a mean's to sack the city.
Such was the economy of the wife of the agent of my uncle.
These emmet's, how little they are in our eyes!
Childrens minds may be easily overloaded.

EXERCISE III.—ADJECTIVES.

A palmistry at which this vermin are very dexterous.
These kind of knaves I know.—*Shakspeare.*

Vanity has more subjects than any of the passions.
The vain are delighted with fashionable and new dresses.
So highly did they esteem this goods.
Washington has been honoured more than any American.
Which is the loftier of the Asiatic mountains?
This ashes they were very careful to preserve.
Is not she the younger of the three sisters?
Could not some less nobler plunder satisfy thee?
I can assign a more satisfactory and stronger reason.
Peter was older than any of the twelve apostles.
Peace of mind is easier lost than gained.
Of this victuals he was always very fond.
Man has more wants than any animal.
Of all other practical rules this is the most complex.
Is not the French more fashionable than any language?
Vice never leads to old honoured age.
Cloths of a more inferior quality are more salable.
This is found in no book published previous to mine.
He turned away with the most utmost contempt.
Time glides swift and imperceptible away.
Of their more ulterior measures I know nothing.
My three last letters were never answered.
Fortune may frown on the most superior genius.
It becomes a gentleman to speak correct.
The most loftiest mountain is Mont Blanc.
If a man acts foolish, is he to be esteemed wise?
Drop your acquaintance with them bad boys.
They sat silently and motionless an hour and a half.
Quiet minds, like smooth water, reflect clear.

True faith, true policy, united ran;
This was but love of God, and that of man.

EXERCISE IV.—PRONOUNS.

Him that presumes much, has much to fear.
They best can bear reproof, whom merit praise.
A few pupils, older than me, excited my emulation.
Every man will find themselves in the state of Adam.
None are more rich than them who are content.
Scotland and thee did in each other live.
These trifles they do not deserve our attention.
Truth is ever to be preferred for it's own sake.
Thou art afraid—else, what ails you?
It is not Lemuel, but God, whom you have offended.
All things which have life, aspire to God.
So great was the multitude who followed him.

He which would advance, should not look backwards.
It was Sir Billy—who is an other name for a fop.
I take up the arguments in the order they stand.
There is nothing, with respect to me, and such as me.
He that is bribed, the people will abhor.
The day when the accident happened, is not recorded.
We know not who to trust; them who seem fair, are false.
The reason I told it was this: thee was in danger.
I did not know the precise time when it occurred.
Here he answers the question, who asks it.
Who who beheld the outrage, could remain inactive?
This was the prison where we were confined.
I could not believe but what it was a reality.
It was the boys, and not the dog, which broke the basin.
An unprincipled junto is not nice about their means.
The people forced its way, and demanded its rights.
Avoid lightness and frivolity: it is allied to folly.
Either wealth or power may ruin their possessor.
It was Joseph, him whom Pharaoh promoted.
Origen's mother hid his clothes, to prevent him going.
Him that withholdeth corn, the people shall curse him.
He that withholdeth corn the people shall curse.
I have always thought ye honest till now.
Me being but a boy, they took no notice of me.
They that receive me, I will richly reward.
Had it been them, they would have stopped.
Vain pomp and glory of this world, I hate ye.
It was not me, that gave you that answer.
Between you and I, he is a greater thief than author.
Any dunce can copy what you or me shall write.
You seem to forget who you are talking to.
Thee being a stranger, the child was afraid.
This was the most remarkable event which occurred.
Happy are them whose pleasure is their duty.

EXERCISE V.—VERBS.

Where was you standing during the transaction?
Was you there when the pistol was fired?
Thou sees how little difference there are.
If he have failed, it was not through my neglect.
Patience and diligence, like faith, removes mountains.
There was many reasons for not disturbing my repose.
The train of brass artillery and other ordnance, are immense.
Art thou the man that camest from Judah?
What eye those long, long labyrinths dare explore?

Magnus and his friends was barbarously treated.
The propriety of these restrictions, are unquestionable.
And I am one that believe the doctrine.
Thou wast he that leddest out and broughtest in Israel.
Beauty without virtue generally prove a snare.
If thou means to advance, eye those before thee.
A qualification for high offices, come not of indolence.
The desires of right reason is bounded by competency.
Useless studies is nothing but a busy idleness.
Is virtue, then, and piety the same?
So awful an admonition was these miraculous words.
If the great body of the people thinks otherwise.
A committee are a body that have only a delegated power.
In peace of mind consists our strength and happiness.
There is no slander, where love and unity is maintained.
His character, as well as his doctrines, were assailed.
Proof, and not assertion, are what are required.
Right reason and truth is always in unison.
No pains nor cost were spared to make it grand.
Ignorance stupifies, and is the source of many crimes.

> ————————Then wanders forth the sons
> Of Belial, flown with insolence and wine.

What you must chiefly rely on, is the attested facts.
No axe or hammer have ever awakened an echo here.
Did not she send, and gave you this information?
Their honours are departing and come to an end.
Neither wit, nor taste, nor learning, appear in it.
Caligula sat himself up for a deity.
A tortoise requested the eagle to learn him to fly.
'O, that it was always spring!' said little Robert.
I at first intended to have arranged it in a new form.
The gaoler supposed that the prisoners had been fled.
Peter saw a vessel, as it had been a great sheet.
Peace and esteem is all that age can hope.

> Alas! no wife or mother's care
> For him the milk or corn prepare.
>
> Thou bark that sails with man!
> Haste, haste to cleave the seas.

EXERCISE VII.—PARTICIPLES.

What dost thou mean by shaking of thy head?
A good end warrants not using bad means.
Be cautious in forming of connexions.
The worshiping the two calves was still kept up.

In reading of his lecture, he was much embarrassed.
This devoting ourselves to God, must be habitual.
Their estimating the prize too highly, was evident.
He declared the project to be no less than a tempting God.
Every deviation from virtue is approaching to vice.
It is extremely foolish boasting of immoral achievements.
It was the refusing all communion with paganism.
Our deepest knowledge is knowing ourselves.
He wilfully neglects the obtaining unspeakable good.
Retaliating injuries is multiplying offences.
These things are certain : there is no denying facts.
Publicly vindicating error is openly adopting it.
On his father asking him who it was, he answered, 'I.'
Thus shall we escape being defeated and ruined.
Being unjustly liberal is ostentatious pride.
Wisdom teaches justly appreciating of all things.
The procuring these benefits, was a gratuitous act.
Doing good, disinterested good, is not our trade.
Such a renouncing the world is a pernicious delusion.
Freely indulging the appetite impairs the intellect.
The Acts mention Paul preaching of Christ at Damascus.
The Acts mention Paul's preaching Christ at Damascus.
The Acts mention Paul preaching Christ at Damascus.
Constantly beholding objects prevents our admiring them.
We purpose taking that route when we go.
What was the cause of the young woman fainting?
I perceived somebody's creeping through the fence.
I was aware of them intending to arrest me.
We saw some mischievous boys' worrying of a cat.
To pursue fashion, is chasing a bird on the wing.
Being very positive, is no real proof of a stable mind.
By establishing good laws, our peace is secured.
Distinctness is important in delivering orations.
He guarantied the permission we demanded being granted.
For the easier reading the numbers in the table.
Recovering the first surprise, however, we entered boldly,

EXERCISE VII.—ADVERBS, &c.

Respect is lost often by the means used to obtain it.
Such were the views of the then ministry.
Raillery must be very nice to not offend.
Ye know how that it is an unlawful thing.
From hence I infer that they were going there.
Quaint sayings are long remembered often.
I cannot tell you whether this is the fact or no.

Valleys are more fertile generally than mountains.
A qualification of usefulness is acquired with study.
Frequent transgression makes men slaves of sin.
Let nothing induce you ever to utter a falsehood.
The idle are, of necessary consequence, ignorant.
The wind came about so as we could make no way.
Zealots seldom are distinguished by charity.
Study is as necessary and even more so than instruction.
I never have, and never shall be compensated.
Humility neither seeks the first place or the last word.
He has never told me nothing more of the matter.
These men ranked highly among the nobility.
Their bodies are so solid and hard, as you need not fear.
Of her brother's political life previously to this event.
Attainments made easily, are not of much value often.
He has no other merit but that of a compiler.
Venus appears uncommonly brightly to-night.
Men cannot be forced neither into or out-of true faith.
To this man we may commit safely our cause.
One crime cannot be a proper remedy to another.
Venus is not quite as large as the Earth.
It is thinking makes what we read our own.
Quagmires have smooth surfaces commonly.
He was so much offended, as he would not speak to me.
I have put my words in thy mouth.
How wilt thou put thy trust on Egypt for chariots?

EXERCISE VIII.—PROMISCUOUS.

In his fathers reign, they were connected and joined.
What is the Earth and its dimensions?
He is a great deal heavier man than I.
The citizens were never denied the privilege.
Thankful to Heaven that thou wert left behind.
I have met with few who understood men equal to him.
He was then recently returned from the east victorious.
He hoped that money should have been given him.
Laws may, and frequently are made against drunkenness.
He appeared in an human shape.
I do not attempt explaining the mysteries of religion.

> Ere matter, time, or place were known,
> Thou sway'dst these spacious realms alone.

One of the wisest persons that hath been among them.
What is it else but to reject all authority?
They advocate distinctions unworthy any free state.
It would not, and ought not, be felt.

Them who saw the disaster, were greatly alarmed.
He knew none fitter to be their judge but himself.
Record the names of every one present.
We doubt not but we will satisfy the impartial.
But time and chance happeneth to them all.
You was in hopes to have succeeded to the inheritance.
To make light of a small fault, are to commit a greater.
Judge not before hearing of the cause.
Clear articulation is requisite in publicly speaking.
God is the avenger of all breach of faith and injustice.
I had a letter began, and nearly half wrote.
It is better being suspected than being guilty.
Declare the past and present state of things.
To insult the afflicted are impious and barbarous.
Goodness, and not greatness, lead to happiness.
It is pride who whispers, ' What will they think of me?'
In judging of others, charity should be exercised.
Zanies are willing to befool, to please fools.
Questions are easier proposed than answered rightly.

> He forms his schemes the flood of vice to stem,
> But preaching Jesus is not one of them.—*J. Taylor.*

EXERCISE IX.—PROMISCUOUS.

The property of the rebels were confiscated.
He was extreme covetous in all his dealings.
There were no less than thirty islands.
The plot was the easier detected.
Of all the books mine has the fewer blots.
Who does the house belong to?
Is this the person whom you say was present?
Knowledge is only to be acquired by application.
Policy often prevails upon force.
These men were seen enter the house in the night.
These works are Cicero, the most eloquent of men's.
Thomas has bought a bay large horse.
Your gold and silver is cankered.
Now abideth faith, hope, and charity.
And, him destroyed, all this will follow.
There is no need for your assistance.
To whom our fathers would not obey.
Where can we find such an one as this?
They sat out early on their journey.
Philosophers have often mistook the source of happiness.
The books are as old, and perhaps older, than tradition.
This chapter is divided in sections.

I shall treat you as I have them.
A prophet mightier than him.
Neither he or his brother is capable of it.
Richelieu profited of every circumstance.
What was the cause of the girl screaming?
Let him and I have half of them.
I wrote to, and cautioned the captain against it.
Nothing is more lovelier than virtue
He that is diligent, you should commend.
They ride faster than us.
Which of them grammars do you like best?
Neither of these are the meaning intended.
Did you understand who I was speaking of?
Whosoever of you will be chiefest, shall be servant of all.
Remember what thou wert, and be humble.

> Was I deceived? or did a sable cloud
> Turn forth her silver lining on the night?—*Milton.*

EXERCISE X.—PROMISCUOUS.

Changed to a worser shape thou canst not be.

> For him through hostile camps I bend my way,
> For him thus prostrate at thy feet I lay.—*Pope.*
> Thus oft by mariners are shown
> Earl Godwin's castles overflown.—*Swift.*

No civil broils have, since his death, arose.
Nor thou, that flings me floundering from thy back.
Who should I see but the doctor!
That which once was thee.
To wish him wrestle with affection.

> So much she fears for William's life,
> That Mary's fate she dare not mourn.—*Prior.*

Phalaris, who was so much older than her.
They would have given him such satisfaction in other parti-
culars, as a full and happy peace must have ensued.
The woman which we saw, is very amiable.
The three first classes have read.
An union in that which is permanent.
Among every class of people self-interest prevails.
Such conduct is a disgrace of their profession.
His education has been neglected much.
There is no other bridge but the one we saw.
He went and laid down to sleep.
Whom do men say that I am?
Take to you handfuls of ashes of the furnace, and let Moses
sprinkle it towards the heaven in the sight of Pharaoh.

In eulogizing of the dead, he slandered the living.
If a dog both give the first turn and the last, he shall win.
Neither the virtuous or the vicious are exempt from trials.
He spoke as if he was in a passion.
Let him take heed lest he fails.
We have all swerved out-of the path of duty.
I cannot agree with him neither.
He both wrote sermon·, and plays.
If a man say, 'I love God,' and hateth his brother, he is a liar.
He has long ago forsaken that party.
It was proved to be her that opened the letter.
Is not this the same man whom we met before?
I forego my claim for peace's sake.

> For thou art a girl as much brighter than her,
> As she was a poet sublimer than me.—*Prior.*

EXERCISE XI.—PROMISCUOUS.

There remains two points to be settled.
I could not avoid frequently using it.
The Athenians were naturally obliging and agreeable; they
   were cheerful among each other, and humane to their infe-
   riors.—*Goldsmith.*
I hope it is not me thou art displeased with.
I never before saw such large trees.
My paper is Ulysses his bow, in which every man of wit and
   learning may try his strength.—*Addison.*

> 'Twas thee, whom once Stagyra's grove
> Oft with her sage allur'd to rove.—*Scott of Amwell.*

I could not observe by what gradations other men proceeded
   in their acquainting themselves with truth.—*Locke.*
I will show you the way how it is done.
Imprinting, if it signify any thing, is nothing else but the mak-
   ing certain truths to be perceived.—*Locke.*
This arose from the young man associating with bad people.
Him that never thinks, never can be wise.
It was John's the Baptist head that was cut off.
The Jews are Abraham's, Isaac's, and Jacob's posterity.
Two architects were once candidates for the building a certain
   temple at Athens.
This treatise is extreme elaborate.
Them descending, the ladder fell.
The scaling ladder of sugared words are set against them.
One or both was there.
What sort of an animal is that?

These things should be never separated.
His excuse was admitted of by his master.
It is not me that he is engaged with.
I intended to have rewarded him according to his merits.
They would become sooner proficients in Latin.
There is many different opinions concerning it.
There are many in town richer than her.
Let you and I be as little at variance as possible.
A coalman, by waking of one of these gentlemen, saved him
    from ten years imprisonment.
If a man's temper was at his own disposal, he would not choose
    to be of either of these parties.

> The birds their notes renew, and bleating herds
> Attest their joy, that hill and valley rings.—*Milton.*

EXERCISE XII.—PROMISCUOUS.

But we of the nations beg leave to differ with them.
This is so easy and trivial, as it is a shame to mention it.
You was once quite blind; you neither saw your disease or
    your remedy.

> Fluttering his pennons vain, plumb down he drops
> Ten thousand fathom deep.—*Milton.*

The properties of the mirror depends on reflected light.
Was you present at the last meeting?
Hence has arisen much stiffness and affectation.
The nation are powerful both by sea and land.
Those set of books was a valuable present.
The box contained forty piece of muslin.
She is much the taller of the three.
They are both remarkable tall men.
A mans manners may be pleasing, whose morals are bad.
True politeness has it's seat in the heart.
He presented him a humble petition.
I do not intend to turn a critic on this occasion.
At first sight we took it to be they.
The certificate was wrote on parchment.
I have often swam across the river.
I have written four long letters yesterday.
I expected to have seen you last week, but I was disappointed.
We are besat by dangers on all sides.
My father and him were very intimate.
Unless he acts prudently, he will not succeed,
It was no sooner said but done.
Let neither partiality or prejudice appear.

The obligation was ceased long before.
How exquisitely is this all performed in Greek!
Who, when they came to Mount Ephraim, to the house of
   Micah, they lodged there.
I prevailed with your father to consent.
Always act as justice and honour requires.
Them that transgress the rules, will be punished.
With him is wisdom and strength.
My conductor answered, that it was him.

> Be thou, O lovely isle! forever true
> To him who more than faithful was to you.—*Southwick.*

> The joys of love, are they not doubly thine,
> Ye poor! whose health, whose spirits ne'er decline?—*Id.*

EXERCISE XIII.—PROMISCUOUS.

Having once suffered the disgrace, it is felt no longer.
The meanness or the sin will scarce be dissuasives.
Both temper and distemper consists of contraries.
Which is the cause, the writer or the reader's vanity?
The commission of a generalissimo was also given him.
The queen's kindred is styled gentlefolks.
They agree as to the fact, but differ in assigning of reasons.
Their love, and their hatred, and their envy, is now perished.
The inquiry is worthy the attention of every scholar.
Young twigs are easier bent than boughs.
It is not improbable but there are more attractive powers.
By this means an universal ferment was excited.
Who were utterly unable to pronounce some letters, and others
   very indistinctly.—*Sheridan.*
All vessels on board of which any person has been sick or
   died, perform quarantine.
Serverus forbid his subjects to change their religion for that
   of the Christian or Jewish.—*Jones's Ch. Hist.*
Magnus, with four thousand of his supposed accomplices, were
   put to death without a trial.—*Id.*
Art not thou that Egyptian which before these days madest an
   uproar, and leddest out into the wilderness four thousand
   men that were murderers?—*Acts,* xxiii, 38.
Attempting to deceive children into instruction of this kind,
   is only deceiving ourselves.—*Goldsmith.*
There came a woman, having an alabaster box of ointment
   of spikenard, very precious; and she brake the box and
   poured it on his head.—*Mark,* xiv, 3.
My essays, of all my other works, are the most current.

We would suggest the importance of every member, individually, using his influence.

> Thy sumptuous buildings, and thy wife's attire,
> Hath cost a mass of public treasure.—*Shakspeare.*

EXERCISE XIV.—PROMISCUOUS.

This people who knoweth not the law, are cursed.
The people shall be forgiven their iniquity.—*Bible.*
Having been denied the favours which they were promised.

> Hold, Rosaline, this favour thou shalt wear;
> Hold, take you this, my sweet, and give me thine.

Rely not on any man's fidelity, who is unfaithful to God.
The rules are full as concise, and more clear than before.
For they knew all that his father was a Greek.—*Acts.*
Thrice was Cæsar offered the crown.
For a mine undiscovered, neither the owner of the ground, or
any body else, are ever the richer.
Death may be sudden to him, though it comes by never so
slow degrees.
A brute or a man are an other thing when they are alive, from
what they are when dead.—*Hale.*
I have known the having confessed inability, become the occa-
sion of confirmed impotence.—*Taylor.*
I am exceeding joyful in all our tribulation.—2 *Cor.*, vii, 4.
If so much power, wisdom, goodness, and magnificence, is displayed in the material creation, which is the least considerable part of the universe; how great, how wise, how good
must he be, who made and governs the whole!
A good poet no sooner communicates his works, but it is imagined he is a vain young creature, given up to the ambition of fame.—*Pope.*
This was a tax upon himself for the not executing the laws.
O my people, that dwellest in Zion! be not afraid.—*Bible.*

> As rushing out-of-doors, to be resolved,
> If Brutus so unkindly knock'd or no.—*Shakspeare.*

His wrath, which one day will destroy ye both.—*Milton.*

> I know thee not—nor ever saw, till now,
> Sight more detestable than him and thee.—*Id.*

> The season when to come, and when to go,
> To sing, or cease to sing, we never know.—*Pope.*

PART IV.

PROSODY.

PROSODY treats of punctuation, utterance, figures, and versification.

CHAPTER I.—PUNCTUATION.

Punctuation is the art of dividing composition, by points, or stops, for the purpose of showing more clearly the sense and relation of the words, and of noting the different pauses and inflections required in reading.

The following are the principal points, or marks; the Comma [,], the Semicolon [;], the Colon [:], the Period [.], the Dash [—], the Eroteme, or Note of Interrogation [?], the Ecphoneme, or Note of Exclamation [!], and the Curves, or Marks of Parenthesis [()].

OBS.—The pauses that are made in the natural flow of speech, have, in reality, no definite and invariable proportions. Children are often told to pause at a comma while they might count *one ;* at a semicolon, *one, two ;* at a colon, *one, two, three ;* at a period, *one, two, three, four.* This may be of some use, as teaching them to observe their stops that they may catch the sense; but the standard itself is variable, and so are the times which good sense gives to the points. As a final stop, the period is immeasurable. The following general direction is as good as any that can be given.

The Comma denotes the shortest pause; the Semicolon, a pause double that of the comma; the Colon, a pause double that of the semicolon; and the Period, or Full Stop, a pause double that of the colon. The pauses required by the other marks, vary according to the structure of the sentence, and their place in it. They may be equal to any of the foregoing.

SECTION I.—OF THE COMMA.

The Comma is used to separate those parts of a sentence, which are so nearly connected in sense, as to be only one degree removed from that close connexion which admits no point.

11*

Rule I.—Simple Sentences.

A simple sentence does not, in general, admit the comma; as, " The weakest reasoners are the most positive."— *W. Allen.*

Exception.—When the nominative in a long simple sentence is accompanied by inseparable adjuncts, a comma should be placed before the verb; as, " The assemblage of these vast bodies, is divided into different systems."

Rule II.—Simple Members.

The simple members of a compound sentence, whether successive or involved, elliptical or complete, are generally divided by the comma; as,

1. " He speaks eloquently, and he acts wisely."
2. " The man, when he saw this, departed."
3. " It may, and it often does happen."
4. " That life is long, which answers life's great end."
5. " As thy days, so shall thy strength be."

Exception 1.—When a relative immediately follows its antecedent, and is taken in a restrictive sense, the comma should not be introduced before it; as, " The things *which are seen,* are temporal ; but the things *which are not seen,* are eternal." —2 *Cor.,* iv, 18.

Exception 2.—When the simple members are short, and closely connected by a conjunction or a conjunctive adverb, the comma is generally omitted; as, " Infamy is worse *than* death." —" Let him tell me *whether* the number of the stars be even or odd."

Rule III.—More than Two Words.

When more than two words or terms are connected in the same construction, by conjunctions expressed or understood, the comma should be inserted after every one of them but the last ; and if they are nominatives before a verb, the comma should follow the last also : as,

1. " Who, to the enraptur'd heart, and ear, and eye,
    Teach beauty, virtue, truth, and love, and melody."
2. " Ah ! what avails *   *   *   *   *   *
    All that art, fortune, enterprise, can bring,
    If envy, scorn, remorse, or pride, the bosom wring ?"
3. " Women are soft, mild, pitiful, and flexible ;
    Thou, stern, obdurate, flinty, rough, remorseless."
4. " She plans, provides, expatiates, triumphs there."

Obs.—Two or more words are in the *same construction,* when they have a common dependence on some other term, and are parsed alike.

RULE IV.—ONLY TWO WORDS.

When only two words or terms are connected by a conjunction, they should not be separated by the comma; as, "Despair and anguish fled the struggling soul."—*Goldsmith.*

Exception 1.—When the two words connected have several adjuncts, or when one of them has an adjunct that relates not to both, the comma is inserted; as, "Honesty in his dealings, and attention to his business, procured him both esteem and wealth."—"*Who* is applied to persons, or things personified." —*Bullions.*

Exception 2.—When the two words connected are emphatically distinguished, the comma is inserted; as,

"Liberal, not lavish, is kind Nature's hand."—*Beattie.*

"'Tis certain he could write, and cipher too."—*Goldsmith.*

Exception 3.—When there is merely an alternative of words, the comma is inserted; as, "We saw a large opening, or inlet."

Exception 4.—When the conjunction is understood, the comma is inserted; as,

"She thought the isle that gave her birth,
The sweetest, wildest land on earth."—*Hogg.*

RULE V.—WORDS IN PAIRS.

When successive words are joined in pairs by conjunctions, they should be separated in pairs by the comma; as, "Interest and ambition, honour and shame, friendship and enmity, gratitude and revenge, are the prime movers in public transactions."—*W. Allen.*

RULE VI.—WORDS PUT ABSOLUTE.

Nouns or pronouns put absolute, should, with their adjuncts, be set off by the comma; as, "The prince, *his father being dead,* succeeded."—"*This done,* we parted."—"*Zaccheus,* make haste and come down."—"*His prætorship in Sicily,* what did it produce?"—*Cicero.*

RULE VII.—WORDS IN APPOSITION.

Words put in apposition, (especially if they have adjuncts,) are generally set off by the comma; as, "He that now calls upon thee, is Theodore, *the hermit of Teneriffe.*"—*Johnson.*

Exception 1.—When several words, in their common order, are used as one compound name, the comma is not inserted; as, "Samuel Johnson,"—"Publius Gavius Cosanus."

Exception 2.—When a common and a proper name are closely united, the comma is not inserted; as, "The brook

Kidron,"—" The river Don,"—" The empress Catharine,"—
" Paul the apostle."

Exception 3.—When a pronoun is added to another word merely for emphasis and distinction, the comma is not inserted; as, " Ye men of Athens,"—" I myself,"—" Thou flaming minister,"—" You princes."

Exception 4.—When a name acquired by some action or relation, is put in apposition with a preceding noun or pronoun, the comma is not inserted: as, " I made the *ground* my *bed;*" —" To make *him king;*"—" *Whom* they revered as *God;*"— " With *modesty* thy *guide.*"—*Pope.*

RULE VIII.—ADJECTIVES.

Adjectives, when something depends on them, or when they have the import of a dependent clause, should, with their adjuncts, be set off by the comma; as,

1. ———————————" Among the roots
Of hazel, *pendent o'er the plaintive stream,*
They frame the first foundation of their domes."—*Thom.*

2. ————————————" Up springs the lark,
Shrill-voic'd and *loud,* the messenger of morn."—*Id.*

Exception.—When an adjective immediately follows its noun, and is taken in a restrictive sense, the comma should not be used before it; as,

   " On the coast *averse from entrance.*"—*Milton.*

RULE IX.—FINITE VERBS.

Where a finite verb is understood, a comma is generally required: as, " From law arises security; from security, curiosity; from curiosity, knowledge."—*Murray.*

RULE X.—INFINITIVES.

The infinitive mood, when it follows a verb from which it must be separated, or when it depends on something remote or understood, is generally, with its adjuncts, set off by the comma; as, " His delight was, *to assist the distressed.*"—" *To conclude,* I was reduced to beggary."

   " The Governor of all—has interposed,
   Not seldom, his avenging arm, *to smite*
   The injurious trampler upon nature's law."—*Cowper.*

RULE XI.—PARTICIPLES.

Participles, when something depends on them, when they have the import of a dependent clause, or when they relate to something understood, should, with their adjuncts, be set off by the comma; as,

1. " Young Edwin, *lighted by the evening star,*
     Ling'ring and list'ning, wander'd down the vale."—*Beattie.*
2. "*United,* we stand ; *divided,* we fall."
3. "*Properly speaking,* there is no such thing as chance."

Exception.—When a participle immediately follows its noun, and is taken in a restrictive sense, the comma should not be used before it; as,

> " A man *renown'd for repartee,*
>   Will seldom scruple to make free
>   With friendship's finest feeling."—*Cowper.*

RULE XII.—ADVERBS.

Adverbs, when they break the connexion of a simple sentence, or when they have not a close dependence on some particular word in the context, should be set off by the comma; as, " We must not. *however,* confound this gentleness with the artificial courtesy of the world."—"*Besides,* the mind must be employed."—*Gilpin.* "*Most unquestionably,* no fraud was equal to all this."—*Lyttelton.*

RULE XIII.—CONJUNCTIONS.

Conjunctions, when they are separated from the principal clause that depends on them, or when they introduce an example, are generally set off by the comma; as, "*But,* by a timely call upon Religion, the force of Habit was eluded."—*Johnson.*

RULE XIV.—PREPOSITIONS.

Prepositions and their objects, when they break the connexion of a simple sentence, or when they do not closely follow the words on which they depend, are generally set off by the comma; as, " Fashion is, *for the most part,* nothing but the ostentation of riches."—"*By reading,* we add the experience of others to our own."

RULE XV.—INTERJECTIONS.

Interjections are sometimes set off by the comma; as, "For, *lo,* I will call all the families of the kingdoms of the north."—*Jeremiah,* i, 15.

RULE XVI.—WORDS REPEATED.

A word emphatically repeated, is generally set off by the comma; as, "Happy, happy, happy pair !"—*Dryden.* "Ah! no, no, no."—*Id.*

Rule XVII.—Dependent Quotations.

A quotation or observation, when it is introduced by a verb, (as, *say*, *reply*, and the like,) is generally separated from the rest of the sentence by the comma; as, "'The book of nature,' said he, 'is open before thee.'"—"I say unto all, Watch."

SECTION II.—OF THE SEMICOLON.

The Semicolon is used to separate those parts of a compound sentence, which are neither so closely connected as those which are distinguished by the comma, nor so little dependent as those which require the colon.

Rule I.—Compound Members.

When several compound members, some or all of which require the comma, are constructed into a period, they are generally separated by the semicolon: as, "In the regions inhabited by angelic natures, unmingled felicity foreve: blooms; joy flows there with a perpetual and abundant stream, nor needs any mound to check its course."—*Carter.*

Rule II.—Simple Members.

When several simple members, each of which is complete in sense, are constructed into a period; if they require a pause greater than that of the comma, they are usually separated by the semicolon: as, "Straws swim upon the surface; but pearls lie at the bottom."—*Murray.*

"A longer care man's helpless kind demands;
That longer care contracts more lasting bands."—*Pope.*

Rule III.—Apposition, &c.

Words in apposition, in disjunct pairs, or in any other construction, if they require a pause greater than that of the comma, and less than that of the colon, may be separated by the semicolon: as, "There are five moods; the infinitive, the indicative, the potential, the subjunctive, and the imperative."

SECTION III.—OF THE COLON.

The Colon is used to separate those parts of a compound sentence, which are neither so closely connected as those which are distinguished by the semicolon, nor so little dependent as those which require the period.

Rule I.—Additional Remarks.

When the preceding clause is complete in itself, but is followed by some additional remark or illustration, especially if no conjunction is used, the colon is generally and properly inserted: as, "Avoid evil doers: in such society an honest man may become ashamed of himself."—"See that moth fluttering incessantly round the candle: man of pleasure, behold thy image."—*Kames.*

RULE II.—GREATER PAUSES.

When the semicolon has been introduced, and a still greater pause is required within the period, the colon should be employed: as, "Princes have courtiers, and merchants have partners; the voluptuous have companions, and the wicked have accomplices: none but the virtuous can have friends."

RULE III.—INDEPENDENT QUOTATIONS.

A quotation introduced without dependence on a verb or a conjunction, is generally preceded by the colon; as, "In his last moments he uttered these words: '*I fall a sacrifice to sloth and luxury.*'"

SECTION IV.—OF THE PERIOD.

The Period, or Full Stop, is used to mark an entire and independent sentence, whether simple or compound.

RULE I.—DISTINCT SENTENCES.

When a sentence is complete in respect to sense, and independent in respect to construction, it should be marked with the period: as, "Every deviation from truth is criminal. Abhor a falsehood. Let your words be ingenuous. Sincerity possesses the most powerful charm."

RULE II.—ALLIED SENTENCES.

The period is often employed between two sentences which have a general connexion, expressed by a personal pronoun, a conjunction, or a conjunctive adverb; as, "The selfish man languishes in his narrow circle of pleasures. *They* are confined to what affects his own interests. *He* is obliged to repeat the same gratifications, till they become insipid. *But* the man of virtuous sensibility moves in a wider sphere of felicity."— *Blair.*

RULE III.—ABBREVIATIONS.

The period is generally used after abbreviations, and very often to the exclusion of other points; but, as in this case it is not a constant sign of pause, other points may properly follow it, if the words written in full would demand them: as, A. D. for *Anno Domini ;*—Pro tem. for *pro tempore ;*—Ult. for *ul-*

timo ;—1. e. for *id est,* that is ;—Add., Spect., No. 285 ; i. e.,
Addison, in the Spectator, Number 285*th.*

"Consult the statute ; 'quart.' I think, it is,
'Edwardi sext.,' or ' prim. et quint. Eliz.' "—*Pope,* p. 399.

SECTION V.—OF THE DASH.

The Dash is mostly used to denote an unexpected or
emphatic pause of variable length ; but sometimes it is
a sign of faltering ; sometimes, of omission : if set after
an other sign of pause, it usually lengthens the interval.

RULE I.—ABRUPT PAUSES.

A sudden interruption or transition should be marked with
the dash ; as, " 'I must inquire into the affair, and if'—'And
if!' interrupted the farmer."

"Here lies the great—false marble, where ?
Nothing but sordid dust lies here."—*Young.*

RULE II.—EMPHATIC PAUSES.

To mark a considerable pause, greater than the structure of
the sentence or the points inserted, would seem to require, the
dash may be employed ; as,

1. " And now they part—to meet no more."
2. " Revere thyself ;—and yet thyself despise."
3. " Behold the picture !—Is it like ?—Like whom ?"

RULE III.—FAULTY DASHES.

Dashes needlessly inserted, or substituted for other stops
more definite, are in general to be treated as errors in punctuation.   Example : " —You shall go home directly, Le Fevre,
said my uncle Toby, to my house,—and we 'll send for a doctor to see what 's the matter,—and we 'll have an apothecary,
—and the corporal shall be your nurse ;—and I 'll be your
servant, Le Fevre."—STERNE : *Enfield's Speaker,* p. 306. Better
thus : " 'You shall go home directly, Le Fevre,' said my uncle
Toby, ' to my house ; and we 'll send for a doctor to see what 's
the matter ; and we 'll have an apothecary ; and the corporal
shall be your nurse : and I 'll be your servant, Le Fevre.' "

SECTION VI.—OF THE EROTEME.

The Eroteme, or Note of Interrogation, is used to
designate a question.

RULE I.—QUESTIONS DIRECT.

Questions expressed directly as such, if finished, should always be followed by the note of interrogation ; as,

"In life, can love be bought with gold?
Are friendship's pleasures to be sold?"—*Johnson.*

RULE II.—QUESTIONS UNITED.

When two or more questions are united in one compound sentence, the comma or semicolon is sometimes placed between them, and the note of interrogation, after the last only; as,

"Truths would you teach, or save a sinking land?
All fear, none aid you, and few understand."—*Pope.*

RULE III.—QUESTIONS INDIRECT.

When a question is mentioned, but not put directly as a question, it loses both the quality and the sign of interrogation; as, "The Cyprians asked me *why I wept.*"—*Murray.*

SECTION VII.—OF THE ECPHONEME.

The Ecphoneme, or Note of Exclamation, is used to denote a pause with some strong or sudden emotion of the mind; and, as a sign of great wonder, it may be repeated!!!

RULE I.—INTERJECTIONS, &c.

Interjections, and other expressions of great emotion, are generally followed by the note of exclamation; as,

"O! let me listen to the words of life!"—*Thomson.*

RULE II.—INVOCATIONS.

After an earnest address or solemn invocation, the note of exclamation is usually preferred to any other point; as, "Whereupon, O king Agrippa! I was not disobedient unto the heavenly vision."—*Acts,* xxvi, 19.

RULE III.—EXCLAMATORY QUESTIONS.

Words uttered with vehemence in the form of a question, but without reference to an answer, should be followed by the note of exclamation; as, "How madly have I talked!"—*Young.*

SECTION VIII.—OF THE CURVES.

The Curves, or Marks of Parenthesis, are used to distinguish a clause or hint that is hastily thrown in between the parts of a sentence to which it does not properly belong; as,

"To others do (the law is not severe)
What to thyself thou wishest to be done."—*Beattie.*

OBS.—The incidental clause should be uttered in a lower tone, and faster than the principal sentence. It always requires a pause as great as that of a comma, or greater.

Rule I.—The Parenthesis.

A clause that breaks the unity of a sentence too much to be
incorporated with it, and only such, should be enclosed as a
parenthesis; as,

"Know then this truth, (enough for man to know,)
Virtue alone is happiness below."—*Pope.*

Rule II.—Included Points.

The curves do not supersede other stops; and, as the parenthesis terminates with a pause equal to that which precedes it,
the same point should be included, except when the sentences
differ in form: as,

1. "Man's thirst of happiness declares it is:
   (For nature never gravitates to nought:)
   That thirst unquench'd, declares it is not here."—*Young.*
2. "Night visions may befriend: (as sung above:)
   Our waking dreams are fatal. How I dreamt
   Of things impossible! (could sleep do more?)
   Of joys perpetual in perpetual change."—*Young.*

SECTION IX.—OF THE OTHER MARKS.

There are also several other marks, which are occasionally used for various purposes, as follow:—

1. ['] The *Apostrophe* usually denotes either the possessive
case of a noun, or the elision of one or more letters of a
word: as, "The *girl's* regard to her *parents'* advice;"—*'gan,
lov'd, e'en, thro'* ; for *began, loved, even, through.*

2. [-] The *Hyphen* connects the parts of many compound
words, especially such as have two accents; as, *ever-living.*
It is also frequently inserted where a word is divided into syllables; as, *con-tem-plate.*   Placed at the end of a line, it shows
that one or more syllables of a word are carried forward to
the next line.

3. [¨] The *Diæresis,* or *Dialysis,* placed over either of two
contiguous vowels, shows that they are not a diphthong; as,
Danäe, aërial.

4. ['] The *Acute Accent* marks the syllable which requires
the principal stress in pronunciation; as, *équal, equal'ity.*   It
is sometimes used in opposition to the grave accent, to distinguish a close or short vowel; as, "*Fáncy:*" (*Murray:*) or to
denote the rising inflection of the voice; as, "Is it *hé?*"

5. [`] The *Grave Accent* is used in opposition to the acute,
to distinguish an open or long vowel; as, "*Fàvour:*" (*Murray:*) or to denote the falling inflection of the voice; as,
"*Yès;* it is *hè.*"

6. [ˆ] The *Circumflex* generally denotes either the broad sound of *a*, or an unusual and long sound given to some other vowel; as in *eclât, âll, hêir, machine, môve, bûll.*

7. [˘] The *Breve*, or *Stenotone*, is used to denote either a close vowel or a syllable of short quantity; as, *răven*, to devour.

8. [ˉ] The *Macron*, or *Macrotone*, is used to denote either an open vowel or a syllable of long quantity; as, *rāven*, a bird.

9. [——] or [****] The *Ellipsis*, or *Suppression*, denotes the omission of some letters or words; as, *K—g,* for *King.*

10. [ʌ] The *Caret*, used only in writing, shows where to insert words or letters that have been accidentally omitted.

11. [⌣⌣] The *Brace* serves to unite a triplet; or to connect several terms with something to which they are all related.

12. [§] The *Section* marks the smaller divisions of a book or chapter; and, with the help of numbers, serves to abridge references.

13. [¶] The *Paragraph* (chiefly used in the Bible) denotes the commencement of a new subject. The parts of discourse which are called paragraphs, are, in general, sufficiently distinguished, by beginning a new line, and carrying the first word a little forwards or backwards.

14. [" "] The *Guillemets*, or *Quotation Points*, distinguish words that are taken from an other author or speaker. A quotation within a quotation is marked with single points; which, when both are employed, are placed within the others.

15. [[]] The *Crotchets*, or *Brackets*, generally enclose some correction or explanation, or the subject to be explained; as, " He [the speaker] was of a different opinion."

16. [☞] The *Index*, or *Hand*, points out something remarkable, or what the reader should particularly observe.

17. [*] The *Asterisk*, or *Star*, [†] the *Obelisk*, or *Dagger*, [‡] the *Diesis*, or *Double Dagger*, and [‖] the *Parallels*, refer to marginal notes. The *Section* also [§], and the *Paragraph* [¶], are often used for marks of reference, the former being usually applied to the fourth, and the latter to the sixth note on a page; for, by the usage of printers, these signs are now commonly introduced in the following order: 1 *, 2 †, 3 ‡, 4 §, 5 ‖, 6 ¶, 7 **, 8 ††, &c. When many references are to be made, the *small letters* of the alphabet, or the *numerical figures*, in their order, may be conveniently used for the same purpose.

18. [*⁎*] The *Asterism*, or *Three Stars*, a sign not very

often used, is placed before a long or general note, to mark it as a note, without giving it a particular reference.

19. [ç] The *Cedilla* is a mark borrowed from the French, by whom it is placed under the letter *c* to give it the sound of *s* before *a* or *o*; as, in the words, "*façade*," "*Alençon*." In Worcester's Dictionary, it is attached to three other letters, to denote their *soft* sounds: viz., "G̡ as J ; Ṣ as Z ; x̧ as gz."

☞ [For oral exercises in punctuation, the teacher may select any well-pointed book, to which the foregoing rules and explanations may be applied by the pupil. An application of the principles of punctuation, either to points rightly inserted, or in the correction of errors, is as easy a process as ordinary syntactical parsing or correcting; and, in proportion to the utility of these principles, as useful. The exercise, in relation to correct pointing, consists in reading some passage, in successive parts, according to its points; naming the latter, as they occur; and repeating the rules or doctrines of punctuation, as the reasons for the marks employed.]

CHAPTER II.—UTTERANCE.

Utterance is the art of vocal expression. It includes the principles of pronunciation and elocution.

SECTION I.—OF PRONUNCIATION.

Pronunciation, as distinguished from elocution, is the utterance of words taken separately.

Pronunciation requires a knowledge of the just powers of the letters in all their combinations, and of the force and seat of the accent.

I. The *Just Powers* of the letters, are those sounds which are given to them by the best readers.

II. *Accent* is the peculiar stress which we lay upon some particular syllable of a word, whereby that syllable is distinguished from the rest; as, *grám-mar*, *gram-má-ri-an*.

Every word of more than one syllable, has one of its syllables accented.

When the word is long, for the sake of harmony or distinctness, we often give a secondary or less forcible accent to another syllable; as, to the last of *tém-per-a-túre*, and to the second of *in-dém-ni-fi-cá-tion*.

A full and open pronunciation of the long vowel sounds, a clear articulation of the consonants, a forcible and well-placed accent, and a distinct utterance of the unaccented syllables, distinguish the elegant speaker.

[☞ For a full explanation of the principles of pronunciation, the learner is referred to Walker's Critical Pronouncing Dictionary; for authorities in reference to variable usage, to the Universal and Critical Dictionary of J. E. Worcester.]

SECTION II.—OF ELOCUTION.

Elocution is the utterance of words that are arranged into sentences, and form discourse.

Elocution requires a knowledge, and right application, of emphasis, pauses, inflections, and tones.

I. *Emphasis* is the peculiar stress of voice which we lay upon some particular word or words in a sentence, which are thereby distinguished from the rest, as being more especially significant.

II. *Pauses* are cessations in utterance, which serve equally to relieve the speaker, and to render language intelligible and pleasing. The duration of the pauses should be proportionate to the degree of connexion between the parts of the discourse.

III. *Inflections* are those peculiar variations of the human voice, by which a continuous sound is made to pass from one note, key, or pitch, into an other. The passage of the voice from a lower to a higher or shriller note, is called the *rising* or *upward inflection*. The passage of the voice from a higher to a lower or graver note, is called the *falling* or *downward inflection*. These two opposite inflections may be heard in the following examples: 1. *The rising*, "Do you mean to go?" 2. *The falling*, "When will you go?"

Obs.—Questions that may be answered by *yes* or *no*, require the rising inflection; those that demand any other answer, must be uttered with the falling inflection.

IV. *Tones* are those modulations of the voice, which depend upon the feelings of the speaker. They are what Sheridan denominates "the language of emotions." And it is of the utmost importance, that they be natural, unaffected, and rightly adapted to the subject and to the occasion : for, upon them, in a great measure, depends all that is pleasing or interesting in elocution.

CHAPTER III.—FIGURES.

A Figure, in grammar, is an intentional deviation from the ordinary spelling, formation, construction, or application, of words. There are, accordingly, figures of Orthography, figures of Etymology, figures of Syntax, and figures of Rhetoric. When figures are judiciously employed, they both strengthen and adorn expression. They occur more frequently in poetry than in prose; and several of them are merely poetic licenses.

SECTION I.—FIGURES OF ORTHOGRAPHY.

A Figure of Orthography is an intentional deviation from the ordinary or true spelling of a word.

The principal figures of Orthography are two; namely, *Mi-me'-sis* and *Ar'-cha-ism.*

I. *Mimesis* is a ludicrous imitation of some mistake or mispronunciation of a word, in which the error is mimicked by a false spelling, or the taking of one word for an other; as, "*Maister*, says he, have you any *wery* good *weal* in your *vállet ?*"—*Columbian Orator*, p. 292. "Ay, he was *porn* at Monmouth, captain Gower."—*Shak.* "I will *description* the matter to you, if you be *capacity* of it."—*Id.*

"*Perdigious !* I can hardly stand."—*Lloyd.*

II. An *Archaism* is a word or phrase expressed according to ancient usage, and not according to our modern orthography ; as, "*Newe grene chese of smalle clammynes comfortethe a hotte stomake.*"—T. PAYNEL : *Tooke's Diversions*, ii, 132.

" With him was rev'rend Contemplation *pight,*
Bow-bent with *eld*, his beard of snowy hue."—*Beattie.*

SECTION II.—FIGURES OF ETYMOLOGY.

A Figure of Etymology is an intentional deviation from the ordinary formation of a word.

The principal figures of Etymology are eight; namely, *A-phær'-e-sis, Pros'-the-sis, Syn'-co-pe, A-poc'-o-pe, Par-a-go'-ge, Di-ær'-e-sis, Syn-ær'-e-sis,* and *Tme'-sis.*

I. *Aphæresis* is the elision of some of the initial letters of a word: as, *'gainst, 'gan, 'neath,*—for *against, began, beneath.*

II. *Prosthesis* is the prefixing of an expletive syllable to a word : as, *a*down, *a*ppaid, *be*strown, *e*vanished, *y*clad,—for *down, paid, strown, vanished, clad.*

III. *Syncopè* is the elision of some of the middle letters of a word : as, *med'cine,* for *medicine ; e'en,* for *even ; o'er,* for *over ; conq'ring,* for *conquering ; se'nnight,* for *sevennight.*

IV. *Apocopè,* is the elision of some of the final letters of a word : as, *tho',* for *though ; th',* for *the ; t'other,* for *the other.*

V. *Paragogè* is the annexing of an expletive syllable to a word : as, *withouten,* for *without* ; *deary,* for *dear ; Johnny,* for *John.*

VI. *Diæresis* is the separating of two vowels that might form a diphthong : as, *coöperate,* not *cooperate ; aëronaut,* not *æronaut ; orthoëpy,* not *orthœpy.*

VII. *Synæresis* is the sinking of two syllables into one : as, *seest,* for *seëst ; tacked,* for *tack-ed ; drowned,* for *drown-ed.*

Obs.—When a vowel is entirely suppressed in pronunciation, (whether retained in writing or not,) the consonants connected with it, fall into an other syllable; thus, *tried, triest, loved* or *lov'd, lovest* or *lov'st*, are monosyllables; except in solemn discourse, in which the *e* is generally retained and made vocal.

VIII. *Tmesis* is the inserting of a word between the parts of a compound; as, " On *which* side *soever ;*"—"*To* us *ward ;*" —"*To* God *ward.*"

SECTION III.—FIGURES OF SYNTAX.

A Figure of Syntax is an intentional deviation from the ordinary construction of words.

The principal figures of Syntax are five; namely, *El-lip'-sis, Ple'-o-nasm, Syl-lep'-sis, En-al'-la-ge,* and *Hy-per'-ba-ton.*

I. *Ellipsis** is the omission of some word or words which are necessary to complete the construction, but not necessary to convey the meaning. Such words are said to be *understood ;* because they are received as belonging to the sentence, though they are not uttered.

Almost all compound sentences are more or less elliptical. There may be an omission of any of the parts of speech, or even of a whole clause; but the omission of articles or interjections can scarcely constitute a proper ellipsis.   Examples:

1. Of the *Article ;* as, " A man and [*a*] woman."—"The day, [*the*] month, and [*the*] year."

2. Of the *Noun ;* as, " The common [*law*] and the statute law."—" The twelve [*apostles*]."—" One [*book*] of my books." —" A dozen [*bottles*] of wine."

3. Of the *Adjective ;* as, " There are subjects proper for the one, and not [*proper*] for the other."—*Kames.*

4. Of the *Pronoun ;* as, " I love [*him*] and [*I*] fear him."— " The estates [*which*] we own."

---

* There never can be an ellipsis of any thing which is either unnecessary to the construction or necessary to the sense, for to say what we mean and nothing more, never can constitute a deviation from the ordinary grammatical construction of words. As a figure of Syntax, therefore, the *ellipsis* can be only of such words as are so evidently suggested to the reader, that the writer is as fully answerable for them as if he had written them.   To suppose an ellipsis where there is none, or to overlook one where 'it really occurs, is to pervert or mutilate the text, in order to accommodate it to the parser's ignorance of the principles of syntax.   There never can be either a general uniformity or a self-consistency in our methods of parsing, or in our notions of grammar, till the true nature of an ellipsis is clearly ascertained; so that the writer shall distinguish it from a *blundering omission* that impairs the sense, and the reader be barred from an *arbitrary insertion* of what would be cumbrous and useless.   By adopting loose and extravagant ideas of the nature of this figure, some pretenders to learning and philosophy have been led into the most whimsical and opposite notions concerning the grammatical construction of language.   Thus, with equal absurdity, *Cardell* and *Sherman,* in their *Philosophic Grammars,* attempt to confute the doctrines of their predecessors, by supposing *ellipses* at pleasure.   And while the former teaches, that prepositions do not govern the objective case, but that every verb is transitive, and governs at least two objects, expressed or *understood,* its own and that 'of a preposition; the latter, with just as good an argument, contends, that no verb is transitive, but that every objective case is governed by a preposition expressed or *understood.*   A world of nonsense for lack of a *definition !*

5. Of the *Verb ;* as, " Who did this ? I" [*did it*].—" To
whom thus Eve, yet sinless" [*spoke*].

6. Of the *Participle ;* as, " That [*being*] o'er, they part."

7. Of the *Adverb ;* as, " He spoke [*wisely*] and acted wisely."
—" Exceedingly great and [*exceedingly*] powerful."

8. Of the *Conjunction ;* as, " The fruit of the Spirit is love,
[*and*] joy, [*and*] peace, [*and*] long-suffering, [*and*] gentleness,
[*and*] goodness, [*and*] faith, [*and*] meekness, [*and*] temperance."— *Gal.*, v, 22.   The repetition of the conjunction is called
Polysyndeton ; and the omission of it, *Asyndeton.*

9. Of the *Preposition ;* as, " [*On*] this day."—" [*In*] next
month."—" He departed [*from*] this life."—" He gave [*to*] me
a book."—" To walk [*through*] a mile."

10. Of the *Interjection ;* as, " Oh! the frailty, [*Oh !*] the
wickedness of men !"

11. Of a *Phrase* or *Clause ;* as, " The active commonly do
more than they are bound to do ; the indolent [*commonly do*]
less" [*than they are bound to do*].

II. *Pleonasm* is the introduction of superfluous words. This
figure is allowable only, when, in animated discourse, it abruptly introduces an emphatic word, or repeats an idea to impress it more strongly ; as, "*He* that hath ears to hear, let him
hear !"—" All ye inhabitants of the world, *and dwellers on the
earth !*"—" There shall not be left one stone upon an other, *that
shall not be thrown down.*"—" I know thee *who thou art.*"—
Bible. A Pleonasm is sometimes impressive and elegant; but
an unemphatic repetition of the same idea, is one of the worst
faults of bad writing.

III. *Syllepsis* is agreement formed according to the figurative sense of a word, or the mental conception of the thing
spoken of, and not according to the literal or common use of
the term; it is therefore, in general, connected with some
figure of rhetoric: as, " The *Word* was made flesh and dwelt
among us, and we beheld *his* glory."--*John*, i, 14. " Then
Philip went down to the *city* of Samaria, and preached Christ
unto *them.*"—*Acts*, viii, 5. " While *Evening* draws *her* crim-
son curtains round."—*Thomson.*

IV. *Enallagè* is the use of one part of speech, or of one
modification for an other. This figure borders closely upon
solecism ;* and, for the stability of the language, it should be

sparingly indulged. There are, however, several forms of it
which can appeal to good authority : as,

1. " *You know* that *you are* Brutus, that *speak* this."—*Shak.*
2. "They fall *successive* [ly], and *successive* [ly] rise."—*Pope.*
3. "Than *whom* [who] none higher sat."—*Milton.*
4. "Sure some disaster has *befell*" [befallen].—*Gay.*
5. "So furious was that onset's shock,
    Destruction's gates at once *unlock.*"—*Hogg.*

V. *Hyperbaton* is the transposition of words; as, " He wanders *earth around.*"—*Cowper.* " *Rings the world* with the vain
stir."—*Id.* "*Whom* therefore ye ignorantly worship, *him declare I* unto you."—*Acts.* This figure is much employed in
poetry. A judicious use of it confers harmony, variety,
strength, and vivacity upon composition. But care should be
taken lest it produce ambiguity or obscurity.

SECTION IV.—FIGURES OF RHETORIC.

A Figure of Rhetoric is an intentional deviation
from the ordinary application of words. Some figures
of this kind are commonly called *Tropes,* i. e., *turns.*

Numerous departures from perfect simplicity of diction,
occur in almost every kind of composition. They are mostly
founded on some similitude or relation of things, which, by
the power of imagination, is rendered conducive to ornament
or illustration.

The principal figures of Rhetoric are fourteen; namely
*Sim'-i-le`, Met'-a-phor, Al'-le-gor-y, Me-ton'-y-my, Syn-ec'-do-che,
Hy-per'-bo-le, Vis'-ion, A-pos'-tro-phe, Per-son'-i-fi-ca'-tion, Er-o-
te'-sis, Ec-pho-ne'-sis, An-tith'-e-sis, Cli'-max,* and *I'-ro-ny.*

I. A *Simile* is a simple and express comparison; and is
generally introduced by *like, as,* or *so :* as,

" At first, *like thunder's distant tone,*
    The rattling din came rolling on."—*Hogg.*

" Man, *like the generous vine,* supported lives;
    The strength he gains, is from th' embrace he gives."—*Pope.*

II. A *Metaphor* is a figure that expresses the resemblance
of two objects by applying either the name, or some attribute
adjunct, or action of the one, directly to the other; as,

1. "His eye was *morning's brightest ray.*"—*Hogg.*
2. "An angler in the *tides* of fame."—*Id.*

---

altogether. There are, however, some changes of this kind, which the grammarian is
not competent to condemn, though they do not accord with the ordinary principles of
construction.

12

3. " Beside him *sleeps* the warrior's bow."—*Langhorne.*
4. " Wild fancies in his moody brain,
    Gambol'd unbridled and *unbound.*"—*Hogg.*
5. "Speechless, and fix'd in all the *death* of wo."—*Thom.*

III. An *Allegory* is a continued narration of fictitious events, designed to represent and illustrate important realities. Thus the Psalmist represents the *Jewish nation* under the symbol of a *vine :* "Thou hast brought a vine out of Egypt: thou hast cast out the heathen and planted it. Thou preparedst room before it, and didst cause it to take deep root; and it filled the land. The hills were covered with the shadow of it, and the boughs thereof were like the goodly cedars."—*Ps.*, lxxx, 8.

Obs.—The *Allegory*, agreeably to the foregoing definition of it, includes most of those similitudes which in the Scriptures are called *parables;* it includes also the better sort of *fables.* The term *allegory* is sometimes applied to a *true history* in which something else is intended, than is contained in the words literally taken. [See *Gal.*, iv, 24.] In the *Scriptures*, the term *fable* denotes an idle and groundless story. [See 1 *Tim.*, iv, 1; and 2 *Pet.*, i, 16.]

IV. A *Metonymy* is a change of names. It is founded on some such relation as that of *cause* and *effect*, of *subject* and *adjunct*, of *place* and *inhabitant*, of *container* and *thing contained*, or of *sign* and *thing signified :* as, "God is our *salvation ;*" i. e., *Saviour.*—" He was the *sigh* of her secret soul ;" i. e., the *youth* she loved.—"They smote the *city ;*" i. e., *citizens.*— "My son, give me thy *heart;*" i. e., *affection.*—"The *sceptre* shall not depart from Judah;" i. e., *kingly power.*

V. *Synedoche* is the naming of the whole for a part, or of a part for the whole; as, "This *roof* [i. e., house] protects you."—" Now the *year* [i. e., summer] is beautiful."

VI. *Hyperbole* is extravagant exaggeration, in which the imagination is indulged beyond the sobriety of truth; as,

"The sky *shrunk upward with unusual dread,*
    And trembling Tiber *div'd beneath his bed.*"—*Dryden.*

VII. *Vision*, or *Imagery*, is a figure by which the speaker represents the objects of his imagination, as actually before his eyes, and present to his senses; as,

"I see the dagger-crest of Mar !
I see the Moray's silver star
Wave o'er the cloud of Saxon war,
That up the lake comes winding far !"—*Scott.*

VIII. *Apostrophe* is a turning from the regular course of the subject, into an animated address; as, "Death is swallowed up in victory. O Death! where is thy sting? O Grave! where is thy victory?"—1 *Cor.*, xv, 54, 55.

IX. *Personification* is a figure by which, in imagination, we

ascribe intelligence and personality to unintelligent beings or
abstract qualities; as,

1. " The *Worm*, aware of his intent,
   Harangued him thus, right eloquent."—*Cowper.*
2. " Lo, steel-clad *War* his gorgeous standard rears !"—*Rog.*
3. " Hark ! *Truth* proclaims, thy triumphs cease."—*Id.*

X. *Erotesis* is a figure in which the speaker adopts the form
of interrogation, not to express a doubt, but, in general, confi-
dently to assert the reverse of what is asked; as, " Hast thou
an arm like God ? or canst thou thunder with a voice like
him ?"—*Job*, xl, 9.   " He that planted the ear, shall he not
hear ? he that formed the eye, shall he not see ?"—*Ps.*, xciv, 9.

XI. *Ecphonesis* is a pathetic exclamation, denoting some
violent emotion of the mind; as, " O liberty !—O sound once
delightful to every Roman ear !—O sacred privilege of Roman
citizenship !—once sacred—now trampled upon !"—*Cicero.*
" O that I had wings like a dove ! for then would I fly away
and be at rest !"—*Ps.*, lv, 6.

XII. *Antithesis* is a placing of things in opposition, to heighten
their effect by contrast; as,

   " Contrasted faults through all his manners reign;
   Though *poor, luxurious;* though *submissive, vain;*
   Though *grave,* yet *trifling; zealous,* yet *untrue;*
   And e'en *in penance, planning sins* anew."—*Goldsmith.*

XIII. *Climax* is a figure in which the sense is made to advance by successive steps, to rise gradually to what is more
and more important and interesting, or to descend to what is
more and more minute and particular; as, " And beside this,
giving all diligence, add to your faith, virtue; and to virtue,
knowledge; and to knowledge, temperance; and to temperance, patience; and to patience, godliness; and to godliness,
brotherly kindness; and to brotherly kindness, charity."—2
Peter, i, 5.

XIV. *Irony* is a figure in which the speaker sneeringly utters the direct reverse of what he intends shall be understood;
as, " We have, to be sure, great reason to believe the modest
man would not ask him for a debt, when he pursues his life."
—*Cicero.*

CHAPTER IV.—VERSIFICATION.

Versification is the art of arranging words into lines
of correspondent length, so as to produce harmony by
the regular alternation of syllables differing in quantity.

SECTION I.—OF QUANTITY.

The *Quantity* of a syllable, is the relative portion of time occupied in uttering it. In poetry, every syllable is considered to be either *long* or *short.* A long syllable is reckoned to be equal to two short ones.

Obs. 1.—The quantity of a syllable does not depend on the sound of the vowel or diphthong, but principally on the degree of accentual force with which the syllable is uttered, whereby a greater or less portion of time is employed. The open vowel sounds are those which are the most easily protracted, yet they often occur in the shortest and feeblest syllables.

Obs. 2.—Most monosyllables are variable, and may be made either long or short, as suits the rhythm. In words of greater length, the accented syllable is always long; and a syllable immediately before or after that which is accented, is always short.

SECTION II.—OF RHYME.

Rhyme is a similarity of sound, between the last syllables of different lines or half lines. *Blank verse* is verse without rhyme.

Obs.—The principal rhyming syllables are almost always long. Double rhyme adds one short syllable; triple rhyme, two. Such syllables are reduundant in iambic and anapestic verses.

SECTION III.—OF POETIC FEET.

A *line of poetry* consists of successive combinations of syllables, called *feet.* A poetic *foot,* in English, consists either of two or of three syllables.

The principal English feet are the *Iambus,* the *Trochee,* the *Anapest,* and the *Dactyl.*

1. The *Iambus,* or *Iamb,* is a poetic foot consisting of a short syllable and a long one; as, *bĕtrāy, cŏnfĕss.*

2. The *Trochee,* or *Choree,* is a poetic foot consisting of a long syllable and a short one; as, *hātefŭl, pēttĭsh.*

3. The *Anapest* is a poetic foot consisting of two short syllables and one long one; as, *cŏntrăvēne, ăcquĭĕsce.*

4. The *Dactyl* is a poetic foot consisting of one long syllable and two short ones; as, *lābŏųrĕr, pŏssĭblĕ.*

We have, accordingly, four principal kinds of verse, or poetic measure; *Iambic, Trochaic, Anapestic,* and *Dactylic.*

Obs. 1.—The more pure these several kinds are preserved, the more exact and complete is the chime of the verse. But poets generally indulge some variety; not so much, however, as to confound the drift of the rhythmical pulsations.

Obs. 2.—Among the occasional diversifications of metre, are sometimes found or supposed sundry other feet, which are called *secondary:* as, the *Spondee,* a foot of two long syllables; the *Pyrrhic,* of two short: the *Moloss,* of three long syllables; the *Tribrach,* of three short: the *Amphibrach,* a long syllable with a short one on each side; the *Amphimac, Amphimacer,* or *Cretic,* a short syllable with a long one on each side: the *Bacchy,* a short syllable and two long ones; the *Antibacchy*, or *Hypobacchy*, two long syllables and a short one. Yet few, if any, of these feet, are really *necessary* to a sufficient explanation of English verse; and the adopting of so many is liable to the great objection, that we thereby produce different modes of measuring the same lines.

Obs. 3.—Sometimes also verses are variegated by what is called the *pedal cæsura*, or *cesure;* (i. e., *cutting;*) which is a single long syllable counted by itself as a foot. For, despite the absurd suggestions of many grammarians and prosodists to the contrary, all metrical deficiencies and redundancies embrace nothing but *short* syllables, and the number of long ones in a line is almost always the number of *feet* which compose it: as,

> "Keeping | *time,* | *time,* | *time,*
> In a | sort of | Runic | *rhyme.*"—*E. A. Poe.*

SECTION IV.—OF SCANNING.

Scanning, or *Scansion,* is the dividing of verses into the feet which compose them, according to the several orders of poetic numbers, or the different kinds of metre.

Obs.—When a syllable is wanting, the verse is said to be *catalectic;* when the measure is exact, the line is *acatalectic;* when there is a redundant syllable, it forms *hypermeter,* or a line *hypercatalectic.*

ORDER I.—IAMBIC VERSE.

In Iambic verse, the stress is laid on the even syllables, and the odd ones are short. It consists of the following measures:—

Measure 1st.—Iambic of Eight Feet, or Octometer.

> " O āll | yĕ pēo|-plĕ, clăp | yŏur hănds, | ănd wĭth | trĭŭm|-phănt vōic|-ĕs sīng;
> No force | the might|-y pow'r | withstands | of God | the u|-nivers|-al King."

Obs.—Each couplet of this verse is now commonly reduced to, or exchanged for, a simple stanza of four tetrameter lines; thus,—

> "The hour | is come | —the cher|-ish'd hour,
> When from | the bus|-y world | set free,
> I seek | at length | my lone|-ly bower,
> And muse | in si|-lent thought | on thee."—*Hook.*

Measure 2d.—Iambic of Seven Feet, or Heptameter.

> "Thĕ Lōrd | dĕscēnd|-ĕd frōm | ăbōve, | ănd bōw'd | thĕ hēav|-ĕns hīgh."

Obs.—Modern poets have divided this kind of verse, into alternate lines of four and of three feet; thus,—

> "O blĭnd | tŏ ēach | ĭndūl|-gĕnt āim
> Of pōw'r | sŭprēme|-lў wīse,
> Who fan|-cy hap|-piness | in aught
> The hand | of heav'n | denies!"

Measure 3d.—Iambic of Six Feet, or Hexameter.

> "Thў rēalm | fŏrēv|-ĕr lāsts, | thў ōwn | Mĕssī|-ăh rēigns."

Obs.—This is the *Alexandrine;* it is seldom used except to complete a stanza in an ode, or occasionally to close a period in heroic rhyme. French heroics are similar to this.

Measure 4th.—Iambic of Five Feet, or Pentameter.

"Fŏr prāise | tŏo dēar|-lў lōv'd | ŏr wārm|-lў sōught,
Enfee|-bles all | inter|-nal strength | of thought."

"Wĭth sōl|-ĕmn ād|-ŏrā|-tiŏn dōwn | thĕy cāst
Their crowns | inwove | with am|-arant | and gold."

Obs. 1.—This is the regular English *heroic*. It is, perhaps, the only measure suitable for blank verse.

Obs. 2.—The *Elegiac Stanza* consists of four heroics rhyming alternately; as,

"Enough | has Heav'n | indulg'd | of joy | below,
To tempt | our tar|-riance in | this lov'd | retreat;
Enough | has Heav'n | ordain'd | of use|-ful wo,
To make | us lang|-uish for | a hap|-pier seat."

Measure 5th.—Iambic of Four Feet, or Tetrameter.

"Thĕ jōys | ăbōve | ăre ūn|-dĕrstōod
And rel|-ish'd on|-ly by | the good."

Measure 6th.—Iambic of Three Feet, or Trimeter.

"Blŭe lĭght|-nĭngs sĭnge | thĕ wāves,
And thun|-der rends | the rock."

Measure 7th.—Iambic of Two Feet, or Dimeter.

"Thĕir lōve | ănd āwe
Supply | the law."

Measure 8th.—Iambic of One Foot, or Monometer.

"Hŏw brĭght,
The light!"

Obs. 1.—Lines of fewer than seven syllables are seldom found, except in connexion with longer verses.

Obs. 2.—In iambic verse, the first foot is often varied, by introducing a trochee; as,

"*Plănĕts* | ănd sŭns | rŭn lăw|-lĕss thrōugh | thĕ skȳ."

Obs. 3.—By a synæresis of the two short syllables, or perhaps by mere substitution, an anapest may sometimes be employed for an iambus; or a dactyl, for a trochee: as,

"*O'er man|-y a fro|-zen, man|-y a fi|-ery Alp.*"

ORDER II.—TROCHAIC VERSE.

In Trochaic verse, the stress is laid on the odd syllables, and the even ones are short. Single-rhymed trochaic omits the final short syllable, that it may end with a long one. This kind of verse is the same as iambic would be without the initial short syllable. Iambics and trochaics often occur in the same poem.

Measure 1st.—Trochaic of Eight Feet, or Octometer.

"Once up|-on a | midnight | dreary, | while I | pondered, |
weak and | weary,
Over | *mănў ă* | quaint and | *cūrĭ̄ǫus* | volume | of for|
-gotten | lore,

While I | nodded, | nearly | napping, | sudden|-ly there | came a | tapping,
As of | some one | gently | rapping, | rapping | at my | chamber | door."

Measure 2d.—Trochaic of Seven Feet, or Heptameter.

"Hasten, | Lord, to | rescue | me, and | set me | safe from | trouble;
Shame thou | those who | seek my | soul, re|-ward their | mischief | double."

Single Rhyme.

"Night   and | morning | were   at | meeting | over | Water| -loo;
Cocks had | sung their | *earliest* | greeting; | faint and | low they | crew."

Measure 3d.—Trochaic of Six Feet, or Hexameter.

" On ă | mōuntăin | strētch'd bĕ|-nēath ă | hōarў | wĭllŏw,
Lay a | shepherd | swain, and | view'd the | rolling | billow."

Single Rhyme.

" Lonely | in the | forest, | subtle | from his | birth,
Lived a | necro|-mancer, | wondrous | son of | earth."

Measure 4th.—Trochaic of Five Feet, or Pentameter.

" Vīrtŭe's | brīght'nĭng | rāy shăll | bēam fŏr | ĕvĕr."

Single Rhyme.

" Idlĕ | āftĕr | dīnnĕr, | ĭn hĭs | chāir,
Sat a | farmer, | ruddy, | fat, and | fair."

Measure 5th.—Trochaic of Four Feet, or Tetrameter.

" Rōund ă | hōlў | cālm dĭf|-fūsĭng,
Love of | peace and | lonely | musing."

Single Rhyme.

" Rĕstlĕss | mōrtăls | tōil fŏr | nāught,
Bliss in | vain from | earth is | sought."

Measure 6th.—Trochaic of Three Feet, or Trimeter.

" Whēn ŏur | heărts ăre | mōurnĭng."

Single Rhyme.

" In thĕ | dāys ŏf | ōld,
Stories | plainly | told."

Measure 7th.—Trochaic of Two Feet, or Dimeter.

" Fāncў | viēwĭng,
Joys en|-suing."

Single Rhyme.
"Tūmŭlt | cēase,
Sink to | peace."

Measure 8th.—Trochaic of One Foot, or Monometer.
" Chāngĭng,
Ranging."

ORDER III.—ANAPESTIC VERSE.

In Anapestic verse the stress is laid on every third syllable.
The first foot of an anapestic line, may be an iambus.

Measure 1st.—Anapestic of Four Feet, or Tetrameter.

" At thĕ clōse | ŏf thĕ dāy, | whĕn thĕ hăm|-lĕt ĭs stĭll,
And mor|-tals the sweets | of forget|-fulness prove."

Hypermeter with Double Rhyme.

" In a word, | so complete|-ly forestall'd | were the wish|-es,
Even har|-mony struck | from the noise | of the dish|-es."

Hypermeter with Triple Rhyme.

" Lean Tom, | when I saw | him, last week, | on his *horse* |
awry,
Threaten'd loud|-ly to turn | me to stone | with his *sor*|-*cery*."

Measure 2d.—Anapestic of Three Feet, or Trimeter.

" I ăm mōn|-ărch ŏf āll | I sŭrvēy ;
My right | there is none | to dispute."

Measure 3d.—Anapestic of Two Feet, or Dimeter.

" Whĕn I lōok | ŏn mў bōys,
They renew | all my joys."

Measure 4th.—Anapestic of One Foot, or Monometer.

" On thĕ lānd
Let me stand."

ORDER IV.—DACTYLIC VERSE.

In pure Dactylic verse, the stress is laid on the first syllable
of each successive three ; that is, on the first, the fourth, the
seventh, the tenth syllable, &c.   Full dactylic generally forms
triple rhyme.   When one of the final short syllables is omitted,
the rhyme is double ; when both, single.   Dactylic with single
rhyme is the same as anapestic would be without its initial
short syllables.   Dactylic measure is rather uncommon ; and,
when employed, is seldom perfectly regular.

Measure 1st.—Dactylic of Eight Feet, or Octometer.

" Nĭmrŏd thĕ | hŭntĕr wăs | mīghtȳ ĭn | hŭntĭng, ănd | fāmed
ăs thĕ | rūlĕr ŏf | cĭtĭes ŏf | yōre;
Babel, and | Erech, and | Accad, and | Calneh, from | Shi-
nar's fair | region his | name afar | bore."

Measure 2d.—Dactylic of Seven Feet, or Heptameter.

" Out of the | kingdom of | Christ shall be | gathered, by |
angels o'er | Satan vic|-torious,
All that of|-fendeth, that | lieth, that | faileth to | honour his
| name ever | glorious."

Example without Rhyme.

" This is the | forest pri|-meval ; but | where are the | hearts
that be|-neath it
Leap'd like the | roe, when he | hears in the | woodland the
| voice of the | huntsman ?"

Measure 3d.—Dactylic of Six Feet, or Hexameter.

" Time, thou art | ever in | motion, on | wheels of the | days,
years, and | ages ;
Restless as | waves of the | ocean, when | Eurus or | Boreas
| rages."

Measure 4th.—Dactylic of Five Feet, or Pentameter.

" Now thou dost | welcome me, | welcome me, | from the
dark | sea,
Land of the | beautiful, | beautiful, | land of the | free."

Measure 5th.—Dactylic of Four Feet, or Tetrameter.

" Bōys wĭll ăn|tĭcĭpăte, | lăvĭsh, ănd | dĭssĭpăte
All thăt yŏur | būsȳ păte | hōardĕd wĭth | cāre ;
And, in their | foolishness, | passion, and | mulishness,
Charge you with | churlishness, | spurning your | pray'r."

Measure 6th.—Dactylic of Three Feet, or Trimeter.

" Evĕr sĭng | mērrĭlȳ, | mērrĭlȳ."

Measure 7th.—Dactylic of Two Feet, or Dimeter.

" Frēe frŏm să|tĭĕtȳ,
Care, and anx|iety,
Charms in va|riety,
Fall to his | share."

Measure 8th.—Dactylic of One Foot, or Monometer.

" Fēarfŭllȳ,
Tearfully."

12*

CHAPTER V.—ORAL EXERCISES.

EXAMPLES FOR PARSING.

PRAXIS VIII.—PROSODICAL.

In the Eighth Praxis, are exemplified the several Figures of Orthography, of Etymology, of Syntax, and of Rhetoric, which the parser may name and define; and by it the pupil may also be exercised in relation to the principles of Punctuation, Utterance, and Versification.

LESSON I.—FIGURES OF ORTHOGRAPHY.

MIMESIS AND ARCHAISM.

"*Fery goot:* I will make a *prief* of it in my note-book; and we will afterwards '*ork* upon the cause with as great *discreetly* as we can."—*Shak.*

"*Vat* is you sing? I do not like *dese* toys. Pray you, go and *vetch* me *in* my closet *un boitier verd;* a box, a *green-a* box. Do *intend vat* I speak? a *green-a* box."—*Id.*

"I *ax'd* you what you had to sell. I am fitting out a *wessel* for *Wenice,* loading her with *warious keinds* of *prowisions,* and *wittualling* her for a long *woyage;* and I want several *undred* weight of *weal, wenison,* &c., with plenty of *inyons* and *winegar,* for the *preserwation* of *ealth.*"—*Columbian Orator,* p. 292.

"None [else are] so desperately *evill,* as they that may *bee* good and will not: or have *beene* good and are not."—*Rev. John Rogers,* 1620.   "A Carpenter finds his work as *hee* left it, but a Minister shall find his *sett* back. You need preach continually."—*Id.*

"Here *whilom ligg'd* th' Esopus of his age,
But call'd by Fame, in soul *ypricked* deep."—*Thomson.*

"It was a fountain of Nepenthe rare,
Whence, as Dan Homer sings, huge *pleasaunce* grew."—*Id,*

LESSON II.—FIGURES OF ETYMOLOGY.

APHÆRESIS, PROSTHESIS, SYNCOPE, APOCOPE, PARAGOGE, DIÆRESIS, SYNÆRESIS, AND TMESIS.

Bend '*gainst* the steepy hill thy breast,
Burst down like torrent from its crest."—*Scott.*

'*Tis* mine to teach *th'* inactive hand to reap
Kind nature's bounties, *o'er* the globe *diffus'd.*—*Dyer.*

Alas! alas! how impotently true
Th' aërial pencil forms the scene anew.—*Cawthorne.*

Here a deformed monster *joy'd* to won,
Which on fell rancour ever was *ybent.—Lloyd.*

Withouten trump was proclamation made.—*Thomson.*

The gentle knight, who saw their rueful case,
Let fall *adown* his silver beard some tears.
'Certes,' quoth he, 'it is not *e'en* in grace,
T' undo the past and eke your broken years.'—*Id.*

Vain *tamp'ring* has but *foster'd* his disease;
'Tis desp'rate, and he sleeps the sleep of death.—*Cowper.*

I have a pain upon my forehead here—
Why *that's* with watching; *'twill* away again.—*Shakspeare.*

I'll to the woods, among the happier brutes;
Come, *let's* away; hark! the shrill horn resounds.—*Smith.*

What prayer and supplication *soever* be made.—*Bible.*

By the grace of God we have had our conversation in the
world, and more abundantly *to* you *ward.—Id.*

LESSON III.—FIGURES OF SYNTAX.

FIGURE I.—ELLIPSIS.

And now he faintly kens the bounding fawn,
And [—] villager [—] abroad at early toil.—*Beattie.*

The cottage curs at [—] early pilgrim bark.—*Id.*

'Tis granted, and no plainer truth appears,
Our most important [—] are our earliest years.—*Cowper.*

To earn her aid, with fix'd and anxious eye,
He looks on nature's [—] and on fortune's course;
Too much in vain.—*Akenside.*

True dignity is his, whose tranquil mind
Virtue has rais'd above the things [—] below;
Who, ev'ry hope and [—] fear to Heav'n resign'd,
Shrinks not, though Fortune aim her deadliest blow.—*Beattie.*

For longer in that paradise to dwell,
The law [—] I gave to nature, him forbids.—*Milton.*

So little mercy shows [—] who needs so much.—*Cowper.*

Bliss is the same [—] in subject, as [—] in king;
In [—] who obtain defence, and [—] who defend.—*Pope.*

Man made for kings! those optics are but dim
That tell you so—say rather, they [—] for him.—*Cowper.*

Man may dismiss compassion from his heart,
But God will never [—————————].—*Id.*

Mortals whose pleasures are their only care,
First wish to be impos'd on, and then are [—].—*Id.*

Vigour [—] from toil, from trouble patience grows.—*Beattie.*

Where now the rill melodious, [—] pure, and cool,
And meads, with life, and mirth, and beauty crown'd?—*Id.*

How dead the vegetable kingdom lies!
How dumb the tuneful [————————]!—*Thomson.*

Self-love and Reason to one end aspire,
Pain [—] their aversion, pleasure [—] their desire;
But greedy that its object would devour,
This [—] taste the honey, and not wound the flower.—*Pope.*

LESSON IV.—FIGURES OF SYNTAX.

FIGURE II.—PLEONASM.

According to their deeds, *accordingly* he will repay; fury to his adversaries, recompense to his enemies.—*Bible.*

My head is filled with dew, *and my locks with the drops of the night.*—*Solomon's Song,* v, 2.

Thou hast chastised me, *and I was chastised,* as a bullock unaccustomed to the yoke: turn thou me, *and I shall be turned;* for thou art the Lord my God.—*Jer.,* xxxi, 18.

Consider the *lilies* of the field how *they* grow.—*Matt.,* vi, 28.
He that glorieth, let *him* glory in the Lord.—2 *Cor.,* x, 17.

He too is witness, noblest of the train
That waits on man, the flight-performing *horse.*—*Cowper.*

FIGURE III.—SYLLEPSIS.

Thou art Simon the son of Jona: thou shalt be called *Cephas;' which* is, by interpretation, a stone.—*John,* i, 42.

Thus saith the Lord of hosts: 'Behold I will break the bow of *Elam,* the chief of *their* might.'—*Jer.,* xlix, 35.

Behold I lay in Zion a *stumbling-stone* and *rock* of offence; and whosoever believeth on *him* shall not be ashamed.—*Rom.,* ix, 33.

Thus *Conscience* pleads *her* cause within the breast,
Though long rebell'd against, not yet suppress'd.—*Cowper.*

Knowledge is proud that *he* has learned so much;
Wisdom is humble that *he* knows no more.—*Id.*

For those the *race* of Israel oft forsook
Their living *strength,* and unfrequented left
His righteous altar, bowing lowly down
To bestial gods.—*Milton.*

LESSON V.—FIGURES OF SYNTAX.

FIGURE IV.—ENALLAGE.

Let me tell *you*, Cassius, *you* yourself
Are much condemned to have an itching palm,
To sell and mart *your* offices for gold.—*Shakspeare.*

Come, Philomelus; let us *instant* go,
O'erturn his bow'rs, and lay his castle low.—*Thomson.*

Then palaces shall rise; the joyful son
Shall finish what the short-lived sire *begun.*—*Pope.*

Such was that temple built by Solomon,
Than *whom* none richer reign'd o'er Israel.—*G. Brown.*

He spoke: with fatal eagerness we *burn,*
And *quit* the shores, undestin'd to return.—*Day.*

Still as he pass'd, the nations he *sublimes.*—*Thomson.*

Sometimes, with early morn, he mounted *gay.*—*Id.*

FIGURE V.—HYPERBATON.

Such *resting found the sole* of unblest feet.—*Milton.*

Yet, though successless, *will the toil* delight.—*Thomson.*

Where, 'midst the changeful scen'ry ever new,
Fancy a thousand wondrous *forms* descries.—*Beattie.*

Yet so much bounty is in God, such grace,
That who advance his glory, not their own,
Them he himself to glory will advance.—*Milton.*

But *apt* the mind or fancy is to rove
Uncheck'd, and of her roving is no *end.*—*Id.*

No quick *reply* to dubious questions make;
Suspense and caution still prevent mistake.—*Denham.*

LESSON VI.—FIGURES OF RHETORIC.

FIGURE I.—SIMILE.

Human greatness is short and transitory, *as the odour of incense in the fire.*—*Dr. Johnson.*

Terrestrial happiness is of short continuance: *the brightness of the flame is wasting its fuel, the fragrant flower is passing away in its own odours.*—*Id.*

Thy nod is *as the earthquake that shakes the mountains*; and thy smile, *as the dawn of the vernal day.*—*Id.*

>   Plants rais'd *with tenderness are seldom strong;*
>   Man's coltish disposition asks the thong;
>   And without discipline, the fav'rite child,
>   *Like a neglected forester,* runs wild.—*Cowper.*

24

FIGURE II.—METAPHOR.

Cathmon, thy name is a pleasant *gale.—Ossian*.

Rolled into himself he flew, wide on the *bosom of winds*. The old *oak felt* his departure, and *shook* its whistling *head.—Id*.

Carazan gradually lost the inclination to do good, as he acquired the power; and as the *hand of time* scattered *snow* upon his head, the *freezing influence* extended to his bosom.—*Hawkesworth*.

The sun *grew weary* of gilding the palaces of Morad; the *clouds of sorrow* gathered round his head; and the *tempest of hatred* roared about his dwelling.—*Dr. Johnson*.

> The *tree of knowledge*, blasted by disputes,
> Produces sapless leaves in stead of fruits.—*Denham*.

LESSON VII.—FIGURES OF RHETORIC.

FIGURE III.—ALLEGORY.

"But what think ye?—A certain man had two sons; and he came to the first, and said, 'Son, go work to-day in my vineyard.' He answered and said, 'I will not:' but afterward he repented, and went. And he came to the second, and said likewise. And he answered and said, 'I go, sir:' and went not. Whether of them twain did the will of his father?" They say unto him, "The first."—*Matt.*, xxi, 28.

FIGURE IV.—METONYMY.

Swifter than a whirlwind, flies the leaden *death.—Hervey*.

'Be all the dead forgot,' said Foldath's bursting *wrath*. 'Did not I fail in the field?'—*Ossian*.

Their *furrow* oft the stubborn glebe has broke.—*Gray*.

> Firm in his love, resistless in his hate,
> His arm is *conquest*, and his frown is *fate.—Day*.

> At length the *world*, renew'd by calm repose,
> Was strong for toil; the dappled morn arose.—*Parnell*.

> What modes of sight betwixt each wide extreme,
> The mole's dim curtain and the lynx's *beam!*
> Of hearing, from the *life* that fills the flood,
> To *that* which warbles through the vernal wood!—*Pope*.

FIGURE V.—SYNECDOCHE.

'Twas then his *threshold* first receiv'd a guest.—*Parnell*.

> For yet by swains alone the world he knew,
> Whose *feet* came wand'ring o'er the nightly dew.—*Id*.

Flush'd by the spirit of the genial *year*,
Now from the virgin's cheek a fresher bloom
Shoots, less and less, the live carnation round.—*Thomson.*

LESSON VIII.—FIGURES OF RHETORIC.

FIGURE VI.—HYPERBOLE.

I saw their chief, tall as a rock of ice; his spear, the blasted fir; his shield, the rising moon; he sat on the shore, like a cloud of mist on the hill.—*Ossian.*

At which the universal host up sent
A shout that tore Hell's concave, and beyond
Frighted the reign of Chaos and old Night.—*Milton.*
Will all great Neptune's ocean wash this blood
Clean from my hand? No; this my hand will rather
The multitudinous seas incarnadine,
Making the green one red.—*Shakspeare.*
Endless tears flow down in streams.—*Swift.*

FIGURE VII.—VISION.

How mighty is their defence who reverently trust in the arm of God! How powerfully do they contend who fight with lawful weapons! Hark! 'Tis the voice of eloquence, pouring forth the living energies of the soul; pleading, with generous indignation, the cause of injured humanity against lawless might, and reading the awful destiny that awaits the oppressor!—I see the stern countenance of despotism overawed! I see the eye fallen that kindled the elements of war! I see the brow relaxed that scowled defiance at hostile thousands! I see the knees tremble that trod with firmness the embattled field! Fear has entered that heart which ambition had betrayed into violence! The tyrant feels himself a man, and subject to the weakness of humanity!—Behold! and tell me, is that power contemptible which can thus find access to the sternest hearts? —*G. Brown.*

LESSON IX.—FIGURES OF RHETORIC.

FIGURE VIII.—APOSTROPHE.

Yet still they breathe destruction, still go on
Inhumanly ingenious to find out
New pains for life, new terrors for the grave;
Artificers of death! Still monarchs dream
Of universal empire growing up
From universal ruin. *Blast the design,*
Great God of Hosts! nor let thy creatures fall
Unpitied victims at Ambition's shrine.—Porteus.

FIGURE IX.—PERSONIFICATION.

Hail, sacred *Polity*, by *Freedom* rear'd!
Hail, sacred *Freedom*, when by *Law* restrain'd!
Without you, what were man?   A grov'ling herd,
In darkness, wretchedness, and want enchain'd.—*Beattie.*

Let cheerful *Mem'ry*, from her purest cells,
Lead forth a goodly train of *Virtues* fair,
Cherish'd in early youth, now paying back
With tenfold usury the pious care.—*Porteus.*

FIGURE X.—EROTESIS.

He that chastiseth the heathen, shall not he correct? he that
teacheth man knowledge, shall not he know?—*Psal.*, xciv, 10.
Can the Ethiopian change his skin, or the leopard his spots?
then may ye also do good, that are accustomed to do evil.—
Jeremiah, xiii, 23.

FIGURE XI.—ECPHONESIS.

O that my head were waters, and mine eyes a fountain of
tears, that I might weep day and night for the slain of the
daughter of my people!   O that I had in the wilderness a
lodging place of way-faring men, that I might leave my people,
and go from them!—*Jeremiah,* ix, 1.

LESSON X.—FIGURES OF RHETORIC.

FIGURE XII.—ANTITHESIS.

On this side, modesty is engaged; on that, impudence: on
this, chastity; on that, lewdness: on this, integrity; on that,
fraud: on this, piety; on that, profaneness: on this, constancy;
on that, fickleness: on this, honour; on that, baseness: on this,
moderation; on that, unbridled passion.—*Cicero.*

She, from the rending earth, and bursting skies,
Saw gods descend, and fiends infernal rise;
Here fix'd the dreadful, there the blest abodes;
Fear made her devils, and weak hope her gods.—*Pope.*

FIGURE XIII.—CLIMAX.

Virtuous actions are necessarily approved by the awakened
conscience; and when they are approved, they are commended
to practice; and when they are practised, they become easy;
and when they become easy, they afford pleasure; and when
they afford pleasure, they are done frequently; and when they
are done frequently, they are confirmed by habit: and confirmed habit is a kind of second nature.

FIGURE XIV.—IRONY.

And it came to pass at noon, that Elijah mocked them, and said, ' Cry aloud; for he is a god : either he is talking, or he is pursuing, or he is in [*on*] a journey, or peradventure he sleepeth, and must be awaked !'—1 *Kings*, xviii, 27.

> Some lead a life unblamable and just,
> Their own dear virtue their unshaken trust;
> They never sin—or if (as all offend)
> Some trivial slips their daily walk attend,
> The poor are near at hand, the charge is small,
> A slight gratuity atones for all.—*Cowper.*

CHAPTER VI.—EXAMINATION.

QUESTIONS ON PROSODY.

LESSON I.—PUNCTUATION.

Of what does Prosody treat ?
What is *Punctuation ?*
What are the principal points, or marks ?
What pauses are denoted by the first four points ?
What pauses are required by the other four ?
What is the general use of the comma ?
How many rules for the comma are there ? and what are their heads ?
What says Rule 1st of *simple sentences ?*—Rule 2d of *simple members ?*—Rule 3d of *more than two words ?*—Rule 4th of *only two words ?*—Rule 5th of *words in pairs ?*—Rule 6th of *words put absolute ?*—Rule 7th of *words in apposition ?*—Rule 8th of *adjectives ?*—Rule 9th of *finite verbs ?*—Rule 10th of *infinitives ?*—Rule 11th of *participles ?*—Rule 12th of *adverbs ?*—Rule 13th of *conjunctions ?*—Rule 14th of *prepositions ?*—Rule 15th of *interjections ?*—Rule 16th of *words repeated ?*—Rule 17th of *dependent quotations ?*

LESSON II.—PUNCTUATION.

How many and what exceptions are there to Rule 1st for the comma ?—to Rule 2d ?—to Rule 3d ?—to Rule 4th ?—to Rule 5th ?—to Rule 6th ?—to Rule 7th ?—to Rule 8th ?—to Rule 9th ?—to Rule 10th ?—to Rule 11th ?—to Rule 12th ?—to Rule 13th ?—to Rule 14th ?—to Rule 15th ?—to Rule 16th ?—to Rule 17th ?
When are different words said to be in the same construction ?

LESSONS III.—PUNCTUATION.

What is the general use of the semicolon ?
How many rules are there for the semicolon ? and what are their heads ?
What says Rule 1st of *compound members ?*—Rule 2d of *simple members ?*—Rule 3d of *words in apposition ?*
What is the general use of the colon ?
How many rules are there for the colon ? and what are their heads ?
What says Rule 1st of *additional remarks ?*—Rule 2d of *greater pauses ?*—Rule 3d of *independent quotations ?*
What is the general use of the period ?
How many rules are there for the period ? and what are their heads ?
What says Rule 1st of *distinct sentences ?*—Rule 2d of *allied sentences ?*—Rule 3d of *abbreviations ?*

LESSON IV.—PUNCTUATION.

What is the use of the dash?
How many rules are there for the dash? and what are their heads?
What says Rule 1st of *abrupt pauses?*—Rule 2d of *emphatic pauses?*—Rule
3d of *faulty dashes?*
What is the use of the eroteme, or note of interrogation?
How many rules are there for it? and what are their heads?
What says Rule 1st of *questions direct?*—Rule 2d of *questions united?*—Rule
3d of *questions indirect?*
What is the use of the ecphoneme, or note of exclamation?
How many rules are there for it? and what are their heads?
What says Rule 1st of *interjections?*—Rule 2d of *invocations?*—Rule 3d of
exclamatory questions?

LESSON V.—PUNCTUATION.

What is the use of the curves, or marks of parenthesis?
How many rules are there for them? and what are their heads?
What says Rule 1st of *the parenthesis?*—Rule 2d of *included points?*
What is said about other marks?
What is the use of the apostrophe?—of the hyphen?—of the diæresis?—of
the acute accent?—of the grave accent?—of the circumflex?—of the breve?
—of the macron?—of the ellipsis?—of the caret?—of the brace?—of the
section?—of the paragraph?—of the quotation points?—of the crotchets?—
of the index?—of the asterisk, the obelisk, the double dagger, and the
parallels?—of the asterism?—of the cedilla?

[Having correctly answered the foregoing questions, the pupil should be taught to
apply what he has learned; and, for this purpose, he may be required to read the preface to this volume, or a portion of any other accurately pointed book, and to assign
a reason for every mark he finds.]

LESSON VI.—UTTERANCE.

What is *Utterance?* and what does it include?
What is pronunciation?—What does pronunciation require?
What are the just powers of the letters?
What is accent?—Is every word accented?
Can a word have more than one accent?
What four things distinguish the elegant speaker?
What is elocution?—What does elocution require?—What is emphasis?
What are pauses? and what is said of their duration?
What are inflections?—What is called the rising inflection?—What is called
the falling inflection?—How are these inflections exemplified?—How are
they used in asking questions?
What are tones? and why do they deserve particular attention?

LESSON VII.—FIGURES.

What is a *Figure* in grammar?—How many kinds of figures are there?
What is a figure of orthography?—Name the figures of this kind.
What is mimesis?—What is an archaism?
What is a figure of etymology?
How many and what are the figures of etymology?
What is aphæresis?—prosthesis?—syncope?—apocope?—paragoge?—diære-
sis?—synæresis?—tmesis?
What is a figure of syntax?—How many and what are the figures of syntax?
What is ellipsis in grammar? Are sentences often elliptical?
How can there be an ellipsis of the article?—the noun?—the adjective?—the
pronoun?—the verb?—the participle?—the adverb?—the conjunction?—
the preposition?—the interjection?—a phrase or clause?
What is pleonasm?—and when is this figure allowable?
What is syllepsis?—enallage?—hyperbaton?—what is said of hyberbaton?

LESSON VIII.—FIGURES.

What is a figure of rhetoric?—What name have some such figures?

Do figures of rhetoric often occur ?—On what are they founded ?
How many and what are the principal figures of rhetoric ?
What is a simile ?—a metaphor ?—an allegory ?—a metonymy ?—synecdoche ?
—hyperbole ?— vision ?— apostrophe ?— personification ?— erotesis ?—ecphonesis ?—antithesis ?—climax ?—irony ?

LESSON IX.—VERSIFICATION.

What is *Versification ?*—What is the *quantity* of a syllable ?
How is quantity denominated ?—How is it said to be proportioned ?
On what does quantity depend ? and what sounds are the most easily
    lengthened ?
What words are variable in quantity ? and what syllables are fixed ?
What is rhyme ?—What is blank verse ?
Of what does a *line* of poetry consist ?—Of what does a *foot* consist ?
What are the principal English feet ?
What is an iambus ?—a trochee ?—an anapest ?—a dactyl ?
How many kinds of verse have we ?
What is scanning, or scansion ?

LESSON X.—VERSIFICATION.

What syllables are accented in an iambic line ?
What are the several measures of iambic verse ?
What syllables are accented in a trochaic line ?
What are the several measures of trochaic verse ?
What syllables are accented in an anapestic line ?
What are the several measures of anapestic verse ?
What syllables are accented in a dactylic line ?
What are the several measures of dactylic verse ?

[Now parse the ten lessons of the *Eighth Praxis;* explaining every thing of which
the teacher may demand an explanation.]

CHAPTER VII.—FOR WRITING.

EXERCISES IN PROSODY.

[When the pupil can readily answer all the questions on Prosody, and apply
the rules of punctuation to any composition in which the points are rightly inserted,
he should *write out* the following exercises, supplying what is required.]

EXERCISE I.—PUNCTUATION.

Copy the following sentences, and insert the COMMA *where it is
requisite.*

Examples under Rule 1.

The dogmatist's assurance is paramount to argument.
The whole course of his argumentation comes to nothing.
The fieldmouse builds her garner under ground.
Exc. The first principles of almost all sciences are few.
What he gave me to publish was but a small part.
To remain insensible to such provocation is apathy.
Minds ashamed of poverty would be proud of affluence.

Under Rule 2.

I was eyes to the blind and feet was I to the lame.
They are gone but the remembrance of them is sweet,

He has passed it is likely through varieties of fortune.
The mind though free has a governor within itself.
They I doubt not oppose the bill on public principles.
Be silent be grateful and adore.
He is an adept in language who always speaks the truth.
The race is not to the swift nor the battle to the strong.
Exc. 1. He that has far to go should not hurry.
Hobbes believed the eternal truths which he opposed.
Feeble are all pleasures in which the heart has no share.
Exc. 2. A good name is better than precious ointment.
Thinkst thou that duty shall have dread to speak?
The spleen is seldom felt were Flora reigns.

Under Rule 3.

The city army court espouse my cause.
Wars pestilences and diseases are terrible instructors.
Walk daily in a pleasant airy and umbrageous garden.
Wit spirits faculties but make it worse.
Men wives and children stare cry out and run.

Under Rule 4.

Hope and fear are essentials in religion.
Praise and adoration are perfective of our souls.
We know bodies and their properties most perfectly.
Satisfy yourselves with what is rational and attainable.
Exc 1. God will rather look to the inward motions of the
mind than to the outward form of the body.
Gentleness is unassuming in opinion and temperate in zeal.
Exc. 2. He has experienced prosperity and adversity.
All sin essentially is and must be mortal.
Exc. 3. One person is chosen chairman or moderator.
Duration or time is measured by motion.
The governor or viceroy is chosen annually.
Exc. 4. Reflection reason still the ties improve.
His neat plain parlour wants our modern style.

Under Rule 5.

I inquired and rejected consulted and deliberated.
Seed-time and harvest cold and heat summer and winter day
and night shall not cease.

EXERCISE II.—PUNCTUATION.

Copy the following sentences, and insert the COMMA *where it is
requisite.*

Under Rule 6.

The night being dark they did not proceed.

There being no other coach we had no alternative.
Remember my son that human life is the journey of a day.
All circumstances considered it seems right.
He that overcometh to him will I give power.
Your land strangers devour it in your presence.
Ah sinful nation a people laden with iniquity!

> With heads declin'd ye cedars homage pay;
> Be smooth ye rocks ye rapid floods give way!

Under Rule 7.

Now Philomel sweet songstress charms the night.
'Tis chanticleer the shepherd's clock announcing day.
The evening star love's harbinger appears.
The queen of night fair Dian smiles serene.
There is yet one man Micaiah the son of Imlah.
Our whole company man by man ventured down.
As a work of wit the Dunciad has few equals.

> In the same temple the resounding wood
> All vocal beings hymned their equal God.

Exc. 1. The last king of Rome was Tarquinius Superbus.
Bossuet highly eulogizes Maria Theresa of Austria.
Exc. 2. For he went and dwelt by the brook Cherith.
Remember the example of the patriarch Joseph.
Exc. 3. I wisdom dwell with prudence.
Ye fools be ye of an understanding heart.
I tell you that which you yourselves do know.
Exc. 4. I crown thee king of intimate delights.
I count the world a stranger for thy sake.
And this makes friends such miracles below.
God has pronounced it death to taste that tree.
Grace makes the slave a freeman.

Under Rule 8.

Deaf with the noise I took my hasty flight.
Him piteous of his youth soft disengage.
I played a while obedient to the fair.
Love free as air spreads his light wings and flies.

> Then active still and unconfined his mind
> Explores the vast extent of ages past.
> But there is yet a liberty unsung
> By poets and by senators unpraised.

Exc. I will marry a wife beautiful as the Houries.
He was a man able to speak upon doubtful questions.
These are the persons anxious for the change.
Are they men worthy of confidence and support?

Under Rule 9.

Poverty wants some things—avarice all things.
Honesty has one face—flattery two.
One king is too soft and easy—an other too fiery.
Mankind's esteem they court—and he his own:
Theirs the wild chase of false felicities;
His the compos'd possession of the true.

EXERCISE III.—PUNCTUATION.

Copy the following sentences, and insert the COMMA *where it is
requisite.*

Under Rule 10.

My desire is to live in peace.
The great difficulty was to compel them to pay their debts.
To strengthen our virtue God bids us trust in him.
I made no bargain with you to live always drudging.
To sum up all her tongue confessed the shrew.
To proceed my own adventure was still more laughable.

We come not with design of wasteful prey
To drive the country force the swains away.

Under Rule 11.

Having given this answer he departed.
Some sunk to beasts find pleasure end in pain.
Eased of her load subjection grows more light.
Death still draws nearer never seeming near.
He lies full low gored with wounds and weltering in his blood.
Kind is fell Lucifer compared to thee.
Man considered in himself is helpless and wretched.
Like scattered down by howling Eurus blown.
He with wide nostrils snorting skims the wave.
Youth is properly speaking introductory to manhood.
Exc. He kept his eye fixed on the country before him.
They have their part assigned them to act.
Years will not repair the injuries done by him.

Under Rule 12.

Yes we both were philosophers.
However providence saw fit to cross our design.
Besides I know that the eye of the public is upon me.
The fact certainly is much otherwise.
For nothing surely can be more inconsistent.

Under Rule 13.

For in such retirement the soul is strengthened.

It engages our desires; and in some degree satisfies them.
But of every Christian virtue piety is an essential part.
The English verb is variable; as *love lovest loves.*

Under Rule 14.

In a word charity is the soul of social life.
By the bowstring I can repress violence and fraud.
Some by being too artful forfeit the reputation of probity.
With regard to morality I was not indifferent.

Under Rule 15.

Lo earth receives him from the bending skies!
Behold I am against thee O inhabitant of the valley!

Under Rule 16.

I would never consent never never never.
His teeth did chatter chatter chatter still.
Come come come come—to bed to bed to bed.

Under Rule 17.

He cried ' Cause every man to go out from me.'
' Almet' said he ' remember what thou hast seen.'
I answered ' Mock not thy servant who is but a worm before
thee.'

EXERCISE IV.—PUNCTUATION.

1. *Copy the following sentences, and insert the comma and the*
   SEMICOLON *where they are requisite.*

Under Rule 1.

' Man is weak' answered his companion ' knowledge is more
than equivalent to force.'
To judge rightly of the present we must oppose it to the past
for all judgment is comparative and of the future nothing
can be known.
' Content is natural wealth' says Socrates to which I shall add
' luxury is artificial poverty.'

Converse and love mankind might strongly draw
When love was liberty and nature law.

Under Rule 2.

Be wise to-day 'tis madness to defer.
The present all their care the future his.
Wit makes an enterpriser sense a man.
Ask thought for joy grow rich and hoard within.
Song soothes our pains and age has pains to soothe.
Here an enemy encounters there a rival supplants him.
Our answer to their reasons is No to their scoffs nothing.

Under Rule 3.

In Latin there are six cases namely the nominative the genitive the dative the accusative the vocative and the ablative.

Most English nouns form the plural by adding *s* as *boy boys nation nations king kings bay boys.*

Bodies are such as are endued with a vegetable soul as plants a sensitive soul as animals or a rational soul as the body of man.

2. *Copy the following sentences, and insert the comma, the semicolon, and the* COLON *where they are requisite.*

Under Rule 1.

Death wounds to cure we fall we rise we reign.

Bliss!—there is none but unprecarious bliss.

That is the gem sell all and purchase that.

Beware of usurpation God is the judge of all.

Under Rule 2.

I have the world here before me I will review it at leisure surely happiness is somewhere to be found.

A melancholy enthusiast courts persecution and when he cannot obtain it afflicts himself with absurd penances but the holiness of St. Paul consisted in the simplicity of a pious life.

> Observe his awful portrait and admire
> Nor stop at wonder imitate and live.

Under Rule 3.

Such is our Lord's injunction " Watch and pray."

He died praying for his persecutors " Father forgive them they know not what they do."

On his cane was inscribed this motto *"Festina lentè."*

3. *Copy the following sentences, and insert the comma, the semicolon, the colon, and the* PERIOD *where they are requisite.*

Under Rule 1.

Then appeared the sea and the dry land the mountains rose and the rivers flowed the sun and moon began their course in the skies herbs and plants clothed the ground the air the earth and the waters were stored with their respective inhabitants at last man was made in the image of God

In general those parents have most reverence who most deserve it for he that lives well cannot be despised

Under Rule 2.

Civil accomplishments frequently give rise to fame but a distinction is to be made between fame and true honour the statesman the orator or the poet may be famous while yet the man himself is far from being honoured

Under Rule 3.

Glass was invented in Eng by Benalt a monk A D 664
The Roman Era U C commenced A C 1753 years
Here is the Literary Life of S T Coleridge Esq

EXERCISE V.—PUNCTUATION.

1. *Copy the following sentences, and insert the* DASH, *and such other points as are necessary.*

Under Rule 1.

You say *famous* very often and I don't know exactly what it means a *famous* uniform *famous* doings What does *famous* mean

O why *famous* means Now don't you know what *famous* means It means It is a word that people say It is the fashion to say it It means it means *famous.*

Under Rule 2.

But this life is not all there is there is full surely an other state abiding us   And if there is what is thy prospect O remorseless obdurate   Thou shalt hear it would be thy wisdom to think thou now hearest the sound of that trumpet which shall awake the dead   Return O yet return to the Father of mercies and live

The future pleases Why The present pains
But that's a secret yes which all men know

2. *Copy the following sentences, and insert the* NOTE OF INTERROGATION, *and such other points as are necessary.*

Under Rule 1.

Does nature bear a tyrant's breast
Is she the friend of stern control
Wears she the despot's purple vest
Or fetters she the free-born soul

Why should a man whose blood is warm within
Sit like his grandsire cut in alabaster

Who art thou courteous stranger and from whence
Why roam thy steps to this abandon'd dale.

13

Under Rule 2.

Who bid the stork Columbus-like explore
Heavens not his own and worlds unknown before
Who calls the council states the certain day
Who forms the phalanx and who points the way

Under Rule 3.

Ask of thy mother Earth why oaks are made
Taller and stronger than the weeds they shade
They asked me who I was and whither I was going

3. *Copy the following sentences, and insert the* NOTE OF EXCLA-MATION, *and such other points as are necessary.*

Under Rule 1.

Alas how is that rugged heart forlorn
Behold the victor vanquish'd by the worm
Bliss sublunary bliss proud words and vain

Under Rule 2.

O Popular Applause what heart of man
Is proof against thy sweet seducing charms
More than thy balm O Gilead heals the wound

Under Rule 3.

How often have I loitered o'er thy green
Where humble happiness endear'd each scene
What black despair what horror fills his heart

4. *Copy the following sentences, and insert the* MARKS OF PAR-ENTHESIS, *and such other points as are necessary.*

Under Rule 1.

And all the question wrangle e'er so long
Is only this If God has placed him wrong
And who what God foretells who speaks in things
Still louder than in words shall dare deny

Under Rule 2.

Say was it virtue more though Heav'n ne'er gave
Lamented Digby sunk thee to the grave
Where is that thrift that avarice of time
O glorious avarice thought of death inspires
And oh the last last what can words express
Thought reach the last last silence of a friend

EXERCISE VI.—PUNCTUATION.

Copy the following PROMISCUOUS *sentences, and insert the points which they require.*

As one of them opened his sack he espied his money
They cried out the more exceedingly Crucify him
The soldiers' counsel was to kill the prisoners
Great injury these vermin mice and rats do in the field
It is my son's coat an evil beast hath devoured him
Peace of all wordly blessings is the most valuable
By this time the very foundation was removed
The only words he uttered were I am a Roman citizen
Some distress either felt or feared gnaws like a worm
How then must I determine Have I no interest If I have not I
    am stationed here to no purpose *Harris*
In the fire the destruction was so swift sudden vast and miser-
    able as to have no parallel in story
Dionysius the tyrant of Sicily was far from being happy
I ask now Verres what thou hast to advance
Excess began and sloth sustains the trade
Fame can never reconcile a man to a death bed
They that sail on the sea tell of the danger
Be doers of the word and not hearers only
The storms of wint'ry time will quickly pass
Here hope that smiling angel stands
Disguise I see thou art a wickedness
There are no tricks in plain and simple faith.
True love strikes root in reason passion's foe
Two gods divide them all Pleasure and Gain
I am satisfied My son has done his duty
Remember Almet the vision which thou hast seen
I beheld an enclosure beautiful as the gardens of paradise
The knowledge which I have received I will communicate
But I am not yet happy and therefore I despair
Wretched mortals said I to what purpose are you busy
Bad as the world is respect is always paid to virtue
In a word he views men in the clear sunshine of charity
This being the case I am astonished and amazed
These men approached him and saluted him king
Excellent and obliging sages these undoubtedly
Yet at the same time the man himself undergoes a change
One constant effect of idleness is to nourish the passions
You heroes regard nothing but glory
Take care lest while you strive to reach the top you fall
Proud and presumptuous they can brook no opposition

Nay some awe of religion may still subsist
Then said he Lo I come to do thy will O God
As for me behold I am in your hand
Now I Paul myself beseech you
He who lives always in public cannot live to his own soul
     whereas he who retires remains calm
Therefore behold I even I will utterly forget you
This text speaks only of those to whom it speaks
Yea he warmeth himself and saith Aha I am warm
King Agrippa believest thou the prophets

EXERCISE VII.—PUNCTUATION.

Copy the following PROMISCUOUS *sentences, and insert the points*
which they require.

To whom can riches give repute or trust
Content or pleasure but the good and just *Pope*

To him no high no low no great no small
He fills he bounds connects and equals all *Id*

Reason's whole pleasure all the joys of sense
Lie in three words health peace and competence *Id*

Not so for once indulg'd they sweep the main
Deaf to the call or hearing hear in vain *Anon*

Say will the falcon stooping from above
Smit with her varying plumage spare the dove *Pope*

Throw Egypt's by and offer in its stead
Offer the crown on Bernice's head *Id*

Falsely luxurious will not man awake
And springing from the bed of sloth enjoy
The cool the fragrant and the silent hour *Thomson*

Yet thus it is nor otherwise can be
So far from aught romantic what I sing *Young*

Thyself first know then love a self there is
Of virtue fond that kindles at her charms *Id*

How far that little candle throws his beams
So shines a good deed in a naughty world *Shakspeare*

You have too much respect upon the world
They lose it that do buy it with much care *Id*

How many things by season season'd are
To their right praise and true perfection *Id*

Canst thou descend from converse with the skies
And seize thy brother's throat for what a clod *Young*

In two short precepts all your business lies
Would you be great *be virtuous and be wise Denham*
But sometimes virtue starves while vice is fed
What then is the reward of virtue bread *Pope*
A life all turbulence and noise may seem
To him that leads it wise and to be prais'd
But wisdom is a pearl with most success
Sought in still waters and beneath clear skies *Cowper*
All but the swellings of the softened heart
That waken not disturb the tranquil mind *Thomson*
Inspiring God who boundless spirit all
And unremitting energy pervades
Adjusts sustains and agitates the whole *Id*
Ye ladies for indiff'rent in your cause
I should deserve to forfeit all applause
Whatever shocks or gives the least offence
To virtue delicacy truth or sense
Try the criterion 'tis a faithful guide
Nor has nor can have Scripture on its side *Cowper*

EXERCISE VIII.—SCANNING.

*Divide the following verses into the feet which compose them, and
distinguish by marks the long and the short syllables.*

DEITY.

Alone thou sitst above the everlasting hills,
  And all immensity of space thy presence fills:
For thou alone art God;—as God thy saints adore thee;
Jehovah is thy name;—they have no gods before thee.—*G. B.*

HEALTH.

Up the dewy mountain, Health is bounding lightly;
  On her brows a garland, twin'd with richest posies:
Gay is she, elate with hope, and smiling sprightly;
  Redder is her cheek, and sweeter, than the rose is.—*G. B.*

IMPENITENCE.

The impenitent sinner whom mercy empowers,
  Dishonours that goodness which seeks to restore;
As the sands of the desert are water'd by showers,
  Yet barren and fruitless remain as before.—*G. Brown.*

PIETY.

Holy and pure are the pleasures of piety,
  Drawn from the fountain of mercy and love;
Endless, exhaustless, exempt from satiety,
  Rising unearthly, and soaring above.—*G. Brown,*

A SIMILE.

The bolt that strikes the tow'ring cedar dead,
Oft passes harmless o'er the hazel's head.—*G. Brown.*

AN OTHER.

" Yet to the general's voice they soon obey'd
Innumerable.   As when the potent rod
Of Amram's son, in Egypt's evil day,
Wav'd round the coast, up call'd a pitchy cloud
Of locusts, warping on the eastern wind,
That o'er the realm of impious Pharaoh hung
Like night, and darken'd all the land of Nile."—*Milton.*

ELEGIAC STANZA.

Thy name is dear—'tis virtue balm'd in love;
Yet e'en thy name a pensive sadness brings.
Ah! wo the day, our hearts were doom'd to prove,
That fondest love but points affliction's stings!—*G. Brown.*

CUPID.

Zephyrs, moving bland, and breathing fragrant
    With the sweetest odours of the spring,
O'er the winged boy, a thoughtless vagrant,
    Slumb'ring in the grove, their perfumes fling.—*G. Brown*

DIVINE POWER.

When the winds o'er Gennesaret roar'd,
    And the billows tremendously rose,
The Saviour but utter'd the word,
    They were hush'd to the calmest repose.—*G. Brown.*

INVITATION.

Come from the mount of the leopard, spouse,
    Come from the den of the lion;
Come to the tent of thy shepherd, spouse,
    Come to the mountain of Zion.—*G. Brown.*

ADMONITION.

In the days of thy youth,
    Remember thy God:
O! forsake not his truth,
    Incur not his rod.—*G. Brown.*

COMMENDATION.

Constant and duteous,
    Meek as the dove,
How art thou beauteous,
    Daughter of love!—*G. Brown.*

EDWIN, AN ODE.

I. STROPHE.

Led by the pow'r of song, and nature's love,
Which raise the soul all vulgar themes above,
    The mountain grove
    Would Edwin rove,
  In pensive mood, alone;
  And seek the woody dell,
  Where noontide shadows fell,
    Cheering,
    Veering,
  Mov'd by the zephyr's swell.
Here nurs'd he thoughts to genius only known,
  When nought was heard around
  But sooth'd the rest profound
Of rural beauty on her mountain throne.
  Nor less he lov'd (rude nature's child)
  The elemental conflict wild;
  When, fold on fold, above was pil'd
The watery swathe, careering on the wind.
    Such scenes he saw
    With solemn awe,
As in the presence of th' Eternal Mind.
    Fix'd he gaz'd,
    Tranc'd and rais'd,
Sublimely rapt in awful pleasure undefin'd.

II. ANTISTROPHE.

Reckless of dainty joys, he finds delight
Where feebler souls but tremble with affright.
  Lo! now, within the deep ravine,
    A black impending cloud
    Infolds him in its shroud,
  And dark and darker glooms the scene.
  Through the thicket streaming,
  Lightnings now are gleaming;
    Thunders rolling dread,
    Shake the mountain's head;
      Nature's war
      Echoes far,
    O'er ether borne.
      That flash
      The ash
    Has scath'd and torn!

Now it rages;
Oaks of ages,
Writhing in the furious blast,
Wide their leafy honours cast;
Their gnarled arms do force to force oppose:
Deep rooted in the crevic'd rock,
The sturdy trunk sustains the shock,
Like dauntless hero firm against assailing foes.

III. EPODE.

' O Thou who sits above these vapours dense,
And rul'st the storm by thine omnipotence!
Making the collied cloud thy car,
Coursing the winds, thou rid'st afar,
Thy blessings to dispense.
The early and the latter rain,
Which fertilize the dusty plain,
Thy bounteous goodness pours.
Dumb be the atheist tongue abhorr'd!
All nature owns thee, sovereign Lord!
And works thy gracious will;
At thy command the tempest roars,
At thy command is still.
Thy mercy o'er this scene sublime presides;
'Tis mercy forms the veil that hides
The ardent solar beam;
While, from the volley'd breast of heaven,
Transient gleams of dazzling light,
Flashing on the balls of sight,
Make darkness darker seem.
Thou mov'st the quick and sulph'rous leven—
The tempest-driven
Cloud is riven;
And the thirsty mountain-side
Drinks gladly of the gushing tide.'
So breath'd young Edwin, when the summer shower
From out that dark o'erchamb'ring cloud,
With lightning flash and thunder loud,
Burst in wild grandeur o'er his solitary bower.—*G. Brown.*

THE END OF PART FOURTH.

KEY

TO THE

EXAMPLES OF FALSE CONSTRUCTION,

DESIGNED FOR ORAL EXERCISES,

UNDER

THE RULES OF SYNTAX AND THE NOTES.

☞ [The examples of False Syntax here explained, should be corrected *orally* by the pupil, according to the formules given under the rules; and the following corrections may afterwards be used as examples for parsing, if necessary.]

UNDER RULE I.—ARTICLES.

Under Note 1.—*An or A.*

This is *a* hard saying.
An humble heart shall find favour.
Passing from au earthly to *a* heavenly diadem.
Few have the happiness of living with such *a* one.
She evinced *a* uniform adherence to the truth.
An hospital is an asylum for the sick.
This is truly *a* wonderful invention.
He is *a* younger man than we supposed.
A humorsome child is never long pleased.
A careless man is unfit for *an* hostler.

Under Note 2.—*Nouns Connected.*

Avoid rude sports: an eye is soon lost, or *a* bone broken.
As the drop of the bucket, and *the* dust of the balance.
Not a word was uttered, nor *a* sign given.
I despise not the doer, but *the* deed.

Under Note 3.—*Adjectives Connected.*

What is the difference between the old and *the* new method ?
The sixth and *the* tenth have a close resemblance.
Is Paris on the right hand, or *the* left ?
Does Peru join the Atlantic, or *the* Pacific ocean ?
He was influenced both by a just and *a* generous principle.
The book was read by the old and *the* young.
I have both the large and *the* small grammar.
Are both the north and *the* south line measured ?
Are the north line and *the* south both measured ?
Are both the north and *the* south lines mensured ?
Are both the north lines and *the* south measured ?

Under Note 4.—*Adjectives Connected.*

Is the north and south line measured ?
Are the two north and south lines both measured ?
A great and good man looks beyond time.

13*

They made but a weak and ineffectual resistance.
The Allegany and Monongahela rivers form the Ohio.
I rejoice that there is an other and better world.
Were God to raise up an other such man as Moses.
The light and worthless kernels will float.

Under Note 5.—*Articles not Requisite.*

Cleon was an other sort of man.
There is a species of animal called seal.
Let us wait in patience and quietness.
The contemplative mind delights in silence.
Arithmetic is a branch of mathematics.
You will never have an other such chance.
I expected some such answer.
And I persecuted this way unto death.

Under Note 6.—*Of Titles and Names.*

He is entitled to the appellation of gentleman.
Cromwell assumed the title of Protector.
Her father is honoured with the title of Earl.
The chief magistrate is styled President.
The highest title in the state is that of Governor.
For *oak*, *pine*, and *ash*, were names of whole classes of objects.

Under Note 7.—*Of Comparisons.*

He is a better writer than reader.
He was an abler mathematician than linguist.
I should rather have an orange than *an* apple.

Under Note 8.—*Nouns with Who or Which.*

The words (or, *Those* words) which are signs of complex ideas, are liable to be
    misunderstood.
The carriages which were formerly in use, were very clumsy.
The place is not mentioned by *the* geographers who wrote at that time.

Under Note 9.—*Participial Nouns.*

Means are always necessary to *the* accomplishing of ends.
By *the* seeing of the eye, and *the* hearing of the ear, learn wisdom.
In *the* keeping of his commandments, there is great reward.
For *the* revealing of a secret, there is no remedy.
Have you no repugnance to *the* torturing of animals?

Under Note 10.—*Participles, not Nouns.*

By breaking the law, you dishonour the lawgiver.
An argument so weak is not worth mentioning.
In letting go our hope, we let all go.
Avoid talking too much of your ancestors.
The cuckoo keeps repeating her unvaried notes.
Forbear boasting of what you can do.

UNDER RULE II.——NOMINATIVES.

He that is studious, will improve.
They that seek wisdom, will be wise.
She and *I* are of the same age.
You are two or three years older than *we.*
Are not John and *thou* cousins?
I can write as handsomely as *thou.*
Nobody said so but *he.*
Who dost thou think was there?

Who broke this slate?   *I.*
We are alone; here's none but *thou* and I.
Them that honour me, I will honour; and *they* that despise me, shall be lightly esteemed.—1 *Sam.*, ii, 30.
He *who* in that instance was deceived, is a man of sound judgement.

UNDER RULE III.—APPOSITION.

The book is a present from my brother Richard, *him* that keeps the book-store.
I am going to see my friends in the country, *them* that we met at the ferry.
This dress was made by Catharine, the milliner, *her* that we saw at work.
Dennis, the gardener, *he* that gave me the tulips, has promised me a piony.

Resolve me, why the cottager and king,
He whom sea-sever'd realms obey, and *he*
Who steals his whole dominion from the waste,
Repelling winter blasts with mud and straw,
Disquieted alike, draw sigh for sigh.—*Young.*

UNDER RULE IV.—ADJECTIVES.

Under Note 1.—*Agreement.*

Things of *this* sort are easily understood.
Who broke *those* tongs?
Where did I drop *these* scissors?
Bring out *those* oats.
Extinguish *those* embers.
I disregard *these* minutiæ.
That kind of injuries we need not fear.
What was the height of *that* gallows which Haman erected?

Under Note 2.—*Fixed Numbers.*

We rode about ten *miles* an hour.
'Tis for a thousand *pounds.*
How deep is the water?   About six *fathoms.*
The lot is twenty-five *feet* wide.
I have bought eight *loads* of wood.

Under Note 3.—*Reciprocals.*

Two negatives, in English, destroy *each other.*—*Lowth cor.*
That the heathens tolerated *one an other*, is allowed.—*Fuller cor.*
David and Jonathan loved *each other* tenderly.
Words are derived *one from an other* in various ways.   Or better: *Derivative* words are *formed from their primitives* in various ways.—*Cooper cor.*
Teachers like to see their pupils polite to *one an other.*—*Webster cor.*
The Graces always hold *one an other* by the hand.

Under Note 4.—*Of Degrees.*

He chose the *last* of these three.
Trissyllables are often accented on the *first* syllable.
Which are the two *most* remarkable isthmuses in the world?

Under Note 5.—*Of Comparatives.*

The Scriptures are more valuable than any *other* writings.
The Russian empire is more extensive than any *other* government in the world.
Israel loved Joseph more than all his *other* children, because he was the son of his old age.

Under Note 6.—*Of Superlatives.*

Of all ill habits idleness is the most incorrigible.

Eve was the fairest of *women*.
Hope is the most constant of all the passions.

Under Note 7.—*Of Extra Comparisons.*

That opinion is too *general* (or *common*) to be easily corrected.
Virtue confers the *greatest* (or *highest*) dignity upon man.
How much *better are ye* than the fowls !—*Tr. of Luke cor.*
Do not thou hasten above the Most *High.*—*Esdras cor.*
This, *this* was the *unkindest* cut of all.—*Enfield*, p. 353.
The waters are frozen *sooner* and *harder.*—*Verstegan cor.*
A *healthier* (or *more healthy*) place cannot be found.
The best and the wisest men often meet with discouragements.

Under Note 8.—*Adjectives Connected.*

He showed us *an easier* and *more agreeable* way.
This was the *plainest* and *most convincing* argument.   .
Some of the *wisest* and *most moderate* of the senators.
This is an *ancient* and *honourable* fraternity.
There vice shall meet *a fatal* and *irrevocable* doom.

Under Note 9.—*Adjectives Prefixed.*

He is *an industrious young* man.
She has *an elegant new* house.
The *first two* classes have read.
The *two oldest* sons have removed to the westward.
England had not seen an *other such* king.

Under Note 10.—*Of Adjectives for Adverbs.*

She reads well and writes *neatly.*
He was *extremely* prodigal.
They went, *conformably* to their engagement.
He speaks very *fluently*, and reasons justly.
The deepest streams run the most *silently.*
These appear to be finished the *most neatly.*
He was *scarcely* gone, when you arrived.
I am *exceedingly* sorry to hear of your misfortunes.
The work was *uncommonly* well executed.
This is not *so large a* cargo as the last.
Thou knowest *how good a* horse mine is.
I cannot think so *meanly* of him.
He acted much *more wisely* than the others.

Under Note 11.—*Of Them for Those.*

I bought *those* books at a very low price.
Go and tell *those* boys to be still.
I have several copies : thou art welcome to *those* two.
Which of *those* three men is the most useful?

Under Note 12.—*Of This and That.*

Hope is as strong an incentive to action, as fear : *that* is the anticipation of
good, *this* of evil.
The poor want some advantages which the rich enjoy ; but we should not
therefore account *these* happy, and *those* miserable.

Memory and forecast just returns engage,
That pointing back to youth, *this* on to age.—*Pope.*

Under Note 13.—*Each, Every One, &c.*

Let each of them be heard in *his* turn.
On the Lord's day, every one of us Christians *keeps* the sabbath.
Is either of these men known?
No : neither of them *has* any connexions here.

Under Note 14.—Any and None.

Did *any* of the company stop to assist you?
Here are six; but *none* of them will answer.

Under Note 15.—Participial Adjectives.

Some crimes are thought deserving *of* death.
Rudeness of speech is very unbecoming *to* [or *in*] a gentleman.
To eat with *unwashed* hands, was disgusting *to* a Jew.

Leave then thy joys, unsuiting *to* such age—or,
Leave then thy joys, *not* suiting such an age,
To a fresh comer, and resign the stage.

UNDER RULE V.—PRONOUNS.

Every one must judge of *his* own feelings.
Can any person, on *his* entrance into the world, be fully secure that *he* shall
not be deceived?
He cannot see one in prosperity, without envying *him*.
I gave him oats, but he would not eat *them*.
Rebecca took goodly raiment, and put *it* on Jacob.
Take up the tongs, and put *them* in *their* place.
Let each esteem others better than *himself*.
A person may make *himself* happy without riches.
Every man should try to provide for *himself*.
The mind of man should not be left without something on which to employ
its energies.

An idler is a watch that wants both hands,
As useless if *it* goes, as when *it* stands.—*Cowper.*

Under Note 1.—Of Pronouns Needless.

Many words darken speech.
These praises he then seemed inclined to retract.
These people are all very ignorant.
Asa's heart was perfect with the Lord.
Who, instead of going about doing good, are perpetually intent upon doing
mischief.
Whom ye delivered up, and denied in the presence of Pontius Pilate.
Whom, when they had washed *her*, they laid in an upper chamber.
There are witnesses of the fact which I have mentioned.
He is now sorry for what he said.
The empress, approving these conditions, immediately ratified them.
Though this incident appears improbable, yet I cannot doubt the author's
veracity.

Under Note 2.—Of Change in Number.

Thou art my father's brother, else would I reprove *thee*—or,
You are my father's brother, else would I reprove *you*.
Your weakness is excusable, but *your* wickedness is not—or,
Thy weakness is excusable, but *thy* wickedness is not.
Now, my son, I forgive *thee*, and freely pardon *thy* fault—or,
Now, my son, I forgive *you*, and freely pardon *your* fault.

You draw the inspiring breath of ancient song,
Till nobly rises emulous *your* own—or,
Thou drawst the inspiring breath of ancient song,
Till nobly rises emulous *thy* own.

Under Note 3.—Of Who and Which.

This is the horse *which* my father imported.
Those are the birds *which* we call gregarious.
He has two brothers, one of *whom* I am acquainted with.

What was that creature *which* Job called leviathan?
Those *who* desire to be safe, should be careful to do that which is right.
A butterfly, *who* thought himself an accomplished traveller, happened to
light upon a bee-hive.
There was a certain householder, *who* planted a vineyard.

Under Note 4.—*Nouns of Multitude.*

He instructed and fed the crowds *that* surrounded him.
The court, *which* has great influence upon the public manners, ought to be
very exemplary.
The wild tribes *that* inhabit the wildnerness, contemplate the ocean with astonishment, and gaze upon the starry heavens with delight.

Under Note 5.—*Of Mere Names.*

Judas (*which* is now an other name for treachery) betrayed his master with
a kiss.
He alluded to Phalaris,—*which* is a name for all that is cruel.

Under Note 6.—*Of the Pronoun That.*

He was the first *that* entered.
He was the drollest fellow *that* I ever saw.
This is the same man *that* we saw before.
Who is she *that* comes clothed in a robe of green?
The wife and fortune *that* he gained, did not aid him.
Men *that* are avaricious, never have enough.
All *that* I have, is thine.
Was it thou, or the wind, *that* shut the door?
It was not I *that* shut it.
The babe *that* was in the cradle, appeared to be healthy.

Under Note 7.—*Relative Clauses Connected.*

He is a man that knows what belongs to good manners, and *that* will not do
a dishonourable act.
The friend who was here, and *who* entertained us so much, will never be
able to visit us again.
The curiosities which he has brought home, and *which* we shall have the
pleasure of seeing, are said to be very rare.

Under Note 8.—*Relative and Preposition.*

Observe them in the order *in which* they stand.
We proceeded immediately to the place *to which* we were directed.
My companion remained a week in the state *in which* I left him.
The way *in which* I do it, is this.

Under Note 9.—*Of Adverbs for Relatives.*

Remember the condition *from which* thou art rescued.
I know of no rule *by which* it may be done.
He drew up a petition, *in which* he too freely represented his own merits.
The hour is hastening, *in which* whatever praise or censure I have acquired,
will be remembered with equal indifference.

Under Note 10.—*Repeat the Noun.*

Many will acknowledge the excellence of religion, who cannot tell wherein
that excellence consists.
Every difference of opinion is not a *difference* of principle.—*Jefferson.*   Better: *Not every* difference of opinion is a difference of principle.
Next to the knowledge of God, this *knowledge* of ourselves seems most
worthy of our endeavour.

Under Note 11.—Place of the Relative.

Thou, who hast thus condemned the act, art thyself the man that committed it.

There is in simplicity a certain *majesty, which* is far above the quaintness of wit.

Thou, who art a party concerned, hast no right to judge.

It is impossible for such men as *those who* are likely to get the appointment, ever to determine this question.

There are, in the empire of China, millions of *people, whose* support is derived almost entirely from rice.

Under Note 12.—Of What for That.

I had no idea but *that* the story was true.

The post-boy is not so weary but *that* he can whistle.

He had no intimation but *that* the men were honest.

Under Note 13.—Of Adjectives for Antecedents.

Some men are too ignorant to be humble; *and* without *humility* there can be no docility.

Judas declared him innocent; *but innocent* he could not be, had he in any respect deceived the disciples.

Be accurate in all you say or do; for *accuracy* is important in all the concerns of life.

Every law supposes the transgressor to be wicked; *and* indeed he is *so*, if the law is just.

UNDER RULE VI.—PRONOUNS.

In youth, the multitude eagerly pursue pleasure, as if it were *their* chief good.

The council were not unanimous, and *they* separated without coming to any determination.

The committee were divided in sentiment, and *they* referred the business to the general meeting.

There happened to the army a very strange accident, which put *them* in great consternation.

The enemy were not able to support the charge, and *they* dispersed and fled.

The defendant's counsel had a difficult task imposed on *them*.

The board of health publish *their* proceeedings.

I saw all the species thus delivered from *their* sorrows.

Under Note 1.—The Idea of Unity.

I saw the whole species thus delivered from *its* sorrows.

This court is famous for the justice of *its* decisions.

The convention then resolved *itself* into a committee of the whole.

The crowd was so great that the judges with difficulty made their way through *it*.

UNDER RULE VII.—PRONOUNS.

Your levity and heedlessness, if *they* continue, will prevent all substantial improvement.

Poverty and obscurity will oppress him only who esteems *them* oppressive.

Good sense and refined policy are obvious to few, because *they* cannot be discovered but by a train of reflection.

Avoid haughtiness of behaviour, and affectation of manners: *they imply* a want of solid merit.

If love and unity continue, *they* will make you partakers of one an other's joy.

Suffer not jealousy and distrust to enter: *they* will destroy, like a canker, every germ of friendship.

Hatred and animosity are inconsistent with Christian charity: guard, therefore, against the slightest indulgence of *them*.

Every man is entitled to liberty of conscience, and freedom of opinion, if he does not pervert *them* to the injury of others.

UNDER RULE VIII.—PRONOUNS.

Neither Sarah, Ann, nor Jane, has performed *her* task.

One or the other must relinquish *his* claim.

A man is not such a machine as a clock or a watch, which will move only as *it is* moved.

Rye or barley, when *it is* scorched, may supply the place of coffee.

A man may see a metaphor or an allegory in a picture, as well as read *it* in a description.

Despise no infirmity of mind or body, nor any condition of life; for *it* may be thy own lot.

UNDER RULE IX.—VERBS.

We *were disappointed*.

She *dares* not oppose it.

His pulse *is* too quick.

Circumstances *alter* cases.

He *needs* not trouble himself.

Twenty-four pence *are* two shillings.

On one side *were* beautiful meadows.

He may pursue what studies he *pleases*.

What *has become* of our cousins?

There *were* more impostors than one.

What *say* his friends on this subject?

Thou *knowst* the urgency of the case.

What *avail* good sentiments with a bad life?

Have those books *been sent* to the school?

There *are* many occasions for the exercise of patience.

What sounds *has* each of the vowels?

There *was* a great number of spectators.

There *is* an abundance of treatises on this easy science.

> While, ever and anon, there *fall*
> Huge heaps of hoary moulder'd walls—or,
> While, ever and anon, there *falls*
> *A heap* of hoary moulder'd walls.

He that *trusts* in the Lord, will never be without a friend.

Errors that *originate* in ignorance, *are* generally excusable.

Be ye not as the horse, or as the mule, which *has* no understanding.

Not one of the authors who *mention* this incident, is entitled to credit.

The man and woman that *were* present, being strangers to him, wondered at his conduct.

There necessarily *follow* from thence these plain and unquestionable consequences.

> O thou, for ever present in my way,
> Who all my motives and my toils *surveyst*—or,
> O thou, for ever present in my way,
> Who *dost* my motives and my toils *survey*.

Under Note 1.—*Nominative with Adjuncts.*

The derivation of these words *is* uncertain.

Four years' interest *was* demanded.

One added to nineteen, *makes* twenty.

The increase of orphans *renders* the addition necessary.

The road to virtue and happiness *is* open to all.

The ship, with all her crew, *was* lost.

A round of vain and foolish pursuits, *delights* some folks.

KEY TO FALSE SYNTAX.—VERBS. 305

Under Note 2.—Composite Subjects.

To obtain the praise of men, *was* their only object.
To steal and then deny it, *is* a double sin.
To copy and claim the writings of others, *is* plagiarism.
To live soberly, righteously, and piously, *is required* of all men.
That it is our duty to promote peace and harmony among men, *admits* of no dispute.

Under Note 3.—Verb between Nominatives.

The reproofs of instruction *are* the way of life.
A diphthong *is* two vowels joined in one syllable.
So great an affliction to him *were* his wicked sons.
What *are* the latitude and longitude of that island?
He churlishly said to me, ' Who *are* you?'

Under Note 4.—Form Adapted to Style.

1. Familiar Style.

Was it thou that *built* that house?
That boy *writes* very elegantly.
Could not thou write without blotting thy book?
Dost not thou think—or, *Don't thou think*, it will rain to-day?
Does not—or, *Don't* your cousin intend to visit you?
That boy *has torn* my book.
Was it thou that *spread* the hay?
Was it James or thou that *let* him in?
He *dares* not say a word.
Thou *stood* in my way and *hindered* me.

2. Solemn Style.

The Lord *hath prepared* his throne in the heavens; and his kingdom ruleth over all.—*Psalms*, ciii, 19.
Thou *answeredst* them, O Lord our God: thou *wast* a God that forgave* them, though thou *tookest* vengeance of their inventions.
Then thou *spakest* in vision to thy Holy One, and *saidst*.—*Psalms*, lxxxix, 19.
So then, it is not of him that *willeth*, nor of him that *runneth*, but of God that *showeth* mercy.—*Rom.*, ix, 16.

Under Note 5.—The Nominative Expressed.

New York, Fifthmonth 3d, 1823.

Dear friend,
　　　I am sorry to hear of thy loss; but *I* hope it may be retrieved. *I* should be happy to render thee any assistance in my power. *I* shall call to see thee to-morrow morning. Accept assurances of my regard.

A. B.

New York, May 3d, P. M., 1823.

Dear sir,
　　　I have just received the kind note *you* favoured me with this morning; and *I* cannot forbear to express my gratitude to you. On further information, *I* find *I* have not lost so much as *I* at first supposed; and *I* believe *I* shall still be able to meet all my engagements. *I* should, however, be happy to see you. Accept, dear sir, my most cordial thanks.　　C. D.

Will martial flames forever fire thy mind,
And *wilt thou* never be to Heaven resign'd?

UNDER RULE X.—VERBS.

The nobility *were assured* that he would not interpose.

---

* *Forgavest* (as in *Psalm* xcix, 8,) appears to be wrong: because the relative *that* and its antecedent *God* are of the third person, and not of the second.

626*

The committee *have attended* to their appointment.
Mankind *were not unite1* by the bonds of civil society.
The majority *were disposed* to adopt the measure.
The peasantry *go* barefoot, and the middle sort *make* use of wooden shoes.
All the world *are* spectators of your conduct.
Blessed *are* the people that know the joyful sound.

Under Note 1.—*The Idea of Unity.*

The church *has* no power to inflict corporal punishments.
The fleet *was seen* sailing up the channel.
The meeting *has established* several salutary regulations.
The regiment *consists* of a thousand men.
A detachment of two hundred men *was* immediately *sent.*
Every auditory *takes* this in good part.
In this business, the house of commons *was* of no weight.
Is the senate *considered* as a separate body?
There *is* a flock of birds.
No society *is* chargeable with the disapproved conduct of particular members.

UNDER RULE XI.—VERBS.

Temperance and exercise *preserve* health.
Time and tide *wait* for no man.
My love and affection towards thee *remain* unaltered.
Wealth, honour, and happiness, *forsake* the indolent.
My flesh and my heart *fail.*
In all his works, there *are* sprightliness and vigour.
Elizabeth's meekness and humility *were* extraordinary.
In unity *consist* the security and welfare of every society.
High pleasures and luxurious living *beget* satiety.
Much *do* human pride and folly *require* correction.
Our conversation and intercourse with the world *are,* in several respects, an
    education for vice.
Occasional release from toil, and indulgence of ease, *are* what nature de-
    mands, and virtue allows.
What generosity, and what humanity, *were* then *displayed?*

> What thou desir'st,
> And what thou fearest, alike *destroy* all hope.

Under Note 1.—*Affirmation with Negation.*

Wisdom, and not wealth, *procures* esteem.
Prudence, and not pomp, *is* the basis of his fame.
Not fear, but labour *has overcome* him.
The decency, and not the abstinence, *makes* the difference.
Not her beauty, but her talents *attract* attention.
It is her talents, and not her beauty, *that attract* attention.
It is her beauty, and not her talents, *that attracts* attention.

Under Note 2.—*As Well As, But, or Save.*

His constitution, as well as his fortune, *requires* care.
Their religion, as well as their manners, *was ridiculed.*
Every one, but thou, *had been* legally *discharged.*
The buyer, as well as the seller, *renders himself* liable.
All songsters, save the hooting owl, *were* mute.
None, but thou, O mighty prince! *can avert* the blow.
Nothing, but frivolous amusements, *pleases* the indolent.
Cæsar, as well as Cicero, *was admired* for *his* eloquence.

Under Note 3.—*Each, Every, or No.*

Each day, and each hour, *brings its* portion of duty.
Every house, and even every cottage, *was plundered.*

Every thought, every word, and every action, will be brought into judgement, whether *it* be good or evil.
The time will come, when no oppressor, no unjust man, will be able to
screen *himself* from punishment.

No bandit fierce, no tyrant mad with pride,
No cavern'd hermit, *rests* self-satisfied.—*Pope.*

Under Note 4.—And Required.

In this affair, perseverance *and* dexterity were requisite.
Town *and* country are equally agreeable to me.
Sobriety *and* humility lead to honour.
The king, the lords, *and* the commons, compose the British parliament.
The man *and* his whole family are dead.
A small house *and* a trifling annuity are still granted him.

Under Note 5.—Distinct Subject Phrases.

To profess, and to possess, *are* very different things.
To do justly, to love mercy, and to walk humbly with God, *are* duties of
universal obligation.
To be round or square, to be solid or fluid, to be large or small, and to be
moved swiftly or slowly, *are* all equally alien from the nature of thought.

UNDER RULE XII.—VERBS.

Neither imprudence, credulity, nor vanity, *has* ever *been imputed* to him.
What the heart or the imagination *dictates*, flows readily.
Neither authority nor analogy *supports* such an opinion.
Either ability or inclination *was* wanting.
Redundant grass or heath *affords* abundance to their cattle.
The returns of kindness are sweet; and there *is* neither honour, nor virtue,
nor utility, in repelling them.
The sense or drift of a proposition, often *depends* upon a single letter.

Under Note 1.—Nominatives that Disagree.

Neither he nor you *were* there.
Either the boys or I *was* in fault.
Neither he nor I *intend* to be present.
Neither the captain nor the sailors *were saved.*
Whether one person or more *were concerned* in the business, does not yet
appear.

Under Note 2.—The Concord Completed.

Are they. or *am* I, expected to be there?
Neither *is* he, nor am I, capable of it.
Either he has been imprudent, or his associates *have been* vindictive.
Neither were their riches, nor *was* their influence great.

Under Note 3.—Place of the First Person.

My *father and I* were riding out.
The premiums were given to *George and me.*
Jane and I are invited.
They ought to invite my *sister and me.*
We dreamed a dream in one night, *he and I.*

Under Note 4.—Distinct Subject Phrases.

To practise tale-bearing, or even to countenance it, *is* great injustice.
To reveal secrets, or to betray one's friends, *is* contemptible perfidy.

UNDER RULE XIII.—VERBS.

Doth he not *leave* the ninety and nine, and *go* into the mountains, and *seek* that which is gone astray?

Did he not *tell* thee his fault, and *entreat* thee to forgive him?

If he *understands* the business, and *attends* to it, wherein is he deficient?

The day *is approaching,* and *is hastening* upon us, in which we must give an account of our stewardship.

If thou *dost* not *turn* unto the Lord, but *dost forget* him who remembered thee in thy distress, great will be thy condemnation—or, better: If thou *turn* not unto the Lord, but *forget* him who remembered thee in thy distress, great will be thy condemnation.

There are a few, who *have kept* their integrity to the Lord, and *who prefer* his truth to all other enjoyments.

This report *was* current yesterday, and *it agrees* with what we heard before.

Virtue *is* generally *praised,* and *it would be* generally *practised* also, if men were wise.

Under Note 1.—Preterits and Participles.

He *would have gone* with us, if we had invited him.

They *have chosen* the part of honour and virtue.

He soon *began* to be weary of having nothing to do.

Somebody *has broken* my slate.

I *saw* him when he *did* it.

Under Note 2.—Form Adapted to Sense.

He *had entered* into the conspiracy.

The American planters *raise* cotton and rice.

The report *is founded* on truth.

I entered the room and *sat* down.

Go and *lie* down, my son.

With such books, it will always be difficult to *teach* children to read.

UNDER RULE XIV.—PARTICIPLES.

Under Note 1.—Of Expunged.

By observing truth, you will command respect.

I could not, for my heart, forbear pitying him.

I heard them discussing this subject.

By consulting the best authors, he became learned.

Here are rules, by observing which, you may avoid error.

Under Note 2.—Of Inserted.

Their consent was necessary for the raising *of* any supplies.

Thus the saving *of* a great nation devolved on a husbandman.

It is an overvaluing *of* ourselves, to decide upon every thing.

The teacher does not allow any calling *of* ill names.

That burning *of* the capitol was a wanton outrage.

May nothing hinder our receiving *of* so great a good.

My admitting *of* the fact will not affect the argument.

Cain's killing *of* his brother originated in envy.

Under Note 3.—Expression Changed.

Cæsar carried off the treasures, which his opponent had neglected *to take* with him.

It is dangerous *to play* with edge tools.

I intend *to return* in a few days.

To suffer needlessly—or, *Needless suffering* is never a duty.

Nor is it wise *to complain.*

I well remember *to have told* you so—or, *that I told* you so.

The doing of good—or, *To do good*, is a Christian's vocation.
Piety is a *constant endeavour* to live to God. It is *an earnest desire* to do his
will, and not our own.

Under Note 4.—*The Leading Word.*

There is no harm in *women's* knowing about these things.
They did not give notice of the *pupil's* leaving.
The *sun*, darting his beams through my window, awoke me.
The maturity of the sago tree is known by the *leaves'* being covered with a
delicate white powder.

Under Note 5.—*Reference of Participles.*

Sailing up the river, *you may see* the whole town.
Being conscious of guilt, *men tremble at death*—or, *Consciousness* of guilt
renders death *terrible.*
By yielding to temptation, *we sacrifice* our peace.
In loving our enemies, *we shed* no man's blood.
By teaching the young, *we prepare them* for usefulness.

Under Note 6.—*Participles, not Preterits.*

A nail well *driven* will support a great weight.
See here a hundred sentences *stolen* from my work.
I found the water entirely *frozen*, and the pitcher *broken.*
Being *forsaken* by my friends, I had no other resource.

Under Note 7.—*Form of Participles.*

Till by barbarian deluges *o'erflowed.*
Like the lustre of diamonds *set* in gold.
A beam ethereal, sullied and *absorb'd.*
With powerless wings around them *wrapp'd.*
Error *learned* from preaching, is held as sacred truth.

UNDER RULE XV.—ADVERBS.

Under Note 1.—*The Placing of Adverbs.*

The work *will never be* completed.
We *should always prefer* our duty to our pleasure.
It is impossible *to be continually* at work.
He *behaved impertinently* to his master.
The heavenly bodies *are perpetually* in motion.
He found her *not only busy,* but *even* pleased and happy.

Under Note 2.—*Adverbs for Adjectives.*

Give him *an early* and decisive answer.
When a substantive is put *absolute.*
Such expressions sound *harsh.*
Such events are of *rare* (or *unfrequent*) occurrence.
Velvet feels very *smooth.*

Under Note 3.—*Of Here for Hither, &c.*

Bring him *hither* to me.
I shall go *thither* again in a few days.
Whither are they all riding in so great haste?

Under Note 4.—*Of From Hence, &c.*

Hence it appears that the statement is incorrect.
Thence arose the misunderstanding.
Do you know *whence* it proceeds?

Under Note 5.—*Of the Adverb How.*

You see *that* not many are required.
I knew *that* they had heard of his misfortunes.
He remarked, *that* time was valuable.

Under Note 6.—*Of the Adverb No.*

Know now, whether this *is* thy son's coat or *not.*
Whether he is in fault or *not,* I cannot tell.
I will ascertain whether it is so or *not.*

Under Note 7.—*Of Double Negatives.*

I will by no means entertain a spy.
Nobody *ever* invented *or* discovered *any* thing, in *any* way to be compared
  with this.
Be honest, *and* take no shape *or* semblance of disguise.
I did not like *either* his temper *or* his principles.
Nothing *ever* can justify ingratitude.

UNDER RULE XVI.——CONJUNCTIONS.

Under Note 1.—*Of Two Terms with One.*

He has made alterations *in* the work, and additions *to it.*
He is more bold *than his companion,* but not so wise.
Sincerity is as valuable *as knowledge,* and even more so.
I always have *been,* and I always shall be, of this opinion.
What is now kept secret, shall be hereafter displayed and *seen* in the clearest
  light.
We pervert the noble faculty of speech, when we use it to *defame* or to dis-
  quiet our neighbours.
Be more anxious to acquire knowledge, than *to show* it.
The court of chancery frequently mitigates and *disarms* the common law.

Under Note 2.—*Of Lest or But for That.*

We were apprehensive *that* some accident had happened.
I do not deny *that* he has merit.
Are you afraid *that* he will forget you?

> These paths and bow'rs, doubt not *that* our joint hands
> Will keep from wilderness.

Under Note 3.—*Prefer Than.*

It was no other *than* his own father.
Have you no further proof *than* this?
I expected something more *than* this.
He no sooner retires *than* his heart burns with devotion.
Such literary filching is nothing else *than* robbery.

Under Note 4.—*Of Correspondents.*

Neither despise *nor* oppose what you do not understand.
He would *neither* do it himself nor let me do it.
The majesty of good things is such, *that* the confines of them are reverend.
Whether he intends to do so *or not,* I cannot tell.
Send me such articles only, *as* are adapted to this market.
So far as I am able to judge, the book is well written.
No errors are so trivial *as not to deserve* correction.
It will *neither* improve the mind, nor delight the fancy.
The one is *as* deserving as the other.
There is no condition so secure *that it* cannot admit of change.
Do you think this is *as* good as that?
The relations are so obscure *that* they require much thought.

None is so fierce *as to dare* stir him up.
There was no man so sanguine *as* not to apprehend some ill consequence.
I must be so candid *as* to own that I do not understand it.
The book is not *so* well printed as it ought to be.

As still he sat as those who wait,
Till judgement speak the doom of fate.

UNDER RULE XVII.—PREPOSITIONS.

Under Note 1.—*Choice of Prepositions.*

She finds a difficulty *in* fixing her mind.
This affair did not fall *under* his cognizance.
He was accused *of* betraying his trust.
There was no water, and he died *of* thirst.
I have no occasion *for* his services.
You may safely confide *in* him.
I entertain no prejudice *against* him.
You may rely *on* what I tell you.
Virtue and vice differ widely *from* each other.
This remark is founded *on* truth.
After many toils, we arrived *at* our journey's end.
I will tell you a story very different *from* that.
Their conduct is agreeable *to* their profession.
Excessive pleasures pass from satiety *into* disgust.
I turned *in* disgust from the spectacle.
They are gone *into* the meadow.
Let this be divided *among* the three.
The shells were broken *into* pieces.
The deception has passed *with* every one.
They never quarrel *with* each other.
Through every difficulty—or, Amidst *all difficulties*, he persevered.
Let us go *up* stairs.
I was *in* London, when this happened.
We were detained *at* home, and disappointed *of* our walk.
This originated *in* mistake.
The Bridewell is situated *on* the west of the City-Hall, and it has no communication *with* the other buildings.
I am disappointed *in* the work; it is very inferior *to* what I expected.

Under Note 2.—*Omission of Prepositions.*

Be worthy *of* me, as I am worthy *of* you.
They cannot but be unworthy *of* the care of others.
Thou shalt have no portion on this side *of* the river.
Sestos and Abydos were exactly opposite *to* each other.
Ovid was banished *from* Rome by his patron Augustus.

UNDER RULE XIX.—POSSESSIVES.

Under Note 1.—*The Possessive Form.*

Man's chief good is an upright mind.
I will not destroy the city for *ten's* sake.
Moses's rod was turned into a serpent.
They are wolves in *sheeps'* clothing.
The tree is known by *its* fruit.
The privilege is not *theirs*, any more than it is *yours*.

Yet he was gentle as soft summer airs,
Had grace for *others'* sins, but none for *theirs.—Cowper.*

Under Note 2.—*Possessives Connected.*

There is but little difference between the *Earth's* and Venus's diameter.
This hat is *John's*, or James's.

The store is opposite to *Morris* and Company's.
This palace has been the grand *Sultan* Mahomet's.
This was the *Apostle* Paul's advice.
Were Cain's occupation and *Abel's* the same?
Were *Cain's* and Abel's occupation the same?
Were *Cain* and Abel's occupations the same?
Were *Cain's* and Abel's parents the same?
Were Cain's parents and *Abel's* the same?
Was *Cain* and Abel's father there?
Were *Cain* and Abel's parents there?

> Thy Maker's will has placed thee here,
> A *Maker* wise and good.

Under Note 3.—*Choice of Forms.*

The government of the world is not left to chance.
He was *heir to the son of* Louis the Sixteenth.
The throne we honour, is the *people's* choice.
We met at *the house of* my brother's partner.
An account of the proceedings of *Alexander's court.*
Here is a copy of the Constitution of the *Teachers' Society in* the city of New-York.

Under Note 4.—*Nouns with Possessives Plural.*

Their *health* perhaps may be pretty well secured.
We all have talents committed to our *charge.*
For your *sake* forgave I it, in the sight of Christ.
We are, for our *part*, well satisfied.
The pious cheerfully submit to their *lot.*
Fools think it not worth their *while* to be wise.

Under Note 5.—*Of Possessives with Participles.*

I rewarded the boy for studying so diligently.
Have you a rule for thus parsing the participle?
He errs in giving the word a double construction.
By offending others, we expose ourselves.
They deserve our thanks for quickly relieving us.

UNDER RULE XX.—OBJECTIVES.

Thee only have I chosen.
Whom shall we send on this errand?
My father allowed my brother and *me* to accompany him.
Him that is idle and mischievous, reprove sharply.
Whom should I meet but my old friend!
He accosts *whomever* he meets.
Whomsoever the court favours, is safe.
Them that honour me, I will honour.
Whom do you think I saw the other day?

Under Note 1.—*An Object Required.*

The ambitious are always seeking to aggrandize *themselves.*
I must *premise three circumstances.*
This society does not *allow personal reflections.*
False accusation cannot *diminish real merit.*
His servants ye are *whom ye obey.*

Under Note 2.—*Of False Transitives.*

Good keeping *fattens* the herd.
We endeavoured to *reconcile* the parties.
Being weary, he *sat* down.
Go, *flee* away into the land of Judah.
The popular lords did not fail to *enlarge* on the subject.

Under Note 3.—Passive Verbs.

The *benefit* of their recantation *was* refused *them*.
Temporal *riches* are not promised *to believers*.
Several beautiful *pictures* were shown *us*.
But, unfortunately, the *favour* was denied *me*.
A high *compliment was* paid *you*.
The *question has* never been asked *me*.

UNDER RULE XXI.—SAME CASES.

We thought it was *thou*.
I would act the same part, if I were *he*.
It could not have been *she*.
It is not *I*, that he is angry with.
They believed it to be *me*.
It was thought to be *he*.
If it had been *she*, she would have told us.
We know it to be *them*.
Who do you think it is ?
Whom do you suppose it to be?
We did not know *who* they were.
Thou art *he* whom they described.
Impossible ! it can't be *I*.
Who did he think you were?
Who say ye that I am?

UNDER RULE XXII.—OBJECTIVES.

Let that remain a secret between you and *me*.
I lent the book to some one, I know not [*to*] *whom*.
Whom did he inquire for ? *Thee*.
From *him* that is needy, turn not away.
We are all accountable, each for his own *acts*.
Does that boy know *whom* he is speaking to?
I bestow my favours on *whomsoever* I will.

UNDER RULE XXIII.—INFINITIVES.

Please *to* excuse my son's absence.
Cause every man *to* go out from me.
Forbid them *to* enter the garden.
Do you not perceive it *to* move?
Allow others *to* discover your merit.
He was seen *to* go in at that gate.
Permit me *to* pass this way.

UNDER RULE XXIV.—INFINITIVES.

I felt a chilling sensation *creep* over me.
I have heard him *mention* the subject.
Bid the boys *come* in immediately.
I dare *say* he has not got home yet.
Let no rash promise *be made*.
We sometimes see bad men *honoured*.
A good reader will make himself distinctly *heard*.

UNDER RULE XXV.—NOM. ABSOLUTE.

I being young, they deceived me.
They refusing to comply, I withdrew.
Thou being present, he would not tell what he knew.
The child is lost; and *I*, whither shall I go?

14

O happy *we!* surrounded thus with blessings !
"*Thou* too ! Brutus, my son !" cried Cæsar overcome.

But *he,* the chieftain of them all,
His sword hangs rusting on the wall.— *W. Scott.*

She quick relapsing to her former state,
With boding fears approach the serving train.

There all thy gifts and graces we display,
Thou, only *thou,* directing all our way.—*Pope.*

UNDER RULE XXVI.—SUBJUNCTIVES.

First Clause—Subjunctive Present.

He will maintain his cause, though he *lose* his estate.
They will fine thee, unless thou *offer* an excuse.
I shall walk out in the afternoon, unless it *rain.*
Let him take heed lest he *fall.*
On condition that he *come,* I consent to stay.
If he *be* but discreet, he will succeed.
Take heed that thou *speak* not to Jacob.
If thou *cast* me off, I shall be miserable.
Send them to me, if thou *please.*
Watch the door of thy lips, lest thou *utter* folly.

Second Clause.—Subjunctive Imperfect.

If I *were* to write, he would not regard it.
If thou *felt* as I do, we should soon decide.
Though thou *shed* thy blood in the cause, it would but prove thee sincerely a fool.
If thou *loved* him, there would be more evidence of it.
I believed, whatever *were* the issue, all would be well.
If love *were* never feigned, it would appear to be scarce.
There fell from his eyes, as it *were* scales.
If he *were* an impostor, he must have been detected.
Were death denied, all men would wish to die.
O that there *were* yet a day to redress thy wrongs !
Though thou *wert* huge as Atlas, thy efforts would be vain.

Last Clause.—Indicative Mood.

Though he *seems* to be artless, he has deceived us.
If he *thinks* as he speaks, he may safely be trusted.
Though this event *is* strange, it certainly did happen.
If thou *lovest* tranquillity of mind, seek it not abroad.
If seasons of idleness *are* dangerous, what must a continued habit of it prove?
Though he *was* a son, yet learned he obedience by the things which he suffered.
I knew thou *wast* not slow to hear.

Under Note 1.— Words of Time.

The work *was finished* last week.
He *has been* out of employment this fortnight.
This mode of expression *was* formerly in use.
I *shall be* much *obliged* to him if he will attend to it.
I will pay the vows which my lips *uttered* when I was in trouble.
I have compassion on the multitude, because they *have continued* with me now three days.
I thought, by the accent, that he *was speaking* to his child.
And he that *had been* dead, sat up and began to speak.
Thou hast borne, and *hast had* patience, and for my name's sake hast laboured, and hast not fainted.

Ye will not come unto me that ye *may have* life—or, Ye *would not come* unto me that ye might have life.
At the end of this quarter, I *shall have been* at school two years.
We have done no more than it was our duty *to do.*

Under Rule 2.—Relative Tenses.

We expected that he *would arrive* last night.
Our friends intended *to meet* us.
We hoped *to see* you.
He would not have been allowed *to enter.*

Under Note 3.—Permanent Propositions.

The doctor affirmed, that fever always *produces* thirst.
The ancients asserted, that virtue *is* its own reward.

PROMISCUOUS EXAMPLES CORRECTED.

LESSON I.

There is a spirit in man; and the inspiration of the Almighty giveth *him* understanding.
My people *do* not consider.
I have never heard *whom* they invited.

> Then hasten thy return; for, *thou* away,
> Nor lustre has the sun, nor joy the day.

I am as well as when you *were* here.
That elderly man, *him* that came in late, I supposed to be the superintendent.
All the virtues of mankind are to be counted upon a few fingers; but *their* follies and vices are innumerable.
It must indeed be confessed, that a lampoon or a satire *does not carry* in *it* robbery or murder.
There *were* more persons than one engaged in this affair.
A man who lacks ceremony, has need *of* great merit.
A wise man avoids the showing *of* any excellence in trifles.   Better—*forbears to show*—or, *is careful not to show,* &c.
The *first* and *most important* female quality is sweetness of temper.
We choose rather *to* lead than *to* follow.
Ignorance is the mother of fear, as well as *of* admiration.
He must fear many, *whom* many fear.
Every one *partakes* of honour bestowed on the worthy.
The king *and* the queen were not at all deceived.—[*Note 4th, Rule* xi.]
Were there no difference, there would be no choice.
I *would* rather *have been informed.*
Must *thou* return this evening?
Life and death *are* in the power of the tongue.
I saw a person that I took to be *her.*
Let him be *who* he may, I shall not stop.
This is certainly *a* useful invention.
That such a spirit as thou *does not understand* me.
'It is no more *than* justice,' quoth the farmer.

LESSON II.

Great improvements *have been made.*
What I have heard, is undoubtedly true.
The nation is torn by feuds which threaten *its* ruin.
The account of these transactions *was* incorrect.
Godliness with contentment *is* great gain.
The number of sufferers *has not been ascertained.*
There *is* one or more of them yet in confinement.

They have *chosen* the wisest part.
He spent his whole life in doing good.
They *scarcely know* that temperance is a virtue.
I am afraid *that* I have laboured in vain.
Mischief *on* itself doth back recoil.
This construction sounds rather *harsh*.
What is the cause of the *leaves'* curling?
Was it *thou*, that made the noise?
Let thy flock *clothe* the naked.
Wisdom and knowledge *are* granted unto thee.
His conduct was *surprisingly* strange.
This woman taught my brother and *me* to read.
Let your promises be such *as* you can perform.
We shall sell them in the state *in which* they now are.
We may, *however*, add this observation.
This came *into* fashion when I was young.
I did not use the leaves, but *the* root of the plant.
We have continually used every *means* in our power.
Pass ye away, *ye inhabitants* of Saphir—or, Pass away, thou inhabitant of
  Saphir.
Give every syllable and every letter *its* proper sound.

LESSON III.

To know exactly how much mischief may be ventured upon with impunity,
  is knowledge enough for some folks.
Every leaf and every twig *teems* with life.
I *rejoiced* at this intelligence.
At this stage of advancement, *the pupil finds little difficulty in understanding*
  the passive and *the* neuter verbs.
I was afraid that I *should lose* the parcel.
Which of all these patterns is the *prettiest?*
They *that* [or *who*] despise instruction, shall not be wise.
Both thou and thy advisers have mistaken *your* interest.
An idle soul shall suffer hunger.
The lips of knowledge *are* a precious jewel.
My cousin and I are requested to attend.
I can only say, that such is my belief.
This is different from the *conscience'* being made to feel.
Here is ground for their leaving *of* the world with peace—or, (better,) Here
  is ground *for leaving* the world with peace.
Whither are you all running so fast?
Man is the noblest work of creation.
Of *all crimes* willful murder is the most atrocious.
The tribes *that* I visited, are partially civilized.
Hence I conclude, they are in error.
The girls' books are neater than the *boys'*.
I intended *to transcribe* it.
Shall a character made up of the very worst passions, pass under the name
  of *gentleman ?*
Rhoda ran in, and told *that* Peter stood before the gate.
What *are* latitude and longitude?
Cicero was more eloquent than any *other* Roman—or, Cicero was *the most*
  eloquent of the Romans.
Who dares apologize for Pizarro ?—*which* is but another name for rapacity.

LESSON IV.

Tell me whether you will do it or *not*.
After the *straitest* [or *strictest*] sect, I lived a Pharisee.
We have no more *than* five loaves and two fishes.
I know not who it was *that* did it.

Doubt not, little though there be,
That I'll cast a crumb to thee.

This rule is the best *that* can be given.
I have never seen *any* other way.
These are poor amends for the men and treasures *that* we have lost.
Dost thou know *those* boys?
This is a part of *the estate of my uncle's father.*
Many people never learn to speak *correctly.*
Some people are rash, and others timid : *these* apprehend too much, *those* too little.
Is it lawful for us to give tribute to Cæsar or *not?*
It was not worth while *to preserve* any permanent enmity.
I no sooner saw my face in it, *than* I was startled at the shortness of it.
Every person is answerable for *his* own conduct.
They are men that scorn a mean action, and *that* will exert themselves to serve you.
I do not recollect ever *to have paid* it—*the paying of* it—*the payment of* it—or, *that I ever paid* it.
The stoics taught that all crimes *are* equal.
Every one of these theories *is* now *exploded.*
Any of these four will answer.
There is no situation *in which* he would be happy.
The boy *that you thought so clever,* has been detected in stealing.
I will meet thee there, if *thou* please.
He is not so sick, but *that* he can laugh.
These clothes *do* not *fit* me.
The audience *were* all very attentive.

Wert thou some star, which from the ruin'd roof
Of shak'd Olympus by mischance *did fall!*

LESSON V.

Was the master, or *were* many of the scholars, in the room?
His *father* and mother's consent was asked.
Who is he supposed to be?
He is *a venerable old* man.
It was then my purpose to *visit* Sicily.
It is *only* to the learner, and *him* that is in doubt, that this assistance is recommended.
There *is* not the least hope of his recovery.
Anger and impatience *are* always unreasonable.
In his letters, there *is* not only correctness, but elegance.
Opportunity to do good is the highest preferment *that* a noble mind desires.
The year *in which* he died is not mentioned.
Had I *known* it, I should not have *gone.*
Was it *thou,* that spoke to me?
The house is *pleasantly* situated.
He did it as *privately* as he possibly could.
To subdue our passions—*The subduing of* our passions—*The subjugation of* our passions—or, *That we subdue* our passions, is the noblest of conquests.
James is more diligent than *thou.*
Words *interwoven* with sighs found out their way.
He appears to be *excessively* diffident.
The number of our days *is* with thee.
As a father pitieth his children, so the Lord pitieth them that fear him.
The circumstances of this case, *are* different.
Well for us, if some *other such* men should rise!
A man that is young in years, may be old in hours, if he *lose* no time.
The chief captain, fearing *that* Paul *would be pulled into* pieces *by* them, commanded the soldiers to go down, and to take him by force from among them.

27*

Nay, weep not, gentle Eros; there *are left* us
Ourselves to end ourselves.

CORRECTIONS UNDER THE GENERAL RULE.

Are there, then, more true *religions* than one ?
The laws of Lycurgus but substituted insensibility *for* enjoyment.
Rain is seldom or *never* seen at Lima.
The young bird raising its open mouth for food, *exhibits* a natural indication
of corporeal want.
There is much truth in *Ascham's* observation.
Adopting the doctrine *in* which he had been taught—or, Adopting the doc-
trine *which had been taught him.*
This library *contained more than five hundred thousand* volumes.
The Coptic alphabet was one of the latest *that were* formed.
There are many evidences of *men's* proneness to vice.
To perceive nothing, *and* not to perceive, are the same—or, To perceive
nothing, is the same *as* not to perceive.
The king of France or *of* England, was to be the umpire.
He may be said to have saved the life of a citizen ; and, consequently, *he is
entitled* [or, *to be entitled*] to the reward.
The men had made inquiry for Simon's house, and *were standing* before the
gate.
Give no more trouble than you *cannot* possibly help.
That the art of printing was then unknown, was a circumstance in some re-
spects favourable to the freedom of the pen.
An other passion which the present age is apt to run into, is *a desire* to
make children learn all things.
It requires few talents to which most men are not born, or *which,* at least,
they may not acquire.
Nor was Philip wanting in his endeavours to corrupt Demosthenes, as he
had corrupted most of the leading men in Greece.
The Greeks, fearing *to be surrounded,* wheeled about and halted, with the
river *behind them.*
Poverty turns our thoughts too much upon the supplying of our wants; and
riches, upon *the enjoying of* our superfluities.

> That brother should not war with brother,
> *Nor one despise and grieve an* other.

> Such is the refuge of our youth and age ;
> *At* first from hope, *at* last from vacancy—or,

> Such is the refuge of our youth and age ;
> *Of that* from hope, *of this* from vacancy.

> Triumphant Sylla! couldst thou then divine,
> By aught *but* Romans Rome should thus be laid ?

END OF THE KEY TO THE ORAL EXERCISES.

APPENDIX I.

(ORTHOGRAPHY.)

OF THE SOUNDS OF THE LETTERS.

In the first chapter of Part I, the powers of the letters, or the elementary sounds of the English language, were duly enumerated and explained; for these, as well as the letters themselves, are few, and may be fully stated in few words: but, since we often express the same sound in many different ways, and also, in some instances, give to the same letter several different sounds,—or, it may be, no sound at all,—any adequate account of the powers of the letters considered severally according to usage,—that is, of the sound or sounds of each letter, with its mute positions, as these occur in practice,—must, it was thought, descend to a minuteness of detail not desirable in the first chapter of Orthography. For this reason, the following particulars have been reserved to be given here as an Appendix, pertaining to the First Part of this English Grammar.

The terms *long* and *short*, which are often used to denote certain *vowel sounds*, being also used, with a different import, to distinguish the *quantity of syllables*, are frequently misunderstood: for which reason, we have often substituted for them the terms *open* and *close*,—the former, to denote the sound usually given to a vowel when it *forms or ends* an accented syllable; as, *ba, be, bi, bo, bu, by*,—the latter, to denote the sound which the vowel commonly takes when *closed by a consonant*; as, *ab, eb, ib, ob, ub*.

I. OF THE LETTER A.

The vowel *A* has *four** sounds properly its own:—
1. The English, open, or long *a*; as in *fame, favour, efficacious*.
2. The French, close, or short *a*; as in *bat, banner, balance*.
3. The Italian, or middle *a*; as in *far, father, aha, comma, scoria, sofa*.
4. The Dutch, Old-Saxon, or broad *a*; as in *wall, warm, water*.

DIPHTHONGS BEGINNING WITH A.

The only proper diphthong in which *a* is put first, is the word *ay*, meaning *yes*; in which *a* has its middle sound, and *y* that of *open e*.

Aa, when pronounced as an improper diphthong, takes the sound of *close a*; as in *Balaam, Canaan, Isaac*.

Æ, a Latin improper diphthong, very common also in Anglo-Saxon, generally has the sound of *open* or *long e*; as in *Cæsar, ænigma, pæan*; sometimes that of *close* or *short e*; as in *aphæresis, diæresis, et cætera*. Some authors reject the *a*, and write *Cesar, enigma*, &c.

Ai, an improper diphthong, generally has the sound of *open* or *long a*; as in *vail, sail, vain*. In a final unaccented syllable, it sometimes preserves the first sound of *a*, as in *chilblain, mortmain*; but oftener takes the sound of *close* or *short i*; as in *certain, curtain, mountain, villain*: in *said, saith, again*, and *against*, that of *close e*; and in the name *Britain*, that of *close u*.

Ao, an improper diphthong, occurs in the word *gaol*; now frequently written, as it is pronounced, *jail*; and in the adjective *extraordinary*, and its derivatives, in which, according to Walker, the *a* is silent.

---

* Some writers distinguish from the first of these sounds the *grave* sound of *a*, heard in *care, fair, there*, &c. But *Walker* teaches no difference.

Au, an improper diphthong, is generally sounded like *broad a;* as in *cause, caught.* Before *n* and an other consonant, it has the sound of *middle a;* as in *aunt, flaunt, launch, laundry.* *Gauge* is pronounced *gage.*

Aw, an improper diphthong, is always sounded like *broad a;* as in *draw, drawn, drawl.*

Ay, an improper diphthong, like *ai*, has the sound of *open* or *long a;* as in *day, pay, delay:* in *sayst* and *says,* that of *close e.*

TRIPHTHONGS BEGINNING WITH A.

Awe is sounded *au*, like *broad a.* *Aye,* an adverb signifying *always,* has the sound of *open a* only, being different, both in sound and spelling, from the adverb *ay,* yes, with which it is often carelessly confounded.

II. OF THE LETTER B.

The consonant *B* has but one sound ; as in *boy, robber, cub.*

B is silent before *t* or after *m* in the same syllable; as in *debt, debtor, doubt, dumb, lamb, climb, tomb.* It is heard in *subtile,* fine, but not in *subtle,* cunning.

III. OF THE LETTER C.

The consonant *C* has two sounds; the one *hard*, like that of *k*, the other *soft*, or rather *hissing*, like that of *s*.

C, before *a, o, u, l, r, t,* or when it ends a syllable, is generally hard like *k;* as in *can, come, curb, clay, crab, act, action, accent, flaccid.*

C before *e, i,* or *y*, is always soft like *s;* as in *cent, civil, decency, acid.*

In a few words *c* takes the flat sound of *s*, like that of *z;* as in *discern, suffice, sacrifice, sice.*

C before *ea, ia, ie, io,* or *eou,* when the accent precedes, sounds like *sh;* as in *ocean, special, species, gracious, cetaceous.*

C is silent in *czar, czarina, victuals, indict, muscle, corpuscle.*

Ch is generally sounded like *tch;* as in *church, chance, child.* But in words derived from the learned languages, it has the sound of *k;* as in *character, scheme, catechise, chorus, chyle, patriarch, drachma, magna charta:* except in *chart, charter, charity.* *Ch*, in words derived from the French, takes the sound of *sh;* as in *chaise, machine.*

Arch, before a vowel, is pronounced *ark;* as in *archives, archangel, archipelago:* except in *arched, archer, archery, archenemy.* Before a consonant, it is pronounced *artch;* as in *archbishop, archduke.*

Ch is silent in *schism, yatch, drachm;* unsettled in *schedule.*

IV. OF THE LETTER D.

The general sound of the consonant *D*, is heard in *dog, eddy, did.*

D, in the termination *ed*, preceded by a sharp consonant, takes the sound of *t*, when the *e* is suppressed: as in *faced, stuffed, cracked, tripped, passed ;* pronounced, *faste, stuft, cract, tript, past.*

D before *ia, ie, io,* or *eou,* when the accent precedes, generally sounds like *j;* as in *Indian, soldier, tedious, hideous.* So in *verdure, arduous, education.*

V. OF THE LETTER E.

The vowel *E* has *three* sounds properly its own:—

1. The open or long; as in *me, mere, menial, melodious.*
2. The close or short; as in *men, merry, ebony.*
3. The obscure or faint; as in *open, garden, shovel, able.* This third sound is scarcely perceptible, and is barely sufficient to articulate the consonant and form a syllable.

E final is mute, and belongs to the syllable formed by the preceding vowel or diphthong; as in *age, eve, ice, ore*. Except—1. In the words, *be, he, me, we, she,* and *the,* in which it has the open sound. 2. In Greek and Latin words, in which it has its open sound, and forms a distinct syllable; as in *Penelope, Pasiphaë, Cyaneë, Gargaphië, Arsinoë, apostrophe, catastrophe, simile, extempore, epitome.* 3. In the terminations *cre, gre, tre,* in which it has the sound of *close u ;* as in *acre, meagre, centre.*

Mute *e,* after a single consonant, or after *st* or *th,* generally preserves the open or long sound of the preceding vowel ; as in *cane, here, pine, cone, tune, thyme, baste, clothe ;* except in syllables unaccented ; as the last of *genuine ;* and in a few monosyllables; as *bade, are, were, gone, shone, one, done, give, live, shove, love.*

DIPHTHONGS BEGINNING WITH E.

E before an other vowel, in general, either forms with it an *improper* diphthong, or else belongs to a separate syllable.

Ea, an improper diphthong, mostly sounds like *open e ;* as in *ear, fear, tea :* frequently, like *close e ;* as in *earl, head, health :* sometimes, like *open a ;* as in *steak, bear, forswear :* rarely, like *middle a ;* as in *heart, hearth, hearken. Ea* unaccented, sounds like *close u ;* as in *vengeance, pageant.*

Ee, an improper diphthong, has the sound of *open e ;* as in *eel, sheep, tree.* The contractions *e'er* and *ne'er,* are pronounced *air* and *nair.*

Ei, an improper diphthong, mostly sounds like *open a ;* as in *reign, veil :* frequently, like *open e ;* as in *deceit, either, neither, seize :* sometimes, like *open i ;* as in *height, sleight :* often, in unaccented syllables, like *close i ;* as in *foreign, forfeit, surfeit, sovereign :* rarely, like *close e ;* as in *heifer, nonpareil.*

Eo, an improper diphthong, in *people* sounds like *open e ;* in *feoff, feoffment, leopard, jeopardy,* like *close e ;* in *yeoman,* like *open o ;* in *George, georgic,* like *close o ;* in *dungeon, puncheon, sturgeon, &c.,* like *close u. Feod, feodal, feodatory,* are now written as they are pronounced, *feud, feudal, feudatory.*

Eu and *ew* have the diphthongal sound of *open u ;* as in *feud, deuce ; jew, dew, few, new.* These diphthongs, when initial, sound like *yu.* Nouns beginning with this sound, require the article *a,* and not *an,* before them ; as, *A European, a ewer.* After *r* or *rh, eu* and *ew* are commonly sounded like *oo ;* as in *drew, grew, screw, rheumatism.*

In *sew* and *Shrewsbury, ew* sounds like *open o. Shew* and *strew* are properly spelled, as they are most commonly pronounced, *show, strow.*

Ey, accented, has the sound of *open a ;* as in *bey, prey, survey :* unaccented, it has the sound of *open e ;* as in *alley, valley, money. Key* and *ley* are pronounced, *kee, lee.*

TRIPHTHONGS BEGINNING WITH E.

Eau, a French triphthong, sounds like *open o ;* as in *beau, flambeau, portmanteau, bureau :* except in *beauty,* and its compounds, in which it is pronounced like *open u.*

Eou is a combination of vowels sometimes heard in one syllable, especially after *c* or *g ;* as in *crus-ta-ceous, gor geous.* Walker, in his Rhyming Dictionary, gives one hundred and twenty words ending in *eous,* in all of which he separates these vowels; as in *extra-ne-ous.* And why, in his Pronouncing Dictionary, he gave us several such anomalies as *fa-ba-ce-ous* in four syllables, and *her-ba-ceous* in three, it is not easy to tell. The best rule is this : after *c* or *g,* unite these vowels; after the other consonants, separate them.

Ewe is a triphthong having the sound of *yu.* The vulgar pronunciation *yoe* should be carefully avoided.

Eye is an improper triphthong, pronounced like *open i.*

VI. OF THE LETTER F.

The consonant *F* has one unvaried sound, which is heard in *fan, effort, staff :* except *of,* which, when simple, is pronounced *ov.*

14*

VII. OF THE LETTER G.

The consonant *G* has two sounds; the one *hard*, guttural, and peculiar to this letter; the other *soft*, like that of *j*.

G before *a, o, u, l, r*, or at the end of a word, is hard; as in *game, gone, gull, glory, grace, log, bog.*

G before *e, i,* or *y,* is soft; as in *gem, ginger, elegy.* Except—1. In *get, give, gewgaw, finger,* and a few other words. 2. When a syllable is added to a word ending in *g:* as, *long, longer; fog, foggy.*

G is silent before *m* or *n* in the same syllable; as in *phlegm, apothegm, gnaw, resign.*

G, when silent, usually lengthens the preceding vowel; as in *resign, impugn, impregn.*

Gh at the beginning of a word has the sound of *g hard;* as in *ghost, ghostly, ghastly :* in other situations, it is generally silent; as in *high, mighty, plough, bough, through.*

Gh final sometimes sounds like *f;* as in *laugh, rough, tough :* and sometimes, like *g hard;* as in *burgh.* In *hough, lough, shough,* it sounds like *k;* thus, *hock, lock, shock.*

VIII. OF THE LETTER H.

The sound of the consonant *H,* (though articulate and audible when properly uttered,) is little more than an aspirate breathing. It is heard in *hat, hit, hot, hut, adhere.*

H at the beginning of words is always sounded; except in *heir, herb, honest, honour, hospital, hostler, hour, humble, humour,* and their compounds.

H after *r,* is always silent; as *rheum, rhetoric.*

H final, preceded by a vowel in the same syllable, is always silent; as in *ah, Sarah, Nineveh.*

IX. OF THE LETTER I.

The vowel *I* has *three* sounds, each perhaps properly its own:—

1. The open or long; as in *life, fine, time, find, bind, child, mild, wild, pint.* This is a diphthongal sound, and is equivalent to the sound of *middle a* and that of *open e* quickly united.

2. The close or short; as in *ink, think, sinking.*

3. The feeble; as in *divest, doctrinal, diversity.* This sound is equivalent to that of *open e* uttered feebly. *I* generally has this sound when it occurs at the end of an unaccented syllable: except at the end of Latin words, where it is open or long; as in *literati.* In some words, (principally from other modern languages,) *i* has the full sound of *open e,* under the accent; as in *Porto Rico, machine, magazine, antique, shire.*

Accented *i* followed by a vowel, has its open sound; and the vowels belong to separate syllables; as in *pliant, diet, satiety, violet, pious.*

Unaccented *i* followed by a vowel, has its feeble sound; as in *expatiate, obedient, various, abstemious.*

DIPHTHONGS BEGINNING WITH I.

I, in the situation last described, readily coalesces with the vowel which follows, and is often sunk into the same syllable, forming a proper diphthong; as in *fustian, quotient, question.* The terminations *cion, sion,* and *tion,* are generally pronounced *shun ; cious* and *tious* are pronounced *shus.*

Ie is commonly an improper diphthong. *Ie final* has the sound of *open i ;* as in *die, lie, pie, tie. Ie medial* generally has the sound of *open e ;* as in *grief, thief, grenadier.* In *friend* and its compounds, it takes the sound of *close e.*

TRIPHTHONGS BEGINNING WITH I.

The triphthongs *ieu* and *iew,* sound like *open u ;* as in *lieu, adieu, view, review.*

The three vowels *iou*, in the termination *ious*, often fall into one syllable and form a triphthong. There are two hundred and forty-five words of this ending; and more than two hundred derivatives from them. Walker has several puzzling inconsistencies in their pronunciation; such as *fas-tid-i-ous* and *per-fid-ious*, *con-ta gi-ous* and *sac-ri-le-gious*. After *c*, *g*, *t*, or *x*, these vowels should coalesce; as in *gra-cious*, *re-li-gious*, *vex-a-tious*, *ob-nox-ious*, and about two hundred other words. After the other consonants, let them form two syllables; (except when there is a synæresis in poetry;) as in *du-bi-ous*, *o-di-ous*, *va-ri-ous*, *en-vi-ous*.

X. OF THE LETTER J.

The consonant *J* always has the sound of *soft g*, or of *dzh*; as in *joy*, *jewel*: except in *hallelujah*, better written as it is pronounced, *halléluiah*.

XI. OF THE LETTER K.

The consonant *K* has the sound of *c hard*; and occurs where *c* would have its soft sound: as in *keep*, *kind*, *smoky*.
K before *n* is silent; as in *knave*, *know*, *knuckle*. It is never doubled in simple English words; but two Kays may come together in certain compounds, or in the separate syllables of some Hebrew names; as, *brickkiln*, *jackknife*, *Akkub*, *Bukki*, *Habakkuk*. *C* before it doubles the sound, and shortens the preceding vowel; as in *cockle*, *wicked*.

XII. OF THE LETTER L.

The consonant *L* has a soft liquid sound; as in *line*, *lily*, *roll*, *follow*.
L is sometimes silent; as in *alms*, *almond*, *calf*, *chalk*, *could*, *would*, *should*.

XIII. OF THE LETTER M.

The consonant *M* has but one sound; as in *map*, *murmur*, *mammon*. *M* before *n*, at the beginning of a word, is silent; as in *Mnason*, *Mnemosyne*, *mnemonics*. *Comptroller* is pronounced *controller*.

XIV. OF THE LETTER N.

The consonant *N* has two sounds: the pure; as in *nun*, *banner*, *cannon*; and the ringing sound of *ng*; as in *think*, *mangle*, *conquer*, *congress*, *singing*, *twinkling*. The latter sound should be carefully preserved in all words ending in *ing*; and in such others as require it.
N final preceded by *m*, is silent; as in *hymn*, *solemn*.

XV. OF THE LETTER O.

The vowel *O* has *three* sounds properly its own:—
1. The open or long; as in *no*, *note*, *opiate*, *opacity*, *domain*.
2. The close or short; as in *not*, *nor*, *torrid*, *dollar*.
3. The slender; as in *prove*, *move*, *who*, *to*, *do*, *tomb*.
O in many words sounds like *close u*; as in *love*, *shove*, *son*, *come*, *nothing*, *dost*, *attorney*, *gallon*, *dragon*. In the termination *on* immediately after the accent, *o* is often sunk into a sound scarcely perceptible like that of *obscure e*; as in *mason*, *person*. *One* is pronounced *wun*; and *once*, *wunce*.

DIPHTHONGS BEGINNING WITH O.

Oa, an improper diphthong, has the sound of *open o*; as in *boat*, *coal*, *roach*: except in *broad* and *groat*, which have the sound of *broad a*.

Oe, an improper diphthong, when *final,* has the sound of *open o;* as in *doe, foe, throe:* except in *canoe, shoe,* pronounced *canoo, shoo.* *Œ,* a Latin diphthong, generally sounds like *open e;* as in *Antœci, fœtus:* sometimes, like *close e;* as in *fœtid.* Some authors reject the *o,* and write *fetid,* &c.

Oi is generally a proper diphthong, uniting the sound of *close o* or *broad a,* and that of *open e;* as in *boil, coil, soil, rejoice.* But the vowels sometimes belong to separate syllables; as in *stoic.* *Oi* unaccented, sometimes has the sound of *close i;* as in *avoirdupois, connoisseur, tortoise.* *Choir* is now frequently written as it is pronounced, *quire.*

Oo, an improper diphthong, generally has the slender sound of *o;* as in *coo, too, woo, fool, room.* It has a shorter sound in *foot, good, wood, stood, wool;* that of *close u,* in *blood* and *flood;* and that of *open o,* in *door* and *floor.*

Ou is generally a proper diphthong, uniting the sound of *close o,* and that of *u* sounded as *slender o* or *oo ;* as in *bound, found, sound, ounce, thou.*

Ou is also an improper diphthong; and, as such, it has six sounds:—
1. That of *close u ;* as in *rough, tough, young, flourish.*
2. That of *broad a ;* as in *ought, bought, thought.*
3. That of *open o ;* as in *court, dough, four, though.*
4. That of *close o ;* only in *cough, trough, lough, shough.*
5. That of *slender o* or *oo ;* as in *soup, you, through.*
6. That of *oo,* shortened; only in *would, could, should.*

Ow generally sounds like the proper diphthong *ou ;* as in *brown, dowry, now, shower:* but it often has the sound of *open o ;* as in *know, show, stow.*

Oy is sounded like *oi ;* as in *joy, toy.*

TRIPHTHONGS BEGINNING WITH O.

Oeu is a French triphthong occurring in the word *manoeuvre,* which is pronounced in English *man-oo-vur.* *Owe* is an improper triphthong, in which the *o* only is heard, and with its long open sound.

XVI. OF THE LETTER P.

The consonant *P* has but one sound ; which is heard in *pen, sup, supper.* It is sometimes silent; as in *psalm, receipt, corps.*

Ph generally sounds like *f ;* as in *philosophy.* In *Stephen* and *nephew, ph* has the sound of *v.* The *h* after *p,* is silent in *diphthong, triphthong, naphtha, ophthalmic;* and both the *p* and the *h* are silent in *apophthegm, phthisis, phthisical.* From the last three words, *ph* is sometimes dropped.

XVII. OF THE LETTER Q.

The consonant *Q* has the sound of *k,* and is always followed by the vowel *u,* which, in words purely *English,* is sounded like *w;* as in *queen, quarter, request.* In some words of *French* origin, the *u* is silent; as in *coquet, liquor, burlesque.*

XVIII. OF THE LETTER R.

The consonant *R,* at the beginning of words, has a rough sound; as in *rose, roam;* in other situations, a smoother one; as in *proud, harrow, barber.*

XIX. OF THE LETTER S.

The consonant *S* has a sharp, hissing sound; as in *sad, sister, thus:* and a flat sound, like that of *z;* as in *rose, dismal.*

S, at the beginning of words, or after any of the sharp consonants, is always sharp; as in *see, steps, cliffs, sits, stocks, smiths.*

S, after any of the flat mutes, or at the end of words when not preceded by a sharp consonant, is generally flat; as in *eyes, trees, beds, bags, calves.* *Ss* is generally sharp.

S, in the termination *sion*, takes the sound of *sh*, after a consonant; as in *aspersion*, *session :* and that of *zh*, after a vowel; as in *invasion*, *elision*.
S is silent in *isle*, *island*, *aisle*, *demesne*, *viscount*.

XX. OF THE LETTER T.

The general sound of the consonant *T*, is heard in *time*, *letter*, *set*.
T, immediately after the accent, takes the sound of *tch*, before *u*, and generally also before *eou :* as in *nature*, *feature*, *virtue*, *righteous*, *courteous :* when *s* or *x* precedes, it takes this sound before *ia* or *io ;* as in *fustian*, *bastion*, *mixtion*. But the general sound of *t* after the accent, when followed by *i* and an other vowel, is that of *sh ;* as in *creation*, *patient*, *cautious*.
T is sometimes silent; as in *often*, *rustle*, *whistle*.
Th represents an elementary sound. It is either sharp, as in *thing*, *ethical*, *thinketh ;* or flat, as in *this*, *whither*, *thither*.
Th initial is sharp; as in *thank :* except in *than*, *that*, *the*, *thee*, *their*, *them*, *then*, *thence*, *there*, *these*, *they*, *thine*, *this*, *thither*, *those*, *thou*, *thus*, *thy*, and their compounds.
Th final is also sharp; as in *south :* except in *beneath*, *booth*, *with*, and several verbs in *th*, which are frequently (and more properly) written with final *e ;* as in *soothe*, *smoothe*, *bequeathe*.
Th medial is sharp, when preceded or followed by a consonant; as in *swarthy*, *athwart :* except in *brethren*, *burthen*, *farther*, *farthing*, *murther*, *northern*, *worthy*.
Th between two vowels, is generally flat in words purely English; as in *gather*, *neither*, *whither :* and sharp in words from the learned languages; as in *atheist*, *ether*, *method*.
Th in *Thames*, *Thomas*, *thyme*, *asthma*, *phthisic*, and their compounds, is pronounced like *t*.

XXI. OF THE LETTER U.

The vowel *U* has *three* sounds properly its own :—
. 1. The open, long, or diphthongal ; as in *tube*, *cubic*, *juvenile*.
2. The close or short ; as in *tub*, *butter*, *justice*.
3. The middle ; as in *pull*, *pulpit*, *artful*.
U forming a syllable by itself, is *nearly* equivalent in sound to *you*, and requires the article *a*, and not *an*, before it; as, *a union*.
Bury and *busy* are pronounced *berry*, *bizzy*. Their compounds are similar.
After *r* or *rh*, open *u*, and the diphthongs *ue* and *ui*, take the sound of *oo ;* as in *rude*, *rhubarb*, *rue*, *rueful*, *fruit*, *fruitful*.

DIPHTHONGS BEGINNING WITH U.

U, in the proper diphthongs *ua*, *ue*, *ui*, *uo*, *uy*, has the sound of *w*, or *oo* *feeble ;* as in *persuade*, *query*, *quell*, *quiet*, *languid*, *quote*, *obloquy*.
Ua, an improper diphthong, has the sound—1. of *middle a ;* as in *guard*, *guardian :* 2. of *close a ;* as in *guarantee*, *piquant :* 3. of *obscure e ;* as in *victuals* and its compounds ; 4. of *open u ;* as in *mantuamaker*.
Ue, an improper diphthong, has the sound—1. of *open u ;* as in *blue*, *ensue*, *ague :* 2. of *close e ;* as in *guest :* 3. of *obscure e ;* as in *league*, *antique*.
Ui, an improper diphthong, has the sound—1. of *open i ;* as *guide*, *guile :* 2. of *close i ;* as in *conduit*, *circuit :* 3. of *open u ;* as in *juice*, *suit.*
Uy, an improper diphthong, has the sound—1. of *open y ;* as in *buy :* 2. of *feeble y*, or *open e feeble ;* as in *plaguy*.

TRIPHTHONGS BEGINNING WITH U.

Uai is pronounced like *way ;* as in *guai-a-cum*, *quail*, *quaint*.
Uaw is sounded like *wa* in *water ;* as in *squaw*, a female Indian.
Uay has the sound of *way*, as in *Pa-ra-guay ·* except in *quay*, which **Walker** pronounces *kee*.

Uea and *uee* are sounded *wee;* as in *queasy, queer, squeal, squeeze.*
Uoi and *uoy* are sounded *woi;* as in *quoit, buoy.*

XXII. OF THE LETTER V.

The consonant *V* always has a sound like that of *f* flattened; as in *love, vulture.* It is never silent.

XXIII. OF THE LETTER W.

W, as a *consonant,* has the sound heard in *wine, win,* being a sound less vocal than that of *oo,* and depending more upon the lips.

W before *h,* is pronounced as if it followed the *h;* as in *what, when.* Before *r* it is always silent; as in *wrath, wrench:* so in *whole, whoop, sword, answer, two.*

W is never used alone as a vowel; except in some Welsh names, in which it is equivalent to *oo;* as in *Cwm Cothy.* In a diphthong, when heard, it has the power of *u;* as in *brow:* but it is frequently silent; as in *flow, snow, &c.*

W, when sounded before vowels, being reckoned a *consonant,* we have no diphthongs or triphthongs *beginning* with this letter.

XXIV. OF THE LETTER X.

The consonant *X* has a *sharp* sound, like *ks;* as in *ox:* and a *flat* one, like *gz;* as in *example.*

X is sharp, when it ends an accented syllable; as in *exit, excellence:* or when it precedes an accented syllable beginning with a consonant; as in *expound, expunge.*

X unaccented, is generally flat when the next syllable begins with a vowel; as in *exist, exotic.*

X initial, in Greek proper names, has the sound of *z;* as in *Xanthus, Xantippe, Xenophon, Xerxes.*

XXV. OF THE LETTER Y.

Y, as a *consonant,* has the sound heard in *yard, youth;* being rather less vocal than the feeble sound of *i* or *y,* and serving merely to modify that of a succeeding vowel, with which it is quickly united.

Y, as a vowel, has the same sounds as *i:*—

1. The open or long; as in *cry, thyme, cycle.*
2. The close or short; as in *system, symptom, cynic.*
3. The feeble; (like *open e feeble;*) as in *cymar, cycloidal, mercy.*

The vowels *i* and *y* have, in general, exactly the same sound under similar circumstances; and, in forming derivatives, we often change one for the other: as in *city, cities; tie, tying; easy, easily.*

Y, before a vowel heard in the same syllable, is reckoned a *consonant;* we have, therefore, no diphthongs or triphthongs *commencing* with this letter.

XXVI. OF THE LETTER Z.

The consonant *Z* always has the sound of *s flat;* as in *breeze, zenith.*

APPENDIX II.

(ETYMOLOGY.)

OF THE DERIVATION OF WORDS.

Derivation is a species of Etymology, which explains the various methods by which those derivative words which are not formed by mere grammatical inflections, are deduced from their primitives.

Most of those words which are regarded as primitives in English, may be traced to ulterior sources, and many of them are found to be compounds or derivatives in other languages. A knowledge of the *Saxon, Latin, Greek,* and *French* languages, will throw much light on this subject. But as the learner is supposed to be unacquainted with those languages, we shall not go beyond the precincts of our own; except to show him the origin and primitive import of some of our definitive and connecting particles, and to explain the prefixes and terminations which are frequently employed to form English derivatives.

The rude and cursory languages of barbarous nations, to whom literature is unknown, are among those transitory things which, by the hand of time, are irrecoverably buried in oblivion. The fabric of the English language is undoubtedly of *Saxon* origin; but what was the form of the language spoken by the *Saxons,* when about the year 450 they entered Britain, cannot now be accurately known. It was probably a dialect of the *Gothic* or *Teutonic.* This *Anglo-Saxon* dialect, being the nucleus, received large accessions from other tongues of the north, from the *Norman French,* and from the more polished languages of *Rome* and *Greece,* to form the modern *English.* The speech of our rude and warlike ancestors thus gradually improved, as Christianity, civilization, and knowledge, advanced the arts of life in Britain; and, as early as the tenth century, it became a language capable of expressing all the sentiments of a civilized people. From the time of *Alfred,* its progress may be traced by means of writings which remain; but it can scarcely be called *English* till about the thirteenth century. And for two or three centuries later, it was so different from the modern English, as to be scarcely intelligible to most readers; but, gradually improving by means upon which we cannot here dilate, it at length became what we now find it, a language, copious, strong, refined, and capable of no inconsiderable degree of harmony.

The following is an explanation of the *Saxon* letters employed below:

a	b	c	d	e	f	g	h	i	j	k	l	m	n	o	p	q
a	b	c	ð	e	ꝼ	ȝ	h	ı		k	l	m	n	o	p	cƿ

r	s	t	th	u	v	w	x	y	z.
ꞃ	ꞃ	ꞇ	ð or þ	u	ᚹ	ƿ	x	ẏ	z.

SECTION I.—DERIVATION OF THE ARTICLES.

1. According to *Horne Tooke,* THE is the Saxon ðe from ðean *to take;* and is nearly equivalent in meaning to *that* or *those.* We find it written in ancient works, ꞃe, ꞃe, ꞃeo, ye, ꞇe, ðe, þe, and ꞇhe; and, tracing it through what we suppose to be the *oldest* of these forms, we rather consider it the imperative of ꞃeon *to see.*

2. AN is the Saxon *œn, ane, an,* ONE; and, by dropping *n* before a consonant, becomes *a. Gawin Douglas,* an ancient English writer, wrote *ane,* even before a consonant; as, "*Ane* book,"—"*Ane* lang spere,"—"*Ane* volume."

SECTION II.—DERIVATION OF NOUNS.

In *English*, Nouns are derived from nouns, from adjectives, from verbs, or from participles.

I. Nouns are derived from *Nouns* in several different ways:—

1. By adding *ship, dom, ri., wick, or, ate, hood,* or *head:* as, *fellow, fellowship; king, kingdom; bishop, bishopric; bailiff,* or *baily, bailiwick; senate, senator; tetrarch, tetrarchate; child, childhood; God, Godhead.* These generally denote dominion, office, or character.

2. By adding *ian:* as, *music, musician; physic, physician.* These generally denote profession.

3. By adding *y* or *ery:* as, *slave, slavery; fool, foolery; scene, scenery; cutler, cutlery; grocer, grocery.* These sometimes denote a state, or habit of action; sometimes, an artificer's wares or shop.

4. By adding *age* or *ade:* as, *patron, patronage; porter, porterage; band, bandage; lemon, lemonade.*

5. By adding *kin, let, ling, ock, el,* or *erel:* as, *lamb, lambkin; river, rivulet; duck, duckling; hill, hillock; run, runnel; cock, cockerel.* These denote little things, and are called diminutives.

6. By adding *ist:* as, *psalm, psalmist; botany, botanist.* These denote persons devoted to, or skilled in, the subject expressed by the primitive.

7. By prefixing an adjective, or an other noun, and forming a compound word; as, *holiday, foreman, statesman, tradesman.*

8. By prefixing *dis, in, non,* or *un,* to reverse the meaning: as, *order, disorder; consistency, inconsistency; observance, nonobservance; truth, untruth.*

9. By prefixing *counter,* signifying *against* or *opposite:* as, *attraction, counter-attraction; bond, counter-bond.*

10. By adding *ess, ix,* or *ine,* to change masculines to feminines: as, *heir, heiress; prophet, prophetess; abbot, abbess; testator, testatrix; hero, heroine.*

II. Nouns are derived from *Adjectives* in several different ways:—

1. By adding *ness, ity, ship, dom,* or *hood:* as, *good, goodness; real, reality; hard, hardship; wise, wisdom; false, falsehood.*

2. By changing *t* into *ce* or *cy:* as, *radiant, radiance; consequent, consequence; flagrant, flagrancy; current, currency.*

3. By changing some of the letters, and adding *t* or *th:* as, *long, length; broad, breadth; high, height.* The nouns included under these three heads, generally denote abstract qualities, and are called abstract nouns.

4. By adding *ard:* as, *drunk, drunkard; dull, dullard.* These denote the character of a person.

5. By adding *ist:* as, *sensual, sensualist; royal, royalist.* These denote persons devoted, addicted, or attached, to something.

6. By adding *a,* the Latin ending of neuter plurals, to certain proper adjectives in *an:* as, *Miltonian, Miltoniana;* i. e., *Miltonian things*—matters relating to *Milton.*

III. Nouns are derived from *Verbs* in several different ways:—

1. By adding *ment, ance, ure,* or *age:* as, *punish, punishment; repent, repentance; forfeit, forfeiture; stow, stowage; equip, equipage.*

2. By changing the termination of the verb, into *se, ce, sion, tion, ation,* or *ition:* as, *expand, expanse, expansion; pretend, pretence, pretension; invent, invention; create, creation; omit, omission; provide, provision; reform, reformation; oppose, opposition.* These denote the act of doing, or the thing done.

3. By adding *er* or *or:* as, *hunt, hunter; write, writer; collect, collector.* These generally denote the doer.

4. Nouns and verbs are sometimes alike in orthography, but different in pronunciation: as, a *house,* to *house;* a *reb'el,* to *rebel';* a *rec'ord,* to *record'.* Sometimes they are wholly alike, and are distinguished only by the construction: as, *love,* to *love; fear,* to *fear; sleep,* to *sleep.*

IV Nouns are often derived from *Participles* in *ing.* Such nouns are usually distinguished from participles, only by their construction: as, a *meeting,* the *understanding, murmurings, disputings.*

SECTION III.—DERIVATION OF ADJECTIVES.

In *English*, Adjectives are derived from nouns, from adjectives, from verbs, or from participles.

I. Adjectives are derived from *Nouns* in several different ways:—

1. By adding *ous, ious, eous, y, ey, ic, al, ical,* or *ine:* (sometimes with an omission or change of some of the final letters:) as, *danger, dangerous; glory, glorious; right, righteous; rock, rocky; clay, clayey; poet, poetic; nation, national; method, methodical; vertex, vertical; clergy, clerical; adamant, adamantine.* Adjectives thus formed, generally apply the properties of their primitives to the nouns to which they relate.

2. By adding *ful:* as, *fear, fearful; cheer, cheerful; grace, graceful.* These denote abundance.

3. By adding *some:* as, *burden, burdensome; game, gamesome.* These denote plenty, but with some diminution.

4. By adding *en:* as, *oak, oaken; silk, silken.* These generally denote the matter of which a thing is made.

5. By adding *ly* or *ish:* as, *friend, friendly; child, childish,* These denote resemblance; for *ly* signifies *like.*

6. By adding *able* or *ible:* as, *fashion, fashionable; access, accessible.* But these terminations are generally added to verbs.

7. By adding *less:* as, *house, houseless; death, deathless.* These denote privation or exemption.

8. Adjectives from proper names, take various terminations: as, *America, American; England, English; Dane, Danish; Portugal, Portuguese; Plato, Platonic.*

9. By adding *ed:* as, *saint, sainted; bigot, bigoted.* These are participial, and are often joined with other adjectives to form compounds; as, *three-sided, bare-footed, long-eared, hundred-handed, flat-nosed.*

10. Nouns are often converted into adjectives, without change of termination: as, *paper* currency; a *gold* chain.

II. Adjectives are derived from *Adjectives* in several different ways:—

1. By adding *ish* or *some:* as, *white, whitish; lone, lonesome.* These denote quality with some diminution.

2. By prefixing *dis, in,* or *un:* as, *honest, dishonest; consistent, inconsistent; wise, unwise.* These express a negation of the quality denoted by their primitives.

3. By adding *y* or *ly:* as, *swarth, swarthy; good, goodly.* Of these there are but few; for almost all derivatives of the latter form, are adverbs.

III. Adjectives are derived from *Verbs* in several different ways:—

1. By adding *able* or *ible:* (sometimes with a change of some of the final letters:) as, *perish, perishable; vary, variable; convert, convertible; divide, divisible.* These denote susceptibility.

2. By adding *ive* or *ory:* (sometimes with a change of some of the final letters:) as, *elect, elective; interrogate, interrogative, interrogatory; defend, defensive; defame, defamatory.*

3. Words ending in *ate,* are mostly verbs: but some of them may be employed as adjectives, in the same form, especially in poetry: as, *reprobate, complicate.*

IV. Adjectives are derived from *Participles* in the following ways:— ·

1. By prefixing *un:* as, *unyielding, unregarded, undeserved.*

2. By combining the participle with some word which does not belong to the verb; as, *way-faring, hollow-sounding, long-drawn.*

3. Participles often become adjectives without change of form. Such adjectives are distinguished from participles only by the construction: as, "A *lasting* ornament;"—"The *starving* chymist;"—"Words of *learned* length."

SECTION IV.—DERIVATION OF THE PRONOUNS.

I. The *English* Pronouns are all of *Saxon* origin. The following appears to be their derivation:—

Eng.	*I,*	*my* or *mine,*	*me;*	*we,*	*our* or *ours,*	*us.*
Sax.	ic,	mın,	me;	pe,	uɲe,	uꞃ.
Eng.	*thou,*	*thy* or *thine,*	*thee;*	*ye,*	*your* or *yours,*	*you.*
Sax.	ðu,	ðin,	ðe;	ȝe,	eoꞃeɲ,	eoꞃ.
Eng.	*he,*	*his,*	*him;*	*they,*	*their* or *theirs,*	*them.*
Sax.	he,	hŷꞃ,	hım;	hı,	hıɲa, *or* heoɲa,	hem.
Eng.	*she,*	*her,* or *hers,*	*her;*	*they,*	*their* or *theirs,*	*them.*
Sax.	heo,	heɲa *or* hŷɲa,	heɲ;	hı,	hıɲa, *or* heoɲa,	hem.
Eng.	*it,*	*its,*	*it;*	*they,*	*their* or *theirs,*	*them.*
Sax.	hıt,	hŷꞃ,	hıt;	hı,	hıɲa, *or* heoɲa,	hem.

The plurals and oblique cases do not all appear to be regular derivatives from the nominative singular. Many of these pronouns, as well as a vast number of other words of frequent use in the language, were variously written by the old English and Anglo-Saxon authors. He who traces the history of our language will meet with them under all the following forms, and perhaps more:—

1. I, J, Y, y, ŷ, ı, ic, che, ich, ıc;—MY, mi, min, MINE, myne, myn, mŷn;—ME, mee, me, meh, mec, mech;—WE, wee, ve, ꞃe;—OUR or OURS, oure, uɲe, ure, urin, uren, urne, user, usser, usses, usse, ussum;—US, ous, vs, uꞃ, uss, usic, usich, usih.

2. THOU, thoue, thow, thowe, thu, ðu, þu;—THY, thi, thin, THINE, thyne, thyn, ðin, þin;—THEE, the, theh, thec, ðe þe;—YE, yee, ze, zee, ȝe, ghe;—YOUR or YOURS, youre, zour, ȝour, ȝoure, hure, coꞃeɲ;—YOU, youe, yow, ȝou, zou, ou, ıu, ıuh, eop, iow, geow, eowih, cowic, iowih.

3. HE, hee, hie, hi, he, se;—HIS, hise, is, hys, hyse, ys, ŷs, hŷs, hŷꞃ;—HIM, hine, hen, hyne, hiene, hion, hym, hŷm, iin, hım;—THEY, thay, thei, the, tha, thai, thii, yai, hi, hii, hie, heo, hig, hyg, hŷ, hiȝ, hı;—THEIR or THEIRS, ther, theyr, theyrs, thair, thare, hare, here, ber, hir, hire, hira, hŷɲa, ðeoɲa, þeoɲa, heora;—THEM, theym, thym, thaym, thaim, thame, tham, em, hem, heom, biom, hom, eom, him, hi, hig.

4. SHE, shee, sche, scho, sho, shoe, rcæ, rco, heo, hio, hiu;—HER, [possessive,] hur, hir, hire, hyr, hyre, hŷɲe, hŷɲa, heɲa;—HER, [objective,] hir, hire, heɲ, hyre, hi.

5. IT, itt, hyt, hytt, yt, yt, hit, ıc, hıt. According to Horne Tooke, this pronoun is from the perfect participle of hǣtan, *to name,* and signifies *the said;* but Dr. Alexander Murray makes it the neuter of a declinable adjective, "he, heo, hita, *this.*"—*Hist. Europ. Lang.,* Vol. i, p. 315.

II. The relatives are derived from the same source, and have passed through similar changes, or varieties in orthography; as,

1. WHO, ho, wha, hwa, wua, hua, qua, quha, hꞃa, hue;—WHOSE, who's, whos, quhois, quhais, quhase, hꞃæꞃ;—WHOM, whome, quhum, quhome, hwom, hꞃam, hwæm, hwæne, hwone.

2. WHICH, whiche, whyche, whilch, wych, quilch, quilk, quhilk, hwile, hꞃile, hwyle, hwelc, whillk, huilic, hvilc.

3. WHAT, hwat, hwæt, hwet, quhat. This pronoun, whether relative or interrogative, is regarded by some as a neuter derivative from the masculine or feminine *wha,* who. It may have been thence derived, but, in modern English, it is not always of the neuter gender.

4. THAT, in Anglo-Saxon, is *thæt,* or þæt. Horne Tooke supposes this word to have been originally the perfect participle of thean, *to take.* This derivation is doubtful.

From its various uses, the word *that* is called sometimes a pronoun, sometimes an adjective, and sometimes a conjunction; but, in respect to derivation, it is, doubtless, one and the same.—As an adjective, it was formerly applicable to a plural noun; as, "*That* holy *ordres.*"—*Dr. Martin.*

SECTION V.—DERIVATION OF VERBS.

In *English,* Verbs are derived from nouns, from adjectives, or from verbs.
I. Verbs are derived from *Nouns* in the following ways:—

1. By adding *ize, ise, en,* or *ate:* as, *author, authorize; critic, criticise; length, lengthen; origin, originate.* The termination *ize* is of Greek origin; and *ise,* of French: the former should be generally preferred in forming English derivatives; but *ise* usually terminates such verbs as are essentially formed by means of prefixes; as, *arise, disguise, advise, circumcise, despise, surmise, comprise, compromise, enterprise.*

2. By changing a consonant, or by adding mute *e:* as, *advice, advise; bath, bathe; breath, breathe.*

II. Verbs are derived from *Adjectives* in the following ways:—

1. By adding *en, ate,* or *ize:* as, *deep, deepen; domestic, domesticate; civil, civilize.*

2. Many adjectives become verbs, without change of form: as, *warm,* to *warm; dry,* to *dry; black,* to *black; forward,* to *forward.*

III. Verbs are derived from *Verbs* in the following ways:—

1. By prefixing *dis* or *un,* to reverse the meaning: as, *please, displease; qualify, disqualify; fasten, unfasten; muzzle, unmuzzle.*

2. By prefixing *a, be, for, fore, mis, over, out, under, up,* or *with:* as, *rise, arise; sprinkle, besprinkle; bid, forbid; see, foresee; take, mistake; look, overlook; run, outrun; go, undergo; hold, uphold; draw, withdraw.*

SECTION VI.—DERIVATION OF PARTICIPLES.

All *English* Participles are derived from *English* verbs, in the manner explained under the head of Etymology; and when foreign participles are introduced into our language, they are not participles with us, but belong to some other part of speech.

SECTION VII.—DERIVATION OF ADVERBS.

1. In *English,* many Adverbs are derived from adjectives by adding *ly,* which is an abbreviation for *like:* as, *candid, candidly; sordid, sordidly.* Most adverbs of manner are thus formed.

2. Many adverbs are compounds formed from two or more English words; as, *herein, thereby, to-day, always, already, elsewhere, sometimes, wherewithal.* The formation and the meaning of these are in general sufficiently obvious.

3. About seventy adverbs are formed by means of the prefix *a;* as, *Abreast, abroad, across, afresh, away, ago, awry, astray.*

4. *Needs,* as an adverb, (meaning *necessarily,*) is a contraction of *need is; prithee,* of *I pray thee; alone,* of *all one; only,* of *one like; anon,* of *in one* [instant]; *never,* of *ne ever;* [not ever].

5. *Very* is from the French *veray,* or *vrai,* true. "*Still,*" says Tooke, "is from the imperative of the Saxon ꝑcellan, *to put;*" and "*Else* is from the imperative of aleꝼan, *to dismiss.*" *Rather* is the comparative of the ancient *rath,* soon.

SECTION VIII.—DERIVATION OF CONJUNCTIONS.

The *English* Conjunctions are mostly of *Saxon* origin. The best dictionaries of our language give us, for the most part, the same words in *Saxon* characters; but *Horne Tooke,* in his *Diversions of Purley,* a learned and curious work which the advanced student may peruse with advantage, traces these and many other English particles to *Saxon verbs* or *participles.* The following derivations, so far as they partake of such speculations, are offered principally on his authority:—

1. ALTHOUGH, signifying *admit, allow,* is from *all* and *though;* the latter being the imperative of an ancient verb, meaning *to allow.*

2. AN, an obsolete conjunction, signifying *if,* or *grant,* is the imperative of the *Saxon* verb anan, *to grant.*

3. AND, denoting *addition,* is said by Tooke to come from an-að, the imperative of anan-að, *to grant to, to add.*

4. As, according to *Dr. Johnson,* is from the Teutonic *als;* but *J. H. Tooke* says that *als* itself is a contraction for *all* and the original particle *es* or *as,* meaning *it, that,* or *which.*

5. BECAUSE, meaning *by cause*, is from *be* (Saxon for *by*) and *cause*.

6. BOTH, *the two*, is from the pronominal adjective *both;* which, according to *Dr. Alex. Murray*, is a contraction of the Visigothic *bagoth*, doubled. The Anglo-Saxons wrote for it *butu, butwu, buta*, and *batwa;* i. e., *ba*, both, *twa*, two.

7. BUT, implying *addition*, is supposed by Tooke to have come from "boᴛ, the imperative of boᴛan, *to boot, to add.*"

8. BUT, denoting *exception*, is conjectured by the same author to have come from "be-uᴛan, the imperative of beon-uᴛan, *to be out.*"

9. EITHER, *one of the two*, is from the Saxon *ægether*, or *egther*.

10. EKE, signifying *also* or *add*, (now nearly obsolete) is from eac, the imperative of eacan, *to add*.

11. EXCEPT, which, as a conjunction, means *unless*, is the imperative, or (according to *Dr. Johnson*) an ancient perfect participle, of the verb *to except*.

12. FOR, meaning *because*, is the Saxon ꝼoꞃ, or the Dutch *voor*, from a Gothic noun signifying *cause* or *sake*.

13. IF, meaning *give, grant, allow*, is from ᵹɪꝼ, [*gif*,] the imperative of ᵹiꝼan, *to give*.

14. LEST, meaning *that not, dismissed*, is from leꞃeꝼ, the perfect participle of leꞃan, *to dismiss*.

15. NEITHER, *not either*, is a union and contraction of *ne either:* our old writers frequently used *ne* for *not*.

16. NOR, *not other, not else*, is a union and contraction of *ne or*.

17. NOTWITHSTANDING, *not hindering*, is an English compound which needs no further explanation.

18. OR has been supposed a contraction of the Saxon oðeꞃ, *other*. Dr. Bosworth gives oððe as its Saxon equivalent.

19. SAVE, [*but, except*,] anciently used as a conjunction, is the imperative of the verb *to save*, meaning *to except*.

20. SINCE [*seeing* or *seen*] is from ꞃineꞃ, or ꞃyne, the perfect participle of ꞃeon, *to see*. *Seeing*, too, is sometimes a copulative conjunction.

21. THAN, which introduces the latter term of a *comparison*, is from the Saxon ðanne, which was used for the same purpose.

22. THAT [*taken*] is from ðæᴛ, the perfect participle of ðean, *to take*.

23. THOUGH [*allow*] is from ðaꝼɪᵹ, the imperative of ðaꝼiᵹan, *to allow*.

24. UNLESS [*except, dismiss*,] is from onleꞃ, the imperative of onleran, *to dismiss*.

25. WHETHER, which introduces the first term of an *alternative*, is the Saxon hꝑæðeꞃ, which was used for the same purpose.

26. YET, [*nevertheless*,] is from ᵹeᴛ, the imperative of ᵹeᴛan, *to get*.

SECTION IX.—DERIVATION OF PREPOSITIONS.

The following is the derivation of most of the *English* Prepositions:—

1. ABOUT [*at circuit*] is from the French *à*, or the English prefix *a*, meaning *at* or *to*, and *bout*, meaning *turn*, or *limit*.

2. ABOVE [*at-by-high*] is from the Saxon, *a*, *be*, and uꝼa, *high*.

3. ACROSS [*at-cross*] is from *a* and the noun *cross*.

4. AFTER [*farther in the rear*] is the comparitive of *aft*, now used only by seamen.

5. AGAINST [*opposed to*] is from on-ᵹeonð, *gone at*.

6. ALONG [*at-long*] is from *a* and *long*.

7. AMID [*at mid* or *middle*] is from *a* and *mid*.

8. AMIDST [*at midst*] is from *a* and *midst*, contracted from *middest*, the superlative of *mid*.

9. AMONG [*a-mixed*] is abbreviated from *amongst*.

10. AMONGST [*a-mixed*] is from *a* and *mongst*, a Saxon participle signifying *mixed*.

11. AROUND [*at circle*] is from *a* and *round*, circle or sphere.

12. AT [*joining*] is supposed by some to come from the Latin *ad;* but Dr. Murray says, "We have in Teutonic AT for AGT, touching or touched, joined, at."—*Hist. Lang.*, i, 349.

13. ATHWART [*across*] is from *a* and *thwart*, cross.

14. BEFORE [*by-fore*] is from the prefix *be* and the adjective *fore*.

15. BEHIND [*by-hind*] is from the prefix *be* and the adjective *hind*.

16. BELOW [*by-low*] is from the prefix *be* and the adjective *low*.

17. BENEATH [*below*] is from *be* and the adjective *neath*, low ; whence the comparative *nether*, lower.

18. BESIDE [*by-side*] is from *be* and the noun *side*.

19. BESIDES* [*by-sides*] is from *be* and the plural noun *sides*.

20. BETWEEN [*by-twain*] is from *be* and *twain*, two.

21. BETWIXT [*between*] is from *be* and *twyx*, a Gothic word signifying *two*, or *twain*.

22. BEYOND [*by-gone*] is from *be* and ȝeonð, the perfect participle of ȝeonðan, *to pass*, or *go*.

23. BY (formerly written *bi* and *be*) is the imperative of *beon*, *to be*.

24. CONCERNING is from the first participle of the verb *to concern*.

25. DOWN [*low*] is from the Anglo-Saxon adjective *dun*, low.

26. DURING [*lasting*] is from an old verb *dure*, to last, formerly in use ; as, " While the world may *dure*."—*Chaucer's Knight's Tale.*

27. EXCEPT is from the imperative, or (according to *Dr. Johnson*) the ancient perfect participle, of the verb *to except*.

28. EXCEPTING is from the first participle of the verb *to except*.

29. FOR [*by cause of*] is from a Gothic noun signifying *cause* or *sake*.

30. FROM is derived from the Saxon ꝼɲum, or ꝼɲam, *beginning*.

31. IN is from the Latin *in :* the Greek is εν, and the French *en*.

32. INTO is a compound of *in* and *to*.

33. NOTWITHSTANDING [*not hindering*] is from the adverb *not*, and the participle *withstanding*.

34. OF is from the Saxon oꝼ, which *H. Tooke* supposes to be from a noun signifying *offspring*.

35. OFF (opposed to *on*) *Dr. Johnson* derives from the Dutch *af*.

36. ON is traced by etymologists to the Gothic *ana*, the German *an*, the Dutch *aan :* but such a derivation does not *fix its meaning*.

37. OUTOF (opposed to *into*) is from the adverb *out* and the preposition *of* —usually written separately, but better joined in some instances.

38. OVER [*above*] is from uꝼeɲu, *higher*.

39. OVERTHWART is a compound of *over* and *thwart*, cross.

40. PAST is a contraction from the perfect participle *passed*.

41. ROUND [*about*] is from the noun or adjective *round*.

42. SINCE [*seen*], says Tooke, is from the perfect participle of ɲeon, *to see*.

43. THROUGH (contracted from *thorough*) is from a Saxon word meaning *door* or *passage*.

44. THROUGHOUT is a compound of *through* and *out*.

45. TILL [*the end*] is from the Saxon ꞇɩl, [Saxon for *till*,] noting end of time.

46. TO is a simple word from the Saxon ꞇo, which is supposed to come from a Gothic noun signifying *end*.

47. TOUCHING is from the first participle of the verb *to touch*.

48. TOWARD or TOWARDS is probably a compound of *to* and *ward*, from paɲðian, *to look*.

49. UNDER [*on nether*] is from the Dutch *on neder*, on lower.

50. UNDERNEATH is a compound from *under* and *neath*, low.

51. UNTIL is a compound from *on* or *un* and *till*, the end.

52. UNTO (now little used) is from *on* or *un* and *to*.

53. UP is from the Saxon *up*, which *H. Tooke* traces to uꝼa, *high*.

54. UPON [*high on*] is from *up* and *on*.

55. WITH [*join*] is probably from the imperative of pɩðan, *to join*.

56. WITHIN [*by-in*] is from *with* and *in*.

57. WITHOUT [*by-out*] is from *with* and *out*.

58. WORTH [*of the value of*] is from the Saxon verb *wyrthan* or *weorthan*, to *be ;* and has, by pedigree, as good a claim to be a preposition as *by* and

---

* *Beside* should be used as a preposition. and *besides* only as an adverb. See reasons for this distinction, in *Campbell's Philosophy of Rhetoric.*

with: the old English writers used *worth* for *be*, in every part of the conjugation. According to *J. H. Tooke*, *with*, in the two compounds *within* and *without*, is from þýnð, the imperative of pynðan, *to be;* and the meaning of the former is *be in*, and of the latter *be out.* Compare the derivations of BY, WITH, and WORTH; and see observations 6th and 7th, on Rule 22d, page 209.

SECTION X.—DERIVATION OF INTERJECTIONS.

Those significant and constructive words which are occasionally used as Interjections, do not require an explanation here; and those mere sounds which are in no wise expressive of thought, scarcely admit of definition or derivation. The interjection HEY is probably a corruption of the adjective *high;*—ALAS is from the French *hélas;*—ALACK is probably a corruption of *alas;*—WELAWAY (which is now corrupted into *welladay*,) is from the Saxon palapa, *wo on wo;*—FIE, from pian, *to hate;*—HEYDAY, from *high day;*—AVAUNT, from the French *avant*, before;—LO, from *look;*—BEGONE, from *be* and *gone;*—WELCOME, from *well* and *come.*

SECTION XI.—EXPLANATION OF THE PREFIXES.

In the formation of words, certain particles are often employed as prefixes; which, as they generally have some peculiar import, may be separately explained. A few of them are of Anglo-Saxon origin; and the greater part of these are still employed as separate words in our language. The rest are Latin, Greek, or French prepositions. The roots to which they are prefixed, are not always proper English words. Those which are such, are called *Separable Radicals;* and those which are not such, *Inseparable Radicals.*

CLASS I.—ENGLISH OR ANGLO-SAXON PREFIXES.

1. A, as an English prefix, signifies *on, in, at,* or *to;* as in *a-board, a-shore, a-sleep, a-fur, a-field.* The French *à*, to, is probably the same particle; as in *a-dieu.* This prefix is sometimes redundant; as in *a-wake, a-rise.*

2. BE signifies *upon, to, by,* or *for;* as in *be-spatter, be-times, be-tide, be-speak.* It is sometimes redundant; as in *be-gird, be-deck, be-loved.*

3. COUNTER means *against* or *opposite;* as in *counter-poise, counter-evidence, counter-natural.*

4. FOR, in composition, seems to signify *from:* it is found in the irregular verbs *for-bear, for-bid, for-get, for-give, for-sake, for-swear;* and in *for-do, for-pass, for-pine, for-say, for-think, for-waste,* which last are now seldom used.

5. FORE, prefixed to verbs, signifies *before;* as in *fore-know, fore-tell:* prefixed to nouns, it is an adjective, and signifies *anterior;* as in *fore-side, fore-part.*

6. HALF, signifying *one of two equal parts,* is much used in composition; and, often, merely to denote imperfection: as, *half-sighted,* seeing imperfectly.

7. MIS signifies *wrong;* as in *mis-do, mis-place.*

8. OUT, prefixed to verbs, generally denotes excess; as in *out-do, out-leap:* prefixed to nouns, it is an adjective, and signifies *exterior;* as in *out-side, out-parish.*

9. OVER usually denotes superiority or excess; as in *over-power, over-strain, over-large, over-dose, over-growth.*

10. SELF signifies *one's own person,* or *belonging to one's own person.* It is much used in composition; as in *self-love, self-abuse, self-affairs, self-willed, self-accusing.* Sometimes *self* means *very;* as in *self-same.*

11. UN denotes negation or contrariety; as in *un-kind, un-load.*

12. UNDER denotes inferiority; as in *under-value, under-clerk.*

13. UP denotes motion upwards; as in *up-lift:* sometimes subversion; as in *up-set.*

14. WITH, as a prefix, (unlike the common preposition *With*,) signifies *against, from,* or *back;* as in *with-stand, with-hold, with-draw.*

CLASS II.—LATIN PREFIXES.

The primitives to which these are prefixed, are not many of them employed separately in English. The final letter of the prefix *ad, con, ex, in, ob,* or *sub,* is often changed before certain consonants.

1. A, AB, or ABS, means from, or away: as, *a-vert*, to turn from; *ab-duce*, to lead from; *abs-tract*, to draw away.

2. AD, *ac, af, al, an, ap, as, at,*—to or at: as, *ad-vert*, to turn to; *ac-cede*, to yield to; *af-flux*, a flowing-to; *al-ly*, to bind to; *an-nex*, to link to; *ap-ply*, to put to; *as-sume*, to take to; *at-test*, to witness to.

3. ANTE,—before: as *ante-cedent*, going before; *ante-mundane*, before the world; *ante-date*, to date before.

4. CIRCUM,—around or about: as, *circum-volve*, to roll around.

5. CON, *com, co, col, cor,*—together: as, *contract*, to draw together; *compel*, to drive together; *co-erce*, to force together; *col-lect*, to gather together; *cor-rade*, to scrape together; *con-junction*, a joining-together.

6. CONTRA,—against: as *contra-dict*, to speak against.

7. DE,—of, from, or down: as, *de-note*, to be a sign of; *de-tract*, to draw from; *de-pend*, to hang down; *de-press*, to press down.

8. DIS, DI,—away or apart: as, *dis-pel*, to drive away; *dis-sect*, to cut apart; *di-vert*, to turn away. *Dis*, before English words, generally reverses their meaning; as, *please, dis-please*.

9. E or EX, *ec, ef,*—out: as, *e-ject*, to cast out; *ex-tract*, to draw out; *ec-stacy*, a raising-out; *ef-face*, to blot out.

10. EXTRA,—beyond: as, *extra-vagant*, wandering beyond.

11. IN, *il, im, ir,*—in, into, against, or upon: as, *in-spire*, to breathe in; *il-lude*, to draw in by deceit; *im-mure*, to wall in; *ir-ruption*, a breaking-in; *in-cur*, to run into; *in-dict*, to declare against; *im-pute*, to charge upon. These syllables, prefixed to nouns or adjectives, generally reverse their meaning; as, *ir-religion, ir-rational, in-secure, in-sane*.

12. INTER,—between: as, *inter-sperse*, to scatter between; *inter-jection*, something thrown in between.

13. INTRO,—within: as, *intro-vert*, to turn within.

14. OB, *oc, of, op,*—against: as, *ob-trude*, to thrust against; *oc-cur*, to run against; *of-fer*, to bring against; *op-pose*, to place against; *ob-ject*, cast against.

15. PER,—through or by: as, *per-vade*, to go through; *per-chance*, by chance; *per-cent*, by the hundred.

16. POST,—after: as, *post-pone*, to place after.

17. PRÆ, or *pre,*—before: as, *pre-sume*, to take before; *pre-position*, a placing-before, or something placed before.

18. PRO,—for, forth, or forwards: as, *pro-vide*, to take care for; *pro-duce*, to bring forth; *pro-trude*, to thrust forwards.

19. PRETER,—past or beyond: as, *preter-it*, gone by; *preter-natural*, beyond what is natural.

20. RE,—again or back: as, *re-view*, to view again; *re-pel*, to drive back.

21. RETRO,—backwards: as, *retro-cession*, a going-backwards.

22. SE,—aside or apart: as, *se-duce*, to lead aside; *se-cede*, to go apart.

23. SEMI,—half: as, *semi-colon*, half a colon; *semi-circle*, half a circle; *semi-vowel*, half a vowel.

24. SUB, *sup, sur,*—under: as, *sub-scribe*, to write under; *sup-ply*, to put under; *sur-reption*, a creeping-under; *sub-ject*, cast under.

25. SUBTER,—beneath: as, *subter-fluous*, flowing beneath.

26. SUPER,—over or above: as, *super-fluous*, flowing over; *super-natant*, swimming above; *super-lative*, carried over.

27. TRANS,—beyond, over, to an other state or place: as, *trans-gress*, to pass beyond or over; *trans-mit*, to send to an other place; *trans-form*, to change to an other shape.

CLASS III.—GREEK PREFIXES.

1. A and AN, in Greek derivatives, denote privation: as, *a-nomalous*, wanting rule; *an-onymous*, wanting name; *an-archy*, want of government.

2. AMPHI,—both or two: as, *amphi-bious*, living in *two* elements.

3. ANTI,—against: as, *anti-acid*, against acidity; *anti-febrile*, against fever; *anti-thesis*, a placing-against.

4. APO, *aph*,—from: as, *apo-strophe*, a turning-from; *aph-æresis*, a taking-from.

5. DIA,—through: as, *dia-gonal*, through the corners; *dia-meter*, the measure through.

6. EPI, *eph*,—upon: as, *epi-demic*, upon the people; *eph-emera*, upon a day.

7. HEMI,—half: as, *hemi-sphere*, half a sphere.

8. HYPER,—over: as, *hyper-critical*, over-critical.

9. HYPO,—under: as, *hypo-stasis*, substance, or that which stands under; *hypo-thesis*, supposition, or a placing-under.

10. META,—beyond, over, to an other state or place: as, *meta-morphose*, to change to an other shape.

11. PARA,—against: as, *para-dox*, something contrary to common opinion.

12. PERI,—around: as, *peri-phery*, the circumference, or measure round.

13. SYN, *sym*, *syl*,—together: as, *syn-tax*, a placing-together; *sym-pathy*, a suffering-together; *syl-lable*, what is taken together.

CLASS IV.—FRENCH PREFIXES.

1. A is a preposition of very frequent use in French, and generally means *to*. We have suggested that it is probably the same as the Anglo-Saxon prefix *a*. It is found in a few English compounds that are of French, and not of Saxon origin: *a-dieu*, to God; *a-bout*, to the end or turn.

2. DE, —of or from: as in *de-mure*, of manners; *de-liver*, to ease from or of.

3. DEMI,—half: as, *demi-man*, half a man; *demi-god*, half a god.

4. EN, *em*,—in, into, or upon: as, *en-chain*, to hold in chains; *em-brace*, to clasp in the arms; *en-tomb*, to put into a tomb; *em-boss*, to stud upon. Many words are yet wavering between the French and the Latin orthography of this prefix: as, *embody*, or *imbody*; *ensurance*, or *insurance*; *ensnare*, or *insnare*; *enquire*, or *inquire*.

5. SUR,—upon, over, or after: as, *sur-name*, a name upon a name; *sur-vey*, to look over; *sur-vive*, to live after, to overlive, to outlive.

APPENDIX III.

(SYNTAX.)

OF THE QUALITIES OF STYLE.

Style is the particular manner in which a person expresses his conceptions by means of language. It is different from mere words, and is not to be regulated altogether by rules of construction. It always has some relation to the author's peculiar manner of thinking; and, being that sort of expression which his thoughts most readily assume, sometimes partakes, not only of what is characteristic of the man, but even of national peculiarity. The words which an author employs, may be proper, and so constructed as to violate no rule of syntax; and yet his style may have great faults.

To designate the general characters of style, such epithets as concise, diffuse,—neat, negligent,—nervous, feeble,—simple, affected,—easy, stiff,—perspicuous, obscure,—elegant, florid,—are employed. A considerable diversity of style, may be found in compositions all equally excellent in their kind. And, indeed, different subjects, as well as the different endowments by which genius is distinguished, require this diversity. But in forming his style, the learner should remember, that a negligent, feeble, affected, stiff, or obscure style, is always faulty; and that perspicuity, ease, simplicity, strength, and neatness, are qualities always to be aimed at.

In order to acquire a good style, the frequent practice of composing and writing something, is indispensably necessary. Without exercise and diligent attention, rules or precepts for the attainment of this object, will be of no avail. When the learner has acquired such a knowledge of grammar, as to be in some degree qualified for the undertaking, he should devote a stated portion of his time to composition. This exercise will bring the powers of his mind into requisition, in a way that is well calculated to strengthen them. And if he has opportunity for reading, he may, by a diligent perusal of the best authors, acquire both language and taste, as well as sentiment; and these three are the essential qualifications of a good writer.

In regard to the qualities which constitute a good style, we can here offer no more than a few brief hints. With respect to words and phrases, particular attention should be paid to *purity, propriety,* and *precision;* and, with respect to sentences, to *perspicuity, unity,* and *strength.* Under each of these heads, we shall arrange in the form of short *precepts* a few of the most important directions for the forming of a good style.

SECTION I.—OF PURITY.

Purity of style consists in the use of such words and phrases only, as belong to the language which we write or speak.

PRECEPT 1. Avoid the unnecessary use of foreign words or idioms: as, *fraicheur, hauteur, delicatesse, politesse, noblesse;* he *repented himself;* it *serves to* an excellent purpose.

PRECEPT 2. Avoid, on ordinary occasions, obsolete or antiquated words; as, *whilom, erewhile, whoso, albeit, moreover, aforetime, methinks.*

PRECEPT 3. Avoid strange or unauthorized words: as, *flutteration, inspectator, judgematical, incumberment, connexity, electerized, martyrized.*

PRECEPT 4. Avoid bombast, or affectation of fine writing. It is ridiculous, however serious the subject: as, "Personifications, however rich the depictions, and unconstrained their latitude; analogies, however imposing the

15

objects of parallel, and the media of comparison; can never expose the consequences of sin to the extent of fact, or the range of demonstration."—*Anonymous.*

SECTION II.—OF PROPRIETY.

Propriety of language consists in the selection and right construction, of such words as the best usage has appropriated to those ideas which we intend to express by them.

PRECEPT 1. Avoid low and provincial expressions: such as, "*Says I;*"—"*Thinks I to myself;*"—"*To get into a scrape;*"—"Stay here *while* I return."

PRECEPT 2. In writing prose, avoid words and phrases that are merely poetical: such as, *morn, eve, plaint, lone, amid, oft, steepy;*—"*what time* the winds arise."

PRECEPT 3. Avoid technical terms: except where they are necessary, in treating of a particular art or science. In technology, they are proper.

PRECEPT 4. Avoid the recurrence of words in different senses, or such a repetition of words as denotes paucity of language: as, "His own *reason* might have suggested better *reasons.*"—"Gregory *favoured* the undertaking, for no other reason than this; that the manager, in countenance, *favoured* his friend."—"I *want* to go and see what he *wants.*"

PRECEPT 5. Supply words that are wanting: thus, in stead of saying, "This action increased his former services," say, "This action increased *the merit of* his former services."

PRECEPT 6. Avoid equivocal or ambiguous expressions: as, "His *memory* shall be lost on the earth."—"I long since learned to like nothing but what you *do.*"

PRECEPT 7. Avoid unintelligible and inconsistent expressions: as, "I have observed that the superiority among these coffee-house politicians, proceeds from *an opinion* of gallantry and fashion."—"These words do not convey even an *opaque* idea of the author's meaning."

PRECEPT 8. Observe the natural order of things or events, and do not *put the cart before the horse:* as, "The scribes *taught and studied* the law of Moses."—"They can neither *return to nor leave* their houses."—"He tumbled, *head over heels,* into the water."

SECTION III.—OF PRECISION.

Precision consists in avoiding all superfluous words, and adapting the expression exactly to the thought, so as to exhibit neither more nor less than is intended by the author.

PRECEPT 1. Avoid a useless tautology, either of expression or sentiment: as in, "Return *again;*—return *back again;*—converse *together;*—rise *up;*—fall *down;*—enter *in;*—a mutual likeness to *each other;*—the *latter* end;—liquid streams;—*grateful* thanks;—the last *of all;*—throughout the *whole* book." "Whenever I go, he *always* meets me there."—"Where is he *at? In* there."—"Nothing *else* but that."—"It is odious *and hateful.*"—"His faithfulness *and fidelity* should be rewarded."

PRECEPT 2. Observe the exact meaning of words accounted synonymous, and employ those which are the most suitable: as, "A diligent scholar may *acquire* knowledge, *gain* celebrity, *obtain* rewards, *win* prizes, and *get* high honour, though he *earn* no money." These six verbs have nearly the same meaning, and yet they cannot well be changed.

SECTION IV.—OF PERSPICUITY.

Perspicuity consists in freedom from obscurity or ambiguity. It is a quality so essential, in every kind of writing, that for the want of it, no merit can atone. "Without this, the richest ornaments of style, only glimmer through the dark, and puzzle instead of pleasing the reader."—*Blair.* Perspicuity, being the most important property of language, and an exemption from the most embarrassing defects, seems even to rise to a degree of positive beauty. We are naturally pleased with a style that frees us from all suspense in regard to the meaning; that "carries us through the subject without embarrassment or confusion; and that always flows like a limpid stream, through which we can see to the very bottom."

PRECEPT 1. Place adjectives, relative pronouns, participles, adverbs, and explanatory phrases, as near as possible to the words to which they relate, and in such a situation as the sense requires. The following sentences are deficient in perspicuity:—"Reverence is the veneration paid to superior sanctity, *intermixed* with a certain degree of awe." "The Romans understood liberty, *at least*, as well as we." "Taste was never *made to cater* for vanity."

PRECEPT 2. In prose, avoid a poetic collocation of words.

PRECEPT 3. Avoid faulty ellipsis, and repeat all words necessary to preserve the sense. The following sentences require the words inserted in crotchets: "Restlessness of mind disqualifies us, both for the enjoyment of peace, and [*for*] the performance of our duty."—*Murray's Key.* "The Christian religion gives a more lovely character of God, than any [*other*] religion ever did."—*Ibid.*

SECTION V.—OF UNITY.

Unity consists in avoiding useless breaks or pauses, and keeping one object predominant throughout a sentence or paragraph. Every sentence, whether its parts be few or many, requires strict unity.

PRECEPT 1. Avoid brokenness and hitching. The following example lacks the very quality of which it speaks: "But most of all, in a single sentence, is required *the strictest unity. It* may consist of parts, *indeed*, but *these parts* must be so closely bound together, as to make the impression upon the mind, *of* one object, not *of* many."—*Murray's Grammar.*

PRECEPT 2. Treat different topics in separate paragraphs, and distinct sentiments in separate sentences. Error: "The two volumes are, indeed, intimately *connected*, and *constitute* one uniform system of English grammar."—*Murray's Preface.*

PRECEPT 3. In the progress of a sentence, do not desert the principal subject in favour of adjuncts. Error: "To substantives belong gender, number, and case; and *they are all* of the third person *when spoken of*, and of the second *when spoken to*."—*Murray's Grammar.*

PRECEPT 4. Do not introduce parentheses, except when a lively remark may be thrown in without diverting the mind too long from the principal subject.

SECTION VI.—OF STRENGTH.

Strength consists in giving to the several words and members of a sentence, such an arrangement as shall bring out the sense to the best advantage, and present every idea in its due importance. A concise style is the most favourable to strength.

PRECEPT 1. Place the most important words in the situation in which they will make the strongest impression.

PRECEPT 2. A weaker assertion should not follow a stronger; and when the sentence consists of two members, the longer should be the concluding one.

PRECEPT 3. When things are to be compared or contrasted, their resemblance or opposition will be rendered more striking, if some resemblance in the language and construction, be preserved.

PRECEPT 4. It is, in general, ungraceful to end a sentence with an adverb, a preposition, or any inconsiderable word or phrase, which may either be omitted or be introduced earlier.

APPENDIX IV.

(PROSODY.)

OF POETIC DICTION.

Poetry, as defined by Dr. Blair, "is the language of passion, or of enlivened imagination, formed, most commonly, into regular numbers." The style of poetry differs, in many respects, from that which is commonly adopted in prose. Poetic diction abounds in bold figures of speech, and unusual collocations of words. A great part of the figures which have been treated of under the head of prosody, are purely poetical. The primary aim of a poet, is to please and to move; and, therefore, it is to the imagination, and the passions, that he speaks. He may, and he ought to have it in his view, to instruct and reform; but it is indirectly, and by pleasing and moving, that he accomplishes this end. The exterior and most obvious distinction of poetry, is versification: yet there are some forms of verse so loose and familiar, as to be hardly distinguishable from prose; and there is also a species of prose, so measured in its cadences, and so much raised in its tone, as to approach very nearly to poetical numbers.

POETICAL PECULIARITIES.

The following are some of the most striking peculiarities in which the poets indulge, and are indulged :—

I. They very often omit the *ARTICLES*; as,

> "What dreadful pleasure ! there to stand sublime,
> Like *shipwreck'd mariner* on *desert coast* !"—*Beattie.*

II. They abbreviate many *NOUNS :* as, *amaze*, for *amazement ; acclaim,* for *acclamation ; consult*, for *consultation ; corse*, for *corpse ; eve*, or *even*, for *evening ; fount*, for *fountain ; helm*, for *helmet ; lament*, for *lamentation ; morn*, for *morning ; plaint*, for *complaint ; targe*, for *target ; weal*, for *wealth.*

III. They employ several nouns that are not used in prose, or are used but rarely; as, *benison, boon, emprise, fane, guerdon, guise, ire, ken, lore, meed, sire, steed, stithy, welkin, yore.*

IV. They introduce the noun *self* after an other noun of the possessive case ; as,

> 1. "Affliction's semblance bends not o'er thy tomb,
>   Affliction's *self* deplores thy youthful doom."—*Byron.*
> 2. "Thoughtless of beauty, she was beauty's *self*."—*Thomson.*

V. They place before the verb, nouns, or other words, that usually come after it ; and, after it, those that usually come before it : as,

> 1. "No jealousy *their dawn of love* o'ercast,
>   Nor blasted *were their wedded days* with strife."—*Beattie.*
> 2. "No *hive* hast *thou* of hoarded sweets."
> 3. "Thy chain *a wretched weight* shall prove."—*Langhorne.*
> 4. "Follows the loosen'd aggravated *roar*."—*Thomson.*
> 5. "That *purple* grows *the primrose pale*."—*Langhorne.*

VI. They often place *ADJECTIVES* after their nouns ; as,

1. "Or where the gorgeous East, with richest hand,
   Showers on her kings *barbaric*, pearl and gold."—*Milton.*
2. "Come, nymph *demure*, with mantle *blue*."

VII. They ascribe qualities to things to which they do not literally belong; as,

1. "Or *drowsy tinklings* lull the distant folds."—*Gray.*
2. "Imbitter'd more and more from *peevish day* to-day."—*Thomson.*
3. "All thin and naked, to the *numb* cold *night.*"—*Shakspeare.*

VIII. They use concrete terms to express abstract qualities; (i. e., adjectives for nouns;) as,

1. "Earth's meanest son, all trembling, prostrate falls,
    And on the *boundless* of thy goodness calls."—*Young.*
2. "Meanwhile, whate'er of *beautiful* or *new,*
    Sublime or *dreadful,* in earth, sea, or sky,
    By chance or search was offered to his view,
    He scann'd with curious and romantic eye."—*Beattie.*
3. "Won from the void and formless *infinite.*"—*Milton.*

IX. They substitute quality for manner; (i. e., adjectives for adverbs;) as,

1. "———————The stately-sailing swan,
    Gives out his snowy plumage to the gale;
    And, arching *proud* his neck, with oary feet
    Bears forward *fierce,* and guards his osier isle."—*Thomson.*
2. "Thither *continual* pilgrims crowded still."—*Id.*

X. They form new compound epithets; as,

1. "In *world-rejoicing* state, it moves sublime."—*Thomson.*
2. "The *dewy-skirted* clouds imbibe the sun."—*Id.*
3. "By brooks and groves in *hollow-whispering* gales."—*Id.*
4. "The violet of *sky-woven* vest."—*Langhorne.*
5. "A league from Epidamnum had we sailed,
    Before the *always-wind-obeying* deep
    Gave any tragic instance of our harm."—*Shakspeare.*

XI. They connect the comparative degree to the positive; as,

1. "*Near and more near* the billows rise."—*Merrick.*
2. "*Wide and wider* spreads the vale."—*Dyer.*
3. "*Wide and more wide,* the o'erflowings of the mind
    Take every creature in, of every kind."—*Pope.*

XII. They form many adjectives in *y,* which are not common in prose; as, A *gleamy* ray,—*towery* height,—*steepy* hill,—*steely* casque,—*heapy* harvests,—*moony* shield,—*writhy* snake,—*stilly* lake,—*vasty* deep,—*paly* circlet.

XIII. They employ adjectives of an abbreviated form: as, *dread,* for *dreadful; drear,* for *dreary; ebon,* for *ebony; hoar,* for *hoary; lone,* for *lonely; scant,* for *scanty; slope,* for *sloping; submiss,* for *submissive; vermil,* for *vermillion; yon,* for *yonder.*

XIV. They employ several adjectives that are not used in prose, or are used but seldom; as, *azure, blithe, boon, dank, darkling, darksome, doughty, dun, fell, rife, rapt, rueful, sear, sylvan, twain, wan.*

XV. They employ personal *PRONOUNS,* and introduce their nouns afterwards; as,

1. "*It* curl'd not Tweed alone, that *breeze.*"—*W. Scott.*
2. "Is it the lightning's quivering glance,
    That on the thicket streams;
    Or do *they* flash on spear and lance,
    The sun's retiring *beams?*"—*Id.*

XVI. They sometimes omit the relative, of the nominative case; as,

"For is there aught in sleep *can charm* the wise?"—*Thomson.*

XVII. They omit the antecedent, or introduce it after the relative; as,

1. "*Who* never fasts, no banquet e'er enjoys,
    Who never toils or watches, never sleeps."—*Armstrong.*

29*

2. " *Who* dares think one thing and an other tell,
   My soul detests *him* as the gates of hell."—*Pope's Homer.*

XVIII. They remove relative pronouns and other connectives, into the body of their clauses ; as,
1. "Parts the fine locks, her graceful head *that* deck."—*Darwin.*
2. "Not half so dreadful rises to the sight
   Orion's dog, the year-*when* autumn weighs."—*Pope's Homer.*

XIX. They make intransitive *VERBS* transitive ; as,
1. "————————A while he stands,
   Gazing the inverted landscape, half afraid
   To *meditate* the blue profound below."—*Thomson.*
2. "Still in harmonious intercourse, they *liv'd*
   The rural day, and *talk'd* the flowing heart."—*Id.*

XX. They give to the imperative mood the first and the third person ; as,
1. " *Turn we* a moment fancy's rapid flight."—*Thomson.*
2. " *Be* man's peculiar *work* his sole delight."—*Beattie.*
3. " And what is reason ?   *Be she* thus *defin'd:*
   Reason is upright stature in the soul !"—*Young.*

XXI. They employ *can, could,* and *would* as principal verbs transitive; as,
1. " *What* for ourselves we *can,* is always ours."
2. " Who does the best his circumstance allows,
   Does well, acts nobly :—angels *could* no *more.*"—*Young.*
3. " *What would* this man ?   Now upward will he soar,
   And, little less than angel, would be more."—*Pope.*

XXII. They place the infinitive before the word on which it depends; as,
   " When first thy sire *to send* on earth
   Virtue, his darling child, *design'd.*"—*Gray.*

XXIII. They place the auxiliary after its principal ; as,
   " No longer *heed* the sunbeam bright
   That plays on Carron's breast he *can.*"—*Langhorne.*

XXIV. Before verbs they sometimes arbitrarily employ or omit prefixes : as, *begird, bedim, evanish, emove;* for *gird, dim, vanish, move :—lure, wail, wilder, reave;* for *allure, bewail, bewilder, bereave.*

XXV. They abbreviate verbs : as, *list,* for *listen ; ope,* for *open.*

XXVI. They employ several verbs that are not used in prose, or are used but rarely ; as, *appal, astound, brook, cower, doff, ken, wend, ween, trow.*

XXVII. They sometimes imitate a Greek construction of the infinitive ; as,
1. " Who would not sing for Lycidas? he knew
   Himself *to sing,* and *build* the lofty rhyme."—*Milton.*
2. " For not, *to have been dipp'd* in Lethe lake,
   Could save the son of Thetis *from to die.*"—*Spenser.*

XXVIII. They employ the *PARTICIPLES* more frequently than prose writers, and in a construction somewhat peculiar ; as,
1. " He came, and, standing in the midst, explain'd
   The peace *rejected,* but the truce *obtain'd.*"—*Pope.*
2. " As a poor miserable captive thrall
   Comes to the place where he before had sat
   Among the prime in splendor, now *depos'd,*
   Ejected, emptied, gaz'd, unpitied, shunn'd,
   A spectacle of ruin or of scorn."—*Milton.*

XXIX. They employ several *ADVERBS* that are not used in prose, or are used but seldom ; as, *oft, haply, inly, blithely, cheerily, deftly, felly, rifely, ruefully, starkly, yarely.*

XXX. They give to adverbs a peculiar location; as,

1. " Peeping from *forth* their alleys green."—*Collins.*
2. " Erect the standard *there* of ancient night."—*Milton.*
3. " The silence *often* of pure innocence
   Persuades, when speaking fails."—*Shakspeare.*
4. " Where universal love *not* smiles around."—*Thomson.*
5. " Robs me of that which *not* enriches him."—*Shakspeare.*

XXXI. They omit the introductory adverb *there;* as,

"*Was* nought around but images of rest."—*Thomson.*

XXXII. They employ the *CONJUNCTIONS,* or—or, and *nor—nor,* as correspondents; as,

1. "*Or* by the lazy Scheldt *or* wandering Po."—*Goldsmith.*
2. " Wealth heap'd on wealth, *nor* truth *nor* safety buys."—*Johnson.*
3. " Who by repentance is not satisfied,
   Is *nor* of heaven, *nor* earth."—*Shakspeare.*

XXXIII. They often place *PREPOSITIONS* and their adjuncts, before the words on which they depend; as,

"*Against* your fame *with* fondness hate combines;
The rival batters, and the lover mines."—*Johnson.*

XXXIV. They sometimes place the preposition after its object; as,

1. " When beauty, *Eden's bowers within,*
   First stretch'd the arm to deeds of sin,
   When passion burn'd, and prudence slept,
   The pitying angels bent and wept."—*Hogg.*
2. " The Muses fair, *these peaceful shades among,*
   With skilful fingers sweep the trembling strings."—*Lloyd.*

XXXV. They employ *INTERJECTIONS* more frequently than prose writers; as,

"O let me gaze!—Of gazing there's no end.
O let me think!—Thought too is wilder'd here."—*Young.*

XXXVI. They employ *ANTIQUATED WORDS* and modes of expression; as,

1. " *Withouten* that would come *an* heavier bale."—*Thomson.*
2. " He was *to weet,* a little roguish page,
   Save sleep and play, who minded nought at all."—*Id.*
3. " Not one *eftsoons* in view was to be found."—*Id.*
4. " To number up the thousands dwelling here,
   An useless were, and *eke* an endless task."—*Id.*
5. " Of clerks good plenty here you *mote espy.*"—*Id.*
6. " But these I *passen* by, with nameless numbers *moe.*"—*Id.*

SCHOOL BOOKS.

BROWN'S FIRST LINES OF ENGLISH GRAMMAR, designed for young learners, and

BROWN'S INSTITUTES OF ENGLISH GRAMMAR for the higher classes,

have been used as *text-books* in the District Schools and Academies for several years past, and have received warm commendation from Teachers and others interested in education. The author having carefully revised these works, and made them conform more strictly with his larger work, they are again offered to the Managers of Schools, as the *best* works extant on the science of Grammar.

BROWN'S GRAMMAR OF ENGLISH GRAMMARS.

"A work of most elaborate finish, and of surprising extent and copiousness. It presents in a form of much originality, and in a style terse and beautiful, all the principles of our language, and developes almost *every peculiarity* of idiom or of construction."—*Norton's Literary Gazette.*

"We advise all who love our language to procure a copy of this comprehensive commentary upon it."—*Common School Journal.*

"This production stands out in bold relief, as *the book of the age*, on the subject of English Grammar. No scholar can regard his library complete without this book. It is destined to be the standard authority in its department, and will therefore be found an indispensable requisite in the office of every professional man, and on the table of every teacher. It must have a place by the side of Webster and Worcester, as a book of reference."—*Massachusetts Teacher.*

COMSTOCK AND COMING'S PRINCIPLES OF PHYSI-OLOGY, for the use of Schools, Academies, Colleges, and the general reader.

"This is by far the best illustrated work of Physiology, designed for schools and popular reading, with which we are acquainted."—*N. Y. Journal of Medicine.*

"It is the best popular work on the subject which we have seen."—*Peninsular Journal of Medicine.*

NEW-YORK READERS, NOS. 1, 2, 3.

Better in some respects than many of the Readers now in use, this series is worthy the attention of Teachers.

NEW-YORK PRIMER.

NEW-YORK SPELLING-BOOK.

Two popular works for the younger classes, filled with pictorial representations of things that ought to be learned early.

NEW-YORK EXPOSITOR.

A selection of the words in common use, with their definitions —better adapted for Common Schools than most of the Dictionaries extant.

www.ingramcontent.com/pod-product-compliance
Lightning Source LLC
Chambersburg PA
CBHW021116270326
41929CB00009B/910